How It Works®

Science and Technology

Third Edition

Marshall Cavendish
99 White Plains Road
Tarrytown, NY 10591

Website: www.marshallcavendish.com

Third edition updated by Brown Reference Group plc.

Library of Congress Cataloging-in-Publication Data
How it works: science and technology.—3rd ed.
p. cm.
Includes index.
ISBN 0-7614-7314-9 (set) ISBN 0-7614-7317-3 (Vol. 3)
1. Technology—Encyclopedias. 2. Science—Encyclopedias.
[1. Technology—Encyclopedias. 2. Science—Encyclopedias.]
T9 .H738 2003
603—dc21 2001028771

Consultant: Donald R. Franceschetti, Ph.D., University of Memphis

Brown Reference Group
Editor: Wendy Horobin
Associate Editors: Paul Thompson, Martin Clowes, Lis Stedman
Managing Editor: Tim Cooke
Design: Alison Gardner
Picture Research: Becky Cox
Illustrations: Mark Walker

Marshall Cavendish
Project Editor: Peter Mavrikis
Production Manager: Alan Tsai
Editorial Director: Paul Bernabeo

Printed in Malaysia
Bound in the United States of America
08 07 06 05 04 6 5 4 3 2

Title picture: Boy receiving chemotherapy, see *Cancer Treatment*

How It Works®

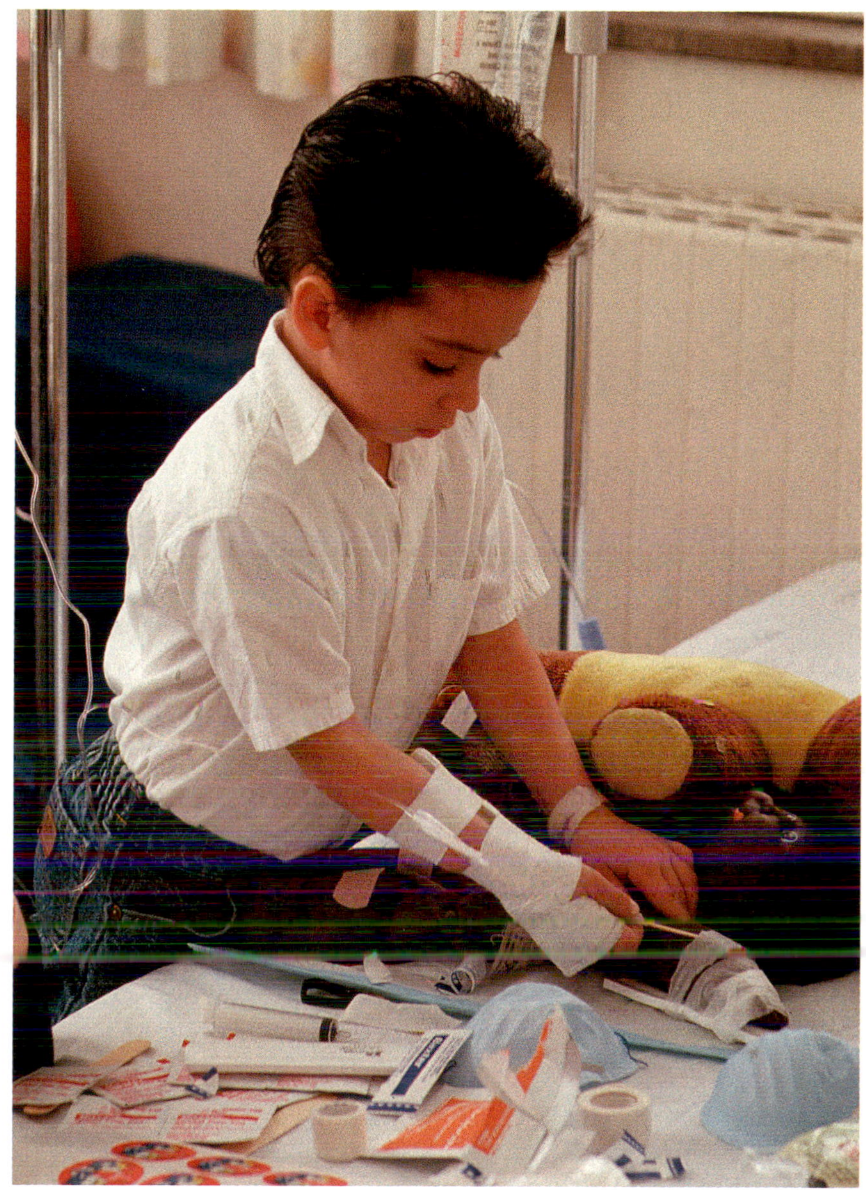

Science and Technology

Volume 3

Bomb and Mine Disposal

Charge-Coupled Device

Marshall Cavendish

New York • London • Toronto • Sydney

Contents

Volume 3

Bomb and Mine Disposal 293
Bones and Fracture Treatment 297
Bookbinding 301
Botany 303
Bow and Arrow 306
Brain 309
Braking System 313
Brass 316
Brass Instrument 318
Breathing Apparatus 321
Brick Manufacture 323
Bridge 325
Bronze 331
Bubble and Cloud Chamber 333
Building Techniques 335
Bunsen Burner 339
Burglar Alarm 340
Bus 342
Cable, Power 344
Cable, Submarine 347
Cable and Rope Manufacture 350
Cable Network 353
Cable Transport Systems 356
Calculator 359
Cam 362
Camera 363
Camera, Digital 370
Canal 373
Cancer Treatment 377
Canning and Bottling 381
Capacitor 386
Carbohydrate 388
Carbon 391
Carbon Fiber 394
Carburetor 396
Car Wash 398
Cash Register 399
Casting 402
Catalyst 405
Cathode-Ray Tube 408
Cell Biology 411
Cellular Telephone 415
Cement Manufacture 417
Centrifuge 422
Ceramics 424
Chain Drive 428
Chaos Theory 430
Charge-Coupled Device 432

Bomb and Mine Disposal

Bomb-disposal techniques date from World War II, when aerial bombing raids on European cities left numerous unexploded devices in their wake. In the same period, antipersonnel and antitank mines were spread over large tracts of land as a deterrent against invasion by hostile forces. These mines had to be cleared before such land could be crossed in safety.

Since the end of World War II, the remnant devices of that conflict have been supplemented by potentially explosive devices from subsequent wars and terrorist campaigns. They range from crudely improvised explosives to sophisticated military devices. Such is the diversity of these weapons—and so specialized the techniques for neutralizing them—that a new term has been coined: explosive ordnance disposal, or EOD.

World War II devices

One of the principal causes of World War II unexploded ordnance (UXO) was the electrical detonation system used in the bombs of the German *Luftwaffe*. As a bomb left an aircraft, it received a charge that was stored in a capacitor in the bomb's fuse. When the bomb landed, the impact would usually close a switch, allowing the current to flow into a detonator and fire the bomb. Occasionally, the switch would fail to close on landing, leaving the bomb unexploded but liable to detonate at the slightest disturbance. The bomb-disposal crews of the time soon learned that this type of fuse could be disarmed by clamping an electric lead on the fuse contacts to discharge the fuse capacitor, making the fuse completely inert and safe to remove.

As well as the electrical switch, some bombs had a clockwork delay timer that could easily be jolted into action by the activity of the disposal squad. Once a bomb had started ticking, the only option was to evacuate the location either until the bomb exploded or until it stopped ticking. To check for ticking, one member of the disposal team would listen with a stethoscope as soon as the bomb was uncovered. One method of preventing the timer from starting to tick was to place a strong magnet near the bomb to prevent its mechanism from moving; another method was to jam the mechanism with a quick-setting plastic or with ice formed from moisture in the air by freezing it with dry ice (solid carbon dioxide).

As bomb-disposal squads became more proficient, bomb designers included booby traps in bomb designs. Each new bomb design called for a new disposal technique to be developed.

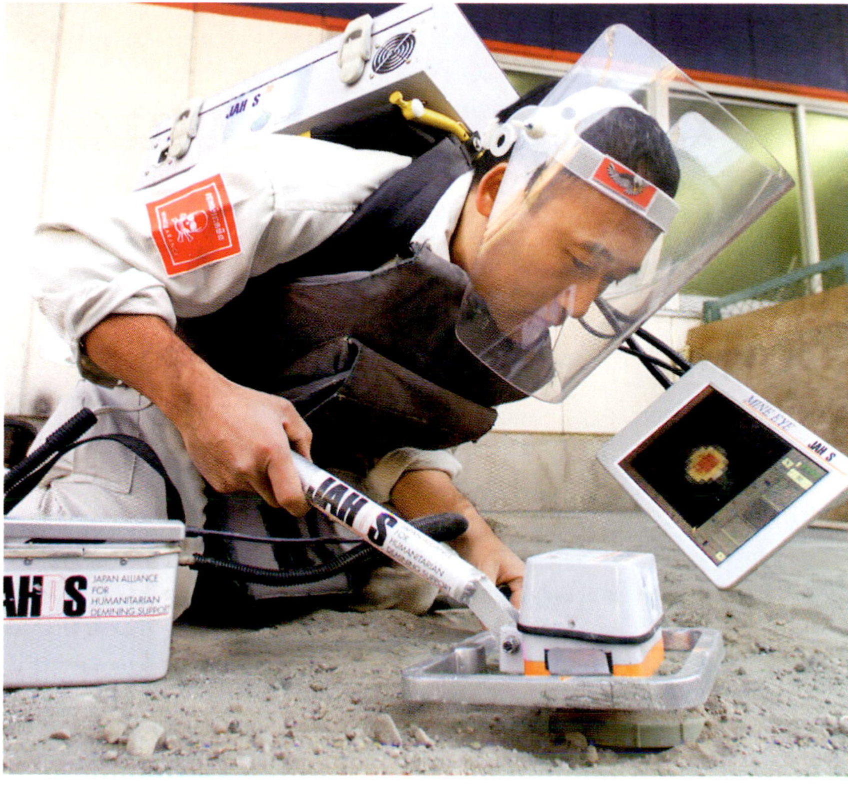

▲ The Mine Eye is a new type of land mine detector that can find even plastic and wooden mines hidden in the ground. Sophisticated electronics provide three-dimensional images that indicate how far down the mine is and its constituent materials, and display the results on a screen right in front of the bomb-disposal expert.

Land mines

Land mines differ from bombs in that they are designed to be detonated by the pressure of a human foot or a tank's track. As such, they have mechanical triggers that are made safe with securing pins until they are in position. A land mine can be made safe by replacing the safety pin or simply by detonating it from a distance. Metal detectors and magnetometers can be used to find hidden mines that contain metal, while techniques such as ground-penetrating radar are necessary to detect nonmetallic mines.

Terrorist bombs

Amateur terrorist bomb makers tend to make many mistakes with their first devices. They often design or assemble bombs inadequately, so the devices either fail to detonate or they explode before their intended detonation time.

Devices that fail to detonate provide an opportunity for bomb-disposal experts to analyze the bomb's intended method of operation. By doing so, bomb-disposal squads gradually became familiar with the characteristic weapons and some of the more common techniques of the bombers.

As a terrorist group becomes more experienced in making bombs—or acquires technical information from other terrorist groups—its techniques become more sophisticated. An example of this type of development occurred with

LARGE-SCALE MINE CLEARANCE

Antipersonnel land mines are relatively cheap weapons that are easy to conceal in rural areas. They cause widespread fear through the deaths and injuries that they cause and the unwitting way in which their victims come across them. These factors have made land mines favored weapons of rural terrorists and civil warriors over the last few decades. Even after a conflict has subsided, large areas of land are left unsafe to traverse as a result of land mine campaigns.

While it is possible to painstakingly locate and disarm or detonate land mines one by one, such an approach would be impractical where huge tracts of land are potential or confirmed minefields. The task is made even more difficult by the absence of records that could help to focus the efforts of land mine-disposal teams.

The only practical method for clearing mines from large areas of land is to use a heavily armored vehicle built to detonate or destroy mines as it goes.

One such vehicle is the Swedish-built Mine-Guzzler demining machine. Weighing in at 50 tons (45 tonnes) and powered by an 870-horsepower (650 kW) engine, the Mine-Guzzler resembles an extremely heavy-duty combine harvester.

At the front of the machine is a row of circular cutting plates, each with tungsten carbide teeth around its circumference. These teeth penetrate to a fixed depth, even on undulating terrain and can clear land mines at depths of up to 19.5 in. (50 cm) below the surface. The mines either explode or are torn to pieces.

The armor of the Mine-Guzzler's body is sufficient to withstand blasts from up to 26 lbs. (12 kg) of high explosive—more than enough to cope with an antitank mine—and the tungsten carbide teeth of its demining roller can be cut off and replaced in the field with an oxyacetylene torch if they become damaged.

The Mine-Guzzler clears a strip 10.5 ft. (3.2 m) wide at a demining speed of 2.5 mph (4 km/h)—equivalent to 3.2 acres (1.28 ha) of land in one hour. It can be driven from a reinforced control cabin at the rear of the vehicle or by remote control using images taken by cameras mounted on the vehicle.

Flailing machines work in a similar way to ground-cutting demining machines: they consist of a heavily armored vehicle that can be driven from a reinforced cab or by remote control. Instead of destroying mines by cutting into them, flailing machines trigger their detonation by using a rotating shaft with flexible chains that simulate the footfalls of human beings.

In the future, it is possible that robot "communities" equipped with metal detectors, magnetometers, and ground-penetrating radar will be used for mine detection. Such communities would forage for land mines by comparing detector data between robots as a way of homing in on hidden mines. Once located, the mines could be disarmed and safely removed. Such communities have already performed well in simulated foraging exercises.

▼ This British Army Aardvark flailing machine is used for clearing large minefields. Chains mounted on an axle are rotated, detonating any mines buried in front of the vehicle. The cab is armored to protect the driver from shrapnel and other debris.

ambush bombs used by the IRA (Irish Republican Army) against British forces in Northern Ireland. To be effective, ambush bombs must be triggered by an operator who keeps the target under surveillance. At first, a landline linked the bomber and the detonator of the bomb.

The weakness of this approach was the ease with which the landlines could be traced to the bomber's position. As a result, detonation by radio signal became a favored terrorist weapon. In response, the British forces developed equipment that swept a range of radio frequencies with a strong signal that caused premature detonation of many bombs and resulted in casualties among the bombers. The terrorists overcame that flaw with switches that responded only to radio signals pulsed according to coded instructions.

▲ Minefields may be an important defensive measure, but clearing them is difficult. To be successful, the operatives must cover every foot of ground, working in a pattern. Once detected, mines are either defused or detonated safely.

Examining a bomb

As a rule, the first step in examining a suspected bomb is an X-ray scan. This reveals the internal mechanism, the arrangement of component parts, and the layout of electrical wiring. A bomb-disposal expert can also use an explosive detector called a sniffer to check that the device really is a bomb and not just a hoax.

The first X-ray equipment used for this task was extremely cumbersome, requiring a truck to move it into position. The miniaturization of electronics has since made possible the development of portable X-ray scanning equipment. If the X-ray scan reveals that a bomb relies on a battery to provide power for the detonator, which most bombs do, then freezing the bomb will render the battery inert. The bomb can then be safely dismantled. Alternatively, a disruptor can be fired at short range at some sensitive part of the bomb revealed by X-ray examination.

In another approach, the bomb container can be pumped full of plastic foam. The foam causes short-circuits in the wiring of the bomb and renders any mechanical devices inert. All these techniques—and several more that are not made public—are available to the EOD team.

FACT FILE

- *After the Falklands War in 1982, the British Royal Engineers charged with bomb disposal set up a children's club to help in the search for suspicious objects—and to prevent the children from touching them. Eventually, 237 of East Falkland's 280 children were enrolled and helped clear Port Stanley. The children received badges and certificates for their role in the bomb-disposal campaign.*

- *Bombers will go to great lengths to complicate the lives of bomb-disposal units. In 1976, a particularly bizarre device was found in Belfast. It consisted of 5 lbs. (2.3 kg) of explosives and a detonator stuffed inside an armchair. The armchair had been placed in an elevator, which had then been made to jam between floors.*

Controlled explosions

Under certain circumstances, the best option for disposing of a bomb is to detonate it in such a way as to keep damage to a minimum, particularly with improvised explosive devices, whose trigger mechanisms can be difficult to identify.

The first step in a controlled explosion is to evacuate all people from the direct vicinity of the bomb. In the case of a small device with a limited blast range, this may be the only precaution necessary: the device can then be detonated by a small charge or a shot from a gun.

The blast damage from larger devices can be minimized by detonating the device inside a reinforced cylinder with an open top. The expanding gases generated by the explosion are directed upwards, while the cylinder retains any fragments thrown out by the exploding bomb. If the bomb is in an awkward space, such as under a vehicle, it must first be removed, using a remote-control robot, to a position where there is enough space to fit the containment cylinder.

If a human has to approach the bomb at any point in the procedure, he or she will probably wear an EOD suit. These are made from a high-strength polyamide, such as Kevlar, and fitted with flexible joints that permit some freedom of motion while providing protection against blasts.

ORDNANCE-DISPOSAL ROBOTS

In the early 1970s, terrorists in Northern Ireland began to arm their bombs with devices that would detonate at the slightest disturbance. Some of these were simple but ingenious: one example was a shallowly bent tube that contained a drop of mercury at the bottom of the bend—the slightest tilt, and the mercury would run up the tube to close a switch that detonated the device. It became clear that EOD personnel should not be subjected to the risk of tampering with such devices.

The British army devised a robot called Wheelbarrow to deal with disturbance-sensitive bombs. It was a small, remotely controlled tracked vehicle with an articulated arm carrying a closed-circuit television camera and floodlight, which allowed bombs to be examined at a safe distance. Wheelbarrow could lift a bomb so that the camera could examine it more closely, or it could carry a bomb to a safe location for detonation. It could also fire a disruptor projectile at a bomb to break the bomb's fuse circuits so quickly that they have no time to detonate the bomb. Wheelbarrow was the forerunner of all modern teleoperated ordnance-disposal systems, or TODs.

▼ Many explosives have a characteristic smell that can be exploited by ordnance-disposal squads. Hidden bombs can be located using sniffer dogs, which have been trained to lead their handlers to explosive devices.

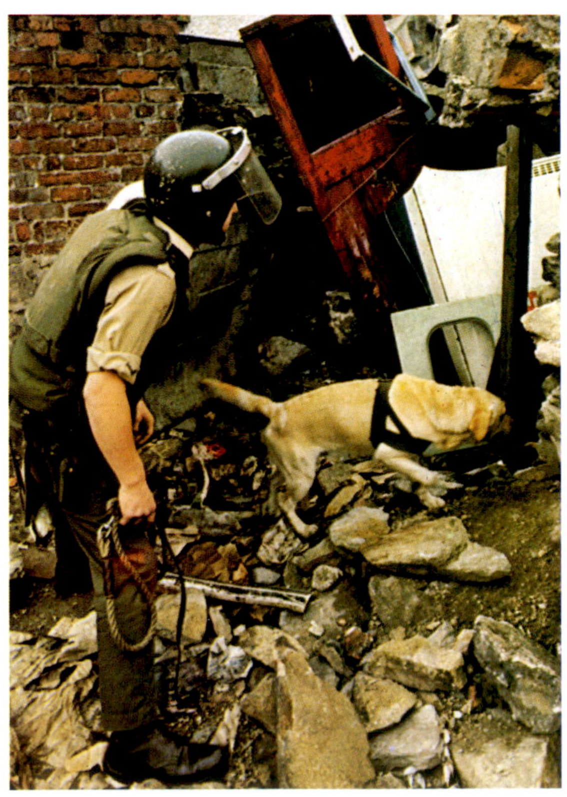

Total-containment vessels

Total-containment vessels, or TCVs, are used where even the slightest amount of blast damage would be unacceptable or where there is a risk of the bomb containing chemical or biological substances, of which even minute quantities could cause widespread injuries or disease. The forerunner of the TCV was an armored vehicle designed to contain the blast of an explosive ordnance device if it exploded on the way to a safe detonation site.

Modern TCVs are spherical chambers of high-strength, high-impact steel that is typically 1½ in. (4 cm) thick. A sphere is used because it is the most effective shape for withstanding high internal pressures. An EOD is placed inside the sphere through a circular hatch, which is then tightly sealed for detonation. Ports in the sphere allow for the post-detonation gases to be sampled and analyzed for chemical or biological agents. If any such agents are identified, neutralizing agents can be introduced and further samples taken to check that any harmful contents have been destroyed before the main hatch is opened.

SEE ALSO: Bomb • Explosive • Magnetometer • Metal detector • Mine, explosive • Remote handling

Bones and Fracture Treatment

The human skeleton consists of an orderly arrangement of rigid, inflexible bones designed to support the body against gravitational forces and protect vulnerable internal organs against injury. The central upright core of the skeleton consists of the skull, backbone, rib cage, and breastbone, collectively known as the axial skeleton, and is aligned in a vertical axis.

Connected to this core are appendages consisting of the shoulder and pelvic girdles and the limbs—the appendicular skeleton. Muscles are attached to the skeleton at strategic points around joints and between bones so that contraction and relaxation of muscle groups with opposing actions control movement at the joint. The characteristic shape of individual bones is controlled by their function. The contour of articular surfaces of joints moving in specified directions and protruberances at muscle insertions are evidence for function controlling the form.

Two main types of bone, flat bones and long bones, can be identified in the axial and appendicular skeletons, respectively. Movement between flat bones is restricted by thick fibrous connections between the bones. The skull of a newborn child consists of several plates of flat bone connected in this way. The joints are known as sutures and gradually disappear as the bones fuse together to form the rigid skull of the adult. The vertebrae of the backbone are irregular flat bones forming an arch around the spinal cord. Some movement between vertebrae is retained throughout life by the insertion of intervertebral disks of cartilage, a firm white fibrous protein. Severe pressure on the spine can displace these disks into contact with nerve roots causing incapacitating pain.

The long bones of the appendicular skeleton have a shaft, or diaphysis, and at least two extremities, or epiphyses. The shaft is usually cylindrical, though it may carry impressions of adjacent nerves and blood vessels, and contributes most of the strength to the bone. Leg bones carry the weight of the body and are thicker and stronger than the arm bones. The extremities are often irregular where muscle tendons are attached and will have a smooth covering of articular cartilage at the joints. The appendicular skeleton also contains a number of small irregularly shaped carpal and tarsal bones at the wrist and ankle joints.

Sesamoid bones are found within the fibrous sheaths of muscle tendons and have a minor supporting function. The kneecap, or patella, is the most easily recognized sesamoid bone.

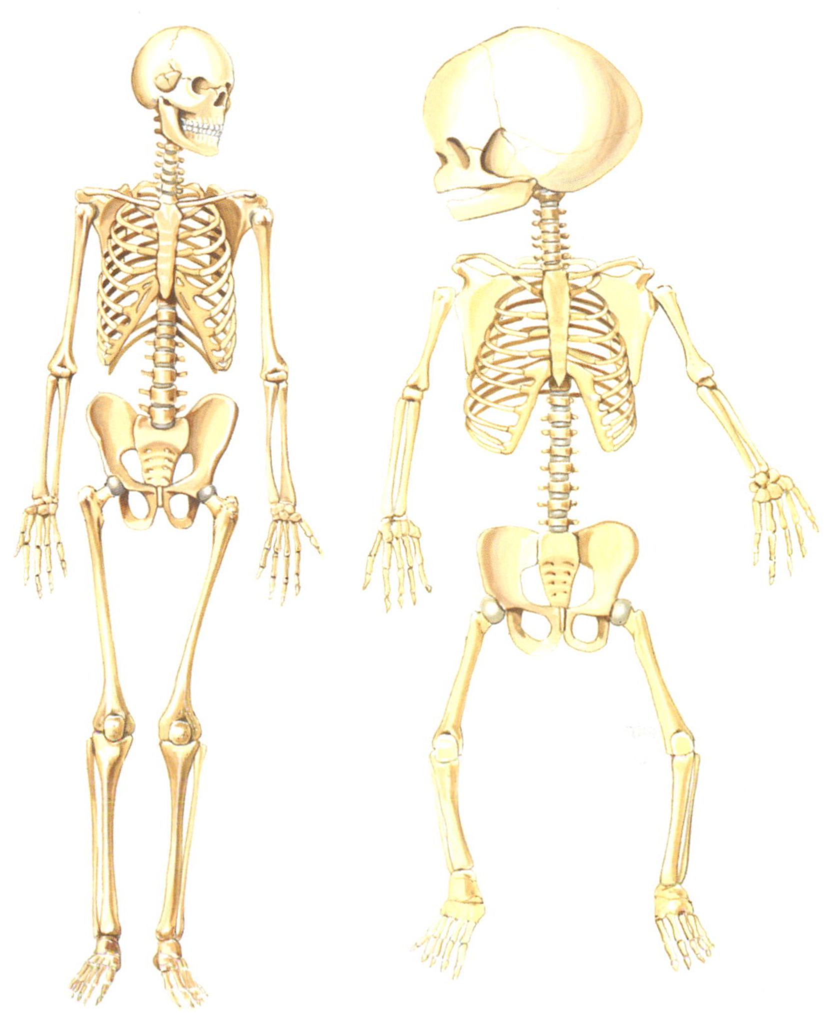

▲ If the skeleton of a newborn baby is magnified in length to that of an adult, the head can be seen to be proportionately much larger. As a child ages, the proportions change dramatically. The mid-point shifts from about the navel of the newborn to below the pelvis of the adult.

Joint movement

A tough but intricate structure connects the articulating surfaces of the limbs and limb girdles. Smooth cartilage covers the bones within the joint, which is lubricated by fluid produced by the synovial membrane located at the edges of the joints. Synovial fluid is continually secreted into the joint and may accumulate excessively when the joint is inflamed, swelling the capsule of the joint. The capsule is a fibrous, nonelastic ligament enclosing the joint in a sleeve and protecting it against injury produced by excessive movement. Load-bearing joints in the shoulder, hip, and knee also contain ligaments within the joint connecting the contiguous bones.

Ability to move in different directions, such as flexion forward or backward, lateral movement, or circular rotation, is built into the structure of different joints. Elbows, knees, and fingers are examples of hinge joints, which move by flexion and are locked when straight by the opposing flat surfaces of the bones and by the joint capsule. Unusual ranges of movement in double-jointed individuals are produced by laxity in the joint capsule. Ball-and-socket joints allow movement in every direction and are found at the shoulder and hip. The socket, or rounded cavity, is produced by the bones of the limb girdle, and the ball is the rounded epiphysis of the long bone.

Pivot joints rotate in a single axis, for example, one is found between the uppermost vertebrae in the neck controlling the side-to-side movement of the head. A condyloid joint such as that between the jawbone and the skull moves in two axes—vertically and horizontally.

Unusual stress on movable joints and aging will eventually erode the cartilage, revealing the rough ends of the bone as well as the nerve fibers within the bone structure. Movement of the joint becomes painful and limited, a process known as osteoarthritis. Weight-bearing joints in the legs are most susceptible to this condition, which can now be remedied by surgical replacement of the joint with an artificial prosthesis.

Growth and aging

The growing child gains height principally by growth in the long bones and, to a lesser extent, in the spine. Long bones contain one or more growth plates, known as the metaphysis, between the shaft and the epiphysis. These areas have a rich blood supply and produce successive layers of new cartilage, which is visible on X rays as a clear zone between the ossification centers of the shaft and extremity where calcium is deposited into the cartilage framework, making new bone. During active growth, cartilage formation outstrips ossification, but illness or malnutrition may interrupt growth and densely ossified growth-arrest lines will appear close to the metaphysis.

In adolescence, a rapid spurt in bone growth occurs under hormonal control and is accompanied by an increased rate of ossification that eventually obliterates the growing plate. This process is normally completed by 18 years of age, when adult height is reached and no further growth in the length of bone is possible. A similar process occurs in flat bones, which enlarge more slowly than long bones and grow at the edges.

The skeleton is not immune from the aging process, though this does not become apparent until the sixth decade of life when fractures occur more readily. Most of the body store of calcium, principally calcium phosphate, is located in the skeleton. Approximately 45 percent of bone consists of calcium salts, but this proportion decreases in later life, partly because the activity of living bone cells declines. Demineralization is accompanied by a gradual bone-thinning process with reduction of the protein framework in which calcium salts are deposited.

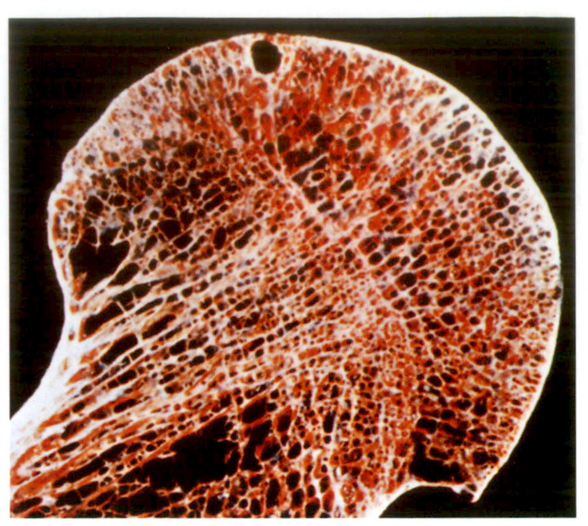

▲ A sectioned femur—the longest and strongest bone in the human body. In normal use, this bone has to withstand pressures of up to two tons per square inch. The lines and ridges in bones are built up during the growth processes in response to the stresses placed on the bone, which enable it to grow stronger where the stresses are greatest. The structure gets its strength from the extensive crosshatching of the bone material, and the spaces ensure the bone is lightweight. The bone is nourished with blood from vessels passing through the canals. These vessels also run to the center of the bone, where the blood-producing marrow is encased in cylindrical sheets of immensely strong bone.

The result of the aging process is often a skeleton that is weak and brittle, and, as a result, breaks in the bone occur at the sites of greater stress. This condition is known as osteoporosis, and is particularly common in women who have gone through menopause. Female reproductive hormones are believed to play a key role in maintaining a woman's bone density, and hormone replacement therapy is often prescribed to prevent the onset of osteoporosis. Teenagers who diet often are also prone to this disease, especially if they cut out dairy and other calcium-rich foods perceived as being high in fat.

Microscopic bone structure

The outer surface of bone is coated with a fibrous membrane, the periosteum. Muscle tendons and joint ligaments are inserted into this membrane, which is firmly attached to the underlying bone. Osteoblasts are bone cells located in large numbers in the periosteum and elsewhere within the bone. They produce a protein known as collagen, which forms a framework in which calcium salts are deposited under the influence of vitamin D. The potential for new bone formation at the bone surface is realized during repair of fractures, where a lumpy aggregation of new bone, known as callus, covers the break.

Examination of a cross section of bone reveals a dense outer layer of compact bone covering a core of cancellous bone. Cancellous bone has a spongy appearance and is quite soft. Compact bone consists of an arrangement of microscopic rods, known as Haversian systems, parallel to the axis of the bone. Each system has a central canal containing blood vessels and bone cells surrounded by circular rings of bone also containing bone cells in microscopic lacunae. The rod system in compact bone provides a greater strength than could be achieved by random calcification of the collagen matrix.

Haversian systems are found in smaller numbers and are larger. Bone marrow is found in cancellous bone, appearing red because of a rich blood supply and the concentration of new blood cells forming in the marrow. In a young child, the marrow is extremely active, occupying the whole of the central core of bones. This marrow is gradually replaced in the adult by an inactive and fatty yellow bone marrow, leaving a residue of red marrow at the extremities of long bones and in most flat bones of the axial skeleton.

The rich internal network of blood vessels within individual bones is fed by one or more nutrient arteries that penetrate into the marrow through the periosteum and compact bone. In contrast, most of the nerve supply to bone is concentrated in the superficial periosteum.

Fracture treatment

A fracture is defined as a break in the normal continuity of a bone caused by stress. For the victim, the most obvious symptoms of a fractured bone are pain, swelling, and tenderness at the site combined with an inability to move the body part. A physician will look for symptoms that include an abnormal mobility of the bone and the presence of grating or grinding of bone fragments. An X ray will confirm the fracture.

Among the many types of fracture are a transverse fracture, which runs across the bone; an oblique fracture, which extends across the bone at an oblique angle; a spiral fracture, which extends across and up a bone; a T-shaped fracture at the end of a bone; an impacted fracture, for example, when the thigh bone is pushed up and through the hip socket; a compound fracture, in which the bone may pierce the skin; and finally, the greenstick fracture. Greenstick fractures are usually caused by the bending of long bones, especially in children who have bones that, while richer in fibrous tissue than adults, are poorer in calcium salts. This phenomenon makes them less resistant to tension than compression.

The healing of the actual bone tissue is quite different from the healing of other body tissue. After a fracture, callus tissue is formed. Callus, also known as fibrocartilage, is soft to begin with as it is uncalcified. It appears between and around the broken ends. The callus contains osteoblasts, which are derived from the connective tissue within a bone, and if pressure is brought to bear on the ends of the broken bone, there will be an increase in the amount of callus formed.

It is necessary, therefore, to immobilize the limb and provide some degree of compression on the fractured bone for satisfactory healing. This technique encourages quick healing and also prevents disfigurement of the bone (misunion). There are several methods of achieving these results, which can be conveniently divided into two approaches: external and internal fixing.

External fixation of fractures

External fixation involves immobilizing the fractured part by the insertion of pins connected externally by plaster, metal devices, or other appliances. The earliest methods recorded used wooden splints bound to the limb in an attempt to immobilize the fracture. This is not a satisfactory solution, however, unless used in an emergency.

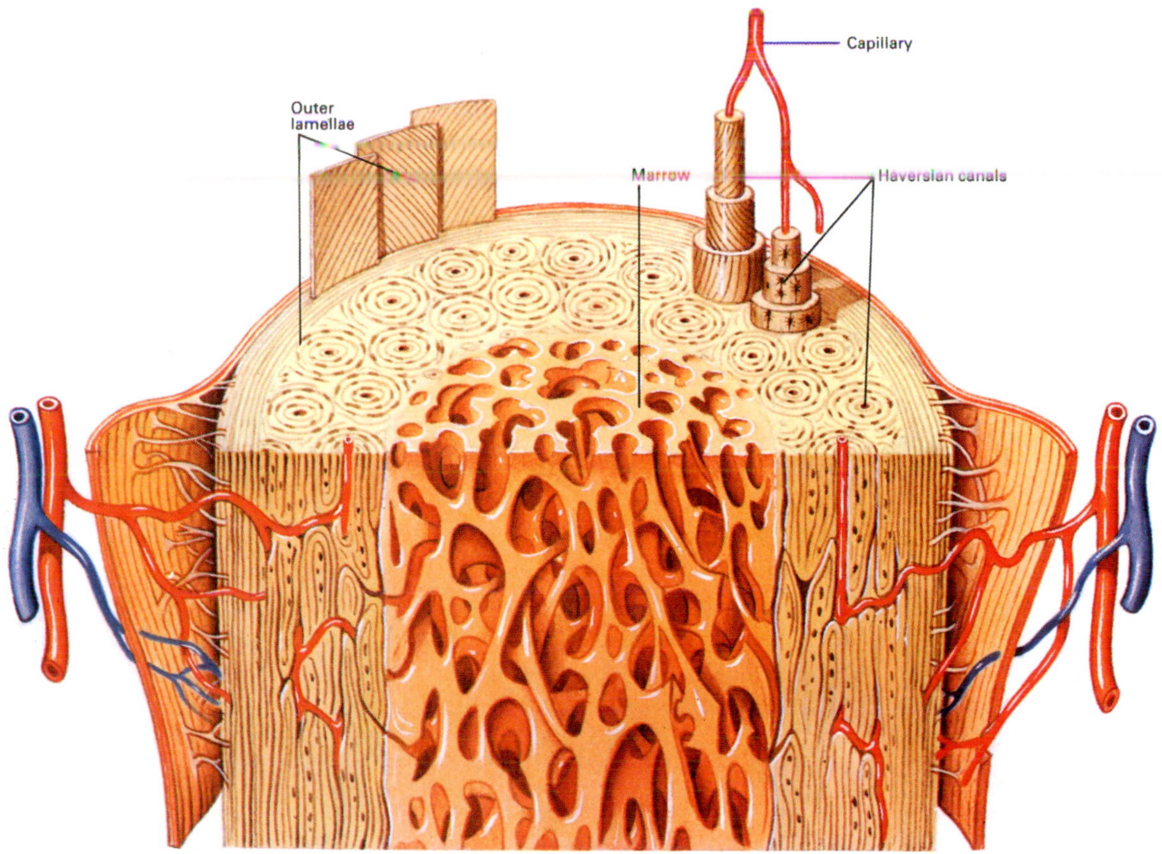

◀ Bone is fed by blood vessels ascending in the Haversian canals through a mass of bone cells that expand into a tracery of strong bone in the center. Here, blood-producing marrow is encased within the central structure.

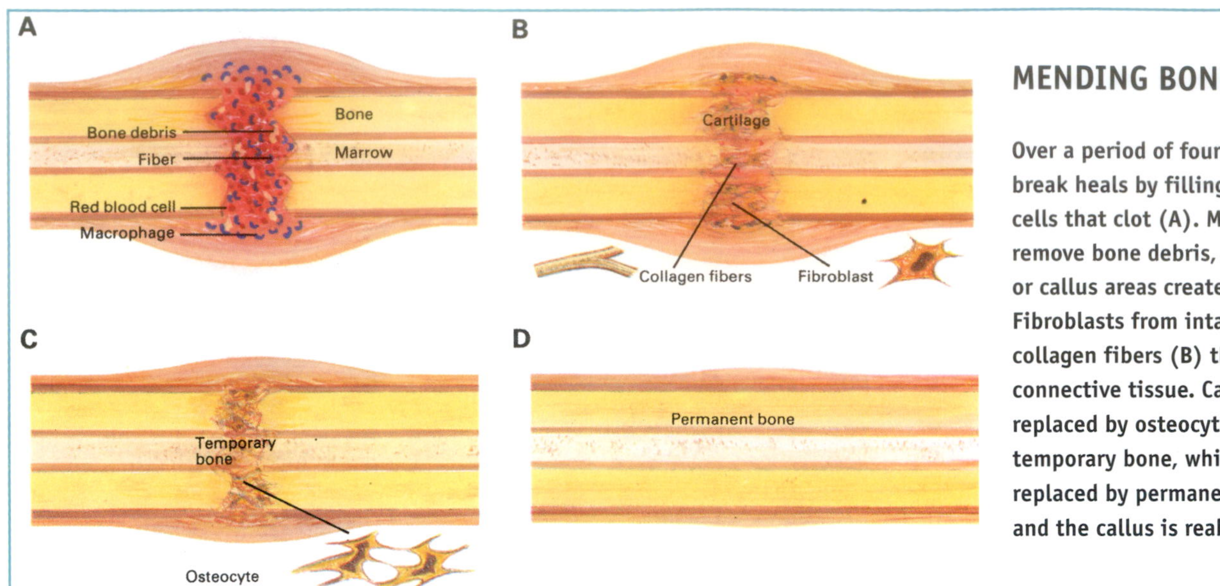

MENDING BONES

Over a period of four to six weeks, a break heals by filling with red blood cells that clot (A). Macrophages remove bone debris, and the swollen or callus areas create new bones. Fibroblasts from intact bone produce collagen fibers (B) that help to make connective tissue. Cartilage is replaced by osteocytes (C), creating temporary bone, which is finally replaced by permanent bone (D), and the callus is reabsorbed.

Until the 1970s, hospital treatment consisted of the use of traction or plaster casts. Traction is a mechanical method of pulling on the limb to encourage healing. Pins or wires with freely attached hooks are inserted into the bone. Cords are then passed through the hooks and pulleys and weights are hung on the end to pull gently on the fractured limb.

Plaster has proved popular all over the world as an inexpensive, practical method of treating fractures and securing correct alignment of the bone, though glass-fiber casts are more commonly used in the United States. As soon as local swelling has been reduced, a stocking is fitted carefully over the affected limb. Bony points are then padded with cotton to prevent chafing and sores developing. Finally, plaster is applied liberally over the limb in such a manner that the fracture cannot be disturbed. While the plaster is setting, the physician holds the limb in as natural a position as possible. This procedure takes a great deal of care and experience; any misalignment will be impossible to correct unless a refracture is effected.

Pinning is a method that requires the physician drilling through the soft tissue and into the bone. The pins are then fitted to a frame to immobilize the limb. The pins can be inserted under local anesthetic into the two parts of the bone. This allows full treatment of any infections, acute fractures, and nonunion alignments.

Internal fixation of fractures

Rigid internal fixation involves the fitting of metal supports inside the limb, which are fixed firmly to the bone. This method has clear advantages over external fixation but can still cause problems during healing.

One of the main advantages is that of early mobility for the patient, thus allowing other tissues to develop through exercise. Psychologically, it can also speed recovery because of the extra mobility. Equally important is the fact that the original bone shape is maintained to a greater degree than with other methods. Use of this method is especially important for the long bones, where any misalignment can have serious effects. Finally, the use of internal fixing devices allows a union of the fragments without the formation of excessive or visible callus, which would otherwise destroy the smooth surface of the bone.

Stable internal fixation can be used, therefore, for a variety of reasons. There are three main ways to compress the fracture: using plates and/or screws, tension band wiring, and intramedullary nailing.

In compression, stainless-steel plates are laid alongside the bone and secured with screws. The plates give an axial compression along the bone and thus give the fracture ideal conditions for knitting. In tension wiring, wire is inserted into the limb and tightly bound over the bone. It is especially good for fractures at a joint and makes use of the fact that forces around such a fracture are transformed into a compression over the fracture gap. Intramedullary nailing involves the fitting of a steel rod for correct alignment of the bone along the shaft axis. It then acts as a stress carrier, substituting for the fractured bone and absorbing all forces that may be applied. One serious drawback of this method is the threat of infection, which may need antibiotic treatment.

▼ X ray of a clear fracture of the tibia (shin bone), the larger of the two bones that form the lower leg. A mass of new bone will form around the fracture as it heals, but the bone will eventually remodel itself into its original smooth shape.

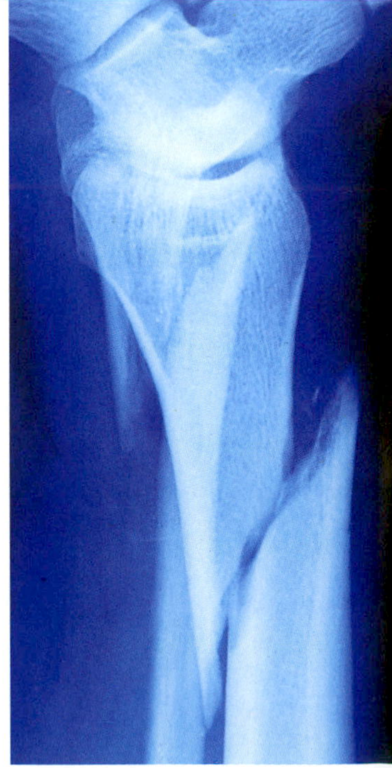

SEE ALSO: Bioengineering • Blood • Osteopathy

Bookbinding

Bookbinding is an old art that developed as manuscripts began to replace parchment rolls. The earliest bindings were produced for Islamic and Christian ecclesiastic use. These early books were laboriously written by hand, taking many years to produce. They were usually elaborately decorated, often with gold, jewels, or lacquer. Today, bookbinding is an extensively automated process, that produces hundreds of books per hour. Hand binding is still done, but only for prestigious books or repair of historical documents.

Pages are printed before they are bound, and the method of printing can affect the first stages of binding. Traditionally, flat sheets of paper are printed, then folded and bound, or, the paper fed from a continuous roll printed, folded, and cut on a single machine. The paper is then passed to the binder.

The pages of the book are printed on sheets according to an imposition. This sets out page positions so that when the sheet is folded the pages are in the right order. The modern book sheet is folded in groups of either 32 or 64 pages, which are called sections. The machine then folds the sheets at a rate of 8,000 to 10,000 per hour. In 1827, William Burn invented the first machine for the binding industry, a rolling press consisting of two large cylinders. One man would turn a handle, another would feed folded sections through, compressing them and squeezing out trapped air.

The sections are then be ready to be made up into a book, but first endpapers need to be affixed to the book cover. At one time, endpapers were stuck onto the first and last sections by hand, which took about 18 minutes per 100 sections; a modern machine takes only two minutes per 100 sections.

Gathering

Gathering puts the sections of pages into the right order. Modern machines have boxes in which the sections are placed. The machine then places one section from each box on a moving belt so that the sections build up into a book.

The sections then pass by conveyor from the gathering machine to a stacker, which counts them and delivers a continuous run of book-sized sections ready for the next stage of the operation—sewing the sections together.

Sewing

Most sewing machines are semiautomatic. An operator places an open section over a saddle and presses a pedal to feed the section through.

◀ Signatures, or book sections, being sewn together. A signature can comprise as few as 8 and as many as 64 pages. Most modern bookbinding equipment works with 32 or 64 page sections.

Semiautomatic machines become automatic with the addition of a feeder, which opens the section and feeds it onto the saddle using a simple computer program.

Nipping

The book blocks are now nipped to recompress the sections. Nipping has not changed greatly over the years; two steel blocks press down to flatten the book and squeeze out the air that has again become trapped inside. Many books have a lining of gauze or strong paper glued along the back of the book block. The lining material is fed into a machine under the book block and pressed onto the book, then dried by infrared or ultrasound.

▼ Folded sections, or signatures, are fed into a machine and gathered—arranged in the sequence required to form the finished book. A careful check is made at this stage to make sure only one of each section is included in each block. The blocks are then fed into a trimmer, which cuts off the three unbound outer edges simultaneously.

Books are cut by three knives on three edges: head and tail (top and bottom) and foredge (front). Modern three-knife trimmers work at 35 to 40 cycles per minute.

Binding

Most books are bound in cloth or printed paper covers. To obtain the required size, the cloth is cut on a machine that cuts length- and sidewise. Printed paper covers are cut to size on a programmable machine with one knife.

Boards are needed to complete the case. They are made mainly from a number of types of paper waste in various sizes and thicknesses. Casemaking machines are extremely complex: they glue a piece of cloth, place two boards and a strip of hollow onto the cloth, turn in the edges, and press to exclude trapped air. The hollow, the part of the case on the spine of the book, is fed from a roll through the machine to the same length as the case board. Modern casemakers run at a rate of 1,000 cases per hour.

Casing-in

The cut book blocks and the completed cases now come together on four machines collectively called an in-line—a backing machine, a casing-in machine, a pressing machine, and a jacketing machine. The backing machine rounds the book, then a joint is backed on to help strengthen it. After this, the book is cased in. Most casing-in machines run at a rate of up to 70 books per minute, although there are now models that are capable of producing up to 120 books per minute.

After casing in, the book is pressed. This is done under hydraulic pressure and with heated nippers gripping into the case where the joint and the case meet. Books are usually pressed for only about 15 seconds, which is a sufficient interval of time to allow the adhesive to dry.

Next, a jacketing machine puts the jacket on the book and then passes it to a stack count. From here, a shrink-wrapping machine packages the book ready for dispatch.

Paperback production

Today paperbacks are produced in vast quantities. The companies that manufacture paperbacks are large with expensive machinery capable of working double shifts to keep overhead down. Costs are crucial in this sector of the book trade.

The majority of today's mass-market paperbacks are unsewn, thus reducing the need for sewing machines or gatherers. The modern paperback machine has a gatherer incorporated that feeds the book into continuously moving jaws. The book passes over a horizontal saw that cuts off the back fold of the sections. The book then passes over a glue wheel, which deposits a layer of adhesive on the spine. The covers are fed automatically from a hopper into the path of the book. As the book passes over the cover, side-nipping jaws nip the book cover together.

The wrapped books are taken to a three-knife guillotine by conveyor, cut as cased books, stacked, and shrink-wrapped. The shrink-wrap machine packs the book the same way that jars of jam are packed for transportation. The process is cheap, fast, and protects the book. Paperback production uses a special adhesive, called hot melt, that works at very high temperatures, from 320 to 345°F (160–175°C), and dries within about five seconds. This process is known as perfect binding.

▶ Full automation of quality books is not always economical because they are not made in as large a quantity as paperbacks, for example. In manual bookbinding book blocks are rounded at the spine (top), which is then spread out on each side. Next the case is formed from boards and liners (center), which are then glued to the sides of the book (bottom).

SEE ALSO: Lithography • Paper manufacture • Printing

Botany

Botany—the study of plants—is undergoing a revolution as a result of genetic engineering, and recent years have seen some of the most impressive advances. New techniques are enabling botanists to design crop plants for improved harvests that are disease resistant and that can tolerate difficult environmental conditions.

Corn, for instance, can now chase off its worst pest, the European corn borer, by utilizing a gene that produces an insecticide within the plant that is toxic only to the bug and harmless to other creatures, including humans. The financial rewards could be considerable, since the insect causes crop losses worth $500 million a year in the United States alone. Another pest, the Colorado beetle, has also been targeted. A variety of potato has been modified to produce a protein that is toxic to the beetle but harmless to humans and animals.

Genes have been implanted into wheat to make it resistant to specific herbicides. In this way, weeds in a field can be attacked and destroyed without harming the crop. More important, genes that enhance protein quality and increase disease resistance can be introduced into wheat in the future. Research is under way to increase the quantity of a protein called lysine in rice, which would reduce one effect of lysine deficiency—childhood blindness—across many Asian countries.

Another advance provided by genetic engineering is the ability to turn the masculinity of plants on or off, which the breeder needs to do in order to raise pedigree crop strains. In crops like corn, for instance, the male anthers have to be removed from each plant, at a yearly cost in the United States of over $200 million, to prevent them from breeding with other neighboring strains, losing or diluting valuable characteristics. By emasculating the plants, breeders can cross them with a pollen of their choice, thus ensuring that they make a good hybrid.

Although some genetically modified crops have become commercial reality in countries like the United States, there is resistance to growing them elsewhere. Of particular concern are "terminator" genes designed to kill second-generation seeds, making it impossible for farmers to save seed for next year's crop. Biotechnology companies often use this gene to prevent other breeders from taking advantage of their genetically modified crop and argue that it lessens the risk of genetically engineered varieties escaping into the environment and contaminating wild species. There are, however, important questions still to be answered about the effects of cross-fertilization with other species and what would happen to organisms foraging on seeds contaminated with terminator toxins.

◀ This African violet, *Saintpaulia ionanther*, has thrown up a purple flower on a normally pink-flowered plant as the result of a transposon, or jumping gene. Transposons are mobile pieces of DNA that can move about within the genome (DNA sequence) of the plant and effect changes depending on where they are at the time. Transposons are thought to be mechanisms by which rapid genetic change can occur, as is required by evolutionary theory.

Genetic engineering is promising other, even more extraordinary, achievements in botany. Farmers may in the future grow plastics as a crop. Genetic engineers in the United States have made thale cress—a plant with no commercial use so far that produces a natural plastic called PHB (polyhydroxybutyrate). This plastic has the great advantage of being biodegradable. ICI (Britain's biggest chemicals company) already uses bacteria to make PHB commercially in fermenters for use in products such as shampoo bottles, garden labels, and medical sutures.

Plants behaving like animals

During the 1980s, plant scientists started to realize that plants behave much more like animals than had been imagined. In particular, it appears that plants have touch sensitivity and even a primitive ability to communicate with each other.

Dozens of plants, such as the Venus's flytrap and the sensitive plant (a species of mimosa), use a sense of touch to trigger their movements, but it is now becoming increasingly clear that botanical peculiarities such as these are far from unusual. In fact, all plants have a sense of touch, and this sense works uncannily like that in animals.

Simply stroking a plant's stem for a few seconds a day is enough to stunt its growth and widen its stem. In natural conditions, this tech-

▲ Tobacco remains an important cash crop despite its narcotic properties, and is a standard testbed for research. Genetic engineering has helped produce bumper tobacco harvests, while food crops such as corn and wheat are now stronger and better able to resist pests and insecticides. One day, in the not too distant future, farmers may even be able to grow plastic as a crop.

nique will enable plants to stand up to the buffeting of the wind and will protect their stems from snapping. Japanese farmers, for example, brush their sugar beet seedlings before transplanting them to the field, thus helping them to survive better. Scientists are now puzzled by other features of plant touch awareness. Stroking the plants also seems to be a sort of plant tonic: it increases their chlorophyll content and helps them endure drought or chilly periods. Horticulturalists are now looking to see how they can use these promising discoveries in greenhouses and crop fields.

How does a plant's sense of touch actually work? In 1989, special touch sensors were discovered in plant cell membranes. When the cells are stretched, the membrane sensors open up and let ions through, upsetting the voltage across the membrane. Exactly the same thing happens in animal cells, telling touch-sensitive nerves when to fire signals to alert the brain. It may seem far-fetched that plants and animals behave in the same way, but in fact, the Venus's flytrap and mimosa actually generate nervelike electric signals when touched, that tell their motor cells to move. Even though plants have no nerves as such, their cells are joined together in a communication link of electric circuits.

It is not clear whether ordinary plants also use electric signals when they detect touch, but scientists are unravelling a string of chemical reactions triggered by the touch sensors, which eventually lead to a change in the plant's growth and development. In 1990, an important discovery was made by chance at Stanford University. Janet Braam and Ronald Davis were studying how plant genes work when they noticed that touching or even simply spraying a plant with water triggered a special set of genes. Chemical detective work revealed that these touch-sensitive genes make a protein involved in identifying and grabbing hold of calcium ions.

These calcium ions are a vital signal for redirecting plant growth, and in 1992, a group of researchers at Edinburgh University turned this chemistry into a practical tool by genetically engineering a "glow" gene into potato plants to make them light up whenever they released calcium under stress. Simply touching the plant makes its cells glow sky-blue. Researchers hope that farmers will eventually use light meters to gauge plant health.

Plant talk

Several remarkable pieces of research have revealed a chemical language between plants. Interest in this began when oak trees being attacked by caterpillars were found to respond by making bitter-tasting tannins, which insects find distasteful. Unexpectedly, nearby unmolested trees also started producing the tannins, as if under caterpillar attack. It appeared that somehow the infested trees had been able to warn their neighbors.

Exactly how one tree can communicate with-another tree remained a mystery until, in 1990, a perfumed signal was discovered in sagebrush, a familiar plant on the plains of the western United States. When a sagebrush is attacked by insects, it not only starts making special insect-fighting proteins but also gives off a hormone perfume rather like the scent of jasmine, which tells neighboring plants to switch on their insect-repelling proteins.

Airborne signals are also used by plants to recruit helpful insects. In 1990, it was found that a scent released by corn plants under attack from caterpillars appeared to act like an SOS signal to attract passing wasps. These were not ordinary wasps, however, but parasitic ones that laid their

▶ The voodoo lily (*Sauromatum venosum*) is one of a number of plants that produces a chemical similar to aspirin. It is thought the chemical is involved in triggering a rise in heat in the poker, attracting insects to pollinate the plant.

eggs on the caterpillars, eventually killing them. The plant was attracting the natural enemies of its own enemy, the caterpillar, by using a chemical language.

Meanwhile, below ground level, desert plants have been discovered "telling" one another to keep their distance. When roots from different plant species grow near each other, they often avoid tangling with one another by giving off warning signals. They pass chemical messages into the soil, which, in effect, reveal if the plant is the same species or a competitor.

▶ Touch-sensitive plants like the Venus's flytrap (*Dionaea muscipula*) are helping scientists to create stronger, more hardy plants.

Aspirin

In addition to airborne hormone signals, many other hormones are being discovered in plants. Probably the most unusual is aspirin, although it has been known for many decades that plants make aspirin—in fact the very name aspirin comes from Spiraea, or meadowsweet. But until recently no one could figure out what function this drug fulfilled in plants.

The answer came, like so many major scientific discoveries, from a completely unexpected source. The voodoo lily is a tropical plant with an extraordinary bloom. On the outside it looks like a purple poker wrapped up in a green sheath, nipped at the bottom into a small chamber. When the bloom becomes fertile, the poker suddenly heats up, exuding a pungent foul-smelling odor. This "perfume" attracts flies, which flock to the poker and crawl down the sheath to the inside of the chamber where the real flowers are hidden and pollinate them.

The signals that trigger the poker to heat up were unknown until the chemistry of the bloom was unraveled in 1987. Of all the chemicals in the plant, only one candidate fitted the bill—salicylic acid, the chemical cousin of aspirin. Its levels surged just before the poker heated up.

This discovery led scientists to investigate how salicylic acid affected ordinary plants. They found that plants attacked by diseases make salicylic acid to fight the infection. It is also thought the chemical allows them to withstand bouts of cold weather. Companies are now looking at ways of either applying the chemical to crops or breeding plants with high levels of their own salicylic acid.

Plant hormones

Although plant-growth hormones have been studied for some time, botanists may be on the threshold of an exciting new wave of plant hormone research. Apart from salicylic acid, dozens of other hormones are being discovered with prospects for future use in agriculture to promote growth and protect plants. Fascinatingly, most of these hormones are closely related to animal hormones.

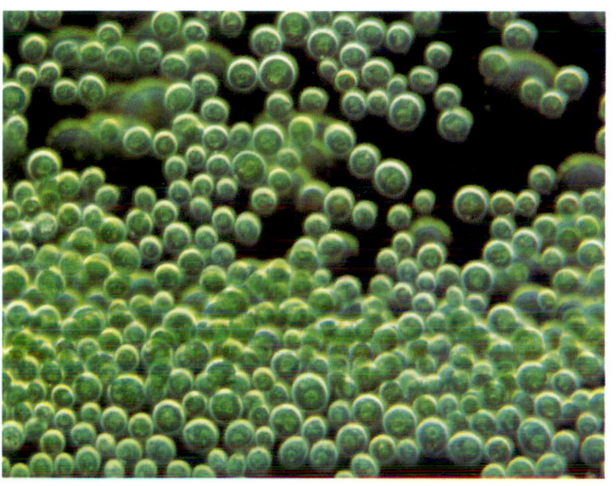

▲ Remarkably, the green algae *Chlamydomonas* contains a chemical light sensor that is almost identical to that found in the eyes of mammals.

Prostaglandins have been found in bean seedlings but are more commonly found in animals, where they trigger pain in wounds and areas of inflammation. Their purpose in plants remains unclear, however. The nerve-transmitting hormones serotonin, norepinephrine, and acetylcholine are found in vegetation from nuts to nettles, but it is not clear what their precise functions are. Acetylcholine seems to be involved in a plant's "clock," communicating the time of day and year by recording the hours of daylight each day. Animals seem to use acetylcholine for the same purpose, as well as for passing messages between nerve fibers.

Steroids are best known for their effects on humans, but estrogens and testosterones are found to help flowering in a wide variety of plants and even mating in fungi. Indeed, one of the most common plant hormones, gibberellic acid, is a close cousin of the animal sex hormones. So, too, are the other plant hormones: indole-acetic acid is related to a nerve-impulse transmitter in animals; cytokinins are found in insects; and abscisic acid, the hormone that makes leaves drop off trees in the fall, has been found in pig brains.

SEE ALSO: Agricultural science • Agriculture, intensive • Agriculture, organic • Genetic engineering • Hormone

Bow and Arrow

Bows and arrows are one of the most primitive, yet long-lived, forms of weaponry. The earliest records of the bow, the first form of stored energy, date from the Upper Paleolithic period (30,000–15,000 B.C.E.) and come from arrowheads found in north Africa and cave paintings in Spain, which clearly depict hunters using bows. Mainly the materials available for its construction and the way that it was used in warfare and hunting governed the development of the bow. Short, sometimes recurved, bows predominated where timber was scarce or stunted in growth or where horn or bone was used as bow material. In addition, shorter bows were easier to use on horseback for both hunting and warfare. In countries with access to long straight timber, the longbow became the weapon of the foot archer. It was about 5 to 6 ft. (1.5–1.8 m) long and provided useful long-range accuracy at about 300 to 400 paces. Although not as powerful in terms of penetration as the crossbow, it could be loosed five to six times more rapidly (with a firing rate of 10 to 20 arrows per minute). It was also simpler and cheaper to make, costing up to five times less than a crossbow of the same period.

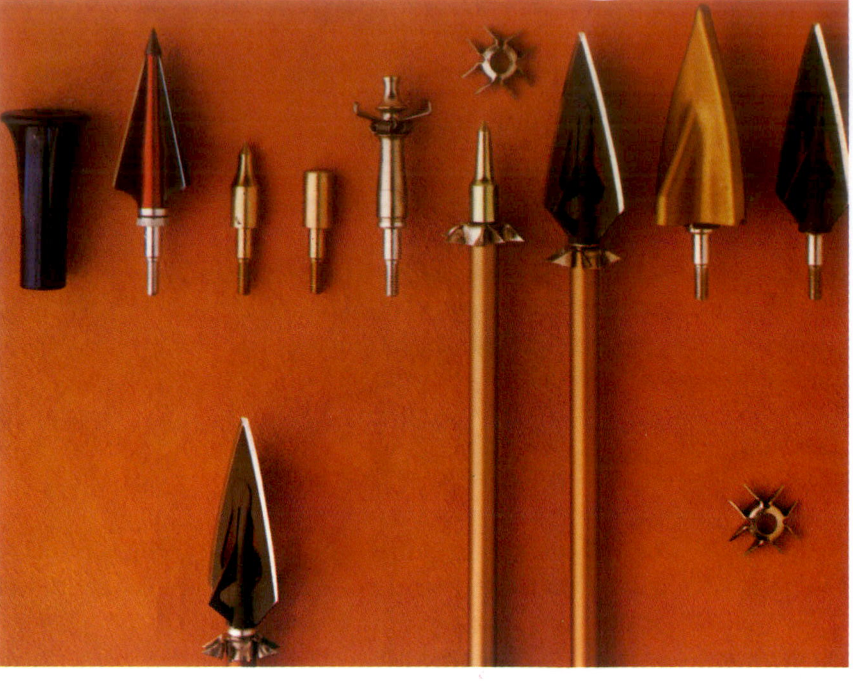

▲ A wide range of poles and arrowheads is available to suit every user's needs.

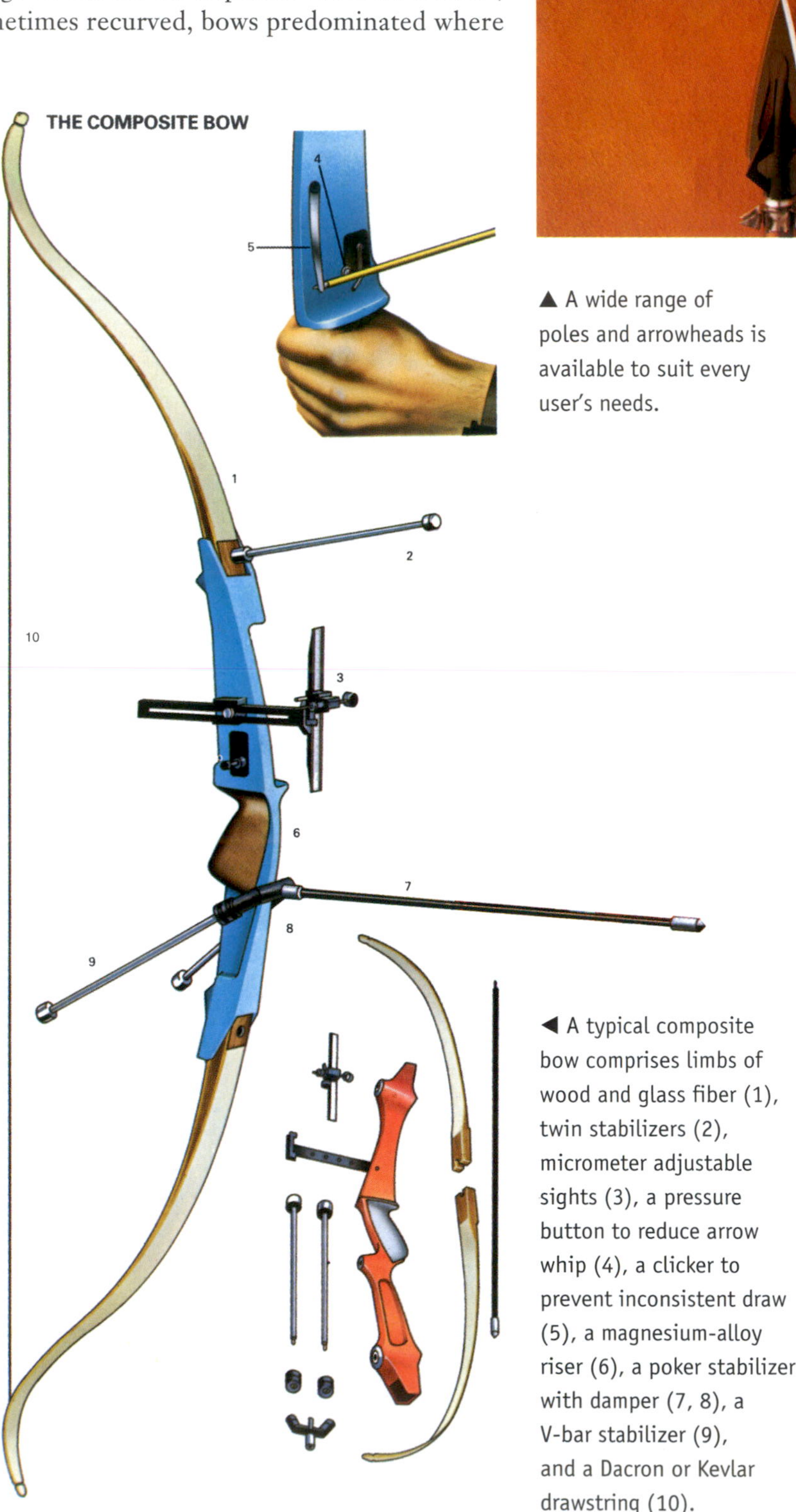

◀ A typical composite bow comprises limbs of wood and glass fiber (1), twin stabilizers (2), micrometer adjustable sights (3), a pressure button to reduce arrow whip (4), a clicker to prevent inconsistent draw (5), a magnesium-alloy riser (6), a poker stabilizer with damper (7, 8), a V-bar stabilizer (9), and a Dacron or Kevlar drawstring (10).

Development of the longbow

As a military weapon, the bow was probably introduced into Britain by the Romans, but it was under the Normans that archery was improved, organized, and diffused throughout the country. The English longbow began to be accepted as a national weapon in the mid-13th century.

Not long after this, laws, rigorously enforced, began to govern the manufacture, distribution, and proficiency of the longbow. Sundays and holidays, for example, were directed to be spent at target practice with the bow, instead of at other pastimes. This rigid regulation of production and use continued through the reign of Elizabeth I and was reinforced at frequent intervals. Despite the improvements made in firearms, the longbow continued to be used in Britain until the 16th century, when its military applications began to decline. As a pastime, however, it retained its popularity until late in the 17th century, when it fell into neglect until its revival as a sport a century later.

Materials used

The wood most favored for the English longbow was Spanish yew, with hazel, ash, and elm as secondary choices. Bowstrings were made of flax, spun and twisted and greased with beeswax: each end was woven into itself and strengthened with stitching and sometimes leather. Arrows were made of good dry timber, with as many as 15 varieties of wood listed as suitable in the middle of the 16th century. By the 19th century, red pine was the wood most frequently used. Arrowheads used with the longbow, mainly of iron or steel, fell into three categories: broad head, fork head (with the barbs facing forward), and blunt head, a type made of wood. The broad head came closest to being an all-purpose type, while the fork heads were used against large game and flying birds, and the blunt heads against small game and birds. The feathers, which stabilize and guide the flight of the arrow, were generally goose or turkey. Arrows were formerly as long as 36 in. (91 cm) but by the 19th century had been reduced in size to about 28 in. (71 cm), a length that remains in common use today.

Using the longbow

The bow must first be strung so that the upper end of the bowstring (which is released from tension when the bow is not in use) is engaged in notches at the upper end of the bow, known as the horn. An arrow is then nocked, or placed in position just above the handle of the bow with the notch of the arrow engaged in the string. The bow is then drawn, the arrow gripped by the first and second fingers and the string by both fingers plus the thumb. The bow was formerly drawn so that the rear of the arrow was level with the ear, but current practice takes it only to the chin. The pull of a bow, or the number of pounds of strength necessary to pull it fully, is now largely a matter of individual preference and ability, while also taking into account the purpose for which it is to be used. Some bows in the United States have 100 lb. (45 kg) pulls, which give enormous power for shooting large game.

A bow exploits the energy stored in its limbs as the archer draws back the string. The energy storage potential of a bow, and hence its power, is measured in terms of the weight required to draw back the bowstring. But the power of a bow is not all that affects how far or fast an arrow will fly. To achieve maximum distance with low draw-weight and short arrows, a shorter bow can be used effectively. The sharper string angle, maximizing mechanical advantage, will thrust the arrow forward with a greater speed and hence achieve greater range.

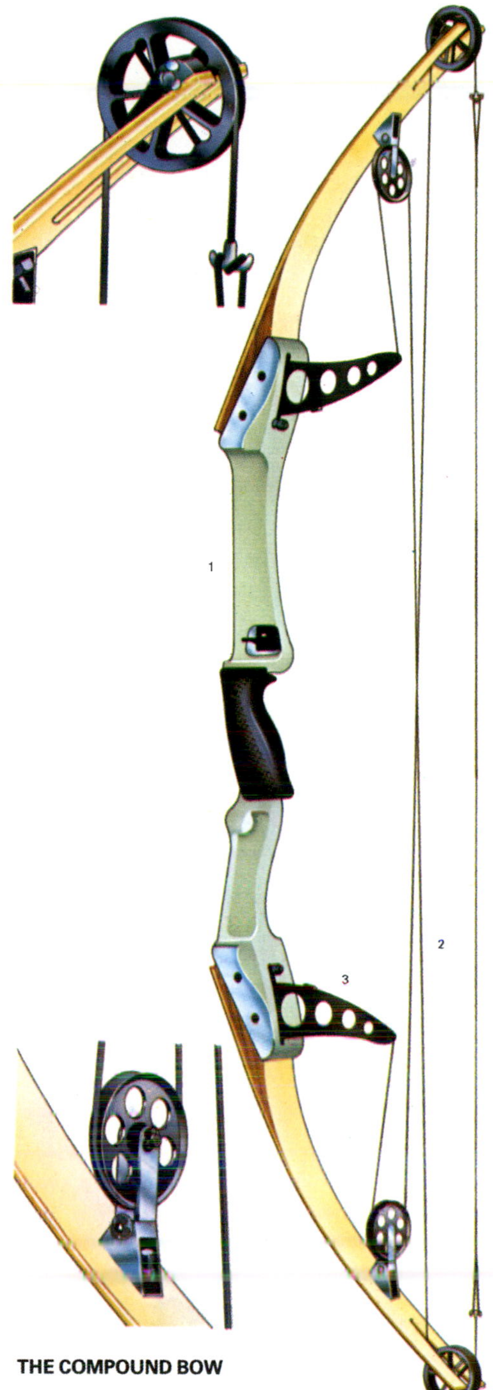

THE COMPOUND BOW

◀ Favored by hunters for its power, the compound bow is short, light, and easy to use. Difficult to draw at first, the bow becomes easier as the mechanical advantage of the pulley comes into play. At full draw, the average archer can hold a high-powered compound bow on target with little effort. This four-pulley bow has a magnesium riser (1), a steel cable (2), and limb-adjustment bars (3).

Archery today

The use of the longbow for target shooting as a pastime was revived about 1780, and the Royal Toxophilite Society was founded in England in 1781 to foster and regulate the sport. Archery has a large following today in Britain and the United States, and frequent competitions are held.

A small number of craftspeople have relearned the art of bowyery (bowmaking) and are capable of recreating most types of bow in use by modern archers. A few archers use a traditional type of longbow made from hardwood and having linen bowstrings, but most use the composite bow. This type of bow is laminated and consists of GRP (glass-reinforced plastic) on the outside with

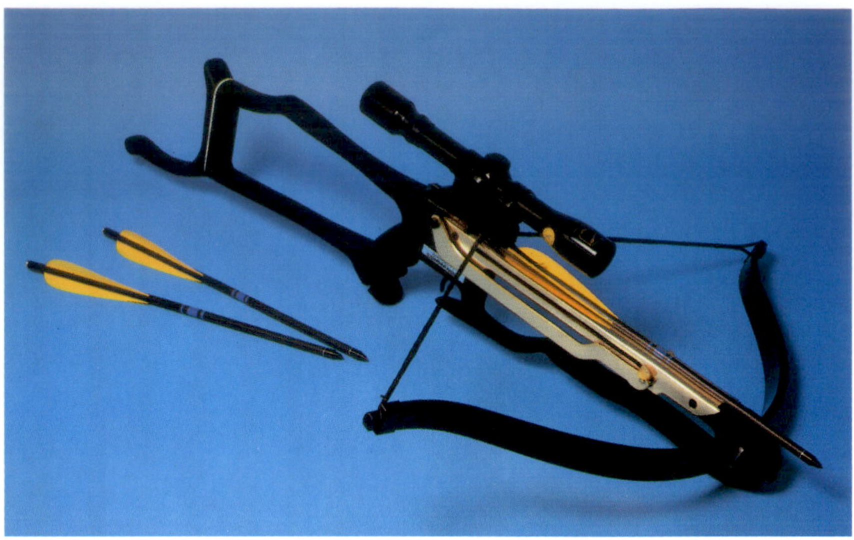

▲ The Barnett Commando crossbow with glass fiber prod, light-alloy body and stock, safety catch, and telescopic sights. The stock breaks to allow the bow to be cocked.

maple laminations inside and hardwood on the riser (handle section). More exotic materials such as magnesium alloys and, ever more commonly, carbon fiber are also being used. Stabilizers are fitted to increase accuracy, with damped units sometimes being used. Compound bows have a pulley system bowstring to give high power from a manageable pull. Lengths vary from 5 to 6 ft. (1.5–1.8 m). The bowstring is made from a synthetic fiber, such as Dacron, and modern arrows are precision-drawn aluminum. Bows for target shooting may also be equipped with adjustable micrometer sights. Competition archers aim at the center gold—9 in. (23 cm) in diameter—at a range of 300 ft. (91 m).

Crossbow

Originally the crossbow was not the light, hand-held weapon common in the late Middle Ages but a heavy device mounted on a sturdy wooden stand. Such weapons appear to have been developed quite independently in China and the countries of the east Mediterranean, and the hand-held crossbow seems to have been a regional modification in both China and the West.

The crossbow consists of three essential components: the bow, the stock, and the trigger mechanism. The bow, originally made of wood or a laminated structure of wood, horn, and sinews, was later made of steel in the West. The bow was attached to the stock, which was grooved down the length of its upper surface to guide the iron-tipped bolt (arrow). The function of the trigger mechanism was to retain the bowstring once it had been drawn and to provide an easy release.

Using a crossbow

At first glance, the crossbow appears to offer no advantage over the conventional bow, having a similar range and penetrating power while being far slower to draw and shoot. Once drawn, however, it can be held drawn and loaded for an indefinite period, and it was an effective weapon in the hands of a relative novice.

Although it existed in the late Roman Empire, the handheld crossbow did not become common in Europe until the Crusades of the 12th century. It appears to have been developed independently of Chinese crossbows, which had a trigger mechanism that used a pair of interlocking levers that automatically cocked the trigger when the bowstring was drawn back. The bowstring of the European crossbow was retained by the tooth of a ratchet wheel, known as a nut, while the trigger—a lever held in position by a leafspring—prevented the nut from turning, either by friction or by engaging with a second tooth.

Early European crossbows had to be drawn by hand, the archer normally placing his feet on the bow and pulling the string upward into position with both hands. The front end of the weapon was provided with a stirrup in which the archer could place his foot, and he often wore a large hook on his waist belt to help draw the bow as he first crouched and then stood upright.

The power of steel

In the 14th century, the wood and horn bow was replaced by a more powerful steel bow, and another means of drawing had to be found. About 1400, a system was introduced whereby the bow was drawn by a rack-and-pinion device called a cranequin that ran along the length of the weapon. A little later a system was introduced using a windlass and pulleys or paired crank handles. Finally, a forked goat's-foot lever was temporarily attached to the weapon.

The rapid development of the handgun rendered the crossbow obsolete as a weapon of war in the 16th century. It remained in use for the next two centuries as a hunting weapon, often ornately embellished, fitted with a butt, and discharged from the shoulder in imitation of the gun.

Today the crossbow has become a popular target weapon and is used by both the military and sportsmen. The high cost of guns and ammunition have been the major causes of this renaissance, although the silent nature of the weapon has proved an attraction to poachers. The modern crossbow normally has a bow of steel, glass-reinforced plastic (GRP), or in the latest models, carbon fiber. The stock and butt, fitted with sights, are of wood, and the bowstring of nylon.

SEE ALSO: Elasticity • Glass fiber • Plastics • Polyamide • Sports equipment

Brain

The complexity and size of the human brain distinguishes humans, the dominant species, from other animal life. The average brain weight of an adult male is 50 oz. (1,400 g) and is estimated to contain 10 billion nerve cells. Female brains are slightly smaller, but the weight difference has no significant effect on function. Four main areas of brain function can be recognized: activities of the mind, perception of sensation, control of movement, and automatic regulation of body functions.

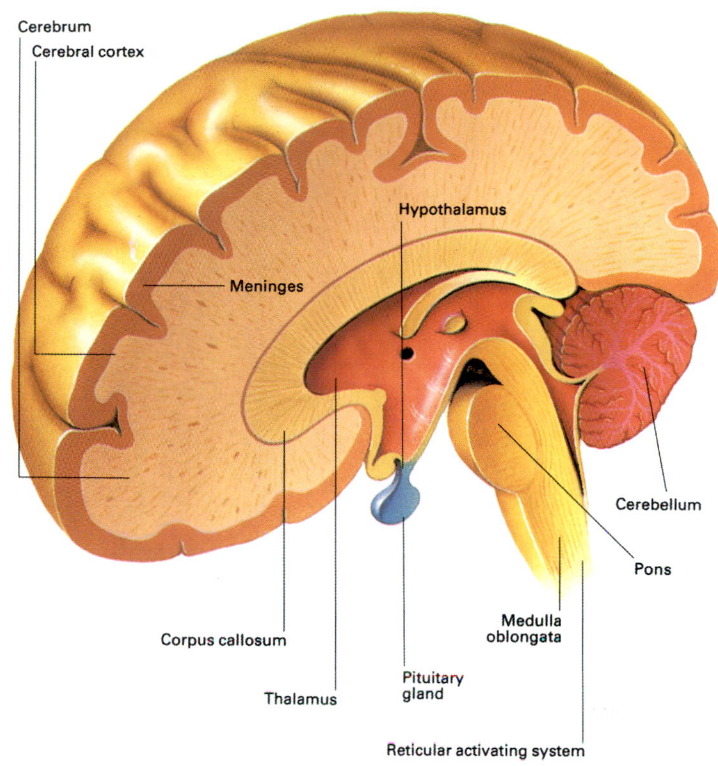

▲ A cross section of the brain, showing the major structures. Within the brain, a network of blood vessels supplies vital oxygen.

Neuroanatomy

The entire human brain consists of neurons, which are characteristic cells with a single nucleus, and long spidery extensions of the cell body known as dendrites. Neurons are arranged in distinctive layers in the brain that are visible to microscopic examination. Numerous connections between neurons exist at the ends of dendrites. Communication of nerve signals occurs at these sites (or synapses), relaying information to and from the brain and, through other connections, to separate areas within the brain. In life, synaptic activity never ceases and results in a continual discharge of electrical impulses over the surface of the brain brought about by the flux of electrically charged molecules through the neuronal cell surface. The small voltage of the electric activity has characteristic fluctuations and rhythms that can be detected by electrodes fixed to the scalp and recorded by an electroencephalograph.

Aggregations of neuronal nuclei have a gray appearance, which can be seen below the surface of the brain when it is examined in cross section. This gray matter is overlaid by white matter consisting of dendritic processes that are coated by individual sheaths of a predominantly fatty material called myelin. The myelin sheath insulates the electrical signal generated in the neuron as it is conducted to the synaptic terminal, which is uncoated—analogous to the bare wires at the end of an electricity cable.

The surface of the brain has a convoluted appearance with numerous grooves and ridges known as *sulci* and *gyri*, respectively. The arrangement enormously increases the surface area of the brain, where a considerable amount of synaptic communication occurs.

A number of deep fissures divide the brain into recognizable parts. The principal division runs in the midline between the front and back separating the two cerebral hemispheres. The hemispheres are joined at the base of the longitudinal fissure by a horizontal band of neuronal tissue, the corpus callosum, so there are important cross connections between the two halves of the brain. Each hemisphere has a frontal, parietal, temporal, and occipital lobe, all of which have distinctive functions. Frontal lobes are separated from the parietal lobes by a central fissure. The area of frontal lobe immediately adjacent to the fissure controls voluntary movement throughout the body. Messages are transmitted through neurons down to the thalamus, which lies below the corpus callosum. The thalamus behaves like a relay station for messages entering and leaving the brain and crosses over information, so that the left side of the body is controlled by the right cerebral hemisphere. Most individuals show a dominance of voluntary movement in the left hemisphere and are right-handed. Large areas of the frontal lobe are not involved with movement and seem to be concerned with emotion, behavior, and intellect. These areas are more highly developed in humans than in other mammalian species.

The occipital lobes lie beneath the back of the skull and are almost entirely concerned with the perception of visual information. Light impulses striking the eyes are transmitted as neuronal impulses along the optic nerves to the thalamus and partly cross over at a junction of the optic nerves, the chiasma. The resulting effect is that objects seen to the left of center reach the right occipital lobe (and conversely for objects to the right). An area in the center of vision of both eyes is perceived simultaneously by both occipital lobes, giving the three-dimensional perspective of binocular vision. The parietal and temporal lobes are located between frontal and occipital areas, with the parietal uppermost. The parietal lobe perceives sensations of touch, pain, pressure, movement, and temperature from the peripheral nerves and accurately locates their source. Interpretation of speech is located in the speech area shared by the parietal and temporal lobes. The dominant speech area is located in the left parietal lobe in right-handed individuals. The temporal lobes perceive and interpret sounds, connect with the speech area, and also participate in our sense of smell.

Memory is not located in a specific area of brain but is retained in the areas involved with different sensory information. A simple example is the recognition by the parietal lobe of a familiar object that is handled but not seen.

Beneath the thalamus, the hypothalamus controls much of the automatic and unconscious nervous system that regulates body functions such as temperature control. Hunger, thirst, and appetite centers are located here. The pituitary gland lies immediately beneath the hypothalamus and controls the output of hormones.

Two areas beneath the cerebral hemispheres can be easily recognized, the cerebellum and midbrain. Cerebellar activity is unconscious but is necessary for maintaining smooth coordination of voluntary movement and balance. The cerebellum connects with the midbrain, where all connections between the cerebral hemispheres and the spinal cord pass. Vital centers regulating sleep, breathing, and heart rate are located in the midbrain together with certain reflex areas regulating vomiting, swallowing, and sneezing.

Membranes and tissues

The brain and spinal cord are covered entirely by three distinct membranous tissues. *Dura mater* is the firm outer membrane of fibrous tissue lying immediately underneath the skull. Infolding of the dura mater between the cerebral hemispheres forms the *falx cerebri*, and folds between the cerebrum and cerebellum form the *tentorium cerebelli*.

A more delicate inner membrane, the *arachnoid mater*, underlies the dura mater and contains cerebrospinal fluid within its subarachnoid space. The innermost layer (*pia mater*) completely coats all the convolutions of the brain, forming the interior boundary of the subarachnoid space.

Cerebrospinal fluid is produced by bundles of capillary blood vessels located in symmetrical cavities within the cerebral hemispheres. These cavities are the cerebral ventricles and are filled with the fluid, which flows out in the region of the midbrain to bathe the exterior of the brain and spinal cord. Cerebrospinal fluid supports and protects the delicate brain by maintaining a constant, uniformly distributed pressure around the brain and acts as a hydraulic shock absorber when the head is subjected to violent motion.

Blood supply is of vital importance to normal functioning of the brain because of the brain's constant requirement for oxygen and glucose,

▼ The limbic system, located within the thalamus, is chiefly concerned with memory, learning, and emotions. Damage to this region of the brain can cause irreversible loss of memory.

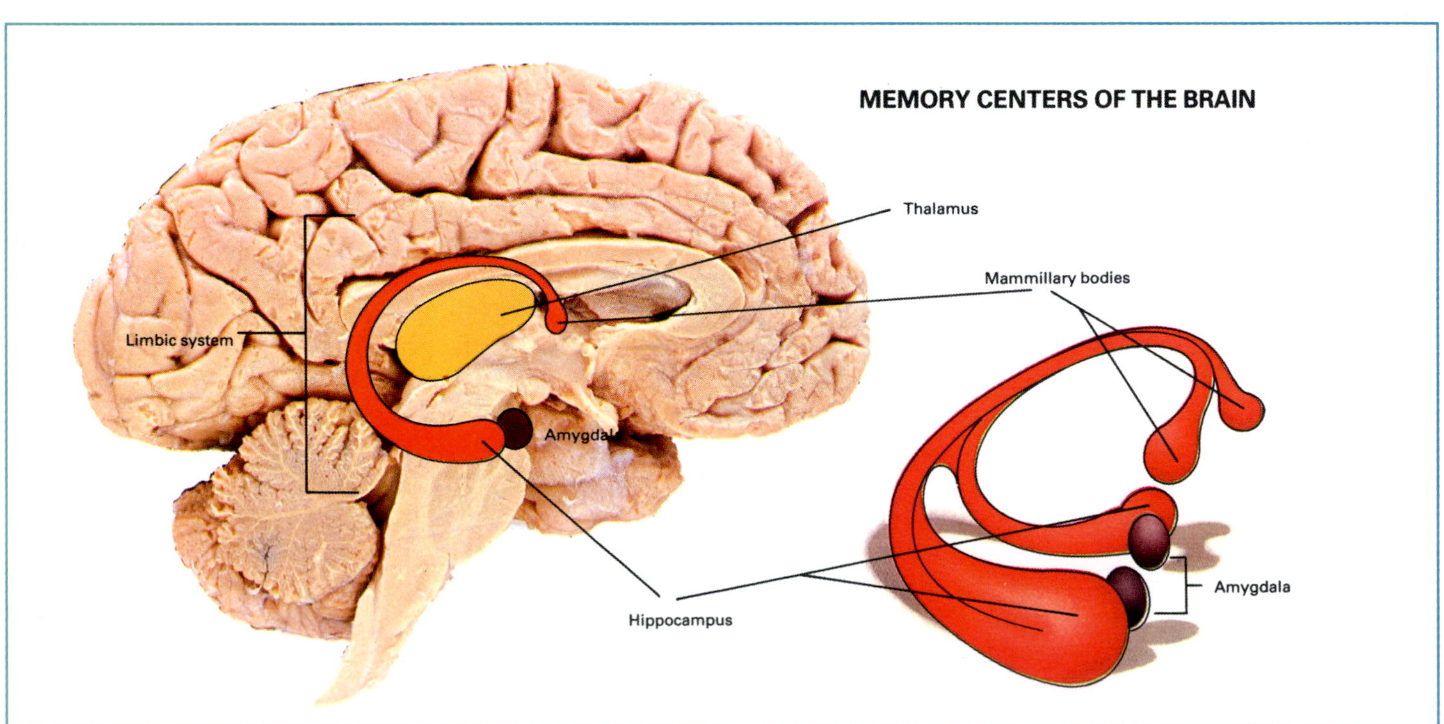

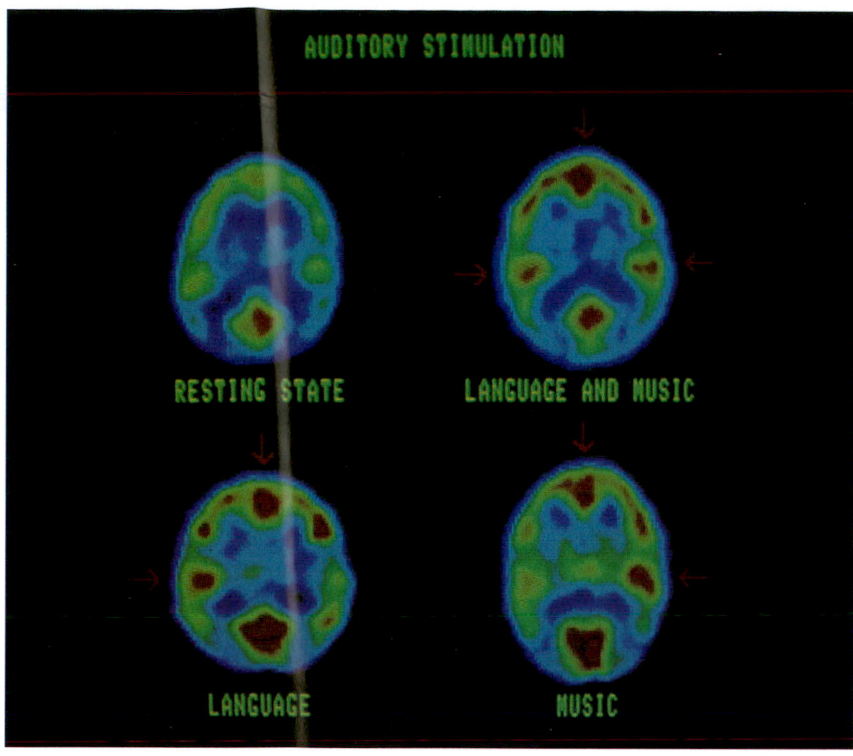

▲ Four scans, made using the technique of Positron Computed Tomography, show how various stimuli affect different parts of the brain.

which is the principal nutrient of brain cells. Approximately 20 percent of the body's total blood volume is circulating through the brain at any one time. Blood enters the skull through two internal carotid arteries in the neck and a basilar artery in the spine. The arteries connect together in a ring at the base of the brain from which three major blood vessels pass to each half of the brain—the anterior, middle, and posterior cerebral arteries. A blood clot arising in any one of these arteries will deprive the adjacent area of brain of its blood supply, causing brain damage, shown by neurological abnormalities arising on the opposite side of the body to the clot.

Although the many branches of the cerebral arteries are in close contact with all areas of the brain, there is a curious impermeability of brain tissue to many potentially toxic substances and drugs that circulate in the blood stream. The precise way in which this blood–brain barrier is achieved is not understood, but it undoubtedly fulfils a protective function. Minerals and glucose essential for brain metabolism are actively taken up and transported through the blood–brain barrier into the brain, but simple chemical diffusion of other substances is prevented.

Neurochemistry

Much information about the normal and abnormal functions of the brain has been revealed by studies of chemical messengers—the monoamines and peptides in brain tissue. Monoamines are small molecules derived from single amino acids. They are produced at synaptic junctions between neurons, released by neuronal excitation, taken up by specific receptors on adjacent neurons, and stimulate energy production in the receptor cell membrane. This sequence of events shows how neuronal impulses are transmitted throughout the brain and spinal cord and even into peripheral nerves. The chemical processes of release, receptor binding, and cell stimulation are almost instantaneous. An elaborate system of enzymes deactivates the monoamine neurotransmitters after they are discharged so that uncontrolled stimulation does not occur. This system consists of monoamine oxidase enzymes; a group of drugs that inhibit the enzymes is useful in the treatment of depressive illness. It is evident that imbalances in the concentration of the several neurotransmitters leads to a wide range of disease, ranging from neurological conditions such as Parkinson's disease to psychiatric illness such as schizophrenia. At least six chemicals are known to have neurotransmitter properties in the brain: 5-hydroxytryptamine, dopamine, noradrenalin, gamma-aminobutyric acid, acetylcholine, and histamine. Individual neurons are probably each capable of releasing a set of neurotransmitters so that differing messages can be transferred along the nerve pathways.

In the 1970s, a new group of peptide substances were found in certain areas of the brain with the property of fixing to specific receptors in the synaptic region in a similar way to the neurotransmitters. In this case, the receptor was shown to be specific for opium-derived drugs. Further, the uptake of these opiumlike peptides could be prevented by specific opium antagonists. The peptides are now known as encephalins and endorphins. They seem to have different effects in the different areas of brain where they are concentrated, affecting emotion, pain perception, mood, and muscle tension.

▶ Neurons in the brain magnified x 200. The average human brain contains 10 billion of these nerve cells, connected to each other by synapses, which transmit electrical impulses across the surface of the brain.

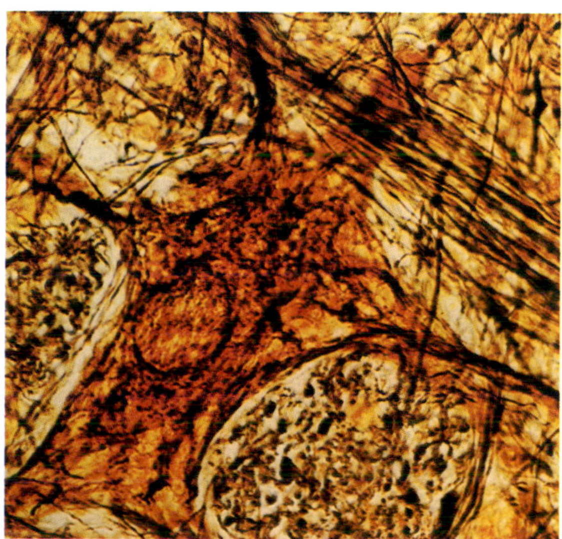

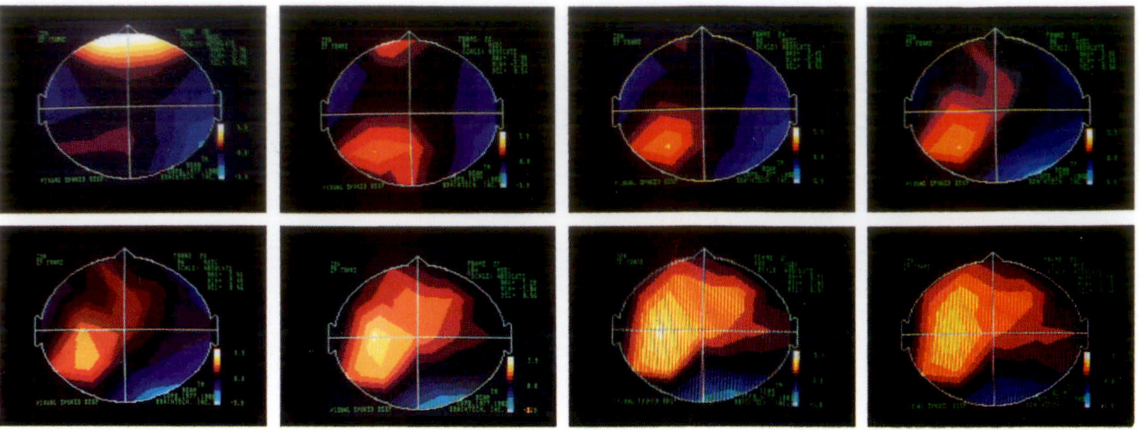

◀ This sequence of frames taken from a BEAM movie reveals that the patient has a tumor (left center area).

Brain growth

When considering the obvious immaturity of the infant human brain, it is surprising to find that almost all the adult number of neuronal cells are already found in the brain of the newborn child. A threefold increase in size and weight of brain after birth is largely caused by growth in the myelin-producing cells that surround the neurons and also by proliferation of dendrites and synaptic connections. Adult brain size is virtually accomplished by two years of age, though maturity of function does not occur until the second decade.

Neurology

Neurology, the study of the brain and the numerous disorders affecting it or arising within it, has been greatly aided by the development of new imaging techniques, particularly magnetic resonance imaging (MRI). MRI has made it possible to observe the inflammatory changes in the white matter of the brain that are typical in multiple sclerosis (MS). Injecting a dye into the patient's blood and then observing the brain with MRI shows the areas of active inflammation. This technique should speed the development of new drugs for MS: doctors will be able to see very rapidly whether drugs they are testing have any effect.

It has been possible to identify which parts of the brain are involved in which function by using a technique called PET (positron-emission tomography) scanning. PET involves exposing the patient to relatively large doses of radiation, however, and needs sophisticated and expensive equipment and expert analysis of the results.

This problem could be solved, however, by MRI linked with a new technique that makes it possible to measure the oxygenation level in a particular part of the brain. If someone is reading, for example, the area of the brain involved will use up oxygen quickly, a fact that will show up on the scan. This method should further improve the accuracy of brain surgery for forms of epilepsy that cannot be controlled with drug treatment. Electroencephalograms (EEGs)—recordings of the electrical activity of the brain— supply further detail.

Brain waves

Recording electric activity from the brain's surface is not a new idea. Since the first encephalogram in the 1920s, however, scientists have struggled to interpret the fluctuating amplitude and frequencies of brain waves. To record a patient's EEG, 20 electrodes are stuck on the scalp, and channels of information representing the activity between different pairs of electrodes are traced out. Until the advent of BEAM (brain electric activity mapping), the problem with the EEG was not that it contained too little information but that it contained too much.

Each EEG tracing contains information in terms of both amplitude and frequency. With multichannel recordings taken from electrodes distributed over the surface of the head, doctors also have to make sense of the patterns of the EEG in terms of both time and space. This mass of interrelated information is difficult even for the most experienced observer to unravel.

The brain's evoked potentials—the electric reaction to a sudden verbal or visual stimulus—are translated by BEAM into a color movie, a visual analogy of the actual voltages. The response during half a second after stimulation is divided up into 128 individual frames. To the top right of each image is the frame number and the time since stimulation, noted in milliseconds. A color chart enables quick and easy conversion of the colors into the actual evoked potential value in microvolts. When the frames are shown in sequence on the TV screen, the positive (red) and negative (blue) waves move to and fro inside the stylized head.

BLOOD • BODY SCANNER • CELL BIOLOGY • ELECTRONICS IN MEDICINE • ENDOCRINOLOGY • PSYCHIATRY • SURGERY

Braking System

A braking system can slow or stop the motion of a machine or vehicle or control its tendency to accelerate. Examples include the friction brakes of automobiles and winding machinery and the electrical systems used to brake trains.

Most brakes act through the frictional force that develops when a fixed surface is brought into contact with the surface of a moving part. As the surfaces rub together, the kinetic energy of the moving part gradually converts into heat energy, which dissipates to the atmosphere. The loss of energy from the moving part is accompanied by the desired reduction of speed.

Band brakes

The band brake is a simple but effective means of controlling motion. It consists of a flexible brake band wrapped around a drum that revolves as a machine operates. As long as the band is loose, it has little grip on the drum, which slips freely under the band. When the band tightens, it grips the drum firmly and develops a powerful braking force. Because the friction between the band and the drum acts to increase the tension in the band—and thus increase the braking force—this type of brake is an example of a self-energizing braking system. Band brakes are used to slow the descent of winched loads, since the force applied using a hand-operated lever is sufficient to start the self-energizing process, which develops a powerful braking force with little effort.

Drum brakes

Drum brakes consist of two or more brake shoes fixed on a pivoted mounting that press against the inside of a rotating drum to slow its rotation. The drum is usually metal and sometimes has metal fins attached to the outside of the drum that dissipate the heat produced by braking.

On a typical drum brake, one shoe is self-energizing and the other is not. As the drum rotates, it pulls one shoe harder against its inner surface so that the braking effect is increased; this shoe is called the leading shoe. The other shoe is pushed off by the drum and has a weaker braking effect; this is called the trailing shoe. The leading shoe wears faster and has to be replaced more often than the trailing shoe, which does less work.

To gain particular advantages of power or wear resistance, drum brakes have also been designed with two leading shoes, with two trailing shoes, or with three or even four shoes.

Drum brakes suffer from an effect called fade, which is a loss of braking efficiency that occurs when the braking surfaces become hot. Drum

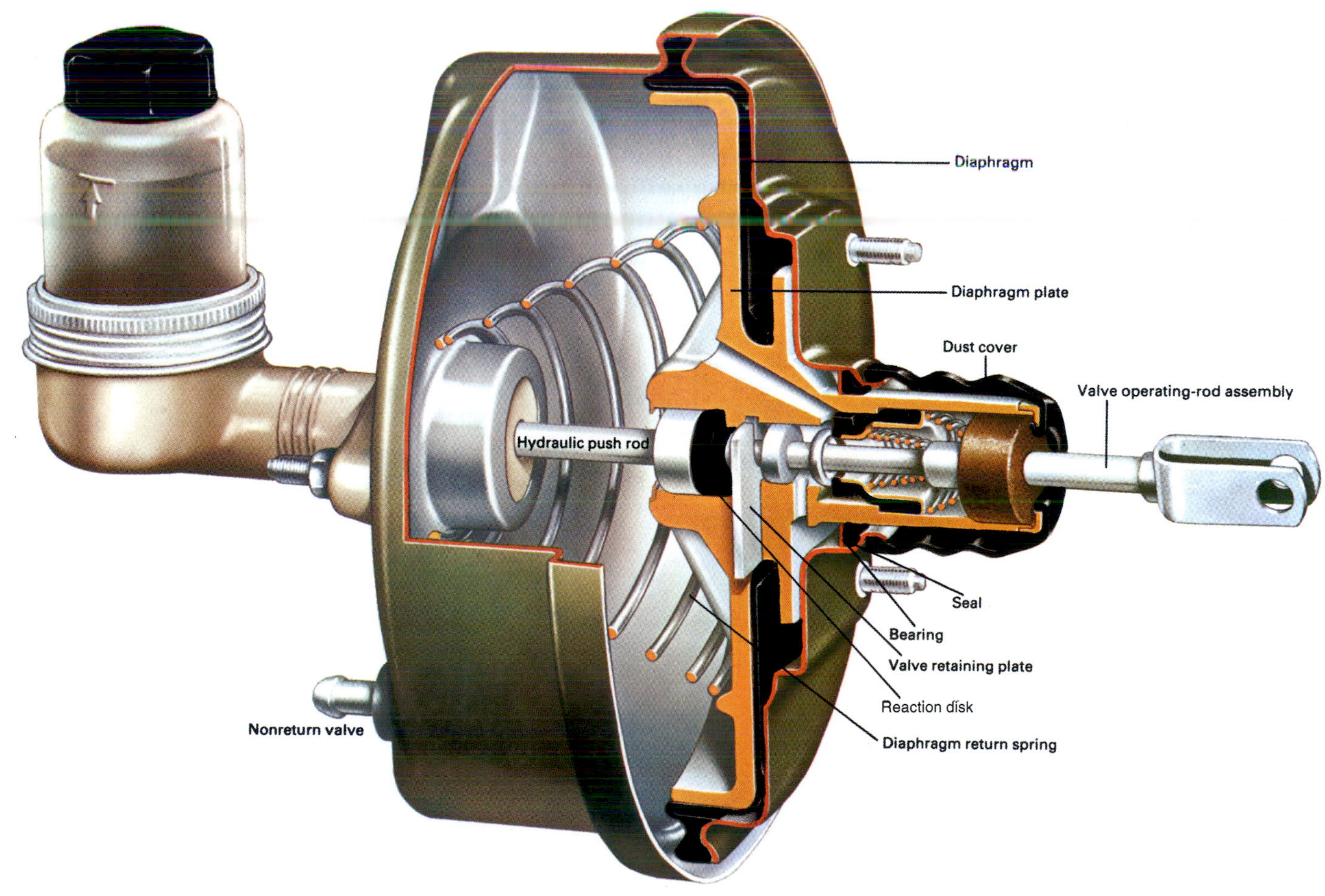

▼ The cylinder of a vacuum-servo braking system relies on a partial vacuum to pull on the brakes. When the vacuum is applied, the diaphragm plate compresses a spring and pulls on the rod that connects to the brake pads. When the vacuum is released, the spring returns the diaphragm to its neutral position.

brakes also lose some of their effect if they become wet. This can occur when an automobile with drum brakes drives through water. The problem is remedied by gently applying the brakes until the heat of braking evaporates all the moisture from the braking surfaces.

Disk brakes

Disk brakes were originally developed for the landing wheels of aircraft. A disk brake consists of a revolving disk that is gripped between two brake pads to apply the braking force. The pads of an automobile disk brake cover between one-sixth and one-ninth of the swept area of the disk. Because a brake disk is less prone to distortion than a brake drum, it can function at much higher temperatures without ill effect; the disk brake can therefore be used for much heavier duty applications than a drum brake, provided an appropriate grade of lining is used on the pads.

Disk brakes are now used extensively on the front axle of cars, where, within a given size of wheel, they dissipate about twice as much energy as the rear brakes. High-performance cars sometimes have disk brakes on both axles. A somewhat different design of disk brake, which has linings equal in size to the full swept area of the disks, is sometimes found on agricultural tractors.

All cars need a mechanically operated parking brake. Although it commonly acts at the rear, in some cases it acts at the front wheels. When the parking brake is on a drum-braked axle, it usually operates the same shoes that are controlled by the foot brake system; when disk brakes are involved, the parking brake often has its own pads in an attachment to the main brakes.

Block brakes

A common system for railroad rolling stock uses block brakes. They consist of shoes that press against the running wheels. The force to apply the brakes is provided by a spring; cylinders operated by compressed air or suction from the locomotive hold the blocks away from the wheels for free running. If a train becomes separated from its locomotive, the failure of the compressed-air or vacuum hose automatically applies the brakes.

Brake materials

The materials used in braking systems have a large coefficient of friction when in contact, which reduces the force that must be applied to generate an adequate braking effect. Brake materials must also be able to conduct heat away from the braking surfaces and be reasonably resistant to wear and high temperatures. Experience has shown that the best results are obtained when the moving part is constructed of metal and the stationary parts are lined with a composition friction material, which may wear much faster than the metal but can readily be replaced.

For general use, such as on vehicle brakes, cast iron has been found to be the most suitable metal surface. Drums can be made of a cast-iron lining with a light alloy body for improved heat conduction; disks can be made with internal passages that allow air to circulate and carry away heat.

Brake linings for general use are made of a composite—a carefully chosen mixture of fiber, metal particles, and nonmetallic ingredients bonded together with a temperature-resistant synthetic resin. Railroad block brakes use either cast-iron or composite blocks, but railroad disk brakes use composite blocks exclusively.

Power brakes

The pressing force that can be generated by hand- or pedal-operated mechanical brakes is seldom sufficient to generate an adequate braking force. When an automobile driver depresses the brake pedal, the brakes are operated by the action of hydraulic pressure or a partial vacuum on the pistons of cylinders attached to the brakes.

Vacuum-servo systems use suction from the inlet manifold of a gasoline engine to apply an equal force to the brakes on all four wheels; hydraulic systems have a master cylinder that forces hydraulic fluid into the cylinders at each of

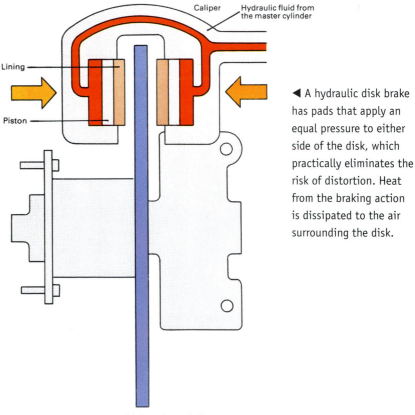

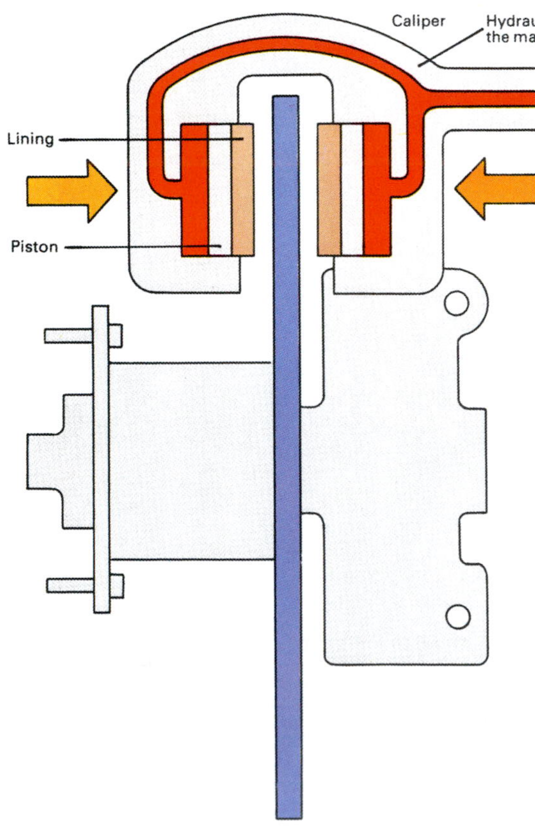

◀ A hydraulic disk brake has pads that apply an equal pressure to either side of the disk, which practically eliminates the risk of distortion. Heat from the braking action is dissipated to the air surrounding the disk.

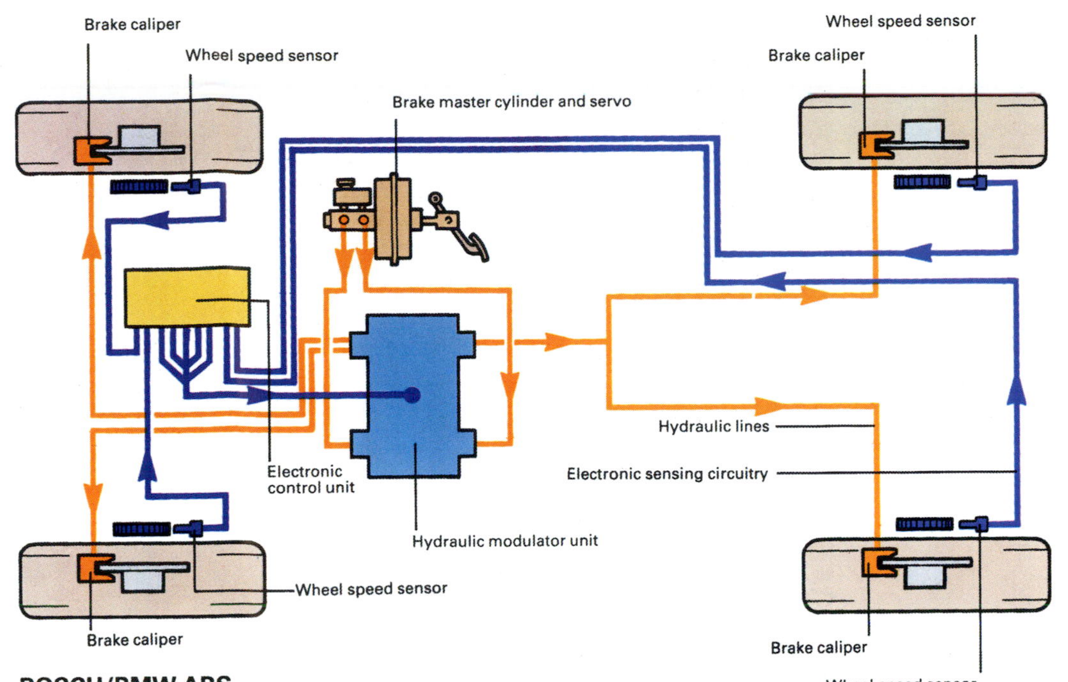

◀ In an antilock braking system, such as this one designed by BMW, a hydraulic modulator acts on inputs from the brake pedal and wheel-lock sensors to moderate braking pressure in the event of wheel lock.

the four wheels. In dual braking systems, separate circuits supply fluid to the cylinders of two pairs of wheels so that an even braking effect continues to be available even if some defect causes a loss of pressure in one of the circuits.

Larger vehicles, such as buses and trucks, have air brakes. These operate in a similar way to hydraulic brakes, but the medium that applies the brakes is compressed air from an engine-driven compressor. Articulated vehicles have their braking systems connected by quick-release hoses. In some cases, the trailer has its own compressed-air reservoir for emergency braking.

Antilock braking systems

Conventional automobile braking systems have the disadvantage that, if the driver uses the brakes too hard on a slippery road, the wheels will lock and the car may go out of control. To solve this problem, many cars are now fitted with antilock braking systems. These systems can sense when one or more of the wheels have locked or are about to lock and reduce the braking effort to the affected wheel or wheels.

Some earlier antilock systems used mechanical sensors to detect wheel lock, but electronic sensors are now used to monitor the speed of each wheel. The information is processed by a central microprocessor control unit, which adjusts the braking effort at each wheel so that maximum braking efficiency is achieved.

The braking system itself uses hydraulic pipes and pistons in just the same way as a car without antilock, so if the electronics in the antilock system should fail, the driver still has the same braking capability as in an ordinary car.

Electric brakes

Electric trains sometimes have auxiliary brakes that operate by altering the wiring of their motors so that they behave as generators (an electric motor and a generator are basically the same machine, except that the first drives and consumes power and the second is driven and provides power). The force needed to drive the generator slows the vehicle down, and the electricity generated is fed back into the overhead supply line or power rail. This type of system, called a regenerative braking system, cuts costs by reducing the power demand of a rail or streetcar network.

Aircraft braking

Aircraft are slowed in flight by air brakes. These are flaps that are extended at right angles above and below the wings or on both sides of the fuselage to break up the airflow and cause drag; that is, they deliberately make the aircraft less aerodynamically efficient. In this situation, the kinetic energy of the aircraft is dissipated to the surrounding air by making it turbulent.

On landing, the wheel brakes are supplemented by reverse thrust of the engines. The propeller blades are twisted round so that they blow forward instead of backward, or in the case of jet engines, scoops are inserted in the exhaust stream to turn this forward. The effect is to push the aircraft in the opposite direction and thus to slow it. Parachutes released on landing are employed to brake some high-performance aircraft.

SEE ALSO: AIRCRAFT DESIGN • AUTOMOBILE • AUTOMOBILE ELECTRONICS SYSTEM • AUTOMOBILE SAFETY • LOCOMOTIVE AND POWER CAR

Brass

Brass is an alloy made from copper and zinc. It was probably discovered sometime after 1000 B.C.E. by a people called the Mossynoeci, who lived near the Black Sea in northeast Turkey. They made brass, or what they thought was white bronze, by heating copper with charcoal and powdered zinc ore. The Persians used it from the fifth century B.C.E., and by the end of the first century B.C.E. the Romans were making brass coins. A flourishing brass industry had developed in northwest Europe by the middle of the fourth century C.E. The first use of brass casting in Britain was at the end of the 17th century, when a foundryman, John Lofting, began making cast-brass thimbles, which until then had been imported from Holland. The output from his factory exceeded 20,000 thimbles per week. The brass casting industry then spread to America, where it was centered in New England.

▲ The centrifugal casting process is a simple means of making symmetrical objects to close tolerances. The molten metal is poured into a cylindrical mold that is spun to force the metal outward against the side of the mold. The spinning also helps to cool the mold so that the melt solidifies quickly. Even large objects such as flanges can be made in this way, with only slight machining required after casting to achieve an exact shape.

Brass manufacture

There is a wide range of brasses, all of them copper alloys containing up to 50 percent zinc and often smaller amounts of other elements such as tin, lead, nickel, manganese, aluminum, and iron. The action of seawater on brass tends to separate the zinc from the copper, and to prevent this from happening, small amounts (0.02 percent to 0.1 percent) of arsenic or antimony—and in the United States, phosphorus—are added to brasses used on ships.

Brasses are classified according to the amount of zinc that they contain. The proportion of zinc in a brass has an important effect on its physical properties. Low-zinc brass, containing between 5 percent and 20 percent zinc, has a reddish color and is known as red brass or low brass. This material is often used for making costume jewelry. When the brass contains about 30 percent zinc, it is called yellow brass or high brass. The uses of yellow brass include making musical instruments and parts for electrical appliances, plumbing equipment, and gun cartridge cases.

Brasses are made in foundries from precisely weighed amounts of pure copper, zinc, and the other constituent elements plus clean high-grade copper scrap. One of the problems in making brass is the difference in melting points between the constituent metals: zinc melts at 786°F (419°C) but copper does not melt until 1981°F (1083°C). If the two metals are heated together, the zinc will boil away before the copper has melted, but if the copper is heated first and then solid zinc is added, most of the zinc will dissolve into the copper. An excess of zinc is added to make up for the small amount that inevitably boils away. The metal is heated in oil or gas-fired crucible furnaces, reverberatory furnaces (in which flames pass over the metals and heat is radiated from the roof of the furnace), and electric arc, or electric induction, furnaces.

The molten brass is poured from the furnace into molds. These molds produce either cylindrical billets, which are used to make tubes and rods, or ingots and slabs, which are used for brass sheets, plates, and strips. The metal is poured carefully to ensure that the molds are properly filled, with no air bubbles in the metal or in the spaces between the casting and the mold. To prevent the casting from sticking to the molds, a coating of a suitable lubricant such as graphite or an oil-based compound is applied to the inside of the mold before the metal is poured in to it.

Brass working

The methods used for making finished items from the ingots, rods, sheets, and so on depend largely on the amount of copper in the alloy. Brasses with a high copper content, usually over 62 percent, are suitable for cold working, which includes rolling, cold forging, and drawing. Drawing involves pulling a bar or rod through a series of dies, each of which has a smaller internal diameter than the previous one.

The cold working of brass causes it to become harder, often making it too hard for further shaping. To restore the softness, it is necessary to anneal the metal by heating it in a furnace or oven. After cooling, the metal must be cleaned to remove the oxides that form on the surface during the heating, otherwise they become embedded in the brass during subsequent working. This removal is commonly done by pickling the metal in solutions containing nitric or sulfuric acid. Annealing takes up to three hours at between 885 and 1380°F (475–750°C), depending on the type and amount of brass and the softness required.

For the hot-working of brass, the workpiece is heated until the metal is soft and plastic, and it is kept at that temperature for a few hours to ensure even heating all the way through. It can then be quickly and easily rolled or extruded into shape, and no annealing is needed. Hot extrusion is carried out by forcing the hot casting through a steel die. The hot-working methods cannot produce items to close tolerances, so a cold process is used to bring the metal to its required dimensions and to harden it.

Brass can be forged either hot or cold into intricate and accurate shapes. Cold-forging works best when the copper content of the brass is above 62 percent. The brass to be forged, hot or cold, is put onto a die bolted to the anvil of a drop forge. The other die is fixed to the bottom of the drop hammer, usually a heavy steel block, which is raised between two vertical guides and then allowed to drop, forcing the brass into shape between the two dies. Bolts, screws, and door and plumbing fittings are among the articles made this way.

High-tensile brass

To increase the tensile strength, hardness, and corrosion resistance of brass, small amounts of manganese, aluminum, iron, lead, and tin are added. These alloys typically contain 55 percent copper, 30 to 34 percent zinc, and various amounts of the other metal depending on the desired properties of the finished brass. High-tensile brass can be worked hot or cold and is very good for casting. One of its most valuable characteristics is its ability to be cast with almost no shrinkage or porosity, no matter how complex the shape. The very high tensile strength of these alloys—44 tons per sq. in. (678 MN/m^2) is typical—allows them to be used for making marine propellers and rudders weighing several tons.

General-purpose brasses

Brasses containing about 40 percent zinc are used for a wide range of goods. They are good for cheap, general-purpose casting with moderate strength and corrosion resistance. The addition of 1 or 2 percent lead, or up to 0.5 percent aluminum, makes these brasses particularly suitable for die casting, and the small amounts of lead improve machinability. Typical castings include valve bodies, building hardware, and engineering fittings. Naval brass is made by adding 1 percent tin to the alloy to improve its resistance to seawater corrosion. Alpha-beta brasses are easily hot-worked and forged to produce a large variety of items, including bathroom hardware, stove fittings and thermostats, oil and fuel systems, gears, steam and water fittings, and terminals for electric cables.

Other brasses

Gilding metal is another copper alloy; it contains up to 95 percent copper and is often used for architectural decoration because of its pleasing appearance. Another member of the brass family is the alloy called nickel silver. It actually contains no silver but is so named because of its silvery appearance. The copper content ranges from 55 to 60 percent, with nickel ranging from 10 to 15 percent, the remainder being zinc. This type of brass is used for the spring relay contacts in telecommunications. It is also used as the base metal in silver-plated tableware or EPNS, which stands for electroplated nickel silver.

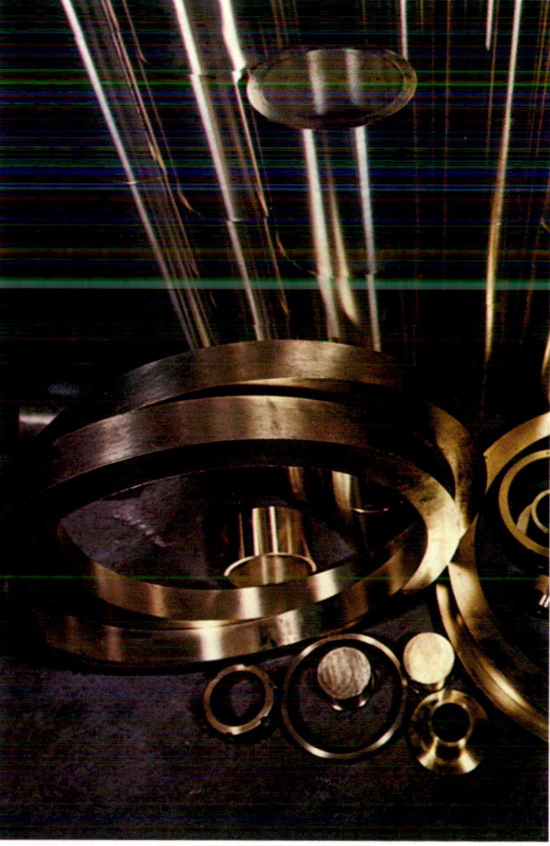

◀ A wide range of brass objects can be made by cylindrical casting, including bushings, tubular sections, and electrical contacts.

SEE ALSO: Alloy • Bronze • Casting • Copper • Metalworking

Brass Instrument

▲ The double- or French-horn has two distinct modes—hence its name. Either F or B-flat mode can be selected by pressing the thumb valve, which diverts the air around extra tubing, making it easier for players to pick out the right note.

Brass instruments consist essentially of a brass tube with a mouthpiece at one end and a flared opening, or bell, at the other. There are a number of variations on this basic theme, however, and the kinds of sounds that can be produced are similarly diverse.

To produce a note on a brass instrument, the player puts his lips against the mouthpiece and buzzes them at the correct frequency, triggering off these vibrations by quickly withdrawing his tongue from between his lips. Simultaneously, he blows into the instrument at the appropriate velocity. On striking the mouthpiece, the air stream produces what is called an edge tone, which sets the air column in the instrument vibrating. The air column vibrates with certain resonant frequencies, or pitches. These resonant frequencies are set up by standing-wave motions in the air column of the tube—they do not move along the tube but consist of a stationary pattern of vibrating air.

Standing waves result from the interaction of two waves traveling in opposite directions that reinforce each other. In the case of brass instruments, the outward-going wave is created by the edge tone in the mouthpiece. Part of this wave, when it reaches the bell, is reflected back down the brass tube toward the mouthpiece. When the edge tone is at the resonant frequency of the tube, a standing wave is set up.

The lowest note available from a given length of tubing is called the fundamental and is produced by the vibration of the entire length of the air column. But the column does not vibrate only as a whole, it also vibrates in exact fractions of its length at the same time.

The longer the vibrating column, the lower the note. The fractions of the vibrating air column therefore give out higher notes than the whole. These notes, called harmonics, are related by simple ratios (such as 3:2, 2:1, 5:2, and so on) to the fundamental. The intervals between them become progressively smaller as they rise in pitch from the fundamental, forming the harmonic series. Only one series can be obtained from a given length of tubing. The player's art lies basically in being able to pick out and sound the desired harmonic with certainty, which he does by pursing his lips and altering their tension.

Timbre

The tone, or timbre, of an instrument relates to the kinds of harmonics that the instrument produces. With brass instruments, this is determined by the shape of the mouthpiece cup, the profile and length of the tubing, and the shape of the bell. A shallow mouthpiece and cylindrical tube widening abruptly into a relatively small diameter bell give the trumpet its brilliance. The conical mouthpiece and profile of the horn together with a widely flaring bell result in its characteristic smooth, mellow sound.

The thickness of the metal used also has some influence, thinner metal giving a more ringing tone. It is difficult to calculate the precise effect of different alloys, although manufacturers have their own secret recipes. Brass is usually clear lacquered or silver plated to improve the appearance of the instrument. The alternative is frequent polishing, which eventually causes wear.

Simple brass instruments are of limited use. A good player can produce seven or eight notes from a bugle, but there are thirty-seven notes available on a piano within the same range (distance between highest and lowest notes).

The slide

The earliest technique for giving brass instruments a greater versatility was to increase the effective length of the tube, as in the trombone. The tubing of the trombone, an instrument basically unchanged since the 16th century, is in the form of two arms joined by a U-shaped tube (the slide), which slides over them. This can be moved to any of seven positions, unmarked on the instrument but chosen through the player's experience, giving seven fundamentals in descending order. These, together with their related harmonic series, enable all the notes within the range to be played.

It proved impractical to apply the same principle to the trumpet beyond a small slide giving one or two extra harmonic series. The horn's tubing is not cylindrical but conical in profile, so a slide is out of the question. By inserting the hand into the bell, however, it was possible to raise the pitch to the next harmonic series. Until the 19th century, all horns in orchestras had to be played this way, with the harmonic notes sounding rather strained unless played by an expert.

The valve

What was needed to liberate the trumpet and horn from the limitations of the bugle call was a mechanism for the instantaneous lengthening of the air column. It appeared in the form of the valve. A patent was taken out in 1818 for a piston valve, and in 1832 the rotary valve was introduced. These are the two types in use today.

Instruments usually have three valves, placed conveniently for the player. They lengthen the air column by diverting it into one or more of three extra lengths of tubing, called valve slides, leading through the valve out to the main tubing and back again. One of these loops causes the pitch of the instrument to descend to the next lower harmonic series; another loop lowers it to the series below that; the third loop lowers it by yet another step. Various combinations of valve give the seven harmonic series produced by the trombone slide.

The piston valve operates inside a cylindrical casing. On being pushed down, it diverts the air through airways in the piston into the valve slide, which it controls. It is returned to its normal position by a spiral spring. To ensure that the airways in the piston remain in line with the ports in the casing, a small projection on the side of the piston runs in a groove in the side of the casing.

The rotary valve consists of a drum-shaped rotor with two curved airways passing through it. Pushing a finger plate causes it to move through 90 degrees, diverting the air stream through the valve slide. In some instruments, an articulated crank transmits the finger-plate movement to the rotor, and in other cases, a string action is used. The rotor is returned to its normal position by either a spiral spring or a small clock spring in an enclosed drum.

The valve slides are adjustable so that each may be tuned individually. There is also an adjustable main slide incorporated into the main tubing of the instrument. It is used to put the instrument in tune with the rest of the orchestra by lengthening or shortening its overall length.

One of the most important results of the invention of the valve was the construction of a large brass instrument which could use its lower harmonics to provide a foundation for the brass section. The bass tuba first appeared in Germany in 1835. Ten years later Adolphe Sax, a German instrument maker, introduced a complete family of valved brass instruments, ranging in pitch from

▼ **The working principle of a valved trumpet.** The normal pitch is B-flat, but some instruments have a slide arrangement by which the pitch is tuned.

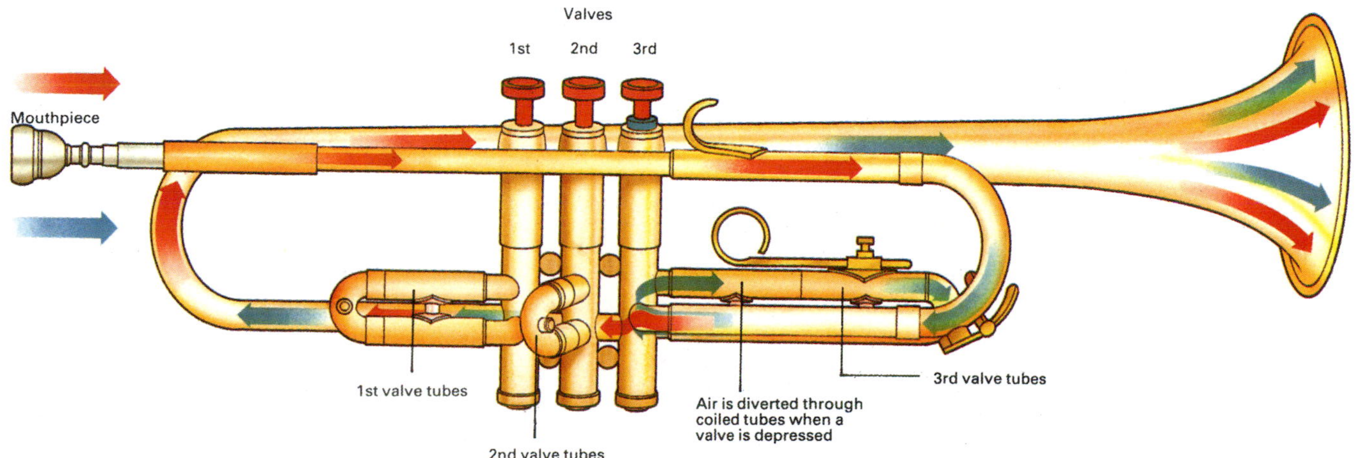

tuba pitch to trumpet pitch, called saxhorns. These saxhorns led to the founding of the British brass band movement and the formation of American wind bands. Valves applied to the post horn produced the cornet, while the flugel horn is a valved bugle. Saxophones, also by Sax, are woodwind instruments, although they are made of brass.

The valve had other uses. Adding a further loop that lowered the pitch by five series enabled the gap between the fundamentals and second harmonics to be filled. This was of most value in the longer instruments; the missing notes in the shorter instruments were already available as higher harmonics on a lower instrument. Brass tubas and the somewhat higher-pitched euphonium are almost always fitted with four valves, and present-day trombones usually have a rotary valve operated by the player's left thumb. Where a trombone has two valves, the second provides the note still missing when the first alone is pressed.

Fifth valves on tubas enable the lower notes to be played in tune. For complex acoustic reasons, they tend to be out of tune—as do also all notes played by a combination of valves. Some makers use a "compensating system" on the larger instruments, where extra tubing is automatically brought into use to correct this deficiency. It is easier for players of smaller instruments to correct the notes by slightly altering the tension of their lips. Even so, orchestral trumpets are sometimes fitted with a finger ring on the third valve slide so that the player can adjust its length while playing if necessary.

There are often one or more additional valves on the horn. This instrument has always made more use of the higher harmonics than any other. Since they are close together, it is easy for the player mistakenly to pick out a wrong note. The problem could be solved by making the tubing shorter so that a note at any given pitch would be a lower harmonic in its new series, but some of the wonderful quality of horn tone is lost in the shorter instrument. In the double horn, a thumb valve cuts out a quarter of the main tubing and diverts the air stream through appropriately shorter valve slides. Both sections of the instrument are operated by the same mouthpiece and valves and terminate in a common bell. The player can decide which to use at will. An extension of the principle gives the five-valved triple horn.

Some sousaphones—the U.S. composer John Philip Sousa's version of the bass tuba, an instrument made in helical form that surrounds the player and rests on a shoulder—are now manufactured with glass fiber bells in order to reduce the weight.

◀ Natural trumpets of the 17th and 18th centuries, before valves were used. Players produced different notes by pursing their lips and varying the speed at which they blew air into the mouthpiece.

Notes may be adversely affected by condensed water formed in the instrument during playing. At least one spit valve is usually found on modern instruments. This is simply a hole with a raised rim in the tubing covered by a pivoted metal key. On depressing the key, the hole is uncovered and water may be drained off. An airtight seal is ensured by a cork that fits into the end of the key over the hole with a spring keeping it pressed in position.

The mute

When a composer wants a drastic change of timbre, he can ask for the instrument to be muted. A mute is a device made from wood, compressed cardboard, fiber, rubber, aluminum, brass, or polystyrene that fits into the bell. It normally diminishes the volume, but by blowing with extra force, the player can make a harsh, strident sound. In addition to the straight mute, there are others available for the trumpet and trombone. More often used in jazz than symphonic music, the main types are the mellow cup mute, the wah-wah mute, and the plunger, which the player holds in his left hand to cover or uncover the bell.

SEE ALSO: Acoustics • Musical scale • Sound • Woodwind instrument

Breathing Apparatus

In many industries and occupations, workers are often exposed to the hazards of airborne dusts and vapors, even though every effort is made to prevent their presence in the atmosphere. Paint sprayers and grinder operators, for example, are always exposed; and firefighters, because of the nature of their job, usually have to work in dangerous and uncontrollable environments. In these and many other cases, some form of equipment is necessary to protect the respiratory system.

Breathing apparatuses can take many forms because of the wide variety of hazards encountered and the degree of protection required. Workers may have to wear the apparatus for long periods, so some equipment is designed for maximum comfort, while some may be designed for emergency use. Atmospheres may be hazardous for one or more of the following reasons: oxygen deficiency; contamination by hazardous dust, mist, or fumes; and contamination by toxic gas or vapor. Breathing apparatuses fall into two main types: respirators that remove contaminants from the surrounding air and equipment that provides the wearer with clean, filtered air or oxygen.

Respirators

Respirators can range from the simple paper-type face mask to sophisticated, powered, positive-pressure hoods and whole-body suits. The choice depends on the contaminant in the atmosphere and the conditions of use.

Respirators cannot be used in atmospheres that are deficient in oxygen (less than 16 percent by volume of oxygen), but they can be specifically designed to prevent the inhalation of selected ranges of contaminants, including, for example, dusts, mists (from aerosols), and some toxic gases and vapors. Respirators have limited service lives because filters, gas-absorbing cartridges, and canisters eventually become clogged or exhausted.

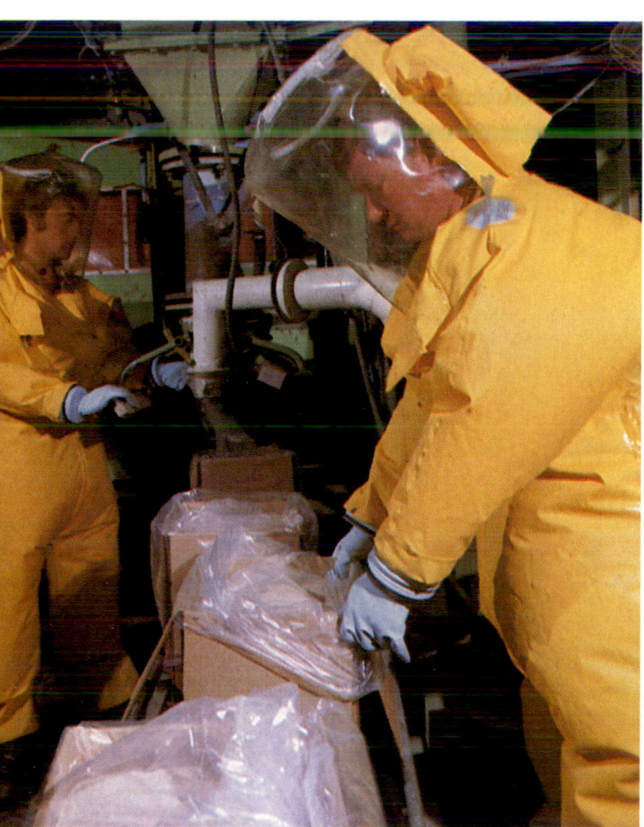

◀ Working with a powdered chemical, where the main hazard is from breathing in or coming into contact with the poisonous dust; a suit and shield serve as a barrier if there is a spillage.

Face pieces

The feature common to all respirators and breathing equipment is the face piece, which connects the purifier or air supply to the user's face. Apart from the simple paper-type mask, respirators usually have contoured soft rubber or plastic face pieces. These are designed to be as airtight as possible, although they all have certain leakage specifications. Face pieces fall into two main types: the half mask, covering nose and mouth only, and the full mask, which covers the nose, mouth, and eyes, and sometimes the ears.

Face pieces can have two nonreturn valves, one for inhalation through the purifier and one for exhalation. The valves make breathing easier by relieving the pressure in the face piece more quickly during exhalation, and they protect the filters from moisture in the exhaled air.

The most common nonreturn valve used in respirators is a rubber diaphragm that is slightly larger than its seat. Under normal or negative pressure, the diaphragm seals against the seat, but when there is positive pressure inside the face piece, the edge of the diaphragm lifts and allows excess air to escape.

Powered respirators

For greater protection and comfort during use, powered respirators are superior to nonpowered types. These devices consist of a face piece supplied with filtered, clean air from a battery operated pack carried by the user.

The power pack delivers air to the face piece in excess of the maximum demand rate of the wearer and thus reduce the respiratory stress and eliminates inward-leakage problems found with nonpowered types.

The air, driven by small vane-type compressor motors in the power pack, can be simply filtered to remove dusts and mists or passed through canisters to remove toxic gases and vapors. Since the power pack is normally worn around the waist, the canisters can be doubled up to improve air flow and purifying efficiency. Because of the slight positive pressure, the face pieces do not need to be too tight fitting and are often incorporated into functional helmets to give the user full facial protection.

Purifiers can be made from a variety of materials. For low-toxicity dusts, they can simply be a filter of paper, resin-impregnated wool, or felt. For toxic gases and vapors, the purifier is usually a cartridge or canister mounted on the face piece or a belt round the waist. The most widely used adsorbent used in canisters is activated carbon, which can be impregnated with metal salts or oxides to remove acid gases or ammonia.

Compressed air line apparatus

This type of apparatus differs from that previously described in that the air is supplied under pressure through a small diameter line from an air compressor or a compressed air cylinder. The compressed air line is connected to a coupling and a pressure reducer near the face piece. The supply usually ranges between 3 and 10 bar, giving a final air flow of about 180 l/min. Compressed air systems offer several advantages: the compressor can be placed outside the contaminated area, avoiding the use of specialized filters, and the same air compressor can be used to supply several workers simultaneously.

Self-contained breathing apparatus

A self-contained breathing apparatus, or SCBA, is used in cases where the atmosphere is deficient in oxygen, such as in a building on fire, or when a contaminant, such as a highly toxic gas, poses an immediate danger to life.

Although SCBA equipment can be fitted with a face piece only, it is normally incorporated into impervious airtight suits because many toxic gases and vapors are able to enter the body through the skin as well as through the respiratory system. There are two types of SCBA: open circuit and closed circuit.

Open-circuit SCBA

An open-circuit SCBA comprises a portable cylinder of compressed air carried by the user by means of a harness and a face piece that vents into the atmosphere. The SCBA's exhalation valve is opened automatically by the pressure in the breathing circuit, and an inhalation valve either supplies a constant air flow to the nose and mouth or supplies air on demand.

The maximum time for which the apparatus can be used without changing the air cylinder is limited to between 20 and 40 minutes, depending on the work rate and therefore the oxygen demand of the user. The size of the air cylinders is limited to avoid excessive weight, and they are much smaller than those used in SCUBA diving, where the greater weight can be compensated for by the buoyancy of the cylinders in water.

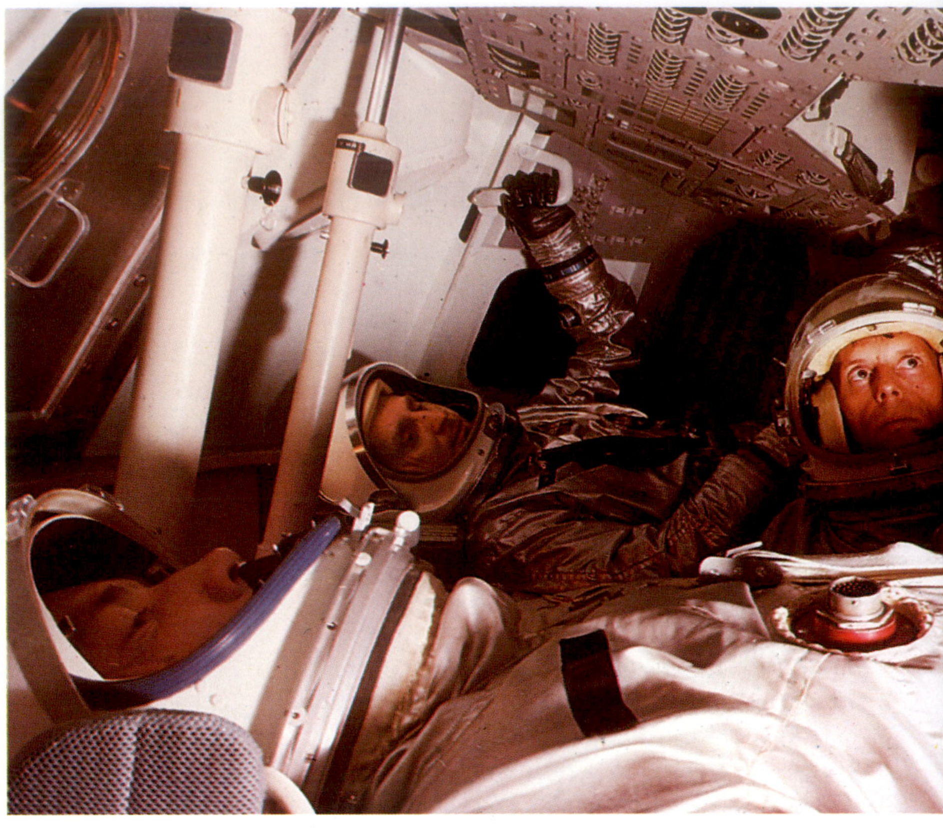

▲ Away from Earth's surface, astronauts have only a spacesuit and back pack, supplemented by the spacecraft's supplies, for life support. To conserve vital materials, such as oxygen and water, the air they breathe is recycled, purified, and enriched—all requiring a complex system of valves and filters. Considering that the suit is designed to meet all these demands and provide a shield against radiation, a spacesuit is a most effective SCBA.

Closed-circuit SCBA

The closed-circuit breathing apparatus differs from the open-circuit type in that the compressed air supply is replaced by either compressed oxygen or oxygen-enriched air. The exhaled air from the face piece passes into a purifier containing chemicals that are able to adsorb the exhaled carbon dioxide. The remainder of the exhaled air, containing nitrogen and unused oxygen, is recycled and then directed into a breathing bag. The negative pressure arising from the adsorbed carbon dioxide causes oxygen to be released into the breathing bag where it mixes with the recycled gases and flows through a cooler to the face piece.

Some types of closed-circuit breathing apparatuses carry no oxygen as such but contain in its place a chemical (usually a peroxide) that reacts with the exhaled carbon dioxide and water vapor to liberate oxygen. A closed-circuit apparatus, although more complicated than the open-circuit types, uses smaller air cylinders and is overall much lighter. It can also be worn for much longer periods before the cylinders (or chemicals) require changing.

SEE ALSO: Aqualung • Chemical and biological warfare • Diving suit • Gas and dust mask • Protective clothing • Space suit

Brick Manufacture

▲ Brick manufacture in Peru dates back many centuries. Scientists have used old samples of local bricks to study how Earth's magnetism has changed over the course of time.

Bricks are widely used as a building material, especially in countries that are particularly rich in different varieties of clay and can therefore produce a wide range of types, strengths, and colors. Bricks are joined together with mortar to form walls (including loadbearing ones), veneers, arches, piers, foundations, and various other structures. The bricks used to line furnaces and fireplaces are made from fireclay, which is refractory—that is, able to withstand very high temperatures without softening. Well-made bricks do not rot and are waterproof, fireproof, and resistant to fungal attack.

Clay is a hydrated silicate of alumina often containing small amounts of impurities such as iron oxide. The clays used in brick manufacture must be sufficiently fine grained and plastic when mixed with water. Firing changes the chemical and physical structure of the clay because the heat fuses the clay particles together into a hard cohesive mass that is virtually indestructible.

History

The earliest bricks were made with mud and straw. They were formed at first by hand and later in a mold and sun-dried. Once the art of pottery was discovered, however, bricks were made from clay and burned or fired in kilns. The earliest known clay bricks were found on sites in Mesopotamia dating from about 2500 B.C.E.

In Europe, bricks were used widely by the Romans. The fall of the empire caused a temporary loss of the art of brick making, but it was revived during the Romanesque and Gothic periods. It was reestablished in England in the 13th century and led to the eventual creation of such masterpieces of brick construction as Hampton Court Palace in the early 16th century. At this time, bricks were still hand made, but in 1619 the first patent was taken out for a clay-working machine. Bricks are known to have been made in the colony of Virginia in 1612.

Development

Mechanization in brick making did not develop until the mid-19th century. Before that, bricks had always been fired in intermittent kilns. In this method, "green" (molded and partially dried) bricks would be loaded into the kiln and fired. After the required time, the fire was put out, the kiln was opened, and the bricks were allowed to cool before they were removed. In 1858, a man called Hoffman introduced the continuous kiln, which was circular and contained from 10 to 20 separate chambers, and in which the fire is led from chamber to chamber in turn so that batches of bricks can be loaded, fired, cooled and removed in permanent rotation. Today the vast majority of bricks are fired in continuous kilns, which are usually arranged in two parallel end-connected sections rather than in a circle.

Brick manufacture

The first stage of manufacture consists of winning the clay—it is usually mechanically excavated from seams between 1 and 100 or more yards thick. At the factory, raw clay is crushed and ground to a suitable grain size and watered to produce a workable consistency. The next stage is shaping the bricks, and there are two basic ways of doing this: either by molding (sometimes referred to as pressing) or by extrusion.

The stiff-plastic molding process is used for clays and shales that do not easily develop high plasticity (stretchability). Here, the clay is formed to a doughlike consistency (15 to 20 percent moisture content) and emerges from a pugmill as a rough "clot," which is then dropped into the mold and pressed. In the semidry molding process, used for clays with low natural plasticity, the clay dust is placed while still comparatively dry directly into the mold.

Clays with good plasticity, again with 15 to 20 percent moisture, are extruded into continuous columns that are then wire-cut into correct brick lengths. These may then be pressed to improve surface texture and must be dried thoroughly before firing.

The soft-mud, or slop-molded, process used for making stocks and multicolored bricks is based on clay combined with lime or chalk in a very wet mix with a moisture content of at least 24 percent. The bricks have to dry over a long period and are either extruded, wire-cut, and pressed into sanded molds or else pressed directly into boxes of three to six molds each.

Plastic clays of high quality are used for handmade bricks. This is a common manufacturing method in less-developed countries and is also used sometimes for surface effects that cannot readily be machine produced. The individual wooden mold is first wetted to create an adhesive film then sanded to impart a pleasing texture to the final surface. Next the craftsman strikes off the amount of clay he needs, rolls it in sand, and "throws" it into the mold—a highly skilled job, since the clay must fill it completely and reach all the awkward corners. Excess clay is bowed off to level the exposed surface, which is then held by a wetted flat piece of wood to keep it smooth while the brick is removed from the mold.

▲ Molded bricks on their way to the firing kilns. Firing will induce changes in the clay that affect the properties and appearance of the finished brick.

Firing

Firing induces chemical and physical changes in the clay, so by varying temperature and firing time, the properties and appearance of the finished bricks can be accurately predetermined. Color, for example, is caused by the interaction of iron oxides with various constituents in the clay and can be modified by varying the amount of air admitted to the kiln at later stages of the firing. It can also be changed by adding a small amount of manganese dioxide, which gives a brown color suitable for facing bricks.

Firing temperatures of 1750 to 2200°F (950–1200°C), depending on the type of clay, are produced in continuous kilns. The fuel, such as coal, oil, or liquefied petroleum gas (LPG), is charged through openings in the floor and burns through shafts that have the green bricks stacked around them. An alternative is provided by car tunnel kilns; here, bricks are placed on the end car of a line at one end of a straight tunnel and then passed slowly through the drying, preheating, firing, and cooling zones before emerging at the other end. Such kilns, typically 400 ft. (130 m) long, are becoming more widely used. Firing time may be from four to ten days, depending on the type of brick and the kiln. Hollow clay blocks are produced by extrusion, dried in tunnel or chamber driers, and fired in tunnel kilns. They have textured faces and are used for external walls on factory or farm buildings or as the inner leaf of cavity walls in housing.

◀ In an automated brick-making process, clots of clay are dropped into a circular molding bay and then pressed to create frogs or surface detail on the brick.

Calcium silicate or sand-lime bricks, of pleasing light colors and popular for mass-housing projects, are made from silica sand, lime, and water. The ingredients are mixed together and mechanically compacted under high pressure into brick shapes. These are subsequently processed by high-pressure steam in an autoclave, a vessel that is designed for high-pressure reactions.

A new development in brick making is the incorporation of waste materials such as digested sewage sludge to make a more "environmentally friendly" brick. Adding sludge reduces the amount of clay needed, and the organic matter in the sludge acts as an extra fuel source during firing. The high firing temperature kills any organisms that may be left in the sludge and renders it inert. These "biobricks" have been used in many buildings, and the technique applied to other ceramic structural materials such as paving slabs.

SEE ALSO: Building techniques • Ceramics • Concrete • Furnace • Vault construction

Bridge

▲ One of London's best-known sights, Tower Bridge, is a road bridge that spans the Thames River. Most of the boats that use the river can easily pass underneath the bridge, but when a big ship needs to travel up-river, the two halves of the central span can be raised almost vertically in just over a minute by hydraulic machinery. This type of bridge is called a bascule bridge, from the French word for "see-saw." On average, the bridge is raised 500 times a year.

Before a bridge is built, the engineers designing it consider various points, such as the best type of bridge for the site—suspension, beam, or arch—the materials to be used, the sort of loads it must carry, environmental conditions such as high winds or earthquakes, and the most suitable construction methods.

Beam bridge

The commonest form of bridge construction is the beam. A plank placed across a ditch is a simple beam bridge, and the action of the load is resisted by bending stresses in the material. For a simple supported beam, which rests on two supports only, any load acting downward puts the bottom part of the beam in tension and the top part in compression. These stresses develop sufficient leverage (the technical term is *bending moment*) to support the load. The forces keeping the beam straight, therefore, equal the load tending to fold it up. For a given amount of material, a deep beam will give more leverage than a thin one, and material near the top and bottom faces works to better effect than material in the middle. So for anything more than the smallest bridges, the beams will be fashioned into I- or T-sections or into a hollow box section (called a box girder bridge).

Cantilever and suspended-span bridge

In a simple supported beam, the maximum bending moment occurs at the center, diminishing to zero at the ends. This construction is inconvenient if a slender, graceful appearance is wanted. The cantilever and suspended-span arrangement has the cantilevers and suspended spans separated by "hinges," which divide the bending moment into two parts, sagging as before in the midspan regions and hogging (tension at the top, compression at the bottom) over the inner supports. If desired, the hogging may be arranged to take more than half the total moment, which fits well with a graceful curved profile. The longest cantilever bridge is the Québec Bridge across the Saint Lawrence River in Canada, with a span of 1,800 ft. (549 m).

Suspension bridge

The suspension bridge can cover a vast span but has a serious drawback: it is very flexible and traffic loading may produce a large deflection, particularly when it acts near the quarter point of the span. For this reason, a stiffening beam or box girder is almost always provided to supplement the cables. Even so, this type is rarely used for railway bridges as trains are heavier and their loading more concentrated than road traffic. Suspension

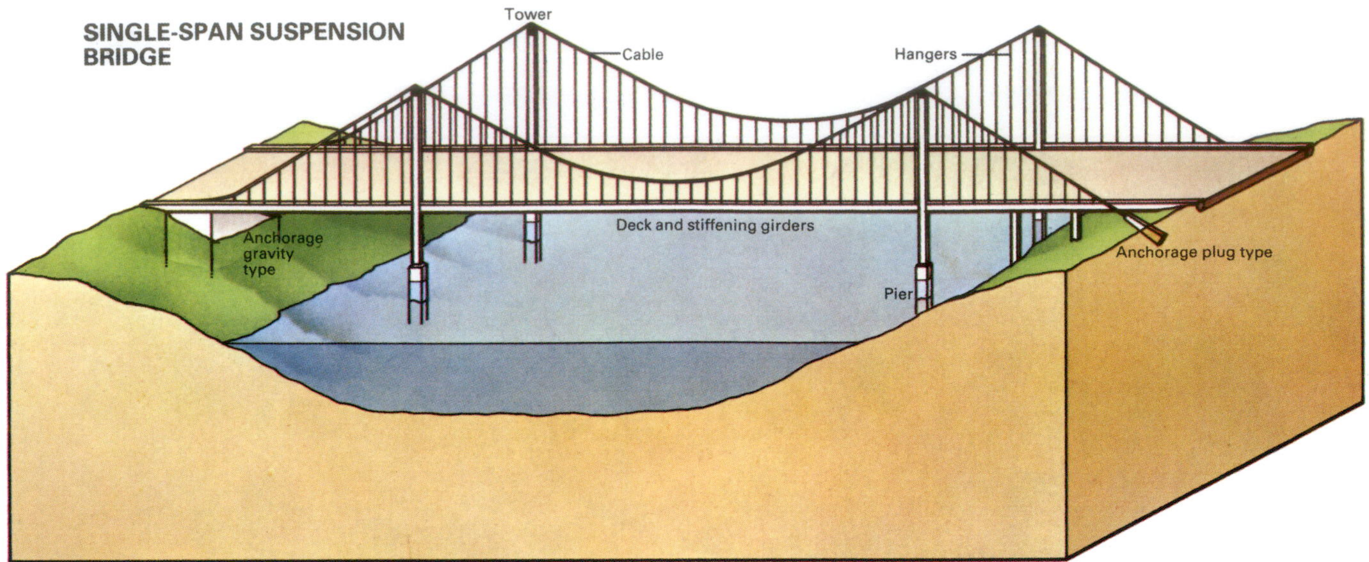

▲ The parts of a typical suspension bridge, with two types of cable anchorage. The plug cable is used when there is sound rock on the bank; the gravity cable relies on massive blocks of concrete.

bridges are, however, the solution for the longest spans, since wire for the cables can be produced cheaply with much greater strength than the steel suitable for beam construction. A compromise that is now popular for intermediate spans is the cable-stayed bridge, which has one or more sets of straight stays joining the towers and deck.

As its name implies, a suspension bridge is supported over most of its length from above by suspension ropes or hangers, which are connected to the main load-carrying elements of the bridge, the cables. These cables, usually two, are firmly anchored to the ground at their ends on each bank of the river or estuary and pass over the tops of two or more vertical supporting towers, hanging in graceful curves between them. Additional supports are often required near the ends of the cables to improve the angle at which they enter the anchorages.

Because they are always in tension (and so will not buckle under small loads as compression members sometimes do), the main cables can be designed with maximum efficiency by using high-tensile steel wire, a type of steel with great tensile strength for its weight. It is in fact the property of steel wire that enables very much longer bridge spans (in excess of 4,500 ft., or 1,400 m) to be achieved with the suspension form of construction than with any other. Because of the inherent flexibility of cables, however, particularly under concentrated loading, the deck of a suspension bridge usually has to be combined with some form of stiffening truss or girder to smooth out deflections and distribute the traffic loads. Railway loading is particularly intense and concentrated, and trusses stiff enough to restrict the deflections of the deck to acceptable values for railway traffic would have to be so deep and heavy, and therefore expensive, that suspension bridges are seldom used for long rail crossings, although several railway suspension bridges have been built.

Anchorages

Where there is good solid rock on or near the surface on the bank of the crossing, the anchorage for each main cable usually takes the form of a wedge-shaped tunnel driven into the rock at an angle of 30 degrees to the horizontal and filled with concrete. Long steel anchor rods or strands are embedded in these concrete plugs with their upper ends protruding so that the wires of the cable, which are splayed out fanwise at its end, can readily be attached to them. Such anchorages depend on the wedge action of the concrete plug and the strength of the surrounding rock to resist the pull from the cables, which for bridges with a span of more than 3,000 ft. (915 m) can be well over 10,000 tons (9,100 tonnes) from each cable.

Where there is no good rock on the banks of the crossing, the cable anchorages take the form of massive blocks of concrete, partly buried below the surface, in which the anchor rods are embedded. This type, usually called a gravity anchorage, depends on the resisting pressure of the ground at the front end of the block and friction along its base to prevent it from being tipped forward toward the river under the inclined pull from the cable. Some suspension bridges, like the George Washington Bridge in New York, have concrete-plug-in-rock cable anchorages at one end and gravity anchorages at the other. With short-span suspension bridges, the cables can be fixed to the ends of the deck, which has to be stiff enough to resist the pull of the cables. Bridges of this type are known as self-anchored.

The towers

The principal function of the main towers is to support the cables on each side of the navigable width of the river at a height sufficient to ensure that the lowest point of the cable and the bridge deck suspended beneath it are clear of all shipping. The towers carry on their tops cast steel blocks called saddles, which have radial grooves in them to contain and guide the wires of the cables smoothly through the change of angle over the tower top. Provision has to be made for cable movement under the action of live loads on the deck, generally achieved by the inclusion of roller bearings in the saddles. For lightness and speed of erection, the tower legs are usually made of steel plates, which are prefabricated on the ground into large sections that can then be lifted into position whole and bolted together one upon the other. In some cases, however, it is cheaper to construct the tower legs in reinforced concrete cast in situ (in its final intended position).

The tower foundations, or piers, have to be capable of sustaining the very heavy loads imposed on them by the weight of the towers and the reactions from the cables, and so must be supported on good rock. Sometimes rock is found near the surface and construction of the reinforced concrete block foundation is relatively simple. But occasionally, when hard rock is found only at great depths, caissons have to be sunk into the bed of the river and pumped up with compressed air so that the deep excavation necessary to construct the tower foundations can be carried out in a dry area.

Cables and hangers

The early metal suspension bridges had cables composed of wrought iron links or chains, but in 1841, John Augustus Roebling, an American of German descent, invented a process for building up cables in situ from parallel steel wires. The process, called cable spinning, consists essentially of bridging an opening by carrying loops of wires on wheels attached to a continuously circulating aerial ropeway that spans the opening. In this way, a cable of any required size can be made up by carrying across and bundling together the required number of wires. Since 1841, almost all major suspension bridges have had their main cables spun in situ this way. The hangers of modern suspension bridges are usually steel wire ropes that are attached to the main cable by means of steel clamps.

◀ A lifting bridge over the Harlem River in New York. The lifting design, in which the central span is hauled up and down the supporting columns, is a particularly economical way to span passages used by large ships. The largest bridge of this type is the Arthur Kill Rail Bridge, New Jersey.

The deck

Up to World War II, it was usual to use reinforced concrete slabs for the decks and deep, heavy steel trusses or lattice girders as the stiffening structures for suspension bridges. The now notorious Tacoma Narrows Bridge in Washington, completed in 1940, was an exception to this in that its deck-stiffening structure was composed of two deep steel girders of I-section. The poor aerodynamics of this structure allow even comparatively light winds to cause oscillations (swaying and twisting) of the deck. About six months after the bridge was opened, the conditions were such that the oscillations built up to resonance and the deck broke up. This disaster led to a review of the theory of deck construction, and today, before a bridge is constructed, designs are tested in a wind tunnel to ensure that the full-size bridge will behave satisfactorily in all likely wind conditions.

A further development, which occurred after the war and originated in Germany, was the use of stiffened steel plate, or battle deck, for bridge decks, instead of reinforced concrete, to save weight. In most recent suspension bridges, the steel deck takes the form of a wide but shallow box girder shaped to act as an airfoil, and with zero lift.

In 1964, the new Verrazano Narrows Bridge in New York was the longest, with a main span of 4,260 ft. (1,298 m), but in 1981, the record passed to the Humber Bridge in England with a 4,625 ft. (1,410 m) span. The Akashi–Kaikyo Bridge between Honshu and Awaji islands in Japan, completed in 1998, is longer still at 6,529 ft. (1,990 m).

The arch

In bridge construction, a suspension bridge could be considered an arch turned upside down. Like the suspension bridge, the arch puts a much larger force on the abutments (the end supports) than a simple beam does, although it pushes rather than pulls. This pushing action makes the ground do part of the work, thereby saving mate-

▲ This double-arched stone bridge was built by the Romans in the Versasca Valley in Tessin, Switzerland. The fact that it is still standing in such a precarious position after 2,000 years is testament to the Romans' building and engineering skills.

rial in the structure, but it requires reliable foundations. Flexibility is less of a problem in this type of construction because ordinary grade steel is used and built up into an arched girder to ensure resistance to buckling. The longest arch bridge is the New River Gorge Bridge in West Virginia, with a span of 1,700 ft. (518 m).

The Bailey bridge

In 1941, the British engineer Sir Donald Bailey introduced a new design of military bridge, as existing types could not support the heavy armored vehicles in use by that time. The Bailey bridge was easy to construct, adaptable, and capable of carrying up to 100 tons (90 tonnes) over spans of 220 ft. (67 m). It was used during World War II, first by the British Army in the North Africa campaign in 1942 and by the U.S. Army in Europe from 1944.

The basic Bailey bridge is made up of sections, each 10 ft. (3 m) long, joined together to form a continuous span. Each section, known as a bay, has two side members (trusses) of girder construction joined by cross pieces (transoms), which support the sheet metal roadway or decking. To increase the load capacity of the basic bridge, extra trusses and sometimes transoms are added to strengthen it. The bridge is easily transportable and is brought to the construction site in component form. For crossing rivers the Bailey bridge can be supported on large plywood floats known as pontoons.

Notable bridges

From the viewpoint of the structural engineer, it is the span, the distance between supports, that counts when designing a bridge. It is relatively easy to build bridges miles long by mass production of short spans. High-speed railways, such as the Japanese Shinkansen, or "bullet train," system, include hundreds of miles of such construction, with little of the interest and problems of the following examples.

The Forth Railway Bridge in Scotland was built between 1883 and 1889 by Sir Benjamin Baker and Sir John Fowler. The first application of steel on such a large scale, it remains the most spectacular cantilever and suspended-span bridge in Britain. The main spans, each 1,700 ft. (520 m) long were constructed by piecemeal assembly of the trusses on the site from quite small elements. More than 50,000 tons (45,000 tonnes) of steel were used, and 4,000 men were needed at certain points in construction.

Steel arches were popular for long spans in the early years of the 20th century. The Hell Gate at

New York was spanned in 1916 by an arch of 973 ft. (297 m) that carried four railway tracks and had a very heavy loading. A similar design was chosen for the Sydney Harbor Bridge. This was built between 1925 and 1931, has a span of 1,650 ft. (500 m), and also carries a very heavy load on a deck that is only 137 ft. (42 m) wide, and includes both a main road and suburban railway line. In 1931, a comparatively lightly loaded steel arch road bridge was opened at Bayonne, near New York, with a span of 1,652 ft. (504 m).

The first bridge to span 1,000 ft. (305 m) was built over the Ohio River in 1849 and was also remarkable as a pioneer in the use of steel wire cables for bridges. The Ohio Bridge used the conventional suspension layout, but for spans this long, the modern solution is usually the cable-stayed bridge.

The Avonmouth Bridge in England is a classic example of the elegant slender appearance that can be obtained by carefully varying the sections of a continuous-beam bridge. The deck is over 100 ft. (30.5 m) wide and is made from steel plate, which works as part of the flanges (top surfaces) of the two boxes beneath. The main span is 570 ft. (174 m) long.

After the 1,000 ft. Ohio Bridge was built and despite its collapse in a storm after only five years, the suspension bridge was used for even greater spans, largely owing to the construction techniques developed in the United States, notably by Roebling. Perhaps the greatest landmark was the 4,200 ft. (1,280 m) clear span of the Golden Gate Bridge, in San Francisco, built between 1933 and 1937. British engineers have since developed suspension bridges with a carefully streamlined box girder as the stiffening beam. The Humber Bridge in Northern England, for example, spans 4,625 ft. (1,410 m) with a clear opening of over 4,500 ft. (1,372 m).

One of the most complex bridge constructions of recent years has been the Store Baelt, which is part of the Oresund Link, joining Malmo in Sweden and Copenhagen in Denmark. Commissioned in 2000, the link is 10 miles (16 km) coast-to-coast. The bridge section is 4.8 miles (7.8 km) long, with a cable-stayed central section spanning the Flinte navigation channel. The bridge is on two levels, with a motorway running above a railway.

Materials

The choice of material is basically between steel or concrete, although the distinction is not absolute, as all concrete bridges include a large amount of steel as reinforcement and the majority of steel bridges have concrete decks.

Concrete is the cheapest serviceable material for the job; it can readily be made to have a crushing strength of about 4,500 lbs. per sq. in. (30 N/mm^2). As the actual strength on site varies rather a lot according to the care and supervision of mixing and placing the concrete, the designer would usually include a safety margin in the calculations by treating 30 Newton concrete as if it were only 20 Newton concrete.

Steel is substantially more expensive than concrete but has much greater strength. Structural steel used in bridge building will yield (deform a great deal in the manner of plastic) at about 320 N/mm^2 and fail completely at about 500 N/mm^2. As steel is made under very carefully controlled conditions, the designer need not include such a large safety margin in the calculations. Other materials are much more expensive and can rarely compete effectively with steel and concrete.

The great disadvantage of concrete is that its tensile strength (resistance to pulling) is very small. This trait does not matter much for arch construction, but for most other cases, steel reinforcement must be added to carry all tensile forces wherever they may occur. Round steel bars are usually the cheapest and most convenient form of steel reinforcement. An alternative way to use reinforcement is to stretch it by hydraulic jacks before the concrete is poured around it—or more commonly for bridges, before it is grouted (glued with a cement paste) into place in ducts (long tubular holes) through concrete that has already hardened. When the jacks are released, the concrete is thus prestressed by an equivalent compression and under any subsequent loads behaves as if it were able to resist tension until the net combination of prestress and stress from the added loads exceeds the tensile strength. The principle is the same as that used instinctively when lifting a row of books off a shelf at the same

◀ The attractive cable-stayed box girder bridge over the Rhine in Bonn, Germany. The box girder construction prevents twisting. The bridge is called *Rheinharfe*, meaning Rhine Harp.

time by pressing them together. To be economical, prestressing requires higher-strength materials than ordinary reinforced concrete. Fortunately steel can be shaped into wires and small-diameter bars of the required strength at only moderate extra cost, so the method continues to be used extensively.

Concrete is about four times heavier than steel per unit of strength. For short-span bridges, the traffic load is large compared with the structure weight, so this does not much matter. For long spans the converse is true; for a 660 ft. (200 m) span the structure weight would be perhaps three times any added load, even with all-steel construction. Sufficient strength must be provided to resist the total effect so for such spans steel is almost certain to be cheaper in total cost. Steel also gains because less material has to be handled and supported during the construction process, and it avoids or reduces the amount of formwork (molds and temporary supports) required.

Erecting bridges

Much ingenuity is used in erecting big bridges. A good designer considers the characteristics of the site very carefully, with erection in mind, at an early stage of the design: can large pieces be brought into position from below, or from above; are very large cranes likely to be available; what is the premium for speed of erection?

The simplest method, perhaps, is to assemble a complete span in a workshop or on some convenient level ground and lift it into position in one piece. This method is clearly more suitable for small bridges, but the main span of the Ohnoura Bay Bridge in Japan, which is 640 ft. (195 m) long and has a mass of nearly 1,000 tons (910 tonnes), was preassembled in Tokyo, shipped complete several hundred miles, and set down gently on its piers as the tide went down.

The next easiest method is erection on scaffolding, where the height is not too great and there is no objection to the obstruction caused. Falsework can become complex and very expensive, using tubular scaffolding or prefabricated metal panels something like a scaled-up version of children's constructional toys. One spectacular example in Britain was the Wentworth Viaduct in Yorkshire, with a main span 310 ft. (95 m) long and 98 ft. (30 m) above ground—125 miles (200 km) of scaffold tube was used to make a complete working platform across the valley.

Finally the bridge can be built out piece by piece, cantilevering forward from the section already completed. For steel-girder bridges, the sections are usually preassembled into lengths of 49 to 65 ft. (15–20 m) and then carried forward and suspended on a carriage beyond the end previously reached. When the new unit has been bolted or welded into position, the process is repeated. This is a very tricky method technically, as the stresses induced are high and, in many places, quite different from the stresses that will act in the permanent condition, so there is every temptation to work to a narrow margin of safety to minimize costs. The structure may be alarmingly flexible at the point of full stretch just before the two halves meet in the middle. The deflection of the two halves of the Wye Bridge in England —(with a main span of 770 ft. or 235 m)—caused by their own weight was over 10 ft. (3 m), which had to be allowed for to enable the parts to be joined smoothly.

Similar methods can be used for concrete bridges although the sections must be much shorter because of the greater weight of the material. Precast sections can be joined on by the prestressing method, or alternatively the concrete can be cast on the spot.

▼ This bridge over the Hooghly River in India is being built out piece by piece using preassembled sections that are cantilevered forward and bolted or welded into position. The process is repeated until it meets the part of the bridge being built from the other side. With some types of suspension bridge the cables and hangers are put in place first, and preformed spans are then hung from the center out toward the towers.

SEE ALSO: Building techniques • Civil engineering • Concrete • Geodesic structures • Vault construction

Bronze

The name bronze originally applied to an alloy of copper with about 25 percent tin, but it now applies to a wide range of copper-based alloys, some of which contain little or no tin. The Bronze Age was the period following the New Stone Age (Neolithic Age), when men first began using metals. At first, they exploited naturally occurring copper, gold, and silver, but about 3000 B.C.E. bronze was discovered, and its strength and flexibility for making implements were quickly appreciated.

The tin needed for making bronze was first found in ancient Anatolia (Turkey), and early civilizations such as those of the Phoenicians (from what are now Syria and Lebanon) and the Romans imported it from as far away as present-day Britain, Spain, and northern France. The contents of late Bronze Age burial sites in Greece, Britain, Germany, and elsewhere include bronze items that show these early people had a relatively high degree of skill in smelting and casting. Bronze continued to be used widely throughout the Iron Age for making ornaments and domestic utensils and later became the main metal for the manufacture of cannons and church bells.

Bronze manufacture

Bronze is made in a similar way to brass. Pure copper and scrap copper are melted in a furnace, and then tin and other alloying metals are added. The molten bronze is run out of the furnace into molds to make ingots for subsequent casting and forming. Several types of furnace are used, the main ones being electric induction furnaces and crucible furnaces, where the metal is melted in a large bowl or crucible heated by oil or gas.

▶ Unpolished marine propellers made from bronze. Often, the metal is further alloyed with aluminum and traces of manganese and nickel.

◀ Many of the world's most famous statues are made from bronze. The French sculptor Rodin used it on many occasions, most notably in sculpting his contemplative figure, *The Thinker*.

Gunmetals

Gunmetal is a bronze to which zinc has been added and is so called because it was originally used to make cannon and other pieces of ordnance. It is made from approximately 88 percent copper with 8 to 10 percent tin and 2 to 4 percent zinc. It has excellent casting properties, and apart from its numerous engineering applications, such as fittings for steam equipment, it is widely used for bearings, gears, and ornamental bronze work. Leaded and nickel gunmetals contain up to 5 percent lead and nickel, respectively. Different grades of these gunmetals are made by varying the relative proportions of the constituent metals. The 88–10–2 (i.e., percentages of copper, tin, and zinc) alloy is often called Admiralty gunmetal, and it is well suited for use in heavily loaded, low-speed bearings. It has good corrosion resistance and is often used for pumps and valves.

As with brass, the addition of lead makes bronze easier to machine because the metal being removed—for instance, using a lathe—comes off in small chips instead of curling into long spirals that could damage the cutting tool. The presence of lead means that higher cutting speeds can be used without damaging the tools or the workpiece. Leaded gunmetals such as the 85–5–5–5 (copper–tin–zinc–lead) alloy are also used for making castings in sand molds, and the addition of up to 0.05 percent phosphorus helps to remove oxygen from the alloy and prevent the formation of bubbles in the castings.

Phosphor bronze

The addition of 0.1 to 0.5 percent phosphorus to the basic copper and tin alloy produces one of the most important types of bronze. When the phosphorus content exceeds 0.3 percent, some of it combines chemically with the copper to form copper phosphide (Cu_3P), which makes the alloy harder. The copper content of phosphor bronze is generally between 85 and 90 percent, and leaded phosphor bronze is made with about 3.5 percent lead. The phosphor bronzes with less than 0.3 percent phosphorus are springy, nonmagnetic, and resistant to corrosion, making them useful for contacts in relays and other electric switchgear.

The bronzes with a higher phosphorus content are extensively used in bearings, the leaded versions being especially good for bearings subjected to very high speeds and pressures, where the lubricating oil film tends to break down and the soft lead metal acts as a lubricant. The hardness of these alloys enables them to withstand the heavy loads imposed on the bearings of steel-rolling mills, turntables, and heavy machinery.

Leaded tin bronzes

Leaded-tin bronzes are basic copper–tin alloys with up to 20 percent lead. Proportions range from 0.5 to 6 percent lead in the low-leaded types to as much as 20 percent lead in the high-leaded forms, and each type has many uses in industry and engineering. Low-leaded bronzes are used for steam and water fittings, ornamental bronze, bolts, nuts, carburetors, gears, and oil pumps. High-leaded bronzes are used in high-speed, heavy-duty bearings and pumps.

Aluminum bronze

Aluminum bronze is made by adding aluminum to copper, often together with a few percent of iron or nickel. This alloy is called a bronze even though it contains no tin, and with an aluminum content of 10 percent, it is as strong as mild steel. It has an attractive golden color and resistance to corrosion, which makes it popular for ornamental work, ships' propellers and fittings, and imitation gold for jewelry. Its strength and toughness make it suitable for pump components, bearings, gears, and aircraft landing gear. There is also a range of bronzes made from copper alloyed with aluminum, manganese, nickel, and iron, which are used for ships' propellers, cams, and hydraulic equipment. The propellers for the ocean liner *Queen Elizabeth II* were cast from one of these alloys. One of the strongest and most durable aluminum bronzes consists of about 80 percent copper, 10 percent aluminum, 5 percent nickel, and 5 percent iron.

Aluminum bronze is not affected by the dilute acids used in many industrial processes, such as dilute hydrochloric and sulfuric acids, so it is widely used for pickling baskets and tanks and acid-resistant pumps.

Bronze coins

Bronze coinage has been used since the seventh century B.C.E. and is common throughout the world today. The alloys used have a high copper content (often as much as 97 percent) with a few percent of tin and zinc. During the French Revolution of 1789 many churches were destroyed, and the bronze bells were melted down, mixed with an equal amount of copper, and made into coins. The composition of the alloy changed over the next half century until the coins contained 95 percent copper, 4 percent tin, and 1 percent zinc. By 1860, this alloy was being used in France, Britain, and many other countries, and it remained standard until the 1920s, when the changing prices of tin, zinc, and copper caused most countries to change the proportions of these metals in their coins.

◀ The *Gates of Paradise* were created in gilded bronze for the door of the Baptistry in Florence by the 15th-century Renaissance sculptor Lorenzo Ghiberti.

SEE ALSO: ALLOY • ALUMINUM • BRASS • CASTING • COINS AND MINTING • COPPER • FURNACE • METALWORKING

Bubble and Cloud Chamber

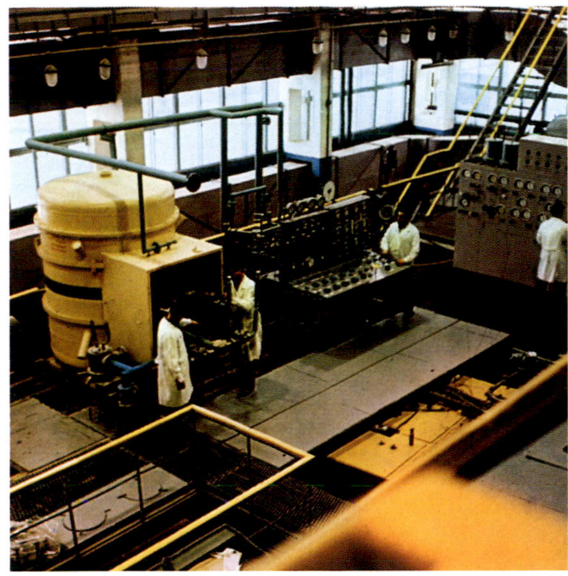

◀ The Lyudmila bubble chamber at the Institute for High Energy Physics at Protvino, Russia. The off-white cylindrical vessel contains the chamber and its refrigerant system.

Bubble chambers and cloud chambers are devices used by particle physicists to observe the motions of cosmic rays and of particles produced by radioactive decay or by high-energy collisions of particles at the target of a particle accelerator.

Cloud chambers

The cloud chamber was developed between 1895 and 1911 by a British physicist, Charles Wilson. As its name suggests, a cloud chamber relies on a process similar to that which forms clouds and mist in the atmosphere: the supersaturation of a vapor and formation of liquid droplets.

The amount of water that air can contain as a vapor depends on temperature: the lower the temperature, the lower the concentration. As moist air rises in the atmosphere, its temperature falls. At a certain point, the concentration of water is at the limit of solubility. The air is said to be saturated with water vapor at this point. If the air cools further, it becomes supersaturated as its capacity for water vapor falls below the actual concentration of water. When this happens, dust particles in air seed the formation of tiny water droplets, which form clouds. Cosmic rays and the radiation from radium, for example, form charged particles called ions as they pass through a vapor. These ions seed the formation of droplets along their path.

The subatomic particles created when atoms are bombarded with high-speed nuclei from a particle accelerator are invisible through a microscope and extremely unstable. However, as these particles hurtle through matter, they strip electrons from the atoms in their path and leave a trail of ions behind them. It is this trail of ions that makes it possible to "see" the particles.

Wilson's cloud chambers used the cooling produced by a sudden drop in pressure to produce supersaturation. (A piston in a cylinder attached to the cloud chamber caused the drop in pressure.) The paths of charged particles then appeared as vapor trails. Modern devices use dry ice (solid carbon dioxide) to chill alcohol vapor until it becomes supersaturated.

Bubble chambers

In 1952, the idea behind the bubble chamber came to its inventor, the U.S. physicist Donald Glaser, as he gazed meditatively at the lines of bubbles rising in his glass of beer. The bubble chamber uses a liquid under such conditions of temperature and pressure that it is on the brink of boiling. If the pressure suddenly drops, the liquid will boil. Just as the ions left in the wake of a charged particle stimulate droplet formation in a cloud chamber, so they stimulate bubble formation in a bubble chamber. If a photograph of these first bubbles can be taken before general boiling starts, it provides a record of the paths of the particles. Thus, when the chamber pressure is reduced, the liquid is illuminated by flashes and cameras photograph the tracks of bubbles—all in a few thousandths of a second. The pressure is then increased to stop the boiling and the chamber is ready for another cycle. Since nuclear reactions are somewhat random, numerous cycles might be necessary before the collision of interest appears on film. A magnetic field that passes through the chamber curves the paths of particles in a way that helps calculate their masses and charges.

▶ A heavy-liquid bubble chamber being assembled at CERN—the European Organization for Nuclear Research—near Geneva, Switzerland. The large, flattened metal hoops at right in the background encase electromagnets that produce a magnetic field in the chamber.

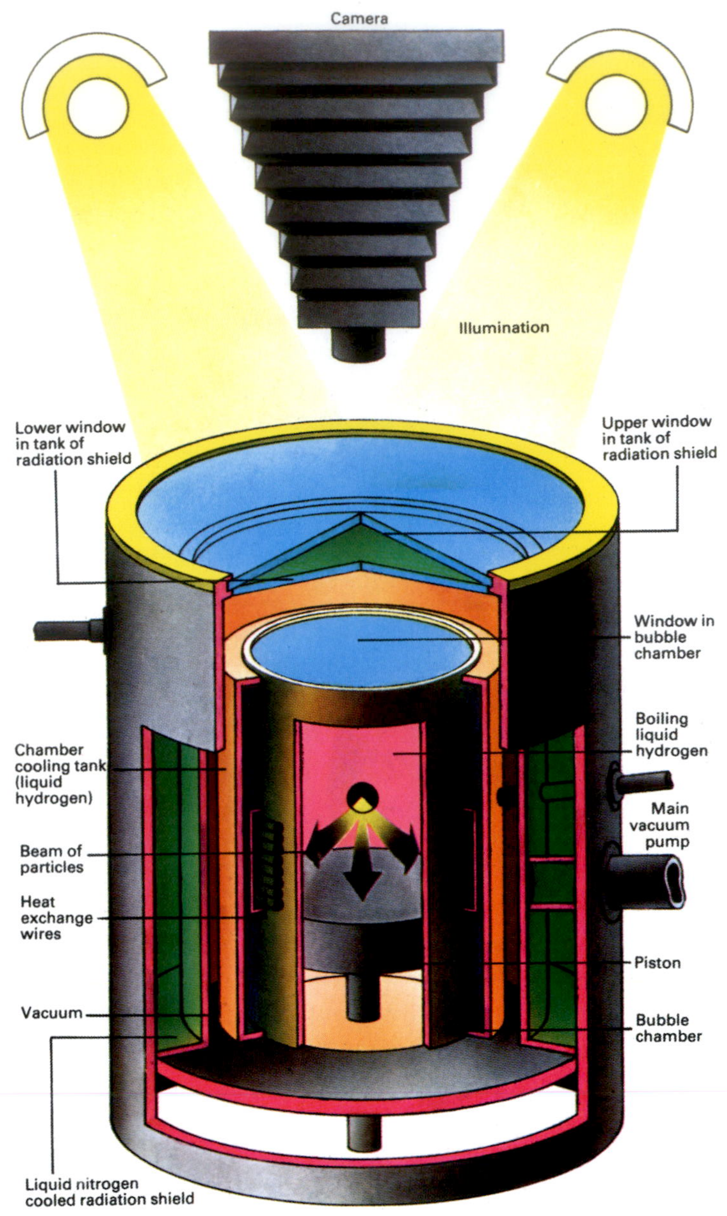

▲ In this diagram of a bubble chamber, the beam of particles originates at a source in the back wall of the chamber. The chamber contains liquid hydrogen at its boiling point. When the piston drops, bubbles of hydrogen gas form around any charged particles in the chamber. At that instant, a flash illuminates the chamber and a camera records any traces in the chamber.

Hydrogen bubble chambers

Hydrogen is the most usual chamber liquid because it provides the simplest target to the incoming particles. The hydrogen atom has just a single proton as its nucleus, so bubble chamber photographs show what happens when a subatomic particle interacts with the proton without the complications of other particles being bound to the proton. Since the incoming particles and the target particles in the chamber are of a known type, it is often possible to work out which particles flew from the collision. The presence of the magnetic field also helps, because the direction the particles curve in the field determines whether they carry a positive or negative charge and the radius of their curved tracks gives an estimate of their mass.

The most recently constructed chambers hold large volumes of liquid hydrogen in stainless steel tanks. Great care has to be taken in the design and operation of these chambers so as to handle such large volumes of potentially explosive hydrogen in safety. The tank has several windows. One is the access for the particles, the others are the peepholes for cameras. There are at least three cameras so that a three-dimensional picture of what, if anything, has happened in the chamber can be worked out from the photographs. Another opening into the tank is for a piston to apply pressure to the liquid.

The typical conditions to hold hydrogen at the point of boiling are a pressure of five atmospheres and a temperature of –412.6°F (–247°C). Pressurization and refrigeration systems are therefore also needed. Powerful electromagnets outside the chamber provide the magnetic field that helps identify the particles from their traces.

By the time all these features have been incorporated, the bubble chamber can measure perhaps 32 ft. (10 m) high and about 20 ft. (6 m) across. Individual chambers are usually known by their dimension along the direction in which the particles fly into the chamber. The first important chamber to be used for physics was the 72 in. (183 cm) chamber at Berkeley, California, which came into action in 1954; the largest chambers in use today include a 12 ft. (3.7 m) chamber at CERN near Geneva, Switzerland, and a 15 ft. (4.6 m) chamber at the National Accelerator Laboratory, Batavia, Illinois.

Bubble chambers are supported by powerful cameras that analyze sometimes millions of photographs from a single session. The particle traces they detect sometimes confirm the existence of subatomic particles predicted by new theories of matter, thereby supporting the theories.

Heavy-liquid bubble chambers

Some of the particles produced in collisions are neutral. Since they carry no electrical charge, such particles cause no ionization in the liquid, leave no identifying trail of bubbles, and complicate the task of analyzing interactions.

In a short time, neutral species decay to form charged particles that can then be spotted. The time of flight in a hydrogen bubble chamber is often too short for this decay to occur, however, so neutral particles escape from the chamber without being detected. Heavy-liquid bubble chambers use liquids such as propane to slow the neutral particles sufficiently for this decay to occur within the chamber, but the simplicity of hydrogen interactions is sacrificed to some extent.

SEE ALSO: Atomic structure • Magnetism • Particle accelerator • Particle detector • Particle physics • Quantum theory

Building Techniques

The origins of modern building techniques and materials can be traced back to the latter part of the 18th century, to the birth of the Industrial Revolution. Stone and timber were the dominant materials of construction, and the structure of buildings was essentially timber floors supported by stone walls or timber framing. Although a scientific attitude toward the design of structures was well established in the European schools of engineering, few builders possessed the necessary technical knowledge to calculate the strength of structures, and they relied instead on intuition and rules of thumb based on medieval and Renaissance precedents.

Technological developments in the 20th century produced a new range of materials, including plastics. Of more importance is the extension of the structural potential of traditional building materials, such as timber and brickwork, and the development of steel and reinforced concrete, both of which were well established at the end of the 19th century. Concrete and steel are today's most important building materials.

▲ This remarkable building is part of a shopping complex in Sacramento, California. The door to the building is an entire corner section, which slides out on rails to provide the entrance and serves as a separate but related focus of interest. Part of its attraction comes from the apparent insecurity of the building, but in fact, the brickwork is merely a cladding on a cantilevered steel support structure and is perfectly stable.

Reinforced concrete

Concrete is usually made by mixing cement with sand, crushed rock, and water. The cement combines chemically with water to form a cement paste around the sand and crushed rock (known as aggregate). The cement paste gradually hardens into a strong material. Concrete is now used in greater quantities than any other structural material, and as a result, the manufacture of cement is one of the world's largest industries. The structural properties of concrete are similar to those of masonry—its resistance to compression is high but it has the advantage that it can be poured into molds to form slabs, beams, columns, and structures of shell form.

Concrete is weak in tension, and where tension exists, it is necessary to introduce reinforcement, generally steel. Reinforced concrete is a composite material in which the concrete resists compression, and the steel reinforcement resists the tension and limits the width of cracks that occur in concrete under relatively low loads. The introduction of reinforcement made numerous designs possible, and by the end of the 19th century reinforced concrete frameworks were being used in commercial buildings in Europe and the United States.

By the 1930s, the technique of prestressing concrete had become commercially viable, largely through the pioneering work of the French engineer Eugène Freyssinet. Prestressing consists of inducing a state of compression in the concrete by means of high-tensile steel wires so that any tension that occurs because of subsequent loading of the structural member is counteracted by the initial compression. Thus the cracking of the concrete can be completely eliminated, and therefore the possibility of corrosion of the reinforcement by moisture penetration can be avoided. It also allows a structural member to be made up of a series of small sections that can be stressed together. The principle is similar to that of a voussoir (segmental) arch, which is a self-stressing system, but the advantage of prestressing is that it can be applied to a straight member such as a beam.

Steel

By the end of the 19th century, steel had become an important construction material. Rolled steel sections were available in quantity, and the technique of connecting members by means of rivets or bolts was fully developed. Another important advance made during World War I has now become the standard method of joining steel members, that is, metal arc-welding. An arc is struck between a metal rod (the electrode) and the members to be welded. The metal is fused at both ends of the arc, and the fused electrode is deposited in the joint in a series of layers until it is filled. This technique is used extensively in the construction of modern steel buildings and bridges as it produces smaller and more efficient joints than rivets or bolts. The composite action of steel beams and reinforced concrete floor slabs is a further development in which studs welded to the top flange of steel beams ensure proper interaction between the two materials.

Timber

Although timber is one of the oldest building materials, recent advances in timber engineering have ensured that it can take its place among the modern building materials. Of particular importance, the development of adhesives that are insensitive to heat and moisture has led to the extensive use of plywood for walls and floors of buildings. Plywood consists of laminates or plies, which are peeled from a log and then glued together under pressure with the grain in alternate directions. The strength of timber depends on the direction in which it is stressed, the strength at right angles to the grain direction being much less than that parallel to the grain. The use of plies with alternate grain directions ensures a material of uniform strength and dimensional stability.

Because of the limited size of commercially available timber sections, the use of adhesives is important in the manufacture of built-up beams of I- or box-section and of laminated beams, which consist of a number of layers of relatively thin sections glued together under pressure. Significant developments have also taken place in the techniques of nailing and bolting timber sections and the use of special metal connecting devices. Timber used for structural elements has the advantage of being light weight, the density of timber being about one-fifth that of concrete, plus it has a relatively high tensile strength—both of which are desirable properties.

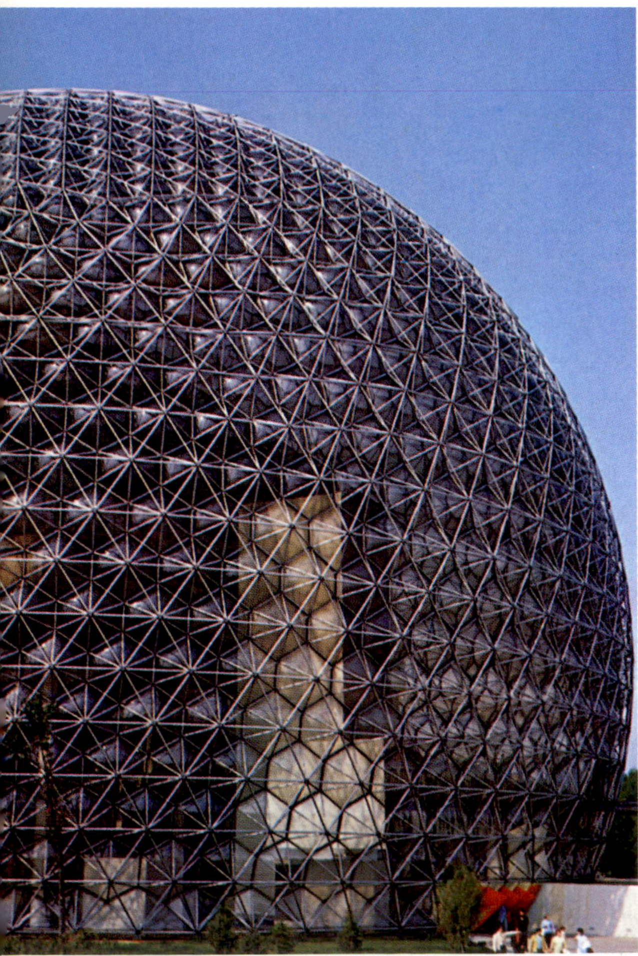

◀ The lightweight but strong enveloping sphere of Montreal's geodesic dome. Frame constructions like this can be prefabricated and the components connected together on-site.

Ceramics

A large section of the structural ceramic industry is involved with brick manufacturing. Like timber, this traditional building material has undergone extensive rationalization with regard to its manufacture, handling, laying, and load-bearing capacity.

Detailed studies of the strength of brickwork have made it possible to construct buildings up to 18 stories in height with a brick thickness at ground level of 15 in. (38 cm). The stiffening influence of brick infill panels on the strength of steel and concrete frames has been used in designs, as has the interaction between wall panels and supporting beams. Design principles similar to those for reinforced concrete have also been established for reinforced brickwork, enabling it to accept both tensile and compressive stresses.

Aluminum

Aluminum in its commercially pure state is a soft, ductile metal, but with the addition of alloying elements, which increase its strength, it is suitable for structural applications. In contrast to steel, it is very durable because of the thin layer of oxide that forms spontaneously on its surface and acts as a barrier against further oxidation. The density of aluminum is roughly one-third that of steel, but its resistance to deformation is also considerably less. The deflection of an aluminum framework will be nearly three times that of an identical framework in steel under the same loads. This fact plus its high cost compared with other building materials have meant that aluminum has found only limited structural application, except in situations where minimum weight is essential. The structural sections available are similar in form to those for steel.

◀ London's Millennium Dome is an example of a tensile structure in which 12 steel columns are supported by tensioned cables from a central core and anchor points around the perimeter. The covering of the Dome is made from Teflon- (PTFE) coated glass fiber sections and is stretched over a network of cables. When completed, the Dome was now the biggest fabric-covered structure in the world.

Plastics

Plastics are produced from basic natural products such as coal, air, water, and oil by complex chemical processes. Because of their synthetic composition, many kinds of plastics can be produced with differing properties, but for structural applications, they normally need to be reinforced with various types of filler or fibers. One of the commonest types of structural plastic is glass-reinforced polyester (GRP), which will withstand high tensile and compressive stresses. This material has the advantage that it can be formed into curved or folded load-bearing elements with relative ease.

There have been a number of structural applications of sandwich panels consisting of a strong skin bonded to a low-density insulating core. Another interesting application is the use of plastics for air-supported structures (such as inflatable domes), which are supported by a small pressure difference between the outside and inside maintained by a continuous flow of low-pressure air from a fan. There is even a footbridge made of composite plastic in Aberfeldy, Scotland.

Modern building design

Modern building design is a complex process that involves the interaction of many skills, in particular those of the architect and engineer. Steel frameworks of up to 200 ft. (61 m) in height were constructed in the 1890s. Typical examples of developments in this form of construction in the period up to 1940 were the Woolworth Building, at 792 ft. (241 m), and the Empire State Building, at 1,472 ft. (449 m). These structures, both in New York, involve the transmission of immense loads to the ground, and the design of foundations is a vital aspect of the building process. Buildings of this size can be built only on ground with a high bearing capacity such as rock. In cities such as London, where the ground is relatively soft, few buildings exceeded a height of 400 ft. (122 m) until the 1990s, when several taller structures, including the Cesar Pelli tower on Canary Wharf, some 800 ft. (244 m) tall, were constructed. This construction was made possible by using long tubular steel piles that support the buildings' foundations by driving them down to sound rock beneath the soft ground. Tall buildings are subjected to high lateral loads. Their stability under gale-force winds is a major structural problem.

Design standards with regard to structural stability, durability, fire resistance, and environmental control and cost have become much more stringent. These standards, coupled with an increasing awareness of the shortage of natural resources, have forced engineers to minimize the quantities of structural materials used in the building process, which in turn calls for more refined analytical and constructional techniques. After World War II, the economic climate favored

▶ This solar home in Corrales, New Mexico, makes use of abundant sunlight to heat water in drums, which is circulated around the house using power generated by a windmill. The reflective walls keep the home cool during the day, while the small windows prevent sunlight from heating the interior by day and heat escaping at night.

the use of concrete, and for high-rise buildings, the core structure was developed. Tall buildings with the core structure are similar in structural form to a tree. Both are essentially large vertical columns rigidly anchored into the ground supporting a series of cantilever projections. The erection of a typical core structure building starts with the construction of the foundation. On soft ground, piles are commonly used to distribute the load over a wide area to avoid overstressing the soil. The piles are capped with a larger concrete slab upon which is built the concrete core. A tower crane is erected at the top of the core and is used to raise large cantilever beams. Ties are hung from these beams to support the floors, which are cast at ground level and then raised.

In the construction of high- and low-rise buildings, extensive use is now made of prefabricated components and site mechanization. Standardized structural components are now available in concrete, timber, and steel, and extensive use of these is made in the construction of houses, schools, office buildings, and hospitals. In some cases, it is possible to prefabricate complete building units including finishes and services. These units can be transported to the site and erected quickly with the minimum plant and in adverse weather conditions. The rapidly increasing demand for buildings has forced the industry to mechanize the construction process to the level at which assembly line production of components and structural units has become standard practice.

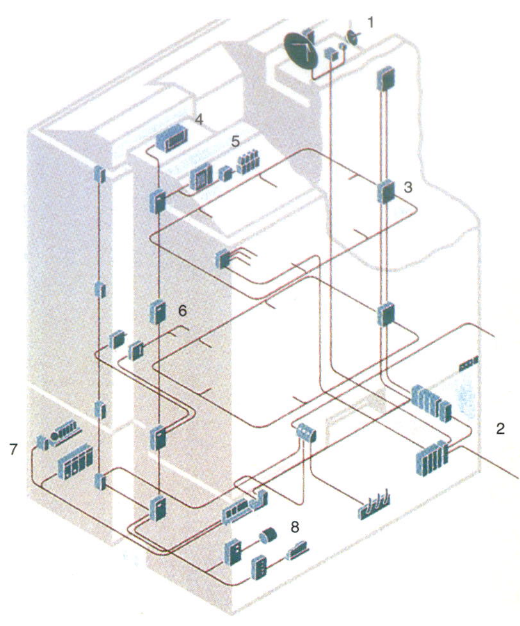

▲ An "intelligent building" in which all communication and supply systems are linked: (1) telecommunications; (2) computers; (3) communications outlets; (4) heat pump chiller; (5) building management controllers; (6) environmental controllers; (7) power supplies; (8) heating, ventilation, and air-conditioning.

FACT FILE

- *In Japan, a building technique known as capsule architecture was developed to deal with the problems of construction in crowded city sites. The 1972 Nakagin Capsule Tower is a hotel system consisting of steel framing and concrete towers to which have been added identical, completely prefabricated living capsules of welded steel.*

- *Tensile structures are a means of using masts and frames clad in flexible, dynamically stressed materials to provide airy, large-scale buildings that are easily erected, dismantled, or replaced. At the Olympic Games in Munich in 1972, the roofs of the main stadium and arenas consisted of huge cable nets stretched over a series of masts, beneath which was hung a weather-resistant membrane skin. The most notable modern example of this technique is the Millennium Dome in London.*

- *Biotecture is the name of an experimental attempt to build human habitats from renewable sources. The Symbiotic Process Laboratory of the University of Texas has artificially stimulated mineral and shell-growth on wire structures beneath the Caribbean by sending electric charges through them. A crop of organic forms is envisaged, which could be used for offshore work sites and habitations.*

Intelligent buildings

The 1990s saw the beginning of the move towards thrifty, environmentally friendly, and healthy buildings, amounting to a "green revolution" in architecture. This new type of building primarily uses little or none of Earth's dwindling supply of fossil fuels or electricity.

The most obvious way of saving energy in buildings is to prevent heat from escaping through external walls, roofs, windows, and doors; also the services can be made more efficient so that they use less energy. On a more sophisticated level, the entire energy consumption of a building can be controlled, minute by minute, night and day, by a centralized electronic building management system that can sense when a room has been vacated and then turn off heating and lights.

An "intelligent building," with such energy efficiency, is arguably the most revolutionary building type of the 1990s. Innovations in the form of advances in microelectronics are incorporated inconspicuously into the fabric and workings of the building. In an intelligent building, heating, lighting, air conditioning, power supply, and security systems are all monitored and automatically controlled by a central computer or building management system.

SEE ALSO: Brick manufacture • Civil engineering • Concrete • Geodesic structures • Skyscraper • Tensile structure • Vault construction • Wood composite

Bunsen Burner

◀ Different types of Bunsen burner, as used in laboratories for over one hundred years.

The Bunsen burner, one of the most useful laboratory tools, is named for the 19th-century German chemist Robert Wilhelm Bunsen—though he did not invent it but only contributed to its development. It is designed to give an extremely hot, nonluminous flame, which does not produce sooty deposits on the articles being heated. The burner consists of a metal tube into which gas is injected under pressure through a narrow jet near the bottom of the burner. As it enters the tube, it causes air to be drawn in through holes level with the jet. The gas and air mix in the barrel of the burner and are ignited at the top. The proportions of the mixture are usually three parts air to one part gas, which burn with a blue flame. If the volume of air is reduced, by rotating a collar that partly covers the air holes, the burner produces a luminous, smoky flame.

When the burner is operated with a three to one gas mixture, the flame will consist of two distinct zones. The inner cone of the flame, or reducing zone, consists of partly-burned gas. This partial ignition results in a mixture of carbon monoxide, hydrogen, carbon dioxide, and nitrogen (whatever the type of feeder gas being used). In the outer cone, or oxidizing zone, this mixture of gases is completely burned, using the oxygen present in the surrounding air. This is the hottest part of the flame. This type of burner can be made to operate on almost any type of flammable gas, such as natural gas, coal gas, butane, or oil gas.

Other designs

With simple modifications, the Bunsen burner's efficiency can be considerably increased. In the Tirril burner, both gas and air supply can be adjusted to give optimum burning, and a flame temperature of over 1600°F (900°C) can be achieved. In the Meker burner, the barrel is much wider and a grid is attached to the top. This produces a number of tiny Bunsen flames, with the outer zones fused to give a "solid" flame without the cooler central zone. This burner produces temperatures in excess of 1830°F (1000°C). A further modification is the blast lamp, in which air or oxygen is fed in under pressure. This type of burner can be used for glass blowing in the laboratory or for brazing and silver soldering of metals. It produces temperatures of up to 3330°F (1830°C).

The burners used in gas cookers and gas fires operate on the principle of the Bunsen burner or of its derivatives. The Welsbach burner is another variant that is used in conjunction with a gas mantle to produce incandescent light.

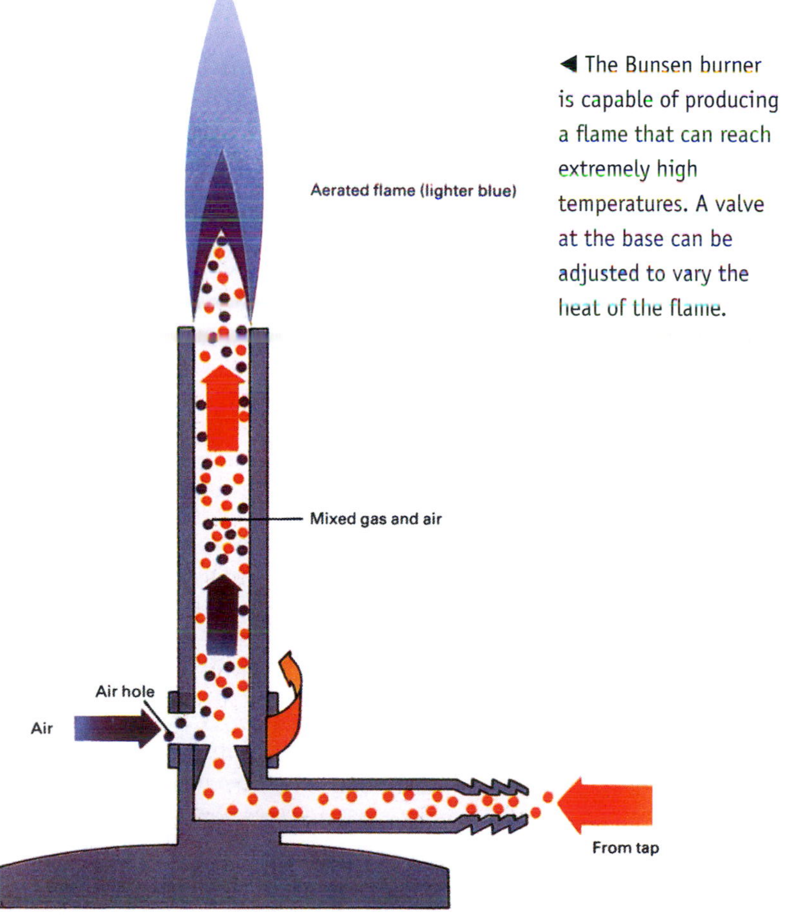

◀ The Bunsen burner is capable of producing a flame that can reach extremely high temperatures. A valve at the base can be adjusted to vary the heat of the flame.

SEE ALSO: Flame and ignition

Burglar Alarm

Burglar alarms are sensor-driven systems that activate audible or visible alarms if they detect intruders or any attempt to remove protected items. The alarms may be located at the protected premises, or they may be at a remote monitoring station that supervises numerous alarm systems.

Mechanical sensors

The most commonly used sensor devices for the protection of doors and windows are magnetic reed switches encapsulated in the framework of a door or window and activated by a magnet fitted in the door or window itself. The switch remains closed as long as the magnet and reed are within ¼ in. (6 mm) of each other. If the magnetic field is removed by opening the protected door or window, the switch opens and activates an alarm.

A different type of sensor detects vibrations caused by intrusion or drilling. This type of alarm is commonly fitted to cars. False alarms owing to traffic noise or thunder can be minimized by carefully adjusting the sensitivity of the detector or by inserting a frequency-sensitive circuit between the sensors and the control.

Pressure mats, which detect the weight of an intruder, are generally constructed from two pieces of foil held apart by a sheet of perforated foam. The switch created by this arrangement is open until pressure forces the two pieces of foil into contact. A current then flows between the two sheets and the alarm is activated.

Movement sensors

A variety of ultrasonic and microwave movement sensors have now become standard for detecting the presence of intruders in protected rooms. The majority of these systems use the Doppler effect, whereby an ultrasonic or microwave signal transmitted by the system is altered in frequency when it is reflected off a moving object back to a detector. The change in the frequency of the return signal is detected and used to activate an alarm. In outdoor areas, this type of system can activate a floodlight that exposes intruders.

Ultrasonic and microwave movement sensors are prone to false alarms under certain conditions. Microwave signals, for example, penetrate glass and thin partitions, so movement outside the limits of a protected area may raise an alarm. Ultrasonics are contained within the protected area, but the system can be set off by high winds or by vibrations from, say, a doorbell ringing. In both types of systems, false alarms can be kept to a minimum by careful design and adjustment.

▼ A typical alarm system receives inputs from a variety of devices that detect intruders. Manually operated panic buttons can be located at strategic points, and a key system is used to enable, disable, or test the system. Such an alarm system usually has a backup battery so that it can function in the event of a power failure.

Closed-circuit television

Closed-circuit television (CCTV) systems are increasingly used in stores, office buildings, and public places. The views of several cameras can be shown in rotation on a screen, or an operator can select one particular camera when suspicious activity is identified. Video recordings can be used in evidence or in identifying an offender, either through public appeals for witnesses or through record searches.

In their early years, CCTV systems were useful only in well-illuminated areas. More recent systems use image intensifiers to produce images of reasonable quality using starlight and light reflected by clouds in the night sky. Another type of system uses infrared illumination and detection to produce images at night.

Infrared beams

Infrared radiation occupies the part of the electromagnetic spectrum between the highest microwave frequencies and the lowest frequencies of visible light. The fact that infrared rays cannot be seen by the human eye makes them useful for intruder-detection systems.

Infrared-beam systems consist of a source of infrared radiation, a focusing system that forms a beam of radiation, and a photocell that detects infrared radiation. The source may be a gallium–arsenide light-emitting diode or an incandescent bulb with a filter that absorbs visible light. The photocell produces a voltage as long as the beam

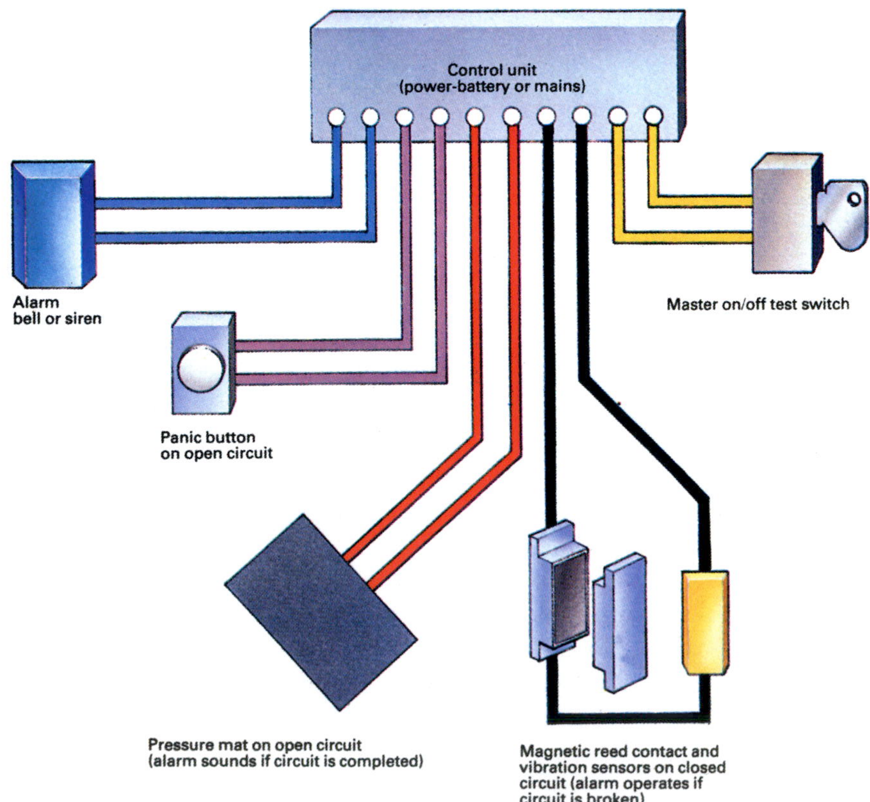

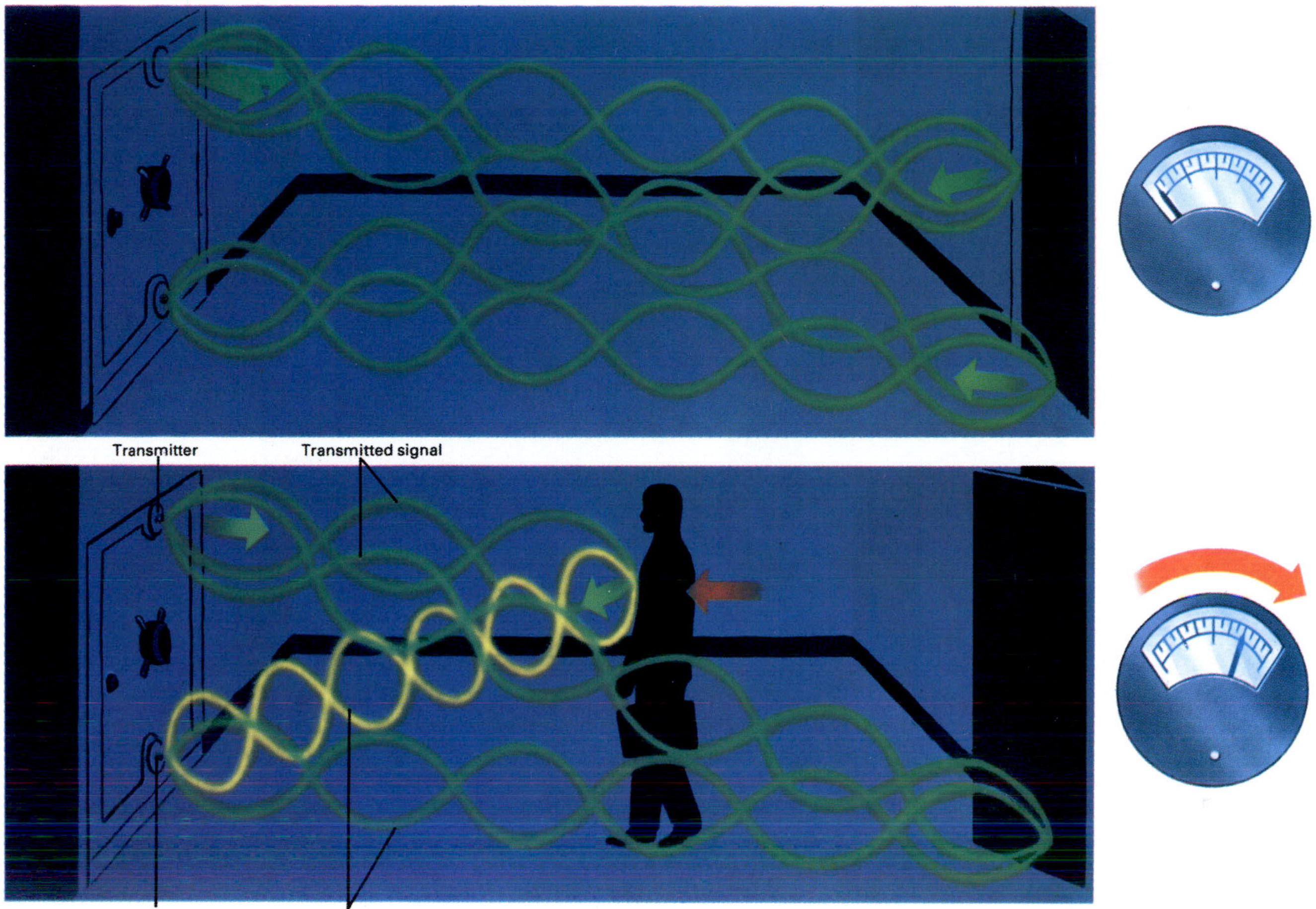

▲ A microwave motion-sensing system uses the Doppler effect to detect intruders. The microwaves bouncing off an approaching intruder have slightly shorter wavelengths than the transmitted signals, and this frequency shift triggers the alarm.

falls on it. If the invisible beam is interrupted by an intruder—however briefly—the drop in the photocell output voltage triggers the alarm.

Item protection

A number of devices are available to protect specific items of value within a premises. These devices include cables that can be threaded through valuable items in such a way that the cable must be disconnected to remove an item. This action triggers an alarm when the electrical circuit of the cable is broken. Such systems are used for antitheft devices in electrical stores.

Larger items, such as games machines or desktop computers, can be fitted with alarms that activate if the item moves or its power supply is disconnected. More sophisticated systems use radio tags, which broadcast a distress signal if the tagged item is moved. Radio transceivers in strategic locations around the premises detect these signals and raise the alarm. The same system can perform automatic routine inventories.

Recognition systems

High-security buildings require systems that deny access to unauthorized persons while allowing free movement for authorized personnel. The most basic of these systems use identity cards with magnetic strips that identify their carriers when passed through a magnetic reader. Systems that use this type of card can control access to buildings, rooms, and computer networks according to the carrier's security clearance. The disadvantage of this type of system is that it assumes that the person using the card is its genuine owner. Stolen or borrowed cards can be used until they are blocked from the system. More secure systems are being developed that will recognize unique patterns in the irises of eyes, fingerprints, or vocal characteristics of security-cleared personnel. Fraudulent access attempts trigger an alarm.

Remote alarm systems

Any alarm system can be remotely monitored by a central security desk in a building, by a remote security company, or by the police. With a remote system the intruder is unaware of being detected, so the chance of arrest is increased. Remote systems send a constant signal to the monitoring point by radio, telephone, or dedicated line. Any change in the signal triggers the alarm system.

SEE ALSO: Doppler effect • Electromagnetic radiation • Electronic surveillance • Lock, security • Photoelectric cell and photometry • Security system

Bus

◀ One of the most innovative bus designs is Volvo's Environmental Concept Bus (ECB). The electrically driven bus uses a gas turbine power unit to drive a generator that charges a series of storage batteries when out on the open road. When in the city, the driver switches to battery power. The electric motor can also act as a generator—energy from the motion of the bus is used to recharge the batteries or act as a brake. Operation of the battery is controlled by computer. The bus has four-wheel, power-assisted, speed-dependent steering, which the driver controls from a cab located in the center of the front of the bus. The rear-view mirrors have been replaced by an internal camera system, and the headlights are supplemented by long-range ultraviolet lamps on the roof that can illuminate distant objects without dazzling other road users. More than 60 passengers can travel on the ECB, half seated, half standing.

People on the move have many options available to them—bicycles, cars, trains, and trolley cars are among the many ways to travel long and short distances. They do have drawbacks, however, in that some limit the number of people that can be carried at one time, and others require infrastructure such as rails and power cables to be in place. Buses, with their large seating capacity and independent power supply, have proved to be an ideal form of transportation in bridging this gap.

Modern motorized buses evolved out of the development of the U.S. automobile industry at the end of the 19th century. They were mainly used for local sightseeing tours because they needed good roads, which were rare beyond city limits. Early models used a truck chassis and could seat up to 20 people. The body was separate, and operators often switched between carrying passengers and freight.

Purpose-built buses first appeared in 1920. The Fageol Safety Coach Company's bus chassis was lower, longer, and wider, making it easier for passengers to get on and off and much more stable on the road. Improvements were also made to the brakes and engine, and passengers benefited from more comfortable seats. Soon afterward came the integral-frame bus, which combined body and chassis, thus distributing weight, as stresses were spread throughout the structure in the roof, floor, and sides of the bus. Power was supplied by two diesel engines mounted in the center of the floor.

The popularity of this mode of transport and the ability to adapt the basic design to different purposes have led to its adoption all over the world. They range from simple school buses to highly sophisticated vehicles carrying kitchens, rest rooms, and in some cases, beds.

Transit buses

Local transit buses usually have low chassis to allow easy access and may also have a platform or sliding ramp to help the disabled and wheelchair users to board. Some modern buses even have a "kneeling function" and can lower the boarding height by up to 4 in. (9 cm) to meet the curb by means of a hydraulic suspension system. There may be one or two entrances on the curb side of the bus, and more in articulated versions. The integrated frame and chassis are usually made of steel, though glass-fiber reinforced resin composite bodies are now being made, which have extremely good tensile and impact properties and are better at resisting corrosion. Smaller buses seating less than 30 people are also becoming popular, particularly for serving suburban and village communities on an economic scale.

Most transit buses run on diesel or natural gas. Engines and transmissions are cradle mounted so that they can be removed or installed by maintenance engineers in less than an hour. In some buses, power is transmitted to the wheels indirectly through a generator that powers electric motors that drive the wheels. Power steering and antilock brakes are now standard features, and telescopic shock absorbers help give a more comfortable ride.

Intercity buses

Long-distance vehicles, as epitomized by the Greyhound bus, first appeared in the United States in 1928. They have become increasingly luxurious with reclining seats, video players, air conditioning, washrooms, and refreshment facilities. Design modifications have made them lighter, stronger, and more aerodynamic to reduce fuel consumption. The internal floor is higher than in transit buses to allow extra baggage to be carried beneath, and some companies carry freight to supplement revenues. Up to 50 passengers can be accommodated.

Carrying extra baggage can put strain on the suspension. Air springs are used in some buses to counteract strain. A central reservoir supplies pressurized air to a series of heavy rubber bellows. As the weight of passengers and baggage increases, a system of valves maintains pressure in the springs, keeping the bus level and at a constant height. But it only works for vertical loads—to cope with the lateral movements that occur when cornering or braking, the axles are connected by suspension links to the body of the bus.

Double-deck buses

Double-deckers are less common around the world than might be expected, given their greater carrying capacity. In some countries, there is concern about their stability; in others, existing infrastructure, such as low bridges and overhead cables, restricts use. Nevertheless, Los Angeles has introduced this type of bus for its express service on freeways, and a small fleet operates in New York City. The greatest use of double-deckers can be found in Britain, where they are widely used for local transport and, in their more luxurious forms, intercity runs.

Buses of the future

Reducing pollution, particularly the noxious emissions from road traffic, is of great importance to urban planners, and bus manufacturers are responding to the challenge to make their vehicles more environmentally friendly. New diesel engine technology produces lower particulate and nitrogen oxide emissions than 20 years ago, and many operators are switching to compressed natural gas mounted in roof tanks to power their buses. Other cleaner-burning fuels being developed include biogas, which is methane derived from natural decomposition of organic material; dimethylether (DME), made using natural gas or forestry biomass as a feedstock; and liquid petroleum gas (LPG) obtained through the distillation of crude oil and "wet" North Sea gas.

In the longer term, fuel cells and hybrid-fuel buses will become more prevalent. Hybrid buses use a fuel engine supplemented with an electric motor, generator, and batteries to smooth out the fluctuations in power experienced when operating in the stop-start conditions found in cities. Trolleybuses, which pick up power from overhead cables, produce no emissions, and are very quiet, are another option—Arnhem in the Netherlands has been using them for fifty years.

A number of specialized road systems especially for buses have been tried. Germany's O-bahn, set up by Daimler-Benz in the early 1980s, sectioned off parts of city-center roads for bus use. Buses were guided between concrete barriers by means of side-mounted wheels, allowing them to operate safely in a narrower stretch of road. A similar system, again tried in Germany, by AEG, used wires set in grooves in the road for guidance.

Perhaps the most radical system so far is the integrated transport network set up in the Brazilian city of Curitiba. Here, some 150 miles of special busways have been built, with long, tubular shelters at the stops where passengers can buy tickets. Bi-articulated buses pull alongside the shelter, which has sliding doors that only open when the bus is correctly aligned. The floor of the shelter is level with the floor of the bus to allow wheelchair users easy access. Assessments of the city's total fuel consumption show that Curitiba uses 30 percent less fuel than comparable cities.

▼ The yellow school bus is a familiar sight across the United States. This type of bus is very unsophisticated by comparison with the luxury touring vehicles used by rock stars, but it is hard wearing and economical to run on local journeys.

SEE ALSO: Battery • Fuel cell • Generator • Internal combustion engine • Low-emission road vehicle • Mass transit and subway • Transmission, automobile

Cable, Power

▲ Three types of oil-filled cable used to carry high-power direct current electricity. The oil is fed through the center of the cable.

There is no precise distinction between wire and cable, but the name cable normally describes two or more electric conductors, or cores, that are individually insulated and contained within a protective sheath. The cores are of stranded construction using twisted copper or aluminum wires. This configuration provides greater flexibility than a single solid conductor of similar rating.

Copper is the classic conductor material, but rising prices resulted in aluminum being widely used. Aluminum cables have a greater bulk but much less weight for a given current capacity. For equal electric resistance, an aluminum conductor has a cross section about 1.6 times that of a copper conductor.

Distribution systems

Electricity from generating plants is distributed at high voltage by means of overhead conductors carried on pylons (transmission towers). The conductors are not insulated themselves but are suspended from the pylons by strings of insulators.

Aluminum conductor, steel-reinforced (ACSR) cables have been used widely. They are comparatively inexpensive to produce but have a number of disadvantages: they are relatively heavy, the steel cores need to be galvanized and greased to resist corrosion, and they require complex terminations. More modern designs use either aluminum conductor, alloy reinforced (ACAR) or all aluminum alloy cable (AAAC) construction. The proportion of aluminum conductors in use increased after the development of improved jointing methods using an inert gas–metal deposition process.

The overhead distribution circuits are three-phase alternating current, with a separate conductor (or pair, or sometimes a group of four spaced conductors) for each phase of the power supply. The overhead system feeds at intervals into substations from which supplies are distributed to the surrounding area at lower voltages. Underground supply systems are still three-phased, but the three conductors are contained in one cable.

Insulation

Individual conductors are insulated in a number of ways according to the function of the cable. Rubber insulation was once used in lower voltage cables for domestic installation, but plastic (PVC) insulation is now used extensively.

In 1967, a fire in the power plant at La Spezia, Italy, spread through the large amounts of PVC-insulated wiring within the building. Alternative materials, which are less susceptible to combustion and do not produce large quantities of acrid smoke when they do burn, have been used since that time in areas where fire prevention is more important than cost, such as underground railways, aircraft, hospitals, and military installations.

Suitable materials include polytetrafluoroethylene (PTFE), silicone rubber, and a range of proprietary mixed and filled polymers. Extreme heat resistance is provided by the use of magnesium oxide powder as insulation. This substance is compressed around the conductors within a copper sheath, forming a cable that is impervious to moisture and resistant to attack by oil and gasoline. It will also carry large currents because the magnesium oxide is quite a good conductor of heat. Cable with this form of insulation is known as MICS (mineral-insulated, copper-sheathed) cable and is specially useful to industry for installations in boiler houses and other areas of high ambient temperature.

If the cable is for underground distribution at high voltage, oil-impregnated paper insulation is applied to the conductors using multihead lapping machines—each head carries several reels of paper that rotate around the conductor as it passes through the machine. For very high voltages, as many as 200 layers may be applied to one conductor. After the individual conductors have been insulated, further layers of paper are applied to the assembly. Following this procedure, a lead or, more often, an aluminum sheath is extruded over the cable to exclude moisture. The sheath may be armored with steel tape or steel wire and further protected by an outer wrapping of burlap or extruded PVC.

Oil-filled cables

Power cables heat up and expand when carrying large currents. During periods of lighter load, they cool down, and there is the risk of spaces, or voids, being left in the wrappings of paper insulation, creating areas of weakness where an internal electrical discharge may occur. In these conditions, the insulation may eventually break down and the cable will need to be replaced. This problem is overcome in oil-filled cable, which has a hollow center containing a spiral duct permanently filled with low-viscosity insulating oil. The oil is free to move longitudinally as it expands or contracts with temperature changes in the cable. The duct is connected to reservoirs along the cable route into which the oil flows when it expands and from which it returns to the cable after cooling. In this way, the insulation remains fully impregnated with oil under all operating conditions. The thickness of paper insulation in an oil-filled cable need be only half that of a cable with oil-impregnated paper insulation alone. This technique is used in cables carrying from 30 kV to 400 kV. It is particularly useful for the feeder cables of electric railways since these are subject to wide variations of load at different times of day.

An alternative to oil-filled cables is gas-filled cables. This type is adopted on cable routes where there are considerable differences of level or where there are long distances over which it is impracticable to install oil reservoirs along the route. These cables are then filled with pressurized nitrogen gas.

Pipe-type cables

In some areas, for example where mining subsidence is likely to occur, the mechanical strength of a cable is very important. In these circumstances a cable may be laid inside a steel pipe with a protective covering of bitumen and glass-fiber fleece. Where there is a high corrosion risk, there may be an external plastic sheath as well. These cables may be nitrogen filled, the pressure of the gas on the cable sheath helping to restore the insulation to its proper position, since it tends to shift when the cable expands with rising temperature.

▼ A typical domestic supply cable (left) and two high-voltage (600 to 1,000 V) cables. The center cable has four plastic-insulated solid aluminum conductors (three single-phase supplies and one neutral). The conductors are taped together and covered with steel wire armor and a plastic sheath. The cable on the right is of similar construction and the same working voltage, but the conductors are of stranded copper. The stranding helps the copper to flex, and the cross-sectional area can be much smaller than with the aluminum, for the same power rating.

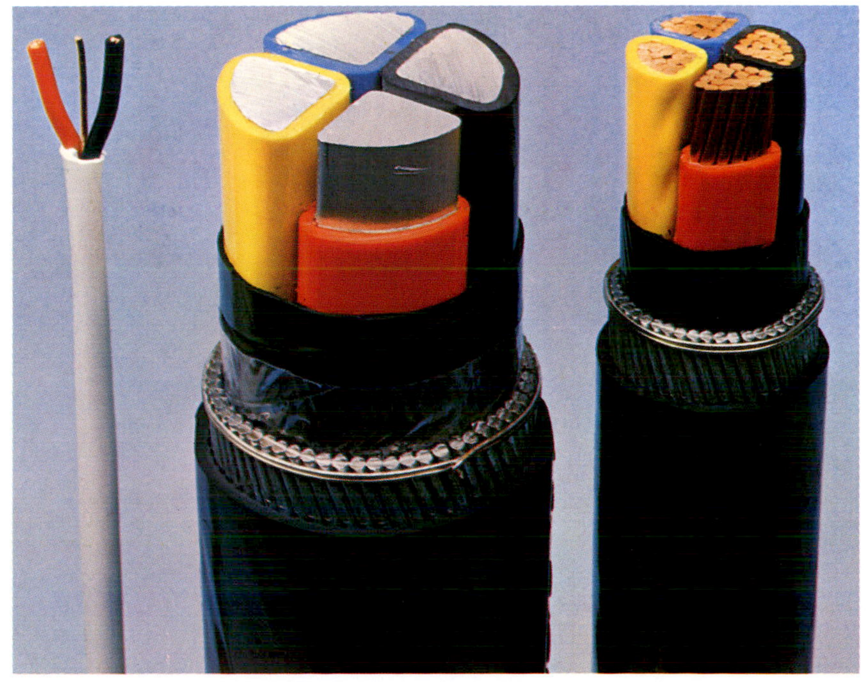

Superconducting cables

For most power cables, the maximum load they can safely carry is limited by internal temperature rises caused by resistive heating of the conductors. Materials such as niobium tin (Nb_3Sn) cooled below 18 K become superconducting—their electrical resistance drops to zero—removing this limitation on load capacity. There were originally many technical problems in cooling the cables, but research in Austria, Russia, and the Brookhaven National Laboratory in New York has established the technology required to overcome these problems.

Power cable installation

Power cables can be buried in a trench, pulled into pipes or ducts, laid in concrete surface troughs, or routed on posts or in tunnels. In some European countries, most of the power cables are buried in trenches that vary in width and depth depending on the type of installation. For high-voltage cables (30 kV and over), a typical trench would be about 30 in. (75 cm) wide and 36 in. (91 cm) deep, although in many cases a larger trench is required, especially if several cable circuits are being laid together with normal spacing between the cables.

When a cable route crosses a busy main road, however, it is not always possible to dig a trench across the whole of the road at once, and so ducts or pipes are installed under each side of the road in turn, then the cables are pulled through. More recently, nondisruptive trenchless methods such as directional drilling and moling have been used as installation techniques. In directional drilling, a string of metal drilling rods is used to create a highly accurate pathway for a cable or pipe, which can be pulled into place behind the drill head as the rods are retracted following the initial bore. Moling is less accurate but suitable for installation of short lengths of cable and consists of an air-powered or pneumatic device that is started from a pit on the line and level required, pulling the cable behind it.

In the United States, ducted installations are more commonly used for distribution cables, and some transmission cables, than in Europe. In American cities, the ducts are laid in groups with access holes every so often for inspection and jointing. The narrow layer of air around the cable in a duct has some heat insulating effect (as with double glazing), and as a result, cables in ducts have a lower current rating than cables laid directly in the ground.

Concrete surface troughs can be used in such places as canal tow paths, railway embankments, and electricity substations. Here, space is usually limited and it is not often possible to open up a deep trench for any length of time. When cables are buried in a trench, the heat generated in the cable by the current flowing through the conductor has to escape through the ground. If it cannot, overheating and breakdown could occur. The troughs can be filled around the cables or left unfilled and ventilated. As a general rule, a filling (called a backfill) is used for major cable installations, which helps to remove heat from the cable.

▶ Overhead power cables are insulated from the metal pylons by ceramics. The conduction route is then completed by short loops of cable. Where a number of lines are carried between pylons, they are often separated by spacers, which prevent the lines coming too close together and causing the current to jump in a process known as arcing.

Dangers of overheating cables

Power cables that overheat have obvious risks, particularly if their use has safety implications. Automobiles, airplanes, and ships are just some examples that use bundles of wires to transmit power to instruments or machine parts. If the insulation of a wire becomes damaged, arcing may occur, causing a fire to start. A new aircraft wire, BMS 13-60, has been designed to resist arcing and produces a smoke density of only 2 percent. It has been introduced only on certain types of airplanes as yet, but its widespread use could reduce the risks of fires on board considerably.

SEE ALSO: Aluminum • Cable, submarine • Cable and rope manufacture • Electricity • Insulator, electric • Power supply

Cable, Submarine

Modern land and submarine communications cables are coaxial—consisting of a copper wire held centrally inside a copper tube by a layer of insulation, a design that is particularly suited to handling high-frequency signals.

When air is used as the insulator between the inner wire and the surrounding copper tube, land cables can be designed to handle frequencies up to 60 MHz (60 million cycles per second). Modern electronic techniques permit over 10,000 high-quality one-way telephone channels or more than 250,000 telegraph channels, to be transmitted simultaneously.

With submarine cables, however, such high-frequency handling characteristics are not possible because of the special construction technique required to protect cables in the sea.

Early cables

The first successful transatlantic cable was laid by the Great Eastern in 1866. It was insulated with gutta percha, a natural resin, and was protected and strengthened with galvanized iron armor wires, even in the deepest laid sections where protection was unnecessary, a practice that was continued in all submarine cables for almost a century. The early cables were telegraph cables with a bandwidth of only a few Hz (cycles per second); they were not coaxial since they had only a single conductor. The direct or very low frequency currents of a telegraph signal return via the sea, which has negligible electrical resistance. At higher frequencies, the return currents tend to crowd closer to the center conductor and to travel in the high-resistance armor wires. A new type of cable was therefore required that could handle higher frequencies.

In 1921, the U.S. physicists J.R. Carson and J.J. Gilbert pointed out that for efficient transmission of high-frequency currents, a submarine cable should have a return conductor of low-resistance material closely surrounding the insulation—thus setting out the principle of the submarine coaxial cable.

Repeaters

No matter how good the design and materials, any practical cable will attenuate (reduce) high-frequency signals more than low-frequency ones. Unless the cable is very short, these high-frequency signals will become so feeble when received as to be indistinguishable from the electronic background noise. The remedy is to insert amplifiers, or repeaters, at regular intervals to ensure the signal-to-noise ratio is kept high. Such amplifiers must be very efficient and stable and use the principle of negative feedback, by which any distortion or change in amplification cancels itself out. Power for operating the repeaters is provided

▼ A cable-laying ship pays out cable from tanks in its hold through regulated feed mechanisms.

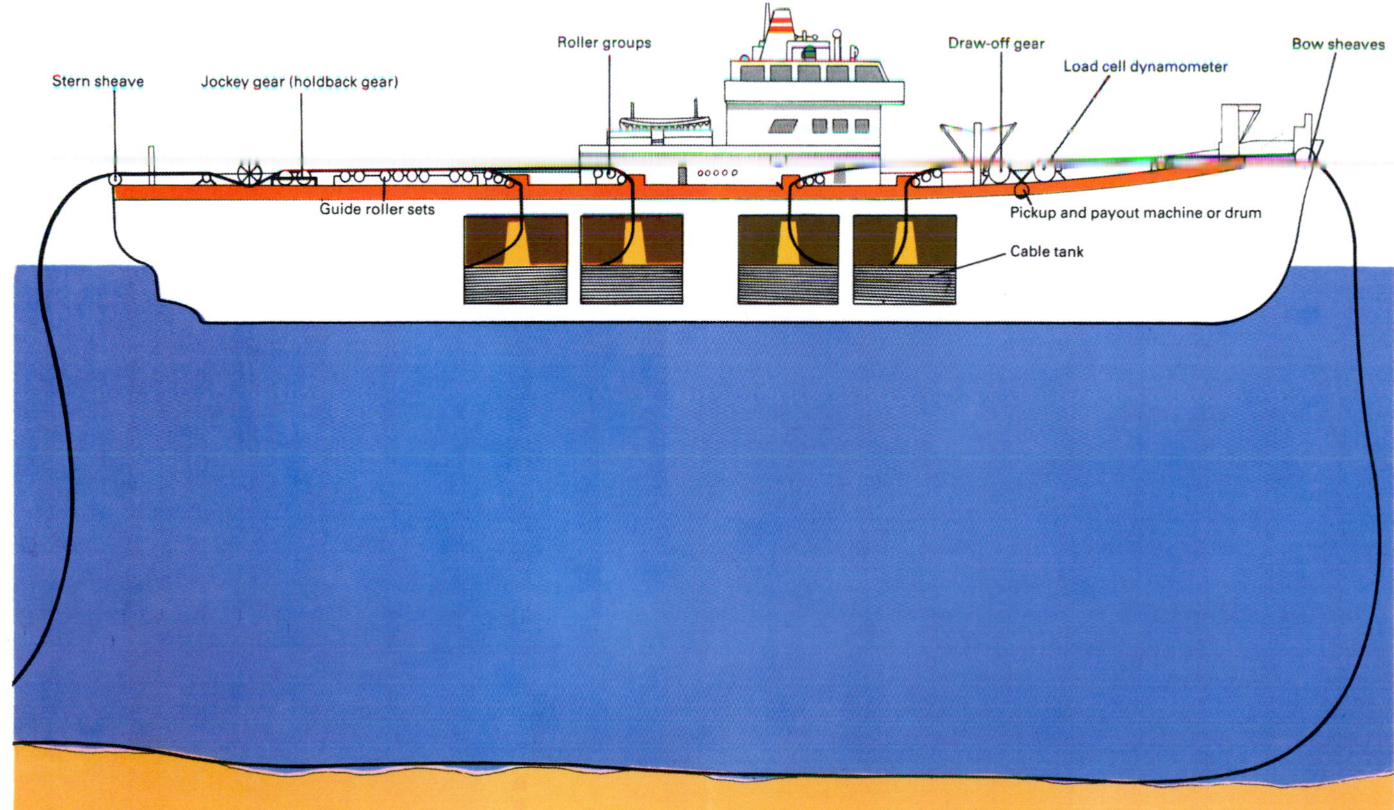

from the land terminals in the form of direct current at several thousand volts and about 0.5 A.

In 1951, a new sea cable was invented in which the supporting member was placed in the center. The first experimental sample was built on a neutral (that is, a nontwisting), steel wire rope with the center conductor, a thin copper strip, folded around it. Its edges were locked in a box seam like that of a tin can. The insulator was a polyethylene tube with a 0.8 in. (2 cm) outside diameter, and the outer conductor consisted of six helical aluminum tapes. To guard against the risk of corrosion by sea water if the outer sheath were punctured, the tapes were bound with a cotton tape impregnated with a corrosion inhibitor. A low-density polyethylene oversheath was extruded over the cotton tape.

This cable, known as lightweight cable, was more efficient and weighed little more than one-third that of the conventional armored cable used in 1956 for the first transatlantic telephone cable, (TAT 1). The new cable was used for CANTAT 1, the first Anglo-Canadian transatlantic cable, in 1961, the New York–Bermuda cable, and the COMPAC and SEACOM networks linking Vancouver, Hawaii, Fiji, New Zealand, Australia, New Guinea, and South East Asia in the following years.

Manufacturing methods

Since 1961, there have been changes in cable design as a result of new requirements and improvements in the materials and methods of manufacture. Two important improvements have been the elimination of the box seam on the center conductor and the substitution of a single longitudinal seam conductor for the six helical tapes.

In the latest version, the steel strand and the flat copper tape for the center conductor are fed into a machine that consists of a number of pairs of forming rollers, which shape the tape into a tube rather larger than, and surrounding, the strand so that its edges butt together. The edges are welded electrically in an inert gas atmosphere, and the complete tube is drawn out, which shrinks it onto the steel.

After inspection for weld faults and a thorough chemical cleaning, the hot polyethylene core is extruded onto the composite center conductor. It is cooled slowly in a long, temperature-controlled water trough, generally under pressure. Following inspection, the core is shaved to a closely controlled diameter either by a circular die or rotary cutters.

Finally, the outer conductor is applied in a manner similar to that used for the center conductor, the main difference being that the edges of the tape are overlapped instead of welded. The oversheath is then extruded on while the cable is still in a straight line. This step is important because without the compressive support of the oversheath, the thin outer conductor tape would buckle when the cable was bent.

▲ One of a cable-laying ship's four cable tanks with a lightweight transatlantic telephone cable, laid in 1958. Today the world is spanned not only by cables, but by a network of communications satellites.

It has been found that with larger, stiffer cables a neutral steel strand is not essential, and an alternative strand design has 41 wires all with the same direction of lay, or twist.

Also, while the first lightweight cable used aluminum for the outer conductor because it was cheaper and lighter than copper, copper is now favored in some applications because the higher electric resistance of aluminum increases the number of repeaters needed by about 5 percent.

Laying submarine cables

The laying of the first successful transatlantic submarine cable in 1866, after several failures, was rightly hailed as a great achievement. Nevertheless, compared with the laying of modern high-capacity submarine telephone cable, it was a relatively simple operation. One reason for the increased complexity is the need for submerged repeaters, or amplifiers, to be spliced into the cable at regular intervals, which nowadays may be as little as 5 miles (8 km).

The very earliest repeaters (1943) were spliced into cable laid previously, a cable ship having to grapple for it and bring it on board to carry out the jointing operation. This method could only be used in shallow water. In deep water, the jointing and laying of cable needed to be done as one continuous operation.

In the early 1950s when consideration was first being given to a transatlantic telephone cable, the cable-laying machinery on cable ships differed little in principle from that of the *Great Eastern*. The only repeaters that such machines could handle were flexible ones, and the first transatlantic telephone cable, TAT 1, laid in 1956, used flexible repeaters of American design and manufacture. Of necessity, they had to be electrically simple and could only amplify in one direction. Two cables, each with 51 repeaters, were required to provide 36 two-way telephone circuits.

Meanwhile, in Britain, a different approach had been taken: that of developing the most efficient repeater possible with suitable means for laying it. The design adopted could amplify in both directions and provide 60 two-way circuits over a single cable. It was sealed in a cylindrical steel case 10.5 in. (26.7 cm) in diameter and 10 ft. (3 m) in length and weighed 1,700 lbs. (760 kg) with the cable entering at one end and leaving at the other. Sixteen of these repeaters were laid by HMTS (Her Majesty's Telegraph Ship) *Monarch* for the Newfoundland–Nova Scotia section of TAT 1. They were fed over the bows laboriously by removing several turns of cable from the drum to allow the repeater to pass, then replacing them. Clearly a better method was badly needed.

The method adopted was known as the Post Office Five Sheave Gear. It involved a fairly simple modification to the existing stern cable engine on the *Monarch* that enabled a repeater to by-pass it. The single drum was replaced by four 6 ft. (1.8 m) diameter V-grooved sheaves (pulley wheels) and one plain sheave, all mounted in a fore-and-aft line, three of the V-sheaves being coupled directly to the drum shaft. The cable passed alternately under and over the sheaves so that it was gripped firmly but did not actually go right around any of them. A flexible steel rope called the bypass rope was spliced to the cable ahead of and behind the repeater, which was mounted on a light trolley. As the trolley neared the first sheave, the cable and repeater were diverted to one side, but the rope continued to pass under and over the sheaves. After rope and repeater had passed, the cable was led back into the sheaves, rope and repeater being laid over the stern together, at a speed of 1.5 to 2 knots.

The machine was first used in 1958 and proved so successful that between 1959 and 1970 all British and Commonwealth cables and some U.S. deep-water cables were laid by this method.

TAT 2, like TAT 1, used flexible repeaters for the main Atlantic crossing, but thereafter the United States changed to lightweight cable and rigid repeaters, shorter and fatter than British ones. The United States also designed a new cable ship equipped with a new caterpillarlike cable engine. This engine was capable of laying cable and repeaters at 8 knots. Cable was gripped by two V-grooved caterpillar tracks that were pressed together by inflated air bags, which allowed the tracks to open up to accept the 13 in. (33 cm) diameter repeater.

Although submarine electric cables are still in use, satellites are being used increasingly for telephony, and fiber-optic cables are taking the place of electric cables for underground and undersea installations.

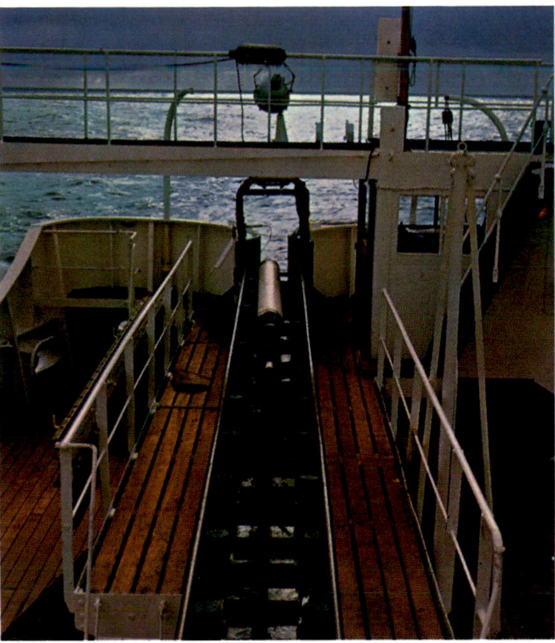

▲ A repeater in a section of a transatlantic cable. Repeaters can be either flexible or rigid. Aboard the cable ship, there are procedures for splicing the cable and tracing electrical faults.

Fiber optics

Optical fibers are also being used as submarine cables. Using fibers only micrometers in diameter, these cables can carry thousands of channels per pair of fibers, which gives it a very advantageous cost-per-channel ratio over conventional cables.

Optical fiber cables transmit light through fibers or thin rods of glass or some other transparent, highly refractive material. Their ability to carry significantly more information than conventional cables has made them valuable for transmitting data between computers and for other data-intensive uses, such as telephony. Optical fibers are not affected by electromagnetic interference, and the signal does not deteriorate as quickly as one sent along a conventional cable.

FACT FILE

- *Sections of submarine cable passing over continental shelves close to shore are sometimes in danger of being trawled by fishing vessels. The Bell Company has developed a cable plow that slides on runners and can bury cable at depths up to 500 fathoms (915 m). Seafloor conditions are monitored by TV cameras mounted on the plow.*

- *Submarine power cables carrying direct current can cause significant compass errors in ships passing over them, particularly if the cable is laid on a north–south axis. In bipolar schemes using twin cables, the problem is solved by laying the two cables close together. An England–France cross-channel link was installed in 1965, spaced at a maximum of 20 in. (50 cm) to keep compass error down to 2 percent.*

SEE ALSO: Amplifier • Cable, power • Cable and rope manufacture • Fiber optics • Satellite, artificial • Telecommunications

Cable and Rope Manufacture

◀ Armoring a submarine communications cable on a special armoring machine that twists the separate wire strands—which have themselves been plaited—around a central core consisting of several plaited strands of conductor material. After plaiting, an oversheath is extruded on while the cable is in a straight line. The finished cable is water-resistant, and the tough wire armor protects it from possible damage by such things as trawl nets.

A rope may be described as any cord at least 0.16 in. (4 mm) in diameter made by closing (twisting together) three or more strands that are themselves formed of twisted yarns or metal wires.

Rope was one of the earliest inventions, and in many respects, it has changed very little over the centuries. Materials, however, have varied and today some 90 percent of all ropes are made from synthetic fibers. Many vegetable fibers have been used in ropemaking, including date palm, flax, jute, cotton, and coir (coconut fiber). Toward the end of the 19th century, Manila hemp was introduced and this soon became the most popular fiber and led to improved processing machinery.

Another hard fiber, sisal, was introduced in the early 1900s and, although not as popular as Manila hemp, was a very useful alternative during and after the two world wars. It was chiefly used for baler twine, but it has been largely replaced by synthetic materials. In the 1950s, nylon and the polyester fabric Dacron were found to be excellent synthetic fibers for rope-making, and these are the strongest materials available for normal commercial purposes.

Modern rope-making processes

Natural fiber rope and certain synthetic ropes are made from yarn that has been spun from raw fibers. The material is fed into a goods, or hackling, machine that combs the fibers with steel pins and produces a coarse sliver. This process is repeated on other machines, the spacing between the pins being reduced each time so that the sliver is brought into a more regular form. The sliver is then condensed in drawing machines before being spun and wound onto bobbins. The resulting yarn can have a right-handed (Z) or left-handed (S) twist.

Synthetic yarns, such as nylon and polyester, are extruded by the manufacturers in the form of continuous filaments, and these have to be built up to a suitably sized composite yarn by plying together a number of the filaments. This is known as doubling or throwing. The yarns are then set onto a creel (a frame holding bobbins of yarn) for forming the strand of a rope. For a conventional three-stranded, right-handed rope, Z yarns would be used. The ends are fed through a register plate, which ensures the correct formation of the strand, keeping the inside yarns located in the center, thus obtaining optimum strength and reducing strand failure. The yarns then enter a compression tube, which locates the point of twisting and helps to form a smooth strand with a compact cross section. The formed strand is drawn through the tube and an S twist is applied, the opposite direction of the yarn twist, before being wound onto strand bobbins. Once these bobbins are filled with strand, they are transferred to the closing machine. They are mounted individually at one end of the closer, and the strands are brought together at the other end. The rope is then passed through a die. Now Z twist is applied and the rope is closed, the finished rope being drawn through again by means of capstans, or haul pulleys, and wound onto a reel. To assist the closing process, the individual strands receive extra twisting to compensate for the loss of turn when the ends are tucked back into the rope.

Another method of making rope is by means of a ropewalk, which is a path along which rope-forming strands are laid. The strands are drawn out by a traveler, and when they have been drawn to the correct length, the rope is closed by means of a top-cart, which is returned from the traveler end to the register plate end at a regulated speed.

Structure of rope

The amount of twist in a rope is called the lay, a hard-laid rope having more twist put into the strand and rope than a soft-laid rope. A three-stranded rope is known as plain, or hawser, laid, and a four-stranded rope, useful for rope ladders, is known as shroud laid. Cable-laid ropes are constructed from ropes of three or more strands, and the twist direction is again reversed.

In recent years, large braided ropes have been developed for mooring ships; this type of rope reduces wastage by eliminating kinking. The most widely used of these ropes, called cross plait, is one in which eight strands are formed: four S direction strands using Z yarn and four Z direction strands using S yarn. The strands are produced on normal stranding machines, and a special closing machine then plaits the rope in pairs of strands—two Z strands followed by two S strands and so on. This construction produces a very flexible rope and is particularly suitable for nylon and polyester ropes, where wastage is expensive.

Wire rope

In the manufacture of wire rope, a number of wires are twisted helically (often around a core) to make a strand, and several strands are then twisted around a larger core to form the rope; the technique is generally similar to that used for fiber ropes. Wire rope has tremendous strength for its size and weight; for example, it is used for haulage and hoisting applications in cranes, cable railways, well digging, and excavation. A number of metals are used for wire ropes, depending on the characteristics required, and the most common material is steel wire. Cores may be made of wire, which gives higher strength, or fiber, which gives greater flexibility.

The wire is wound on bobbins and set up in the stranding machine where the individual wires are pulled together and twisted (generally around

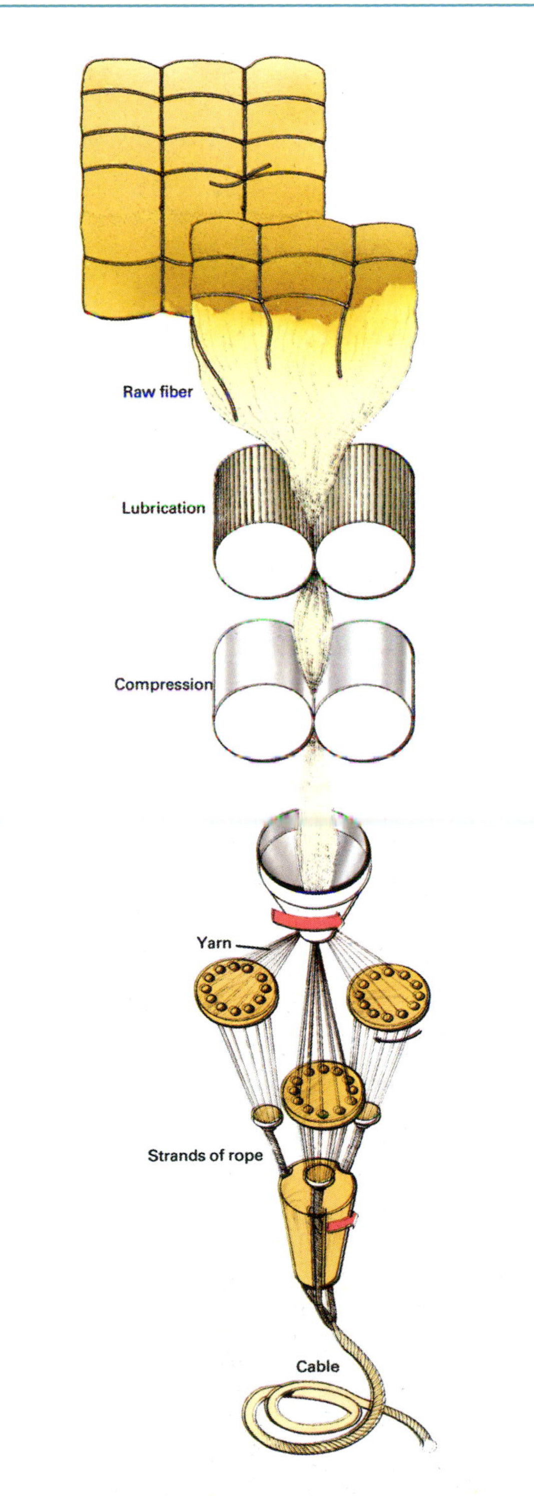

◀ The manufacture of ropes and cables begins with raw fibers being compressed into a sliver. The sliver is given a right-handed or left-handed twist to form a yarn, which in turn is twisted in the opposite direction into rope. Finally, the rope is formed into cable, the direction of twist again being reversed.

a core) to give the strand, which is wound onto a reel after forming. On the basis of the machine design, the twisting action may be achieved by rotation of the bobbin assemblies or by rotation of the take-up reel. The strands are wound onto larger bobbins that are mounted in a closing, or laying, machine where they are compacted together and twisted around the core to give the finished rope. The twisting action is provided by rotation of the bobbin assembly, and the finished rope is pulled out of the machine by means of a capstan arrangement and wound onto a drum.

There are two common ways to twist, or lay, wire rope: the regular lay and the Lang lay. In the regular lay, the helical twist of the strands is opposite in direction to that of the twist in the wires of the strand: in the Lang lay, both twists are in the same direction. Lang lay rope is more flexible and wears better on the pulley or sheave (a grooved wheel in a pulley) but has a tendency to unwind under load.

Wire rope is most commonly made from round wires with the basic arrangement using wires of the same diameter twisted in successive layers to form a strand. The number of wires in each layer is 1, 6, 12, 18, and 24, and the required strand diameter is achieved by appropriate combination of the wire thickness and the number of layers. Use of a small number of large-diameter wires gives a rope good wear characteristics, and the use of a large number of small wires gives a flexible cable. Other types of construction use wires of different diameters to achieve closer packing and better contact between individual wires.

There are four commonly used types of wire rope, which are generally referred to by two numbers that describe their construction. The first number is the number of strands in the rope; the second is the number of wires in each strand. A 6 x 7 rope is called a standard course-laid rope and is used for heavy-duty hauling, such as for well drilling and in operating streetcars; 6 x 9 is used more often than all others for hoisting; 6 x 37 is an extra-flexible hoisting rope for use on small sheaves; and 8 x 19 is interchangeable with 6 x 37 except that it distorts from its construction more readily, and therefore conditions of service that cause crushing of the rope require the six-strand design.

An indication of the strength of steel wire rope is given by the breaking strength of two sizes of 6 x 37 rope: a ¼ in. (6 mm) wire rope has a nominal breaking load of 5,500 lbs. (2,495 kg), whereas the figure for a 3 in. (76.2 mm) rope is over 650,000 lbs. (295,000 kg). In practice, however, the working stress should be restricted to one-fifth of the breaking weight; in other words, there should be a safety factor of five, and even higher factors than this are required for some applications.

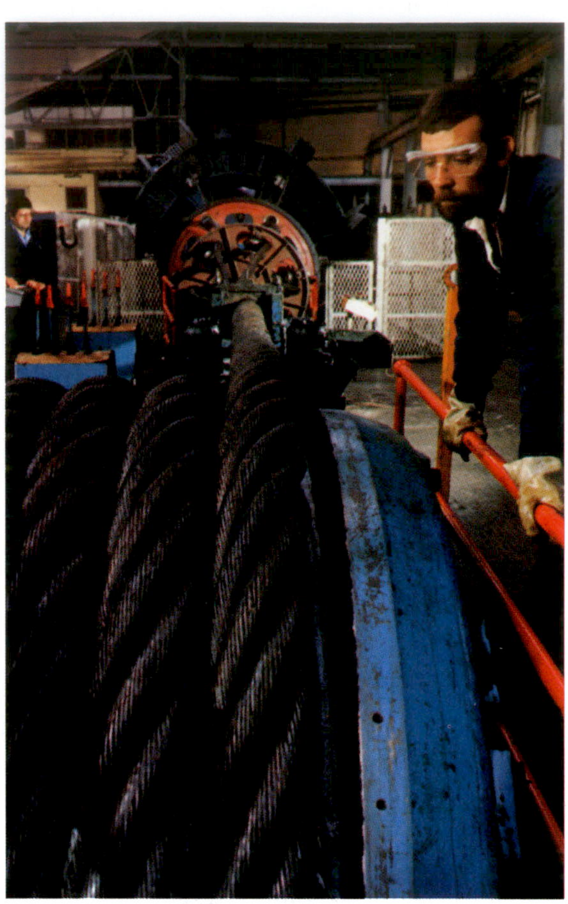

◀ One of the largest six-strand wire ropes ever made: a mooring bridle, 7.6 in. (19.3 cm) in diameter, designed for use during the crucial final construction phase of an offshore oil platform. Wire rope is made by twisting individual strands of steel wire together on a special machine.

In use, the individual wires making up the rope move relative to one another, and this movement is eased by the use of a suitable lubricant. The core of a wire rope is greased (and fiber cores are normally impregnated with lubricant to act as a reservoir) and the strands lubricated during manufacture, but the initial treatment will not normally last for the service life of the rope. It must be kept clean to avoid corrosion by wiping it with waste (rags) or burlap, but solvents such as kerosene should not be used. The rope should then be regreased with an acid-free lubricant such as petroleum jelly worked well into the spaces between the strands.

Failure of wire rope is caused by tensile stress if the rope is overloaded, by high compressive stress as the wires press in on each other, as in running in a V groove, and by the wires rubbing against each other when bending around a sheave. Kinks and small loops should be avoided, while a rope that is subjected to reverse bends (by being wound first around one pulley in one direction, then around another pulley in the opposite direction) will have its effective lifespan halved.

SEE ALSO: Cable, submarine • Cable transport system • Fiber, natural • Fiber, synthetic • Metalworking • Polyamide

Cable Network

▲ Video conferencing is a useful development of the advances in cable technology. At this meeting of the International Olympic Committee, members are able to talk to delegates overseas directly, without them having to travel. The video camera on top of the screen in front of the chairman enables him to be seen and heard by people at the other end of the video link, and the whole room can be viewed by the tripod-mounted camera. The chairman can also see the meeting room the on-screen delegate is speaking from.

Cabling of one kind or another has been used to convey information almost from the time that it was discovered that electricity could be conducted along wires. Information, in the technical sense of the term, includes all knowledge, news, data, instructions, software, and entertainment material. Information is now regarded as a commodity of the greatest social and commercial importance. Because of its importance, an unrestricted supply of information to domestic or business environments is becoming recognized as being comparable in importance to the supply of water, electricity, and heating fuel. The supply of this new commodity is the principal function of cable networks. A secondary but growing function is communication.

Sending signals

The first use of cabling to transmit information appears to have been achieved by a German anatomy professor, S.T. Sommering, in 1809. Sommering used a cable of 27 insulated wires bound together. Twenty-six of these represented the letters of the alphabet, and the 27th was the return wire. At the receiving end, all the wires were dipped into slightly acid water. The letters were sent one at a time by connecting a voltaic pile—a primitive electric battery—to the appropriate wire and were detected at the other end of the cable by the gas bubbles that were formed by electrolysis at the end of the same wire. This device actually worked over a distance of 65 yards (600 m), but it was too expensive and too slow for practical success.

The first successful electric telegraph was invented in 1837 by the American inventor Samuel Morse and simultaneously by the British scientist Charles Wheatstone. The Morse telegraph carried information along a single copper wire and used Earth as the return conductor, and Morse invented a code of short and long pulses of current (dots and dashes) for the purpose. The Morse key became familiar to millions of telegraph and, later, radio operators for well over a century. The electrical resistance of the wire limited the range to about 20 miles (32 km), and relay stations were necessary.

In 1874, the U.S. inventor Thomas Edison developed a method of sending two telegraph messages simultaneously, and by 1915, this number had been extended to eight or more simultaneous messages, largely as a result of the work of the French engineer Jean-Marie-Emile Baudot whose multiplex telegraphy involved synchronized clockwork switches at each end of the cable. Baudot also developed a five-bit code that was used for years for teleprinting in the form of groups of holes punched in paper tape. This code was the forerunner of the seven- and eight-bit digital codes in use today. Baudot is honored in the unit of signaling speed—the number of bits transmitted per minute—known as the baud rate. Later it was discovered that single cables could be made to carry numerous different channels, each consisting of an alternating current carrier wave at a unique frequency, as in radio transmission.

The rise of the television in the 1950s saw a need for improved cable, mainly because the high frequencies being used resulted in severe losses. This need led to the development of low-loss coaxial cable capable of carrying larger amounts of pulsed information at high speed. As the demand grew for ever more channels carrying masses of information, engineers turned to fiber optic cable, which abandoned electricity and opened up a new world of communication using beams of light.

Cable television

The first real impact of the cable network revolution on the domestic scene was the introduction of cable television into the United States in the 1970s. By laying broad-band coaxial or fiber optic cables with links to private homes, cable television companies were able to offer a pay-as-you-view and a video-on-demand service that provided a much larger range of TV channels and other facilities than was possible from other sources. Cable television is in competition with normal terrestrial TV services and with direct-to-home (DTH) television from artificial satellites. Most of the purely TV material supplied on cable is derived from satellites, but whereas most domestic users can accept signals from only one satellite, the cable companies, using more complex equipment, can offer material from several. In addition, the technical quality of cable TV is often better than that provided by way of the domestic satellite antenna.

The most significant difference between the earlier TV systems and cable TV is in the range of other facilities that can be offered by the latter. Video-on-demand allows access to virtually the whole range of available video recorded material. Users are presented with enormous catalogues of titles, and, as video tapes are progressively replaced by digital video discs, the costs of providing such a range will drop. Unlike tapes, video discs suffer no degradation during use, so the technical quality of the program remains at its original level.

The majority of cable users are interested primarily in entertainment, and the demand for interactive entertainment—such as mass voting or personal intervention into the direction of a story—will grow. Also, other extended TV facilities will be accelerated by the growing development of digital television. Already, the proportion of cable network use for purposes other than pure entertainment is growing. Wide-band cabling, such as is provided by fiber optics, allows immediate access to an almost unlimited range of facilities. These include a high-speed linkage to the Internet, much faster than an ISDN link; home shopping for a wide range of commodities; home banking; stock trading; voice and video communication; video conferencing; and many other amenities and resources.

Technology

Currently the most widely used types of cabling are simple twisted, insulated copper wire pairs and coaxial cable. Plain copper wire has severe limitations and is rapidly being replaced by better media.

Coaxial cable may be flexible or semirigid and consists of a central conductor, commonly of braided or solid copper, surrounded by and insulated from a tubular outer conductor. The insulant between the two conductors may be air or a plastic such as polyethylene. The cable's symmetry and its design make it a shielded structure, and it is largely immune to interference from external electromagnetic fields. Coaxial cables can carry considerable electrical power at high frequencies without radiating significant electromagnetic energy.

A better, although more expensive, alternative to coaxial cable, however, is the fiber optic cable.

▼ Watching television need no longer be a passive activity—cable networks have opened up a whole range of interactive services such as home-shopping channels, video-on-demand, and home banking. For people without computers, cable networks can also provide Internet facilities for sending and receiving e-mail.

This is by far the most efficient form of cabling when signals of very high frequency and great bandwidth are to be transmitted, and it uses light as the medium of communication rather than pulsed electricity. Light is an electromagnetic wave form with a higher frequency than any other known entity. Visible light propagated by the Sun covers a band of wavelengths between about 400 nanometers (violet light) and 770 nanometers (red light). A nanometer is 10^{-9} meters, and because light travels at about 300 million meters per second, these very short wavelengths correspond to frequencies of about 10^{15} cycles per second (hertz, or Hz). A frequency of 10^{15} Hz provides plenty of room for a large number of bands, even if each of them takes up several hundred million hertz (MHz). The carrying power of light can be multiplied by using several beams of pure one-color (monochrome) light at different frequencies.

Fiber optic cables depend on the fact that a beam of light passing along a fine glass or plastic fiber does not escape from the fiber but is reflected off the interface between the fiber surface and the exterior. Fibers used in communications have a very small diameter of 0.0002 to 0.0005 in. (5–10 thousandths of a millimeter). Cables can be made up of many fibers, and these are much less heavy than cables using copper conductors. Two pairs of these fine glass fibers can carry 120,000 simultaneous two-way voice circuits.

Digital square-wave pulses of electric current from a computer or other source are used to drive a simple semiconductor device known as a light-emitting diode that converts an electrical pulse into a pulse of light. This light is then focused with a lens onto the end of the optical fiber. At the receiving end of the fiber, the emerging light is focused with a lens onto another semiconductor device called a photodiode, the output of which is a string of electrical pulses identical to the input. Conventional error-checking protocols, as in computers, are applied. Glass fiber cable has the additional advantage over electrical conductors that it emits no electromagnetic radiation, as is the case with metal conductors, so eavesdropping with electromagnetic pickups used in the vicinity of the cable is impossible.

The shortest and simplest fiber optic links use plastic fibers and visible light of about 665 nanometers wavelength. But because of the rapid drop in the brightness of light passing along a plastic fiber, the usable length is seriously limited. Such cable is suitable only for such purposes as local area networking. For transmission over longer distances, high-quality pure glass (silica) fibers must be used. These fibers are more expensive than plastic fibers but produce much less attenuation of the light. A range of light-emitting diodes that produce light pulses of different color are used. Glass fiber cabling commonly uses 820 or 1300 nm light. These wavelengths are in the invisible infrared region.

▲ A lineman installing new cables. Cables can be carried overhead by poles or run through trunking underground. The amount of information that can be carried depends on the type of cable being used —fiber optic cables can carry significantly more information than ordinary coaxial cable.

The world standard for rate of transmission (baud rate) has rapidly increased since the late 1990s, approaching 10 billion bits per second. Laboratory devices under development are, however, capable of up to 40 billion bits per second. The value of and confidence placed in fiber optic communication is illustrated by the fact that, in spite of the cost, a fiber optic cable now extends two-thirds of the way round Earth. This cable is known as FLAG (fiber optic link around the globe), and it can transmit data at the rate of over 5 billion bits per second.

Future developments

As it develops, the cable network is likely to have as much impact on society as did the advent of television in the 1950s and the Internet in the 1990s. It is not improbable that a wide-band cable link will come to be regarded as being as essential to normal domestic functioning as the telephone is today. Once a home is linked into the wide-band cable network, it is connected to the whole world of information and control. Cable is a conduit to this world, and its only serious rival is likely to be some form of radio link.

SEE ALSO: Analog and digital systems • Computer • Computer network • Fiber optics • Internet • Radio • Telecommunications • Transmission, broadcasting

Cable Transport Systems

◀ An "airbus" cable system in Mannheim, Germany. The cable is stationary and the car is electrically driven, much like a subway car.

Cable transport has always been associated with hills and mountains. In the late 1700s and early 1800s, the wagonways used for moving coal from mines to river or sea ports were hauled by cable up and down inclined tracks.

Stationary steam engines built near the top of the incline drove the cables. Today, a few cable-worked inclines survive at industrial sites and in such unique forms of transport as the San Francisco streetcar system. Every cable car is pulled along its track by an underground cable, which is gripped by a viselike mechanism operated by a lever in the front of the car. These heavy cars have three separate braking mechanisms to ensure they do not slip on the city's steep hills—the main track brakes, operated by a lever in the front of the car; the front wheel brakes, operated by a foot pedal; and the rear wheel brakes, which are operated by a crank at the back of the car. Because the cables have a restricted carrying capacity, the cars have to run at regulated intervals to ensure the limit is not exceeded. Generally speaking, other forms of cable haulage are now confined to tourist transport because the system has proved unsuited to modern cities and industry.

Cliff railways

From the 1870s onward, a number of British seaside resorts built cliff railways on steep gradients of about 50 percent (1 in 2) to provide quick travel from cliff tops to sea level. Gradients used to be expressed in British terms by a constant vertical unit in a varying horizontal unit; 1 in 20 for example, is a rise of 1 ft. in 20 ft. (or 1 m in 20 m). This system has now been harmonized with the American equivalent, in which the horizontal unit is constant at 100 (percent). Thus 1 in 20 is equivalent to 5 in 100, that is 5 percent.

Normally a double track is provided with a single car on each track, connected by a cable, with one car balancing the other. The car bodies are like short railroad carriages carried on a wedge-shaped underframe so that they remain level even though the wheels rest on the steeply inclined railway track. When one car is at the top, the other is at the bottom. At the top station, the cable passes around a winding drum, which is used for power and braking.

Some early cliff railways had a simple power source if a water supply was available at the top station. Each car carried a water tank in its underframe. The tank was filled while the car was at the

◀ A chairlift is more comfortable than a ski lift, and because the passengers need not be in contact with the ground, it can be routed over uneven terrain.

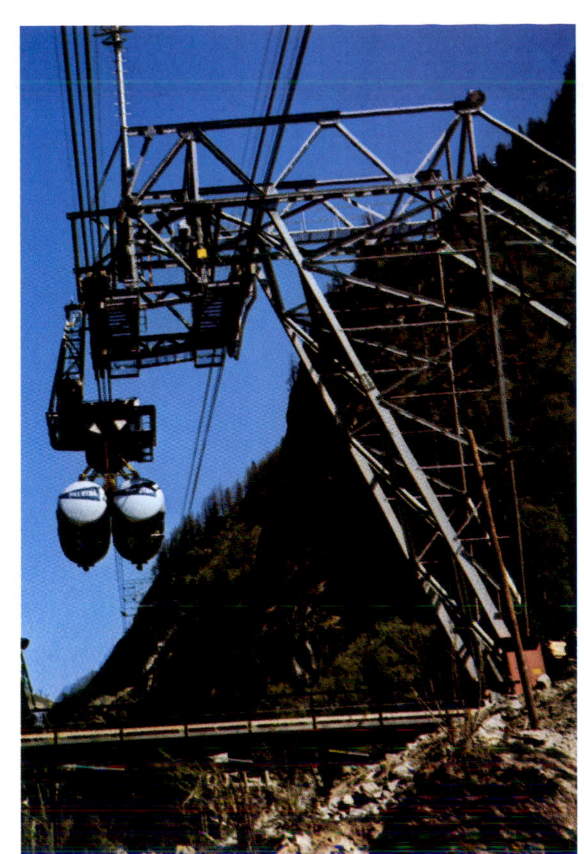

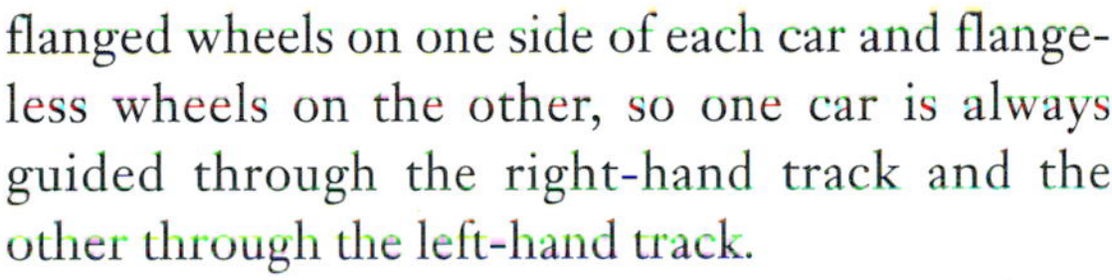

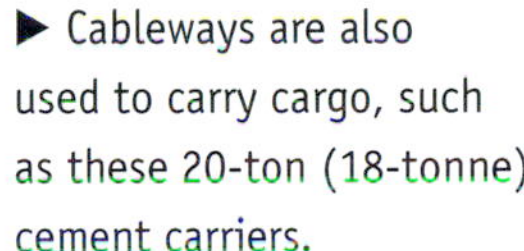

▶ Cableways are also used to carry cargo, such as these 20-ton (18-tonne) cement carriers.

top station and was emptied while at the bottom station. Thus, the car coming down with the full tank of water was heavier, enabling it to pull the lighter car coming up. This form of propulsion is still used today in one or two places, but most cliff railways are now electrically powered.

Funiculars

The first true mountain railways using steam locomotives running on a track equipped for rack-and-pinion (cogwheel) propulsion were built to climb Mount Washington in New Hampshire, in 1869, and Mount Rigi in Switzerland, in 1871. The latter was the pioneer of what today has become the most extensive mountain transport system in the world. Switzerland is extremely mountainous, with some peaks exceeding 14,000 ft. (4,250 m). From this development in mountain transport, other methods were devised, and in the following 20 years until the turn of the century, funicular railways were built on a number of mountain slopes. Most worked on a similar principle to the cliff lift, with two cars connected by cable balancing each other.

Because of the length of some lines—one mile (1.6 km) or more in a few cases—usually only a single track is provided over most of the route, but a short length of double track is laid down at the halfway point where the cars cross each other. The switching of cars through the double-track section is achieved automatically by using double-flanged wheels on one side of each car and flangeless wheels on the other, so one car is always guided through the right-hand track and the other through the left-hand track.

Funiculars vary in steepness according to location and may have gentle curves; some are no steeper than 10 percent, others reach a maximum incline of 88 percent. On less steep lines, the cars are little different from, but smaller than, ordinary railway carriages. On the steeper lines, the cars have a number of separate compartments stepped up one from another, which means that while floors and seats are level, a compartment at

▼ Winding mechanisms are usually located at the bottom station, so they can be easily reached by maintenance crews with their equipment. Electricity is the most commonly used source of power.

the higher end may be 10 or even 15 ft. (3 or 4 m) higher than the lowest compartment at the other end.

The capacity of funicular railways is limited to the two cars, which normally do not travel at more than about 5 to 10 mph (8–16 km/h). Thus, on some mountain lines the railway is divided into sections, with two or even three pairs of cars covering shorter lengths.

Aerial cable cars

There are three distinct types of aerial cable transport: first, large cabins accommodating 100 or more passengers, normally with two cabins on the route balancing each other in the same manner as a funicular and with cable lengths of up to 1 or 2 miles (1.6 to 3.2 km). Second, the chairlift, consisting of open chairs with either single or twin seats, with a large number of chairs spaced at intervals and normally not carried above 20 to 30 ft. (6–10 m) from the ground over distances of up to 2 miles (3 km). Third, the enclosed chairlift, usually containing four seats, and like the open chairlifts, having numerous cabins on the line. These often run at treetop height.

Large cable cars consist of a passenger cabin, usually with very few seats but plenty of standing room because of the short duration of the journey, suspended from a framework embodying a truck that contains a number of grooved pulley wheels. The wheels ride on carrying cables, which themselves are anchored at both ends of the line and resupported en route by pylons built up from the ground, mountain sides, or ridges. Some lines with large-capacity cabins have two carrying cables for each car. Smaller cabins may be carried on only one cable.

Unlike a funicular, which runs mainly on a single track, each cabin on an aerial cable line has its own track throughout. The route between pylons must be straight but may increase or decrease in steepness from one pylon to the next. Cabins are moved by traction cables rigidly attached to the suspension frame and driven by electrically powered winding units. The traction cables are continuous, passing around winding wheels at both ends of the line and attached to both ends of each cabin. The spacing of the cabins is carefully calculated to ensure that the cabins reach the opposite ends of the line together.

Chairlifts are usually carried by a single continuous cable that serves both carrying and traction functions. Some chairs are permanently attached to the cables, which normally run without stopping: passengers must get on and off at each end while the chair is moving. An attendant is usually present to help passengers in and out of seats. The two-seat chairs are normally independent and are attached to the moving cable by grippers. At the start and end of the journey, there are short lengths of rail that allow the chairs to run on and off the moving cable. Some of the larger enclosed chairlifts have one carrying cable and a separate traction cable.

Where chairs are not permanently attached to the cable, control lights advise the operator when it is safe to launch a second chair at the starting station, since they must be spaced at minimum distances apart. A development of the chairlift is the ski-lift, which tows skiers uphill on their skis.

▲ One reason cable car systems of the San Francisco type have not been widely used in the United States and elsewhere is the high cost of installation. More important, however, the cable generates a large amount of friction, which requires more energy to haul cars up hills, and makes the system expensive to operate compared with buses.

Automatic systems

Many of the more recent cable lines are highly automated, and once the cabin operators have pressed the start button, after exchanging bell signals with each other, the cabins run under automatic control. Although they can travel at up to 15 mph (24 km/h) for much of the run, when passing over pylons on steeply inclined sections of cable or when approaching the end of the run, the speed must be reduced to as little as 1 mph (1.6 km/h) or less to avoid the slightest possibility of the cabins swaying.

Apart from their use in popular tourist areas, cable cars, usually of small capacity, are now bringing many Swiss and Austrian mountain villages within easy reach of valley towns, a journey of minutes sometimes replacing several hours climbing on mountain tracks, which even today are unsuited to road vehicles.

SEE ALSO: Cog railway • Mass transit and subway • Monorail system • Streetcar

Calculator

Since the 1960s, modern technology has entirely transformed our means of manipulating numbers. Today's electronic calculators are a remarkable feat of miniaturization and performance. And they are available at outstandingly low cost.

In operation, calculators rely on the use of a very simple mathematical process. They can only add and subtract using a simple code of ones and zeros, a system known as binary notation. There are ways of carrying out most mathematical computations through long routines of adding, shifting, and testing, all of which are impracticably tedious.

Using a calculator, which can typically perform several million such operations per second, the results of calculations that would take several hours for a human brain to perform appear virtually instantaneously.

▶ A magnified view of a circuit etched onto a typical microchip found in electronic calculators. This circuit occupies only a small fraction of the microchip, which is itself only ¹⁄₁₆th of a square inch.

Semiconductors

It was in the 1960s, when new semiconductor technologies first allowed hundreds of thousands of transistors to be squeezed into small blocks of silicon—a process known as large-scale integration—that the task of building a small electronic calculating machine became feasible. The large-scale integrated circuit, abbreviated to LSI, is a form of silicon chip. Current types contain tens of thousands of transistors that are designed to perform various functions, from mathematical calculations to memory storage, using binary logic.

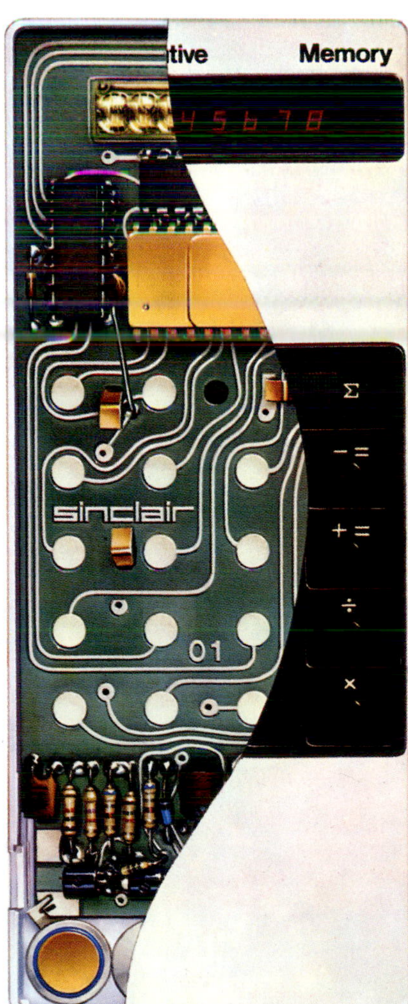

◀ Modern electronic calculators use the same microelectronic technology that makes possible the miniature circuits of home computers. This calculator uses three encapsulated chips of the type shown above to run its programs.

Early models

The first electronic calculators were limited by the number of individual transistors that could be placed on one silicon chip, the amount of electrical power required to drive each function, and the cost of manufacturing the chips. With advances in manufacturing techniques, basic calculator chips have moved from being about the most complex devices produced to some of the simplest; consequently, the costs have fallen rapidly. In a modern basic calculator, the silicon chip represents only a small percentage of the final product cost—the display, keyboard, and case form by far the largest cost elements. Thus it is possible to introduce enhanced calculators with additional functions produced by larger, more complex chips without greatly increasing the overall product cost. Innovations such as biorhythm calculators, music generators, and gameplaying facilities improve sales, are simple to implement, and are therefore very popular with marketing departments.

The earliest and commonest container for integrated circuits was the dual-in-line (DIL) package. For a typical calculator chip of ¹⁄₁₆ sq. in. (less than 0.5 cm^2), this is a relatively enormous package of about 1 sq. in. (7 cm^2). Newer packages such as flat packs and leadless chip carriers require far less space and allow calculators to be built into very confined spaces such as imitation credit cards, rulers, and watches.

Electronic calculators are organized into various functional blocks. The input unit converts decimal keyboard entries into binary code and may hold the information until it can be fed into the central processing unit (CPU), which carries out all calculations. Instructional entries, such as a "divide" command, are routed through to a read-only memory, which then instructs the CPU how to process the data fed in from the keyboard. Finally, an output unit holds the answer from the CPU and turns it into a form that drives a visual display, which can then be read.

Improvements

Not all developments in calculators are connected with their mathematical computing power. Portability, a very important calculator feature, requires the use of small batteries of limited

HOW A CALCULATOR MULTIPLIES FOUR BY TWO

1. Store four in binary coded decimal (bcd) in Register A: A = 0100
2. Store two in bcd in Register B: B = 0010
3. Store zero in Register C: C = 0000
4. Test the right-hand bit of Register A. If it is 1, add the contents of Register B to Register C (in this example, the right-hand bit of Register A is 0, and so no action is taken)
5. Shift the contents of Register A right by one place: A = 0010
6. Test the contents of Register A to determine whether or not they are all 0s. If all 0s, go to step 15
7. Shift the contents of Register B left by one place: B = 0100
8. Test the right-hand bit of Register A. If it is 1, add the content of Register B to Register C (in this example, the right-hand bit of Register A is 0, and so no action is taken)
9. Shift the contents of Register A right by one place: A = 0001
10. Test the contents of Register A to determine whether or not they are all 0s. If all 0s, go to step 15
11. Shift the contents of Register B left by one place: B = 1000
12. Test the right-hand bit of Register A. If it is 1, add the contents of Register B to Register C (in this example, the right-hand bit of Register A is 1, and so register C now contains 1000)
13. Shift the contents of Register A right by one place: A = 0000
14. Test the contents of Register A to determine whether or not they are all 0s. If all 0s, go to step 15
15. Send contents of Register C to the display: C = 1000 = eight

The process above multiplies two single-digit whole numbers together. When multiple digits, fractions, or decimals are involved, the process becomes much more complex.

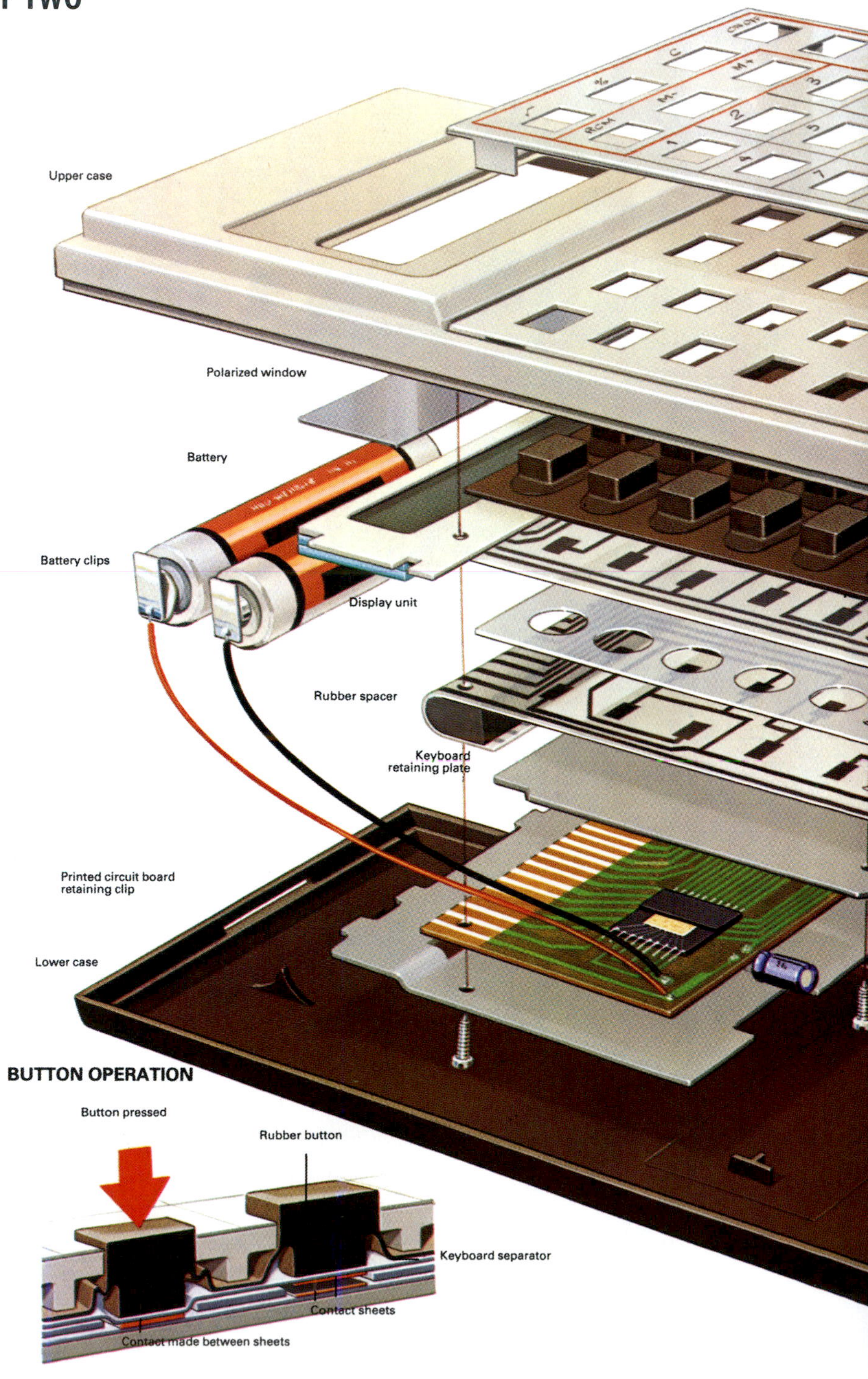

Keyboard panel

Rubber button assembly sheet

Printed circuit contact

Keyboard separator

Lower contact sheet

Assembled printed circuit board

power, which, in turn places restrictions on the display devices. Red light-emitting diode (LED) displays were popular for their low cost and brightness, but they used a lot of power and ran down batteries.

Attractive green vacuum fluorescent displays followed but offered little in the way of power saving. Liquid crystal displays (LCD) have become popular for small portable calculators since they consume one hundred times less power than glowing types. The liquid crystal dot matrix display can depict alphabet characters in addition to numerals (alphanumerics), allowing calculators to deliver messages and so on. Photovoltaic cells have been used in some models to replace batteries, enabling calculators as small and almost as thin as a credit card to be made.

Calculators have already reached the point where their complexity and abilities, in mathematical calculations at least, fully meet the requirements of the market. In practice, most users require little more than basic mathematical functions, and calculators with these simple facilities are available at very little cost. Calculators can also be plugged into a number of accessories such as bar code readers, memory packs, printers, and even fully fledged computers.

Programmable calculators allow highly complex mathematical computations to be carried out repeatedly with great speed, but they must first be programmed (given instructions that will tell them how to carry out the calculations). The gap between a programmable calculator and fully fledged computer is small, and manufacturers have bridged it with small calculator-style computers that have alphanumeric keyboards and can display one line of program or results on a liquid crystal dot matrix display. Scientific and graphical calculators have advanced even further and can cope with complicated mathematical equations. Bigger display screens enable the results of these equations to be shown in statistical forms, such as bar graphs, wave functions, and pie charts.

As memory capacity increases and displays present information in the form of words and symbols in addition to numerals, the role of calculators is expanding. They can store messages, dates, and addresses; tell the time; and even speak and understand speech.

The calculator is becoming less of a mathematician's tool and more of a general-purpose facility for technicians and nonspecialists alike.

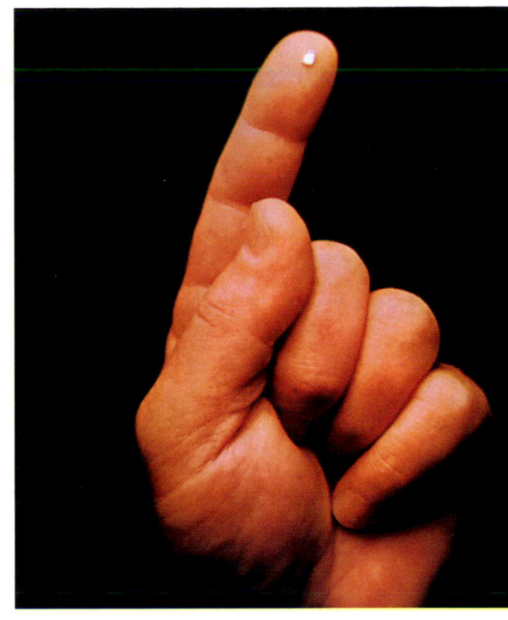

▲ This metal oxide silicon (MOS) integrated circuit, typical of those used in pocket calculators, is only 1⁄16 of a square inch but contains 5,000 transistors.

▼ Using a photovoltaic cell as a power source instead of a battery allows manufacturers to make calculators smaller and lighter.

SEE ALSO: Binary system • Computer • Integrated circuit • Liquid crystal • Mathematics

Cam

A cam is a device for converting rotary motion into linear motion. The simplest form of cam is a rotating disk with a variable radius, so that its profile is not circular but oval or egg-shaped. When the disk rotates, its edge pushes against a cam follower, which may be a small wheel at the end of a lever or the end of the lever or rod itself. The cam follower will thus rise and fall by exactly the same amount as the variation in radius.

By profiling a cam appropriately, any desired cyclic pattern of linear or straight-line motion can be produced. With most cams, some form of spring action ensures that the cam follower remains in contact with the cam. In practice, cams are not necessarily rotary in action. The same form of linear movement can be obtained from a cam profile that oscillates back and forth. In both cases, the output movement will be at right angles to the forces that initiate the motion.

The idea of a cam goes back to the first century Greek scientist Hero of Alexandria, and the cam is one of the basic devices in engineering. It has found many uses throughout history: in the oscillating action of bellows, the timing action of valves (as in steam engines), and the control of windmills.

Today the cam is used in machine tools, electromechanical timing gear, and a wide range of other machinery. In the internal combustion engine, a set of cams on a rotating camshaft controls the opening and closing of the inlet and exhaust valves. The shapes and positions of the cams ensure that the valves are opened and closed in the correct sequence and at the correct time intervals.

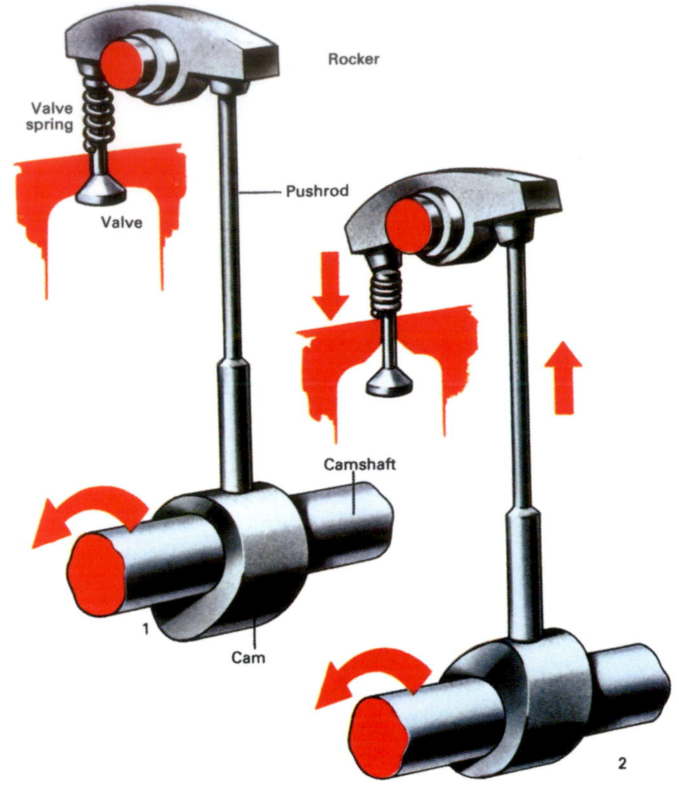

▲ The cam (1) is used to take rotary motion from a machine or engine and turn it into linear motion, such as in the opening or closing of a valve. As the cam rotates (2), it forces up the pushrod, which depresses the valve. In a side-cam automobile engine, the cams are carried on a camshaft located beside the crankshaft. The drive for the camshaft is taken from the crankshaft through a timing chain, which keeps the cams synchronized with the movement of the pistons so that the valves are opened or closed at a precise instant.

Cam systems

Various systems have been adopted over the years, one of the most common being pushrod action, in which the cam acts on a cam follower and from there on a vertical rod in a lubricated sleeve. Movement of this rod is then transmitted in turn through a pivoted rocker arm to the valve's stem. Other systems involve the elimination of the pushrod, as in the overhead camshaft arrangement, where the camshaft is mounted vertically above the crankshaft so that the cams act directly on the valves. The profile of the cams can be modified slightly to vary the time that the valves stay open.

Internal combustion engines operate at high speeds, so the spring force maintaining the cam follower in contact with the cam has to be exceptionally powerful—the faster the engine, the more powerful the spring needs to be. If the spiral spring used is insufficiently powerful, the inertia forces in the valve system will prevent the cam follower from maintaining intimate contact with the cam, and an inefficient condition known as valve bounce will occur, giving a distinctive noise.

Because the cam can be made with any desired profile and in almost any material, it provides a fine controlling device for machine tool-cutting feeds where high stresses are involved. In effect, the cutting tool is made to follow the same path that the cam's profile would follow if it were stretched out in a straight line. Such cams can be expensive to make, but the cost can be justified where the volume of production is large, such as in an automobile factory.

The high manufacturing cost is due to the asymmetric, or even irregular, shape of some cams, which must be machined in extremely tough, durable metals to give sufficient resistance to wear. One technique is to form the cam in mild metal, which is easily worked, then treat the finished cam to harden the metal. Any modifications to the cam profile, however, might require a new cam to be started from mild steel.

SEE ALSO: Internal combustion engine • Valve, mechanical

Camera

Most modern cameras are lightproof boxes in which light-sensitive photographic film is exposed in a controlled manner. The exposure is controlled by adjusting the aperture and the shutter speed. In most cases, the film is loaded in a lightproof cassette; one end of the film is threaded through a slotted spool, and the film is wound one frame forward for each exposure. When all the frames have been exposed, the film is rewound and removed.

▲ Many high-performance cameras have a selection of lenses that can be interchanged for techniques such as wide-angle and zoom photography.

Taking pictures

The technical skill of the photographer lies in selecting the appropriate setting of shutter speed, focus, and lens aperture for a given photograph. These settings depend on the nature of the subject and its distance from the camera, lighting conditions, and the desired effect.

The light for taking a photograph enters through a lens at the front of the camera. The amount of light that enters for a given lighting condition and shutter speed depends on the width of the aperture, which is a hole formed by the blades of an iris diaphragm. Aperture size is measured in terms of a number called an f-ratio, which is inversely related to the width of the aperture. The use of an iris diaphragm allows a single lens to be set at, say, f-2 for full aperture down to f-22 for the smallest aperture setting. Intermediate aperture settings are called stops. The f-ratios of the stops are calculated so that the light-gathering area of the lens alters by a factor of two between adjacent stops, so the f-ratio varies according to the square root of two. In the f-stop series 1.4, 2, 2.8, 4, 5.6, 8, 11, 16, 22, 32, for example, f-4 corresponds to an aperture area twice as large as f-5.6.

The aperture of the camera also controls the depth of field of the image—the range over which it is in focus. At f-22, both near and distant objects will be in focus, while f-2 will only allow sharp focus over a small range of distances. This effect can be used to highlight a sharply focused object against a less well focused background.

If a photographer wishes to increase the depth of field by using a high f-ratio (a small aperture), the shutter speed must be decreased so that the level of exposure remains sufficient to form a good image. The amount by which the shutter speed can be reduced is limited, however, since a slow shutter can result in images that are blurred by camera shake. As a rule, a camera should be mounted on a secure tripod if exposure times longer than 1/60 second are to be attempted.

Shutter speeds are stated in terms of the time for which the shutter is open—usually a fraction of a second. Shutter speed increases in steps that vary by a factor of 2, the usual values in seconds being 1, 1/2, 1/4, 1/8, 1/15, 1/30, 1/60, 1/125, 1/250, 1/500 and 1/1000. This system makes compensating for the similar steps of lens aperture easy: if an exposure of 1/125 second at f-8 is adequate for a given light intensity, then so will be an exposure of 1/60 second at f-11. Apart from helping eliminate camera shake, faster shutter speeds can produce clear images of fast-moving objects such as race cars in motion.

Shutters

Most shutters are either interlens or focal-plane. Interlens shutters have moving metal blades that open and shut between the elements of the lens. The more advanced interlens shutters have speeds from 1 to 1/500 second; simple cameras may have only two settings, such as 1/60 second for sunny weather and 1/30 second for dull lighting.

Focal-plane shutters are located as near to the film as possible. The exposure is made by two blinds moving across the surface of a film in close succession. Light passes through a slit between the blinds, and the exposure time can be varied by altering the width of the slit and the speed of the blind movement. Most focal-plane shutters have speeds from 1 to 1/1000 second; more advanced models can attain speeds as high as 1/4000 second.

A drawback of the interlens shutter design is that cameras with interchangeable lenses require a separate shutter mechanism for each lens. In compensation, interlens shutters can synchronize with a flash at any speed setting: focal-plane shutters have a maximum speed at which correct flash operation is possible—generally 1/60 second but occasionally as fast as 1/250 second.

Lenses and focusing

In the simplest cameras, the focus is fixed on a distance such as 10 ft. (3m) or so, with an aperture chosen so that the focus is acceptably sharp for objects between 5 ft. (1.5m) and infinity from the lens. (In photography, infinity is taken to mean an unspecific large distance.) The simplest lenses are made of molded methyl methacrylate and may have maximum apertures as small as f-14.

More sophisticated cameras have achromatic lens systems that compensate for the slight differences in the focusing of different wavelengths of light. A typical system of this type would have two lens elements at around f-9, three or four elements at around f-2.8, or six elements of f-1.8 or f-2.

Focus is adjusted by changing the distance between the lens assembly and the film. A camera with manual focus has its lens mounted in a case with a spiral screw thread so that it moves in or out as it turns. A scale around the edge of the lens shows the distance of sharpest focus. Some cameras have motorized focusing that responds when focusing buttons are pressed by the photographer.

Focus adjustment can be further simplified by the use of focus confirmation or automatic focusing. Both systems measure the camera-to-subject distance by analyzing the image that will be projected onto the film for sharpness.

In focus-confirmation systems, an LED display indicates whether the subject is in focus and, if not, in which direction the focusing ring on the lens should be turned to bring the subject into focus. Automatic focusing uses these instructions to direct the operation of the motorized focusing system, which adjusts the focusing of the lens.

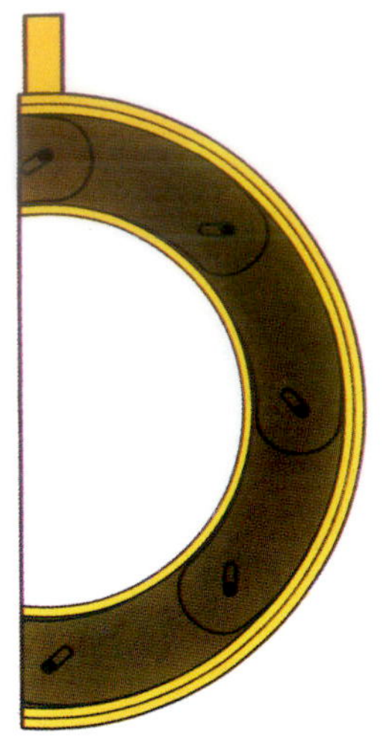
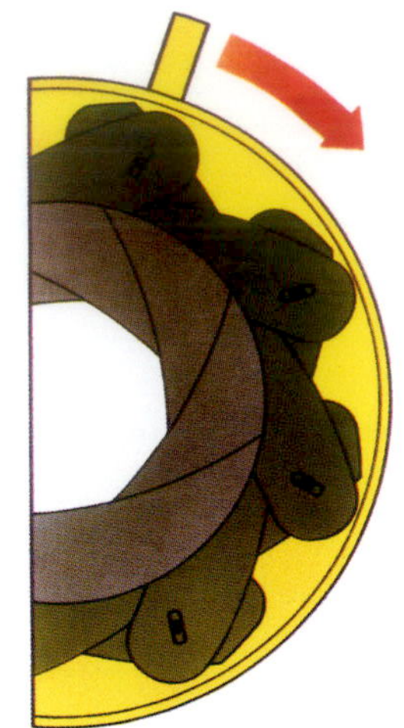
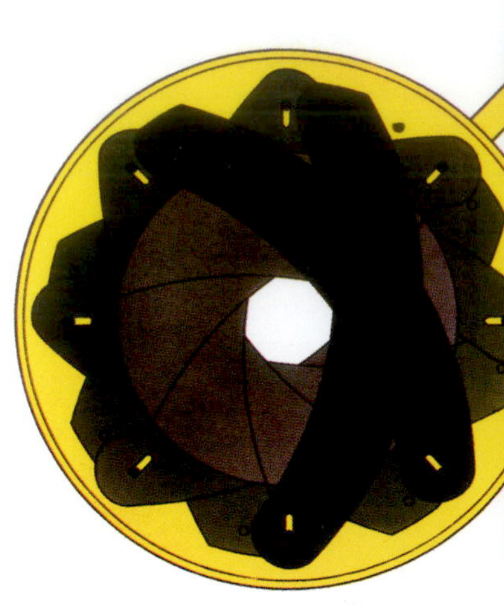

▲ An iris diaphragm forms an aperture, or opening, of variable size between the lens and film in a camera. Its thin metal blades are pivoted at one end and attached to pins on a movable ring at the other end. Turning the ring changes the aperture size.

Autofocus systems take less than a second to cover the entire focusing range of the lens and so, for action photography, are likely to be quicker and more accurate than manual focusing. If flash photography is being used in dark surroundings, many autofocus systems will fail to operate because insufficient light is available. One elegant solution to this problem is to modify the flashgun so that it can emit a brief burst of infrared light for focusing immediately before the main discharge, which is used to illuminate the picture. While automatic focusing has now largely replaced manual focusing in popular cameras, many photographers prefer the extra degree of control offered by manual focusing.

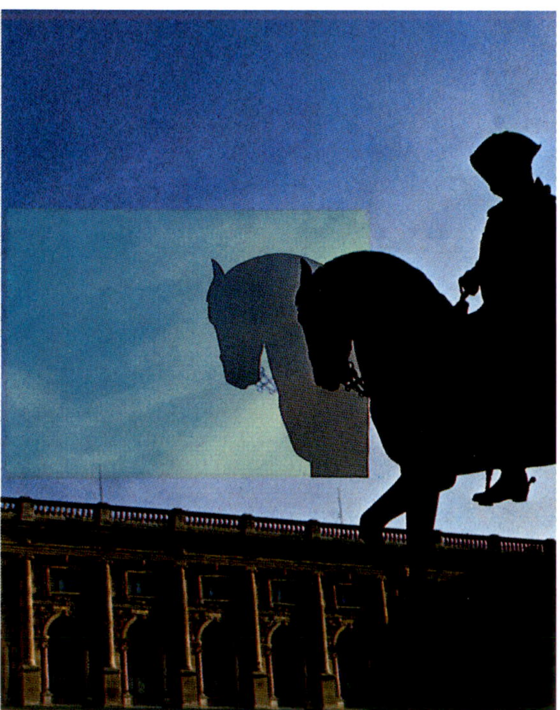
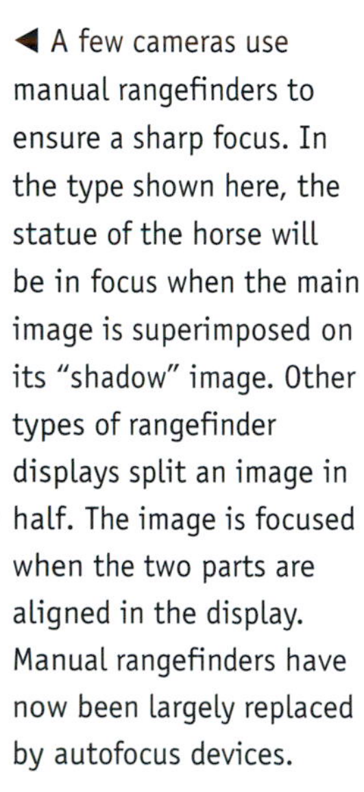

◀ A few cameras use manual rangefinders to ensure a sharp focus. In the type shown here, the statue of the horse will be in focus when the main image is superimposed on its "shadow" image. Other types of rangefinder displays split an image in half. The image is focused when the two parts are aligned in the display. Manual rangefinders have now been largely replaced by autofocus devices.

35 mm cameras

The most popular photographic cameras use strips of film 1.4 in. (35 mm) wide mounted in lightproof cassettes. The standard film lengths—12, 24, and 36 exposures—are based on frames that are 1.4 in. (36 mm) along the length of the film and 0.9 in. (24 mm) across its width. The remaining width of the film is taken up by sprocket holes that help control the movement of the film when loaded. In fact, some cameras are capable of taking images that are longer than the standard frame size so that correspondingly fewer frames fit on a given length of film.

Although film cassettes are nominally lightproof, they are kept in sealed tubes of black plastic that provide additional protection from exposure to light while the cassette is not inside a camera. Cassettes of film are loaded and unloaded through a hatch in the rear of the camera. On loading, a tab of film that protrudes from the cassette is fed through a slit in the uptake spool of the camera, and the first sprocket holes are placed on a sprocket wheel that turns as the film moves.

The film that is pulled out of the cassette during loading is exposed to light and useless for

FLASH PHOTOGRAPHY

Flash photography is used when ambient light intensity is not sufficient to produce a good exposure using a shutter speed that is fast enough to avoid blurring.

The first use of artificial lighting for photography was in 1867, when a U.S. photographer, Timothy O'Sullivan, burned magnesium ribbons to provide light underground for photographs of the Comstock Lode Mine in Nevada. This method gave a brilliant light as long as the ribbon burned. In 1887, a mixture of magnesium powder and potassium chlorate was found to produce an instantaneous flash of white light when it was ignited.

The first electrical flash, developed in 1929, had a filament of aluminum foil in an oxygen-filled bulb. When current from a dry cell passed through the filament, it caused the foil to burn with a bright flash of light. This type of flash bulb was used only once and then replaced.

An electronic flash system uses xenon-filled discharge tubes to produce intense but brief flashes of light. A device called a chopper converts direct current from a dry cell into alternating current that can be transformed to high voltage; a rectifier then converts this current into a direct current that charges two capacitors. One capacitor produces a voltage high enough to strip electrons from xenon atoms in the tube, forming a mixture of free electrons and positive xenon ions. This mixture then conducts a charge from a lower voltage capacitor, emitting light as it does. The duration of the flash is typically 15 to 25 milliseconds, and it is synchronized with the opening of the shutter.

More advanced flash systems produce an initial pulse that causes the irises of the subject's eyes to close before a second flash that is synchronized with the shutter goes off. This action helps reduce "red eye," which is an effect caused by light reflecting off the retina of the eye when the iris is open.

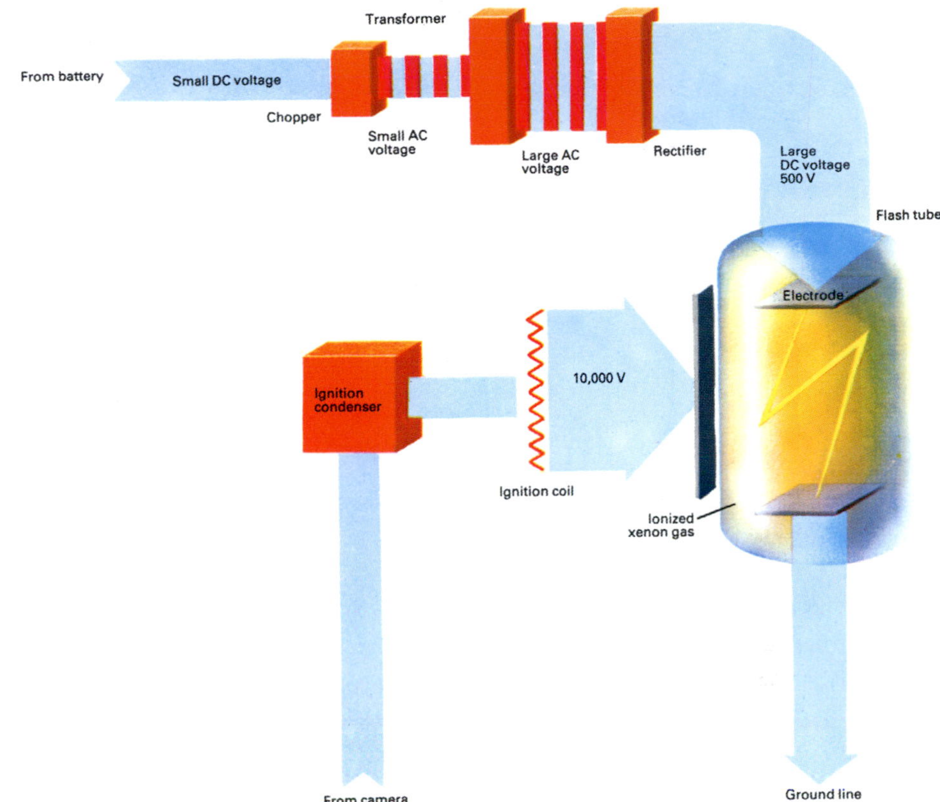

▲ An electronic flash tube produces intense flashes of white light when a current flows through ionized xenon gas. This type of flash tube can be used several thousands of times before it has to be replaced.

photography. When the back of the camera is closed, a motor winds enough film onto the uptake spool to present fresh, unexposed film to the light path; older and more basic cameras have a thumb-operated lever that performs this task.

Once the first frame has been exposed by pressing the shutter release, the motor-driven or manual wind-on mechanism can advance the film to the next frame. The sprocketed wheel turns as the film moves but is stopped by a ratchet when the film has wound on through one frame. It will not turn again until the shutter has been pressed, and the shutter cannot be pressed again until the film has been wound on. This mechanism makes it impossible to expose the same piece of film more than once. Some camera designs include a shutter-lock override that makes multiple exposure of single frames possible.

Once the film has been exposed, the ratchet is disengaged to allow the film to be rewound into its cassette by the motor or by manual winding. Once rewound, the rear hatch of the camera can be opened and the cassette removed.

Roll-film cameras

The roll-film camera was in widespread use until it was superseded by the 35-mm camera. Roll film is backed by a strip of paper. The side of the paper that faces the film is dyed black, while its reverse has numbers that appear through a window on the back of the camera to indicate how many frames have been exposed. Protection from accidental exposure outside the camera is provided by the backing paper, which is longer than the film, and by the ends of the spool.

The earliest roll-film cameras were box shaped. This shape let the photographer view the subject before exposing the film, since the viewing optics require a longer light path than the film-exposure optics. Later models had rigid front and rear plates joined by lightproof bellows, so they could be collapsed when not in use.

Reflex cameras

Reflex camera use a reflection viewing system to provide the additional path length for viewing optics in a compact body. Twin-lens reflex cam-

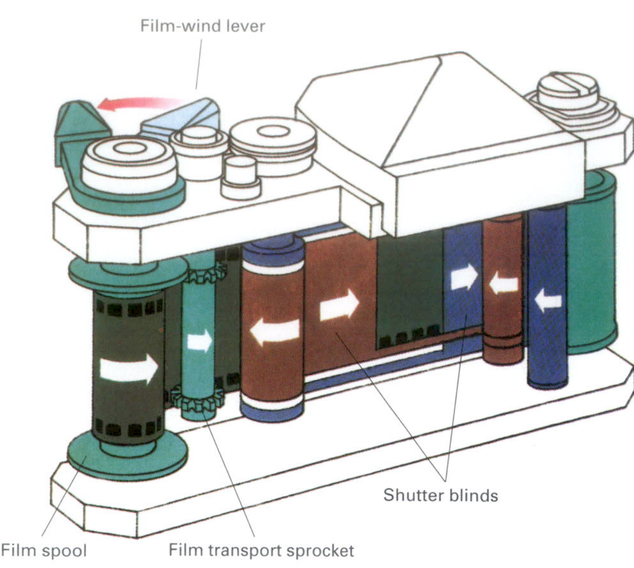

▼ This Canon single-lens reflex camera demonstrates the typical features of early SLRs: a focal-length shutter, a fitting for interchangeable lenses, a power outlet socket for a synchronized electronic flash, and a wheel for adjusting the film-speed setting of the shutter-speed control system.

Battery test button
Electronic flash input
Two stage electromagnetic shutter release
Electronically controlled shutter speeds
Rear lens group
Front lens group
Coated optics

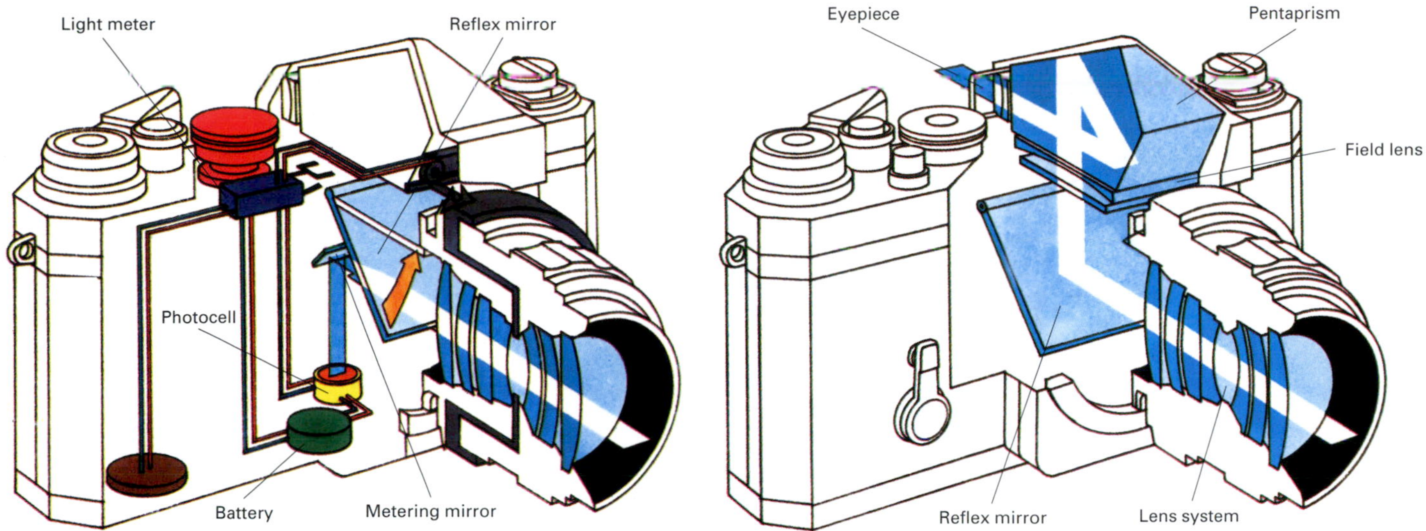

▲ In a single-lens reflex camera, the film and focal-plane shutter are located at the back of the case (left). A light pressure on the shutter release raises the mirror to allow light through to the through-the-lens exposure meter (center). When the mirror is down, it diverts the image to the optics of the viewfinder (right).

eras, such as the Rolleiflex, had two lenses—one mounted above the other on a panel. The bottom lens had a shutter and took the picture; the top lens formed an image on a horizontal viewing screen via a tilted mirror. Correct focusing was achieved by moving the whole lens panel back and forth, so that both lenses had the same focus.

Single-lens reflex cameras

Single-lens reflex cameras, or SLRs, dispense with the need for twin lenses by use of a movable mirror. Between shots, the mirror is angled down, so that it reflects light up onto a horizontal ground-glass viewing screen. A prism above this screen reflects its image into the viewfinder and presents an upright image. Some models include microprisms in the viewing screen. Microprisms break unsharp images into dots, emphasizing the point where the image comes into focus. In other designs, focus-confirmation LEDs appear in the viewfinder display, allowing the photographer to see the image and focus-confirmation.

An instant before the shutter opens, the mirror flips up, allowing the light from the lens to pass through and expose the film. A major advantage of the single-lens reflex system is that the focus in the viewfinder is exactly the same as the focus of the image that reaches the film.

Lens designs

Single-lens reflex cameras use focal-plane shutters rather than interlens shutters; thus the shutter system is contained within the main body of the camera. This arrangement lends itself to interchangeable lenses.

The earliest standard interchangeable lens mount was a 42 mm by 1 mm screw thread. This mount was inexpensive and allowed lenses to be changed reasonably quickly, but it had two major drawbacks: first, care had to be taken to screw the lens fully into position, otherwise it would not focus to infinity; second, because the entire lens had to be rotated several turns as it was fitted, it was difficult to design mechanical couplings between lens and camera. Most manufacturers now use bayonet-style mounts that require less than 90 degrees of rotation to engage the lens, thus simplifing the design of couplings.

The aperture controls on simple lenses control the diaphragm directly. Thus the photographer needs to open the lens to maximum aperture to focus and then carefully stop it down to the required picture-taking aperture before opening the shutter. Many specialized lenses, such as those designed for extreme magnification and close-up work still operate this way. A further refinement was the introduction of a second aperture-control ring on the lens with just two settings: in one position, the lens is always at maximum aperture regardless of the setting of the main aperture-control ring, and in the other position, the lens is stopped down to the setting shown on the main aperture-control ring. Therefore the lens can be stopped down more quickly than the manual system permits. Such lenses are called preset lenses. Few of these lenses are manufactured nowadays, with the exception of some comparatively inexpensive very-long-focal-length designs.

◀ Pocket cameras are becoming ever smaller. Canon's Ixus cameras are less than 4 in. (10 cm) long yet manage to incorporate an electronic flash and a zoom lens. Many modern cameras use the Advanced Photo System, which allows different picture formats to be taken.

EXPOSURE METERING

Exposure is a measure of the amount of light reflected by a subject that passes through the aperture of a camera to form an image on film. Exposure is a critical value in photography, since an image that is underexposed will be too dark, while an overexposed image will have its details "bleached out."

The appropriate level of exposure for a photograph depends on the sensitivity of the film, usually called its speed, and the brightness of the desired image. The amount of light that reaches the film depends on overall light intensity—the ambient intensity and additional light from a flash, if used—the shutter speed, and the aperture width.

Until the 1930s, the only available method for determining light intensity was the use of light-sensitive paper placed in front of the subject. The paper would darken according to the intensity of the light falling on it, giving an indication of the appropriate camera settings.

The first photoelectric exposure meters were introduced in 1932. This type of meter used a selenium cell to produce an electric current in proportion to light intensity, providing a reading on an appropriately marked ammeter.

◀ A modern handheld exposure meter has a silicon photodiode to measure light intensity. The meter calculates and displays the best shutter speed for a given aperture size.

Selenium cells were followed by more sensitive cells that used cadmium sulfide (CdS), whose resistance varies according to light intensity. The cadmium sulfide cell was attached to a battery, and the current that flowed through it would be measured on an indicator. Cadmium sulfide cells suffered from slow recovery time after being exposed to bright light.

Modern exposure meters use silicon photodiodes (SPDs), which function in a similar way to cadmium sulfide cells but have a much faster response time.

SPD meters can be handheld, or they can be an integral part of a camera. Handheld meters can be used to measure variations in lighting conditions across the surface of a subject, which is useful information for an expert photographer. They can also calculate an exposure value for the whole shot. The photographer can then choose to use a slow shutter speed and a narrow aperture—giving depth of field but risking blurring—or a faster shutter speed and a wider aperture.

Integral exposure meters use through-the-lens metering, or TTL, to give a more accurate reading of the light intensity that reaches the film. This reading can be used to make manual adjustments to shutter and aperture settings, or it can form part of an exposure-monitoring system that automatically adjusts camera settings.

Most modern lenses with variable apertures have a coupling between the diaphragm and the camera body. This coupling forces the lens to remain at maximum aperture until the shutter is pressed. While the mirror is moving up, the aperture coupling stops the lens down to the required aperture (which may be set by manually or automatically) the shutter then exposes the film, and finally, the mirror moves down and the lens is opened back to its maximum aperture.

Aperture coupling therefore lets the photographer have the benefit of focusing at maximum aperture—a bright image and clearly defined plane of focus—without having to remember to stop the lens down before taking a picture. For situations where the photographer needs to view using the stopped-down lens—when assessing depth of field, for example—a stopdown lever is sometimes provided on the camera or lens body that can override the aperture coupling.

With the advent of through-the-lens (TTL) exposure meters operating with the lens at full aperture, the camera needs to know how much the lens will stop down by when a picture is taken. This information is transmitted by the meter coupling linkage, normally an extension of the aperture ring on the lens, which mates with a spring-loaded lug on the camera.

The majority of 35 mm SLR cameras use lens mounts that have just these two mechanical couplings. Some recent designs with sophisticated automatic exposure-optimization and focusing systems need more sophisticated communication between lens and camera. In this case, the lens may include a mechanical shaft coupling for transmitting drive from the camera's focusing motor to the lens, a mechanical aperture coupling that incorporates the functions previously performed by the lens aperture control (apertures now being either set by a control on the camera or selected automatically by the camera electronics) and a row of electrical contacts that allow the camera to interrogate a memory chip in the lens in order to discover its maximum and minimum apertures, focal length, and focusing parameters.

A wide range of lenses is available: focal lengths from wide-angle to telephoto, perspective control lenses that correct converging verticals caused by tilting the camera out of the horizontal plane, fisheye lenses that offer a circular perspective, mirror lenses that double back the light path of long focal length lenses to allow more compact designs, macro lenses for producing life-size photographs of small objects, zoom lenses with focal lengths adjustable over a range of up to 5:1 and high-speed lenses that are capable of producing good results in poor lighting conditions.

Exposure control

Many cameras have built-in exposure meters that detect the correct exposure for the lighting conditions. Older types used photoelectric cells, mounted on the camera, that received light from the direction in which the lens pointed and displayed an exposure value. Early through-the-lens exposure meters worked in a similar way using a photocell within the camera body. The photographer then adjusted the camera settings according to the lighting conditions, desired depth of field, and the film speed, or sensitivity.

Automatic and semiautomatic cameras use the exposure value from a through-the-lens exposure meter to calculate aperture and shutter settings for a given combination of lighting conditions and film speed. An automatic camera then installs these settings without further input.

In the case of a semiautomatic camera, the photographer may select either the aperture or shutter speed and leave the other setting for the camera to select; alternatively, the photographer can select both settings, using the camera's exposure reading purely for guidance.

▲ Wildlife photographers sometimes need cameras that are custom built. To photograph insects at close range, Britain's Oxford Scientific Film personnel adapted a snorkel lens system, which works like an inverted periscope.

DX coding

For many years, the speed of a film had to be selected on a dial for automatic exposure control to function. This requirement ended with the advent of DX coding, which indicates a film's speed, number of frames, and tolerance to incorrect exposure. A camera reads a film's DX code from dots of conductive paint on the film cassette.

The amount of information used by a camera depends on its sophistication. A basic camera might use the film speed to set its exposure control in a simple manner; a more complex camera might use the film's exposure tolerance to calculate whether shutter speed can safely be increased in poor lighting conditions to avoid camera shake without risking unacceptable underexposure. Some cameras read the number of frames in a film and automatically start rewinding when the last frame of the film has been exposed.

FACT FILE

- *Electronic cameras are used to photograph hitherto unseen lifeforms, such as the giant tube worms that live in hot-water vents many thousands of feet beneath the sea's surface in the Galapagos Rift in the Pacific. Using a combination of television and computer technology, these cameras produce high-resolution images with the aid of a silicon imaging device and stroboscopic lighting.*

- *In 1903, a German engineer patented a rocket camera built like a giant firework attached to a 15 ft. (4.6 m) stabilizing stick. The camera took a single exposure at its zenith, some 2,600 ft. (793 m), and floated back to ground on a parachute. It was superseded in military reconnaissance by cameras mounted in aircraft.*

SEE ALSO: CAMERA, DIGITAL • DISCHARGE TUBE • INSTANT-PICTURE CAMERA • LENS • PHOTOGRAPHIC FILM AND PROCESSING

Camera, Digital

Although rudimentary digital cameras were available in the early part of the 1990s, an explosion in digital imaging happened in 1997, revolutionizing the photographic industry. That year saw a combination of swift advances in digital camera technology, accessories, and software and a remarkable growth of the Internet as a means of sending messages and photographs. The market potential of such cameras, which capture and store images electronically rather than on film, was immediately recognized by nearly all major camera makers and many electronics manufacturers.

Digital cameras normally use any one of a number of types of removable media to record images, allowing photographs to be downloaded and displayed on an ordinary TV screen or a computer screen soon after they have been taken. There are two main types of removable memory, SmartMedia and CompactFlash, with Sony having its own proprietary Memory Stick. The memory modules can hold a varying number of color pictures, depending on the definition chosen for each shot and the size of the memory module. Some older cameras used standard floppy disks, which could be transferred directly to a computer's floppy disk drive, although recent high-resolution cameras require considerably more memory than is available on a floppy.

Both types allow users to view and either store or delete photographs or browse through a selection of shots before transferring the data to a computer. Cameras with customized removable media require a cable connection to a computer's serial port to enable downloading.

Mass-market digital cameras initially had low image resolution compared with the multi-million-pixel (*pix* plus *el*ement) photographs that

▼ Digital cameras, such as Sony's Mavica, look very like conventional single-lens reflex (SLR) cameras. In practical terms, they are very similar, with a lens, viewfinder, and shutter. The most important difference is the form of the optical recording device—the film. A charge-coupled device records the image as a series of electrical charges that are recorded magnetically onto a floppy disk.

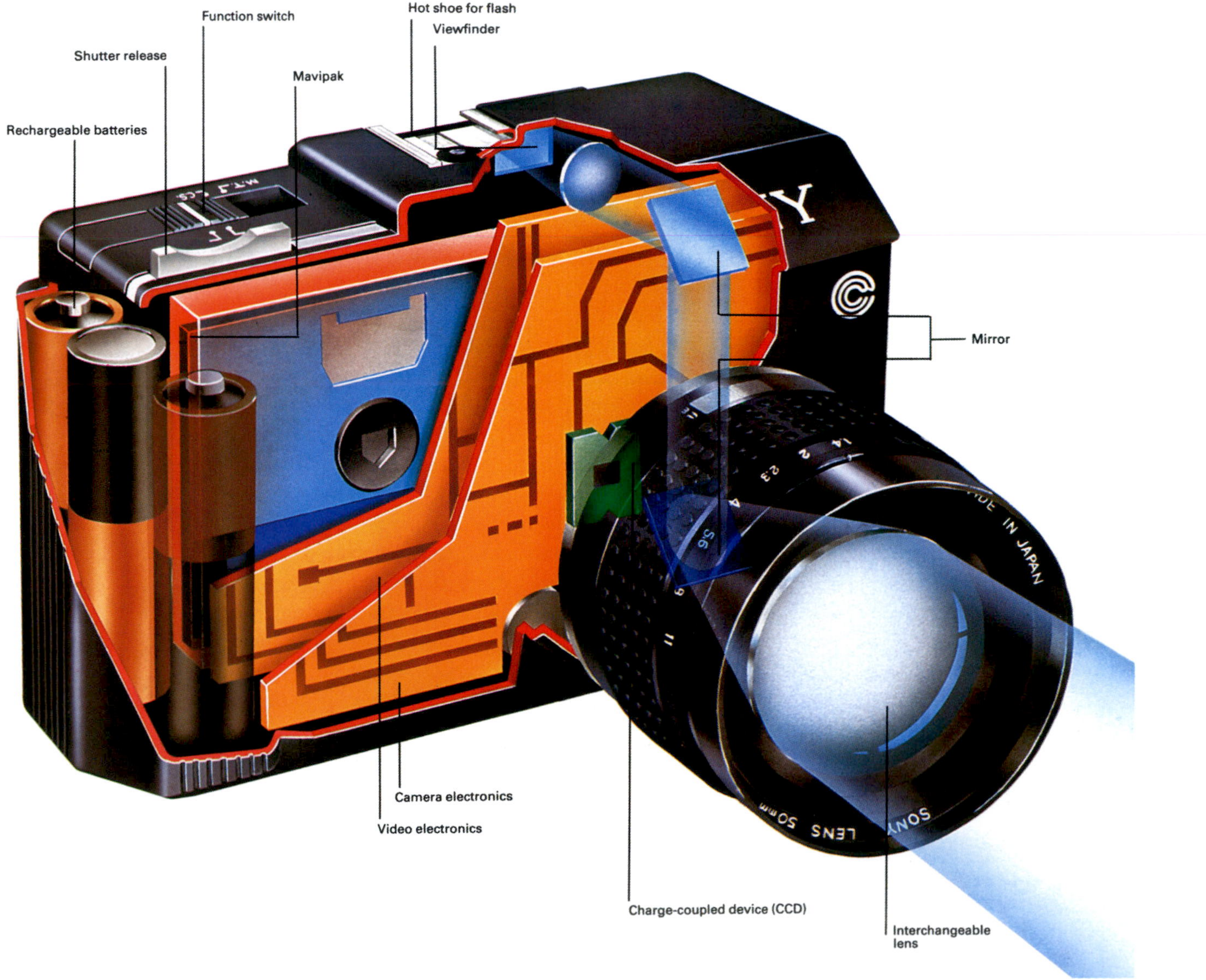

could be obtained from costly professional digital cameras. The low-resolution cameras were mainly intended for Internet users wishing to send low-memory photographs attached to e-mail or for use on websites. The growth in popularity of this type of camera has caused the price to come down and the quality to improve—many top-range consumer digital cameras now have resolutions that provide high-quality snapshots.

Taking digital pictures

How do these cameras work? An ordinary lens focuses the image seen through the viewfinder onto a charge-coupled device (CCD), a silicon microchip that converts the image into a series of electronic pulses. The surface of the CCD is coated in silicon and a metal oxide and is divided into a matrix of minute squares (pixels). When the image is projected onto the CCD, each square generates an electric charge proportional to the amount and color of light falling on it.

Each charge is then transferred square by square across the grid until it reaches the edge. The camera's ancillary electronics record its position in the matrix and its strength before it is passed to the disk for storage. The CCD's light sensitivity is excellent—it easily matches conventional film of about 200 ASA—but in early digital cameras, the squares on the matrix were so much larger than the molecules of light-sensitive emulsion in ordinary camera film that the definition was not impressive.

Mavica, from the electronics giant Sony, was an early example of the new breed of camera. It looked rather like an ordinary 35 mm SLR camera, but instead of inserting a roll of film into the camera, a small flat cassette—the Mavipak—was loaded. This cassette contained the heart of the system, a floppy disk that stored the pictures as varying levels of magnetism.

Many television sets have a definition of about 525 lines; 35 mm film has a definition equivalent to about 1,500 lines; the early Mavipak's definition was equivalent to only 350. However, digital cameras have improved dramatically in the few years since their invention. For example, the Olympus D-620L has a resolution of 1,280 x 1,024 pixels and is a high-quality single-lens reflex (SLR) camera in its own right. There are a multitude of brands on the market, with the price generally reflecting the quality of the lens and the definition of the picture.

The technology continues to develop. Sony's DSC-F1 was said to be the first digital camera with a built-in infrared transceiver, allowing images to be transferred directly from its 4 MB (megabyte) memory to an infrared-enabled computer or printer without needing intermediate cables or disks. Some cameras, such as Nikon's multimedia CoolPix 300, allow images, written text, and sound to be recorded. Digital cameras are constantly improving—for instance, the speed at which a photograph is recorded has decreased significantly. The Olympus D-620L takes 1.7 seconds in its fastest mode, which approaches the speed of a standard 35 mm camera and is about ten times faster than early versions.

◀ Measuring only 2 in. (5 cm), the Mavipak and its successors can record 50 pictures. Once the pictures have been downloaded, information on the disk can be erased and the disk reused for a new batch of pictures. Since its launch in the 1980s, the Mavipak has been superseded by a number of different memory formats.

Manipulating pictures

Possibly the most revolutionary aspect of the digital camera lies in what can be done with the pictures once they are taken. Not only can photographs be downloaded to a PC or viewed on TV, they can also be recorded on videotape. The ability to manipulate the original image is also a major attraction—corresponding developments in computer software allow virtually any type of effect imaginable to be achieved—anything from improving the quality of poor photos (by altering

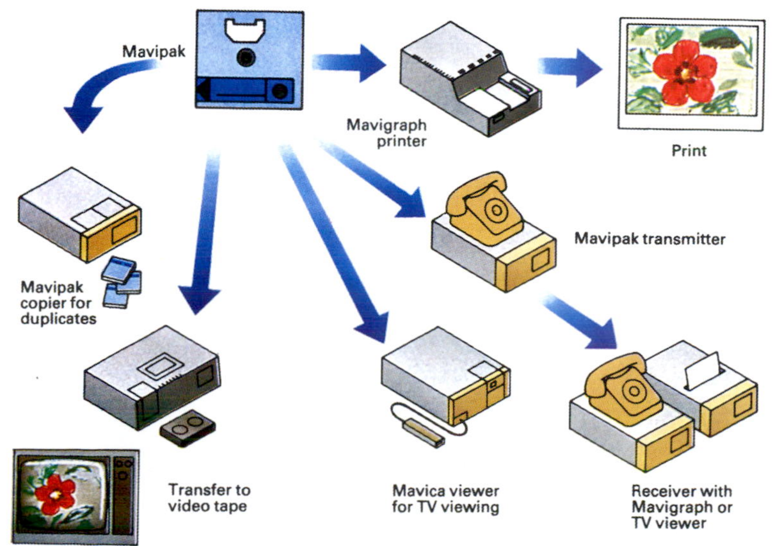

▼ Unlike conventional film, the Mavipak enabled photographers to output images in a variety of different forms by using the digitally-coded information stored on the floppy disk. Its range of outputs anticipated many future developments, including the ability to send pictures down phone lines and through the Internet.

brightness and contrast or eliminating red-eye, for instance) to completely altering the look and colors of a photograph or cutting and pasting parts of one into another.

Printing digital pictures

Printing photographs is also an area that has been revolutionized by the ability to download photographs to a PC. If photographs are loaded onto a computer, printing is a simple matter, and high-quality coated paper, of a similar quality to that used for standard camera pictures, can be used. In combination with a high-quality color ink-jet printer, this paper gives an excellent result that is barely distinguishable from a photograph taken using a standard 35 mm camera. The latest all-purpose printers can produce a photo-quality color print in about one minute. Hewlett-Packard and some camera manufacturers, including Polaroid, Sony, and Olympus, have all introduced dedicated photo printers designed to print directly from a camera. They have slots for CompactFlash, SmartMedia, or, in the case of Sony's Digital Photo Printer, a Memory Stick, and print standard 4 by 6 in. (100 x 150 mm) photos; some can also produce 8 by 10 in. (200 x 250 mm) enlargements.

Another important feature for digital cameras is the video-out port, which enables images to be displayed directly on a television or video recorder simply by attaching a cable. Most cameras can cycle through the images in their memory, so it is possible to have a slide show without using a PC. A few cameras, such as Epson's PhotoPC 600 and some Casio models, accept digital downloads from a PC, too.

Digital cameras are now able to deliver image quality, features, and pricing comparable to ordinary 35 mm cameras. Early digital cameras may have been novelties, but the best are now capable of producing sharp clear prints that reach, and in some cases go beyond, two-megapixel definition. However, conventional film remains a better medium for producing high-quality images at comparatively low cost.

▲ This digital camera, launched in 2000, shows how far technology has advanced since the introduction of the Mavica. This model can produce photorealistic three-dimensional images, and it comes with its own computer software, which enables the viewer to manipulate the pictures.

CAMERA • CHARGE-COUPLED DEVICE • COMPUTER • COMPUTER GRAPHICS • COMPUTER PRINTER • DATA STORAGE • PHOTOGRAPHIC FILM AND PROCESSING

Canal

A canal can be defined as any completely artificial open-water channel, whether it is used for irrigation, land drainage, water supply, or navigation. When the word is used today, however, it is usually in the context of navigation by boats, although many canals may serve a secondary function as a drainage or water-supply channel.

Canals are not to be confused with river navigations. Rivers often have natural characteristics that allow them to be navigable inland; some rivers, however, must be altered and made navigable by the construction of both artificial cuts that bypass a river's acute bends, shallows, and rapids and of locks that regulate water levels to ease navigation when there are abrupt changes in altitude.

▲ Within five years of the building of the Main River section of the linked European inland waterway system, bulk-goods traffic—in this particular case, grain—multiplied more than four times.

Locks

It was on river navigations that the pound lock was evolved, the invention of which was to make the artificial canal possible. The pound lock is said to have been invented in China in 983 C.E., but it is much more probable that it was invented simultaneously in several European countries during the Middle Ages, evolving from the original flash lock employed in early river navigations. The pound lock consisted of a single gate in a weir through which a boat could pass. Naturally, this primitive device was very slow and hazardous in operation. It was eventually realized that such difficulties and dangers could be overcome by building two flash locks close together on a river so that the short reach, or pound, enclosed between them became an equalizing chamber whose water level could, by means of sluices, be raised or lowered to suit that of the river either above or below.

Very early locks had so-called guillotine gates that were raised vertically like a portcullis. The familiar type of lock, consisting of a masonry chamber enclosed by miter gates swinging on a vertical axis, is commonly believed to have been the invention of Leonardo da Vinci, who introduced it on a canal in Italy in 1482 when he was engineer to the Duke of Milan. The miter gates meet at an angle pointing into the flow of the water, making them self-securing. Following this invention, the use of miter-gate locks spread rapidly through France and the Low Countries. The first miter-gate lock in England was built at Waltham Abbey on the Lea River between 1571 and 1574.

◀ The transcontinental waterway passes through a widely varying landscape, linking three major European rivers—the Rhine, Main, and Danube—with a short series of canals from the North Sea to the Black Sea.

Canal routes

The use of modern locks on river navigations was widespread long before canals became popular. The reason for a lack of interest in building canals was that to build a canal over a high watershed involved major civil engineering works for which neither the expertise nor the capital were available. Many early canals are called contour canals because they follow the devious course along the river's natural contours in an effort to avoid the cost of building major earthworks, aqueducts, or tunnels. Even so, such major works were impossible to avoid; equally unavoidable was the problem of supplying the summit, or highest level, of the canal with sufficient water to compensate for that used in lockage. Each boat, as it passes through a contour canal, draws two lock chambers of water away from the topmost level, one as it ascends and another as it descends, and even more water is required for larger lock chambers. To make the problem more difficult for the engineer, this demand for water arises at the precise point where it is most difficult to supply, on an upland plateau.

The first true summit-level canal was built in France to link the Loire River with the Seine River. The Canal de Briare was 21 miles (34 km) long with 40 locks to carry it over a 266 ft. (81 m) summit level. Hugues Cosnier was the brilliant engineer responsible, and from the day it was opened in 1642, his canal was a commercial success. As a prototype, it paved the way for another far more ambitious work, the Canal du Midi, which was built under the direction of the French engineer Pierre Paul Riquet between 1666 and 1681 to link the Garonne at Toulouse with the Mediterranean. It is 149 miles (240 km) long and has 99 locks that lift the canal to a 620 ft. (189 m) summit level. Riquet went to great lengths to ensure that this high summit level had an adequate supply of water. To this end, he drove nearly 40 miles (64 km) of feeder channels and built a huge dam at St. Ferreol in the hills of the Massif Central, an upland area in south-central France.

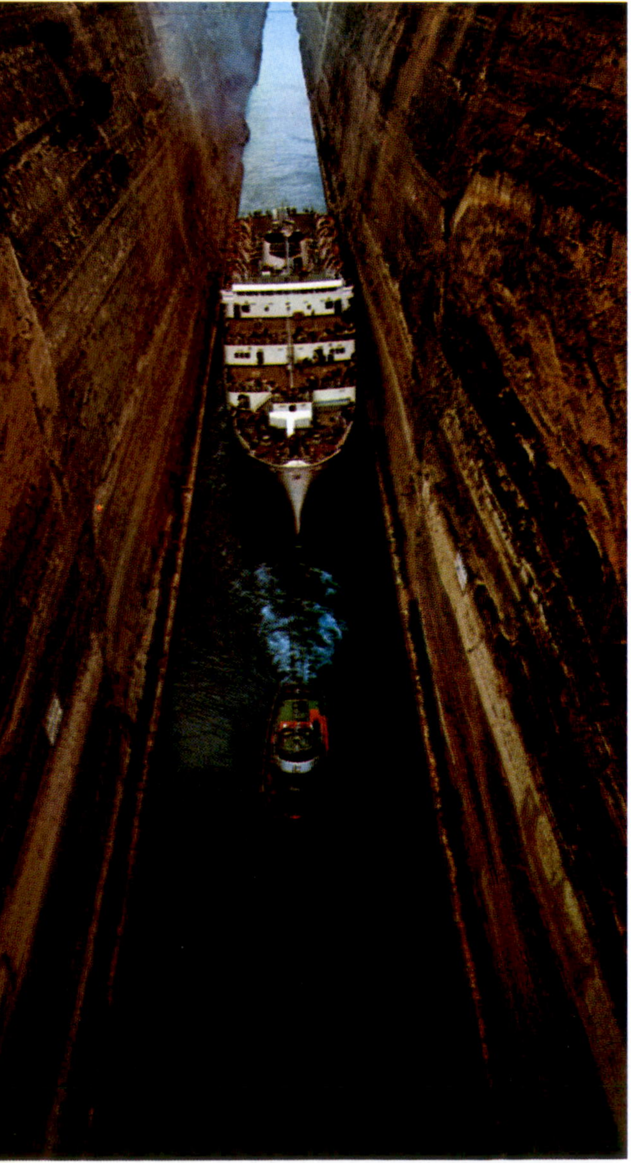

◀ The Corinth Canal in Greece was cut through solid rock at the end of the 19th century. The 3¾-mile (6 km) waterway passes through a narrow strip of land that connects the peninsula of Peloponnesus with the rest of the Greek mainland. The first attempt to build a canal here was made by the Roman emperor Nero in 67 C.E.

History

The Canal du Midi served as a prototype for the rest of the world, spurring Francis Egerton, the Duke of Bridgewater, to embark on the construction of the Bridgewater Canal from his estate at Worsley to Manchester. This began an era of canal building in England that lasted roughly from 1760 to 1830.

First, the four great rivers of England—the Mersey, Trent, Severn, and Thames—were linked by a cross of canals engineered by James Brindley and his assistants using the old contour canal principle. These canals were later supplemented by new and more direct routes, of which the last constructed was Thomas Telford's Birmingham and Liverpool Junction Canal, completed in 1834. In contrast to Brindley's contour canals, the latter was surveyed and built by the "cut and fill" technique adopted by the railway builders, whereby the amount of material excavated in cuttings equalled the amount of material required to raise the embankments sufficiently.

This canal system of the English Midlands as devised by Brindley and his successors played a key role in Britain's industrial revolution by providing an economical method of transport for goods in bulk, especially coal. However, Brindley adopted as standard on his canals a lock chamber 70 ft. (21 m) long but only 7 ft. (2.1 m) wide, which restricted their use to special canal "narrow boats" of similar dimensions carrying only 30 tons (27 tonnes.) Doubtless the water-supply problem was responsible for this slim gauge, but although it proved adequate for 18th-century needs, it became quite inadequate in the 20th century. France, for example, considers a 350 ton- (320-tonne) barge the minimum economic size while the European standard for a self-propelled barge now is 1,350 tons (1,225 tonnes). When it is realized that the 30-tonner, the 350-tonner and the 1,350-tonner cost the same in labor hours to work through a canal, it becomes easy to understand why the greater part of England's canal system today is suitable only for pleasure craft while the wider, deeper, modernized inland waterways of Europe still survive as major arteries of trade.

Just as the Duke of Bridgewater was influenced by the example of the Canal du Midi, so in turn, Americans and Canadians were influenced by canal construction in England. The canal era of the United States was heralded by the opening of the 363 mile (582 km), 82-lock Erie Canal in 1825. Built by the State of New York, mostly through unsettled land, it was begun in 1817 and at that time was the longest in the world. It was widened and deepened throughout as its traffic continued to grow, and in 1883, tolls were abolished. The interlinking Champlain Canal was opened in 1823, but it was not until 1843 that the link to the St. Lawrence River was made with the opening of the Chambly Canal.

Perhaps North America's most remarkable canal was the 394-mile (634 km) link between Philadelphia and Pittsburgh, opened in 1834. This included the 37-mile (59 km) Allegheny Portage, which rose to a summit level at Lemon House of 2,334 ft. (711 m) through five inclined planes, the longest of which was 3,100 ft. (944 m) and the steepest of which had a gradient of 1 in 10. Special boats were constructed, each 20 ft. (6 m) long, that traveled separately on the railroad links but were joined by iron clamps for the canal sections. This facility ceased in 1857 when the Allegheny Portage closed.

Canals today

With significant exceptions, the canal heyday in England and North America was brief. Perhaps because railroads were specifically an English invention, the English-speaking world seems to have lost interest in its canals with the coming of the railroad in the 1830s. This was not the case on the continent of Europe, where both transport systems continued to develop side by side. It was realized that each form of transport was suited to certain traffic and that the particular role of the canal was in carrying low-value bulk cargoes over long distances, provided the canal was capable of passing craft of sufficiently large tonnage. In Europe, therefore, certain trunk canal routes have been progressively enlarged.

In Germany, the completely new 72-mile (117 km) Elbe Lateral Canal was opened in 1977 to convey European standard 1,350-ton (1,225-tonne) craft, so bypassing the old Elbe River navigation, where summer droughts often restricted loads to 400 tons (360 tonnes.) Similarly, in France, the complete canalization of the Rhone River between Lyon and Port St. Louis, by the construction of 12 large locks and dams, was completed in 1980 and now allows 1,500-ton (1,360-tonne) craft and push-tows with loads of 5,000 tons (5,500 tonnes) to complete the 192-mile (310 km) journey.

In North America, the Erie Canal was replaced in 1918 by the New York State Barge Canal, which can accommodate 2,500-ton (2,270-tonne) craft.

▶ A Saturn booster rocket for an Apollo space mission being transported by barge through one of the channels of the Gulf Intracoastal waterway system at Cape Canaveral on the east coast of Florida.

North of this canal is the St. Lawrence Seaway, part canal and part river, which enables seagoing vessels to travel from Montreal to Lake Ontario and from there, via the Welland Canal, into Lake Erie and on past Detroit to Chicago on Lake Michigan or via the Soo Canals to the Lake Superior ports of Duluth and Thunder Bay.

The majority of the other canals in eastern North America have fallen into disuse, but there is the great network of 6,500 miles (10,500 km) of inland waterways formed by the Mississippi and its great tributary the Ohio River. In 1985, the new 234-mile (376 km) Tennessee–Tombigbee Waterway provided a further link in this network. Now all the major parts of the canal system have a common depth of 9 ft. (3 m).

In the southern states and connected with the Mississippi system are the intracoastal waterways. A lock-free mixture of natural channels and artificial canals, they provide waterways for large barges sheltered from the sea. The Gulf Intracoastal runs for over 1,000 miles (1,600 km) from near the Mexican border to Florida, where it is extended by the Atlantic Intracoastal to Norfolk, Virginia.

Farther north, the Cape Cod Canal provides another vital link, between New York and Boston. Opened in 1914, the 7¾-mile (12.4 km) canal, with no locks, is unique in that it often has a considerable current flowing through it when the tides cause different sea levels at the two ends.

In North America today, the normal commercial navigation locks measure at least 600 by 100 ft. (180 by 30 m). All of these large locks are either on or connected to large river systems, so water supply problems do not occur. But even on summit-level canals, the availability of water no longer governs the size of locks, as was the case in Brindley's day. The modern canal engineer thinks in terms of pumping the lockage water back electrically rather than building costly dams to store more water at the summit level.

Boat lifts

Though water can be pumped back, a long flight of locks uses a great deal of another precious commodity—time. Hence, from the earliest days, engineers have schemed to save both water and time by substituting various forms of boat lift for lock flights. Of these, the only one remaining in England is the Anderton Vertical lift of 1875, which lowers boats from the Trent and Mersey Canal to the Weaver River. Ironically, although this is the sole survivor in England and is no longer in commercial use, its English engineers went on to build four much larger lifts of similar type on the Canal du Center in Belgium, which are still used by 400-ton (360-tonne) barges. However they have now been replaced by a single lift of over 240 ft. (73 m) at Strepy. This new lift is similar to another modern lift at Scharnebeck, near Lüneburg on the Elbe Lateral Canal, opened in 1977 and operated on the counterweight principle similar to the lift at Anderton in its modified form.

In Belgium is the huge Ronquières inclined-plane lift on the Brussels–Charleroi Canal, which is the largest canal structure in the world. It is 1 mile (1.6 km) long and lifts 1,350-ton (1,500-tonne) barges 220 ft. (67 m). Another ingenious modern boat lift is the one in operation at Montech in southern France on the Garonne Lateral Canal. This lift consists of an inclined trough of concrete up which the barge, floating on a triangular wedge of water, is pushed by a moving concrete dam propelled by locomotives. A second water slope was built at Béziers on the interlinking Canal du Midi in 1983. Inclined planes are not a new idea—the Chinese had introduced ramps into the Great Canal, which ran between the Chang (Yangtse) and Huai Rivers, as early as 350 C.E. Boats were hauled up and down the ramps by hand.

Perhaps the best American examples of railed inclined planes were to be found on the Allegheny Portage. Others were installed on the Morris and Lehigh Canals. These were designed by James Renwick and were some of the most successful of their kind. Various other inclined planes have been built around the world. Perhaps the most modern of these is the replacement of the Big Chute Marine Railway on the Trent–Severn Canal in Canada, which was opened in 1978. Here the cradle is designed to carry craft of a maximum displacement of 100 tons (90 tonnes), length of 100 ft. (30 m), and beam of 24 ft. (7 m), over a vertical height difference of 58 ft. (17 m).

▲ The Anderton Vertical Lift, which links the Trent and Mersey Canal and the Weaver River 50 ft. (15 m) below, was the first boat lift to be built and the model for similar structures round the world. It was taken out of use because salt, one of the principal cargoes carried on the canal, affected the structure of the lift, but there are plans to restore it to full working order.

FACT FILE

- *China's Grand Canal waterway system, completed by the Mongol ruler Kublai Khan in the 13th century, was already 600 miles (960 km) long by the eighth century, and reportedly carried two million tons of freight per annum. When completed, the system consisted of 1,000 miles of waterways.*
- *In the Low Countries from the 12th century onward, boats of up to 8 tons were transferred between different waterway levels by means of wooden slipways called overdrach. The boats were hauled by winches, which were powered variously by treadmills, waterwheels, horses, and manual windlasses.*

SEE ALSO: BOAT BUILDING • CIVIL ENGINEERING • DOCK • LAND RECLAMATION • LOCK, CANAL

Cancer Treatment

Oncology is the study and treatment of cancer. Though cancer rivals heart disease as a common cause of death, up to a third of all cases can be cured using the latest treatments.

The body is made up of approximately 10 trillion cells. Cancer can start in any one of them and scientists have now discovered why. Each cell has as many as 80,000 genes, which are small segments of DNA (the long threadlike molecule in a cell that carries genetic information). Among the genes are particular sequences of DNA that are responsible for the control of cell growth. Normally, these segments, termed *oncogenes*, are under the control of other genes that act as on/off switches. It is when one of these switches fails to work, perhaps because it has become damaged by radiation or by chemical carcinogens, that cancer develops. Cancer is the result of disordered and disorganized cell growth, a process that can only be understood by looking at what happens in normal cells.

How cancers form

In all tissues, cells are constantly being lost through wear and tear and are replaced by a process of cell division. Occurring under strict control in normal tissues, so that exactly the right number of cells are produced to replace those that are lost, a cell divides in half to create two new cells, each identical to the original.

The cells of a cancer, however, divide and grow at their own speed and in an uncontrolled manner—and they will continue to do so indefinitely unless treatment is given. In time, the cells increase in number until enough are present for the cancer to become visible as a growth.

In addition to growing too rapidly, cancer cells are unable to organize themselves properly, so the mass of tissue that forms does not resemble normal tissue. A cancer obtains its nourishment parasitically from its host and serves no useful purpose for that person.

Not all tumors are cancerous. Although tumor cells will grow at their own speed, tumors can be benign or malignant. Benign tumors tend to push aside normal tissues but do not grow into them. Malignant tumors (cancers) do grow into the surrounding tissue, a process called invasion.

It is the ability of cancer cells to spread inside the body that makes the disease so serious. Fortunately, the stages by which it does so tend to be orderly, with the cancer initially spreading into the surrounding tissues and producing local damage, which in time creates symptoms.

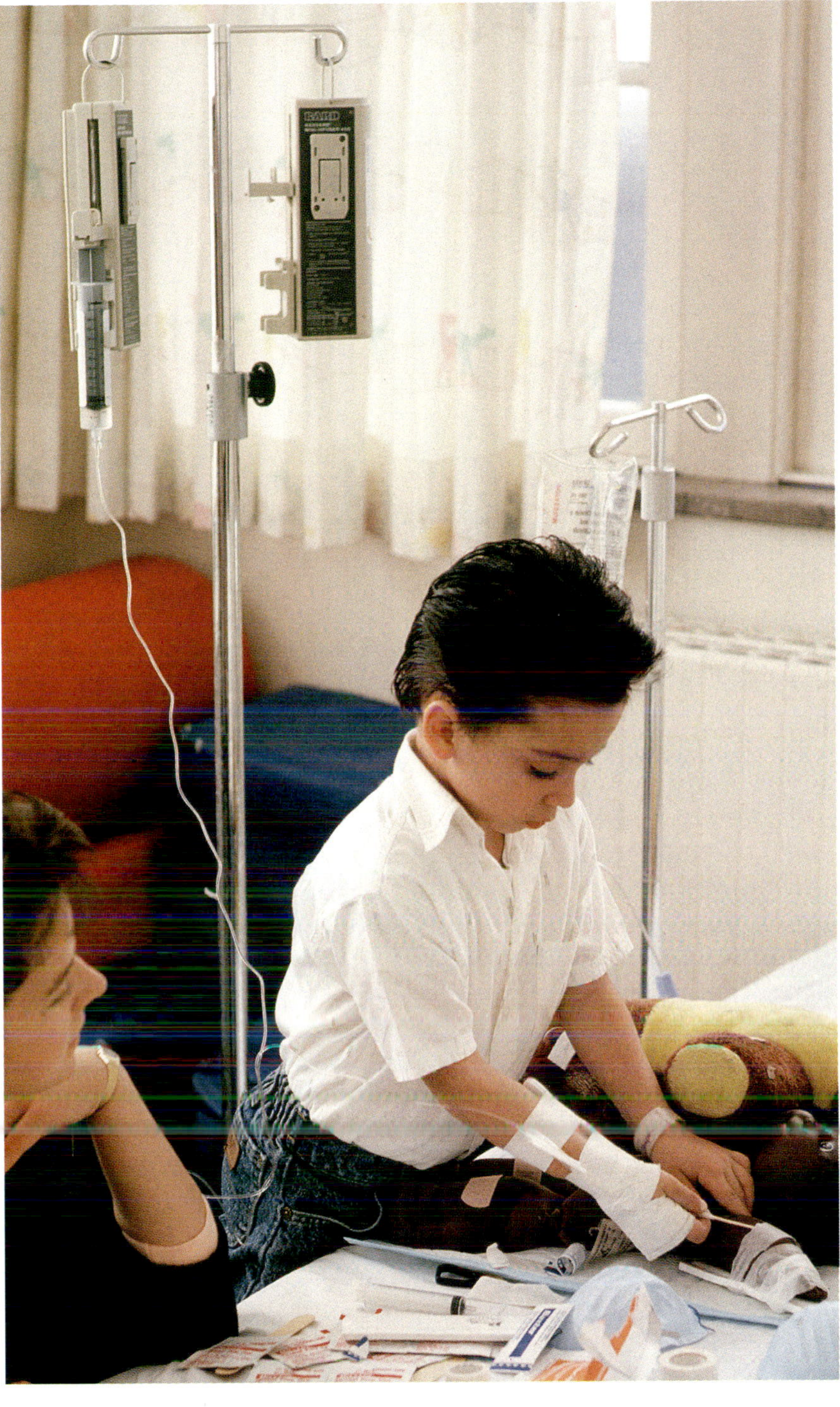

▲ Drip-feed chemotherapy is a good way to administer drugs to small children—they can carry on playing while potentially life-saving chemicals are pumped into their veins.

Next, cells begin to break off from the cancer and float in tissue fluid. In time, this fluid finds its way out of the tissues into a system of channels called lymphatics, which ultimately return the fluid (now called lymph) to the bloodstream. On its journey, the lymph passes through a number of glands called lymph nodes, which filter out dead cells and infection. Cancer cells are usually trapped in the lymph nodes nearest to the cancer, where most die. Sooner or later, however, one will survive and start to grow in the gland, and in this way it will form a secondary growth.

Causes

Environmental factors, such as chemical pollution and exposure to radiation, are thought to lead to cancer, but there are other possibilities. The viral theory states that a cancer cell is infected by a virus, which triggers processes that lead the cell to reproduce uncontrollably.

Alternatively, the immunological theory considers that abnormal cells are constantly being produced by the body and that these cells are destroyed by the body's defenses. When for some unknown reason, this defense system fails, an abnormal cell survives to form a cancer.

▲ False-color scanning electron micrograph of a cancer of the human bronchus (lung).

The chemical theory relies on the knowledge that certain chemicals—tar, for example—will cause cancer when painted on the skin of laboratory animals. These chemicals are irritants that may alter a cell's genetic structure and turn it into a cancer cell. Large numbers of experiments have identified chemicals that will cause cancer in animals; these are called carcinogens. A certain number have been identified, the best known being tobacco smoke. However, despite research, it has not yet been possible to identify carcinogens responsible for many of the common cancers.

Radiation is known to alter the genetic material of a cell. Radiation from the atomic bomb dropped in Japan in 1945 is thought to be a cause of some cancers, even years later.

Diagnosis

A small cancer is much easier to cure than a large one, so early diagnosis is vital. After the diagnosis, confirmation may initially involve X rays and scanning tests to show the presence of a lump. A part of the cancer will then be examined under the microscope. This can be done either by performing a biopsy or by means of a cytological examination.

A biopsy involves the removal, by a surgeon, of a small piece of the tumor, which is then sent for examination by a pathologist, who will determine whether the tissue is cancerous or not. Cytological examination is where body fluids, such as sputum or mucus from the uterine cervix, are studied specifically for cancer cells.

A thorough clinical examination includes taking particular care to check the lymph nodes adjacent to the tumor. Simple blood tests check liver and bone function, and a chest X ray looks for evidence of spread to these sites. If the doctor is suspicious of the cancer spreading to a particular part of the body, that area will also be scanned. Various techniques are used. In isotope scanning a very small amount of a radioactive substance is injected into the body and carried by the blood to the suspected organ or area of tissue. Cancer will take up a different amount of the isotope compared with the rest of the healthy tissue. When the patient is scanned with a special instrument that detects the presence of the radiation, the cancer, if present, can be seen. Many organs of the body can be examined in this way, bone and liver scans being the most commonly performed.

The aim of all cancer treatment is to kill or remove every cancer cell from the patient. With skilled use of the available treatments and sometimes a combination of them, this is often possible.

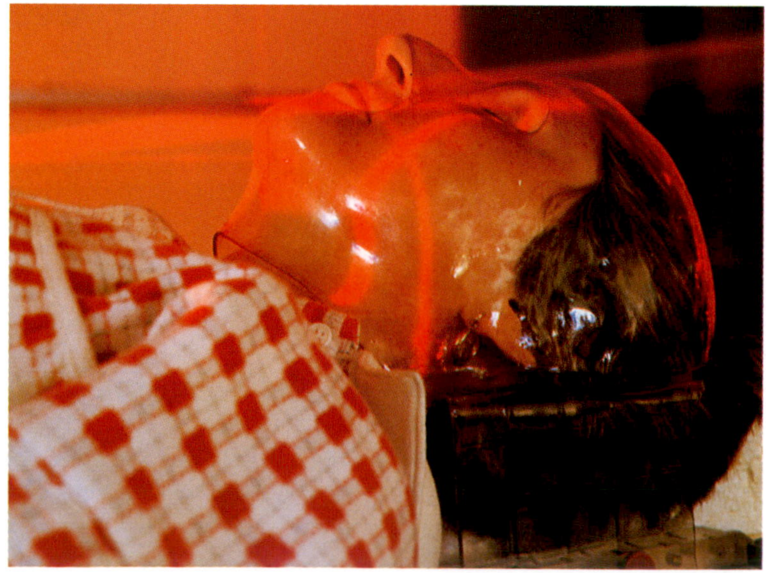

▼ Red laser beams are used to align the head of a patient undergoing radiotherapy for an intracranial tumor. To deliver the radiation beam accurately, the head is immobilized in a plastic mask.

Surgery

Effective cancer surgery aims at removing all of the cancer from the patient. It usually involves removing the visible growth with a wide margin of surrounding normal tissue, to make sure every cancerous cell has been removed.

After removing the tumor, the surgeon will, where possible, reconstruct the patient's anatomy. In some circumstances, reconstruction is not possible. After removal of a cancer of the rectum, for example, the surgeon creates a new opening for the bowel on the abdominal wall—a colostomy—after which bodily waste is collected in a specially designed bag.

Radiotherapy

The aim of radiotherapy is to destroy the cancer with irradiation. Radiation damages the genetic material of cancer cells so that they are unable to divide. Unfortunately it also damages normal cells, but thanks to the body's remarkable ability to repair itself, quite large doses of radiation can be safely given—provided that they are given slowly enough, over a long time period.

Radiotherapy is given in special rooms with thick floors, walls, ceilings, and windows. Radiation leaks are thus prevented and the safety of the hospital staff ensured. The patient lies on a special couch beneath the machine, which is aimed directly at the tumor.

Radiotherapy is used for localized tumors, as is surgery. Some cancers can be cured by radiotherapy alone (for example, some cancers of the head and neck). In other situations, radiotherapy, given either before or after an operation, may increase the chances of a total success—this technique is used in breast cancer cases.

Radiotherapy is also very good at relieving the symptoms of cancer, particularly pain, when cure is not possible. In some circumstances, it is possible to implant radioactive substances into the cancer which give a very large dose to the cancer itself and only a small dose to the surrounding normal tissue. This form of treatment is ideal as the damage to normal tissues is kept to a minimum.

Cytotoxic chemotherapy

If a cancer is too widespread or secondary tumors are present elsewhere in the body, it may not be possible to irradiate the cancer completely or effectively. In this situation, drug treatment is available. These drugs combine with and damage the genetic material of cells so that they cannot divide properly. They were originally developed from mustard gas, when soldiers recovering from this form of poisoning were noticed to have low blood counts. It was realized that the gas was interfering with the division of cells in the bone marrow, where blood is made.

Nitrogen mustard (the active drug in mustard gas) was therefore tried in cancer patients in an attempt to poison the cancer cells. It proved successful. Treatment has now been greatly refined; many new and safer drugs have been discovered and effective combinations of drugs developed. Unfortunately, these drugs poison all dividing cells, hence the term *cytotoxic* (cell poison).

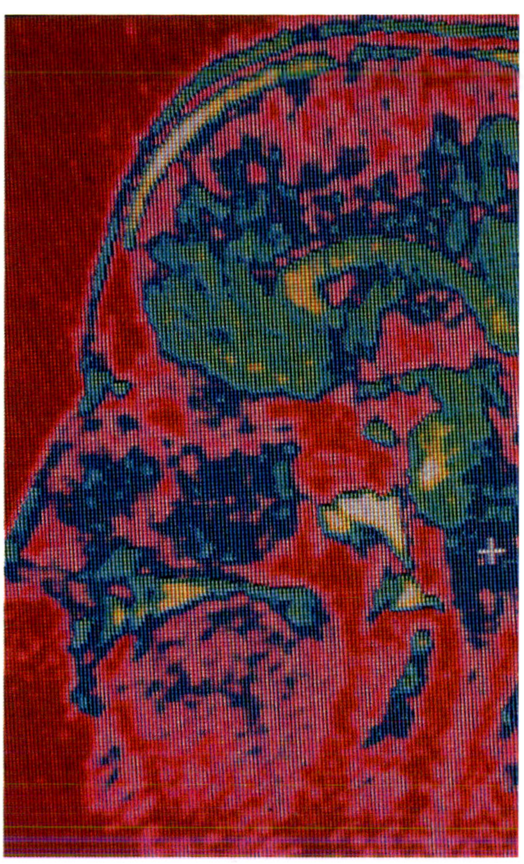

▶ Body scanners are a valuable tool in early cancer diagnosis. In this MRI image, the actual brain tissue is shown clearly enough to diagnose metastatic or tumor cells (indicated by the white cross).

Chemotherapy may be given by different routes, depending on the type of cancer and the drugs used. Most often it is given by injection into a vein (intravenously). Less commonly used ways are by mouth (orally), by injection into a muscle (intramuscularly), or under the skin (subcutaneously). In special cases, chemotherapy may be injected into the fluid around the spine (intrathecally) and in some circumstances, two or more routes may be used together.

Sometimes the drugs are diluted into a large bag of liquid and given via a "drip" into a vein in the arm or hand. The other way of giving intravenous chemotherapy is via a fine plastic tube put into a vein in the chest. Intravenous chemotherapy is given over a period of time, usually from half an hour to a few hours or sometimes a few days. Chemotherapy is not solely used for extensive cancer. It is also used to treat blood cancers such as leukemia, as it has proved effective on bone marrow. Other cancers, like Hodgkin's disease, may also respond better to chemotherapy.

In some cases where there is an inclination to relapse after surgery and/or radiotherapy, chemotherapy is given even when there is no sign of cancer. This is called adjuvant chemotherapy.

Hormone therapy

Hormones are chemical messengers that circulate in the blood to control the growth and metabolism of tissue. If a cancer cell arises in a hormone-

TARGETING CANCER

The body produces its own cancer killers called T lymphocytes, a kind of white blood cell that surrounds and engulfs cancer cells. Some drugs developed to fight cancer are specifically designed to target cancer cells in a similar manner. Antibodies are cultured in the laboratory and attached to anticancer drugs. When injected into the body, the antibodies are attracted to antigens on the surface of the cancer cell and lock the drug directly onto the site. Normal cells have a surface that resists the antibody, and so remain immune from the drug's effects.

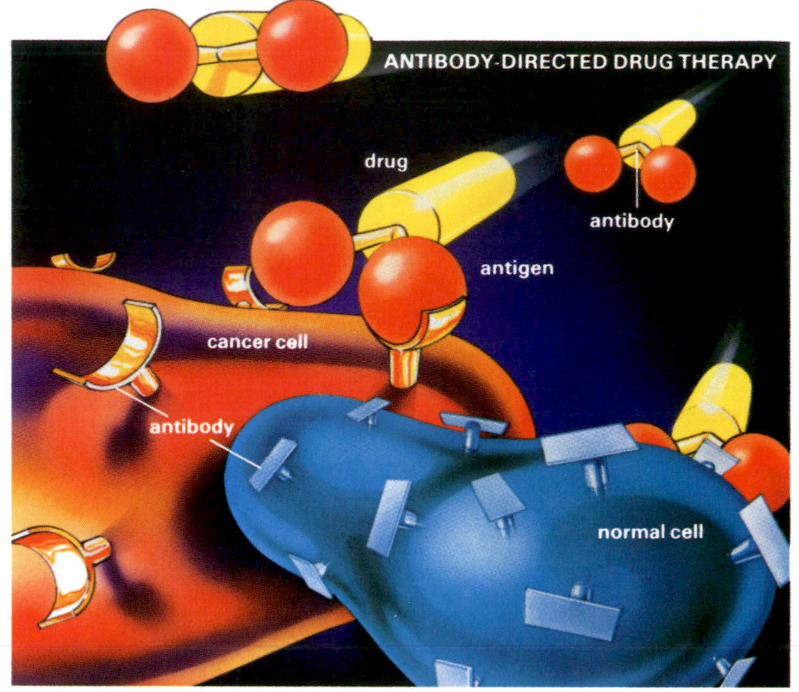

sensitive organ, such as the womb, it may continue to recognize and respond to hormonal messages. If the patient is then given an inhibitory hormone—one that tells the cells to stop dividing—the cancer will stop growing. This type of treatment is particularly useful in breast, uterine, and prostate cancers. The great advantage of hormone therapy is its freedom from unpleasant and possibly dangerous side-effects.

Gene therapy

Many of the gene therapies represent a form of cancer vaccine. The ability to introduce genes into cells is known as gene transfer. Investigators have used these techniques to introduce genes into tumor cells to make them succumb more readily to the patient's own immune system.

These genes contain the building blocks for immune hormones such as interferon, interleukin-2, and granulocyte-macrophage colony-stimulating factor (GM-CSF) or other stimulatory proteins that have been found to enhance the effectiveness of these vaccines in animal studies. Combinations of these can make cancer cells more receptive to treatment.

Bone marrow transplants

In recent years, it has been possible to transplant bone marrow from one person to another. This very specialized procedure requires large doses of radiation to be given to the recipient of the graft beforehand and is only used in rare anemias and leukemia. Cancer therapy is limited by the damage the treatment does to the patient's bone marrow, which forms vital cells that make up the blood and fight infection. Bone marrow transplantation can overcome many of these problems. Marrow is harvested from a close relative by sucking it up through large-bore needles from the center of the hip bones. This marrow is concentrated and infused into the patient's bloodstream. The cells find their way into the bone spaces, where they lodge and start to divide, so creating new marrow.

Photodynamic therapy

Known as PDT, this technique uses specific types or frequencies of light in conjunction with chemicals called "photosensitizing agents" to fight cancer. These photosensitizing agents can destroy single cells such as cancer cells when they are exposed to specific types or frequencies of light.

When PDT is used, the photosensitizing agent is injected into the body and absorbed by all of the cells in the body. The photosensitizing agent remains present within cancer cells for a longer period of time than it remains in healthy cells. When these cancer cells are exposed to a specific type of light, usually directed through fiber-optic devices, the photosensitizing agent reacts by destroying the cells.

Combined treatment

Where more than one treatment is effective in treating a cancer, it is logical to consider combining them in a planned sequence of treatment. In some childhood tumors, surgery is followed by local radiotherapy and then a year of chemotherapy. In head and neck cancer, chemotherapy is followed by local radiotherapy, and then any part of the tumor remaining is removed surgically. Much research has been done to determine the best way of combining treatments to make the best possible use of all of them.

SEE ALSO: Body scanner • Cell biology • Genetic engineering • Pharmacology • Radiotherapy • X-ray imaging

Canning and Bottling

◀ In the first stage of making a drawn and wall-ironed can, a wall-iron press blanks six disks of metal out in one stroke (15,000 an hour) and draws them into half-size cups.

Canning is the heating or processing of food in hermetically sealed containers so that it will keep for years at room temperature. Nicolas Appert, a French inventor in the early 19th century, is generally considered the father of canning, although the reasons why canning preserved foods so successfully were not known until the French chemist and microbiologist Louis Pasteur showed the connection between microorganisms and spoilage some 50 years later.

Microorganisms—bacteria, yeasts, and molds—are present in air, water, soil, and all natural foods. The actively reproducing (vegetative) forms of microorganism are easily killed at relatively low temperatures—around 176°F (80°C)—but some bacteria form "resting bodies" called spores, which can survive much higher temperatures.

Fruits, vegetables, meats, milk, fish, and specialty products (such as soup and baked beans) may be canned. Dangerous spores cannot grow in acidic foods (having a pH less than 4.5), and so fruits, for instance, may be processed at low temperatures up to 212°F (100°C). All products with lower levels of acidity must be processed at higher temperatures, 240°F (116°C) or greater.

Canning operations

Most canning operations are mechanized on a production-line basis. The machinery used, especially in preparation, depends on the nature of the raw material; the aim is to pack the edible portion of the food. With advances in automation much of the preparation process—cleaning and trimming—is also automated.

Blanching, a short preliminary heating at 180 to 212°F (82–100°C), is important for killing the enzymes that can cause unwanted effects such as discoloration or odd flavors; it also removes air from the product and aids filling. Prepared and inspected material is put either manually or automatically into prewashed cans. In multistage operations, solids are placed in first and then topped up with "liquor," or sauce, leaving about a ¼ in. (6 mm) headspace, which prevents excessive pressure forming during processing.

The vacuum in cans is obtained mainly by hot filling, but may be assisted by passing cans through a shallow hot water bath or steam tunnel. This produces water vapor in the headspace, so that when the can is cooled after sealing the vapor condenses, leaving a partial vacuum. Alternatively, the headspace can be swept with steam just before closing, or the can may be seamed in a vacuum chamber. The process of creating the vacuum is called deaeration.

The lid is batch coded and double seamed onto the can in a similar manner to the other end, which is known as the maker's end because it is sealed on by the can manufacturer, not by the food canner.

▶ After the half size cups have been punched out, they then pass to an ironing punch where they are drawn up to full size. They are then trimmed to the same height.

▶ Before they can be filled, the punched and drawn cans are given two washes with detergent, and dried. The cans can be lacquer printed at this stage.

Processing

Cans are processed to destroy all dangerous microorganisms capable of growth in the particular food by either the batch or the continuous method. In the batch method, crates of cans are loaded into autoclaves similar to large domestic pressure cookers. The lid or door is clamped tightly and steam is introduced to purge all air from the autoclave through a vent pipe that is then closed. The vessel is pressurized and heated to the processing temperature, which is maintained by a temperature controller. After heating for a predetermined time, the cans are cooled by adding chlorinated water to the vessel, while initially maintaining processing pressure with compressed air to avoid straining the cans. Autoclaves are operated at 212°F (100°C) for low-acid products. Continuous cookers, capable of processing 2,000 or more cans per minute, can be operated at up to 270°F (132°C). In these machines, cans are introduced into the steam chamber through mechanical valves. Hydrostatic cookers use high columns of water instead of valves to balance the steam pressure.

Free-flowing products, such as vegetables in brine, may be heated directly by rotating the cans over gas burners in flame cookers without damaging the contents. This technique may require heavy cans with reinforced ends to withstand the high internal pressures that develop within them during the heating operation.

In aseptic canning, thin films of homogeneous products are heated and cooled in specially designed heat exchangers. The cooled sterile product is filled into presterilized containers that are then seamed in a sterile atmosphere. Compared with conventional canning, much shorter process times and higher temperatures—up to 300°F (149°C)—can be used to sterilize the food. This method allows sensitive products like puddings to be processed without developing overcooked flavors. It also allows the filling of very large containers for bulk transport.

Advances in plastic technology have resulted in laminated plastic containers that incorporate an aluminum foil layer to provide a gas and moisture barrier, entering the market. These containers are capable of withstanding the high temperatures required to sterilize foods. The most widely used type is the flexible pouch. After filling, the pouch is closed by fusing the inner plastic layer of the laminate in a heat sealer, after which it is processed in an autoclave.

With some types of can, the use of a can opener to remove or puncture the top is necessary. The ring-pull can, originally used for drinks, is now widely used on many different products. The area of the can to be removed is stamped to produce a tear-out panel that is easily removed by hand.

Another development is the peelable foil-end steel can. This type of can uses a heavy foil instead of metal at the top and is designed for individual-portion cans. The foil can be peeled off without the need for a can opener, making it useful for convenience foods. As yet, it has only been used for fruit snacks, but the specially formulated internal coating on the foil makes it suitable for a wide range of other products.

▼ Automatic filler heads filling sterile cans with processed peas and brine on a continuous line. The ribbing in the can wall helps to give the can extra strength.

Making cans

Can manufacture began as a result of Appert's discovery that food could be preserved by heating, though he initially used glass jars. In 1810, Peter Durand took out the patent in England that first mentioned the use of a tin-plated steel container as an alternative to glass, and shortly afterward, Donkin and Hall set up a cannery in London. In those early days, cans were handmade, but by the end of the 19th century an automatic can-making process was introduced, and it has now developed into a highly mechanized and skilled operation performed on continuous lines. Manufacturers can now produce cans at a rate of 400 per minute.

The can is a hermetically sealed container, strongly made to ensure that the contents are kept sterile. For many years, the traditional can has consisted of a soldered body, usually cylindrical, with metal ends, one affixed by the can maker and the other by the canner. It is therefore known as an open-top, or sanitary, can, and it is used for a wide variety of food products and beverages.

Most cans are made from tinplate. This material is often a mild steel strip with a protective layer of tin added, usually by electrodeposition, to prevent the steel from rusting. Aluminum and other forms of steel plate are also used.

Shaping and sealing

The can maker starts with plain or lacquered tinplate sheets that are slit into smaller sheets, or body blanks, appropriate to the can size being made. The blanks pass through a body maker in which they are flexed and notched on one side;

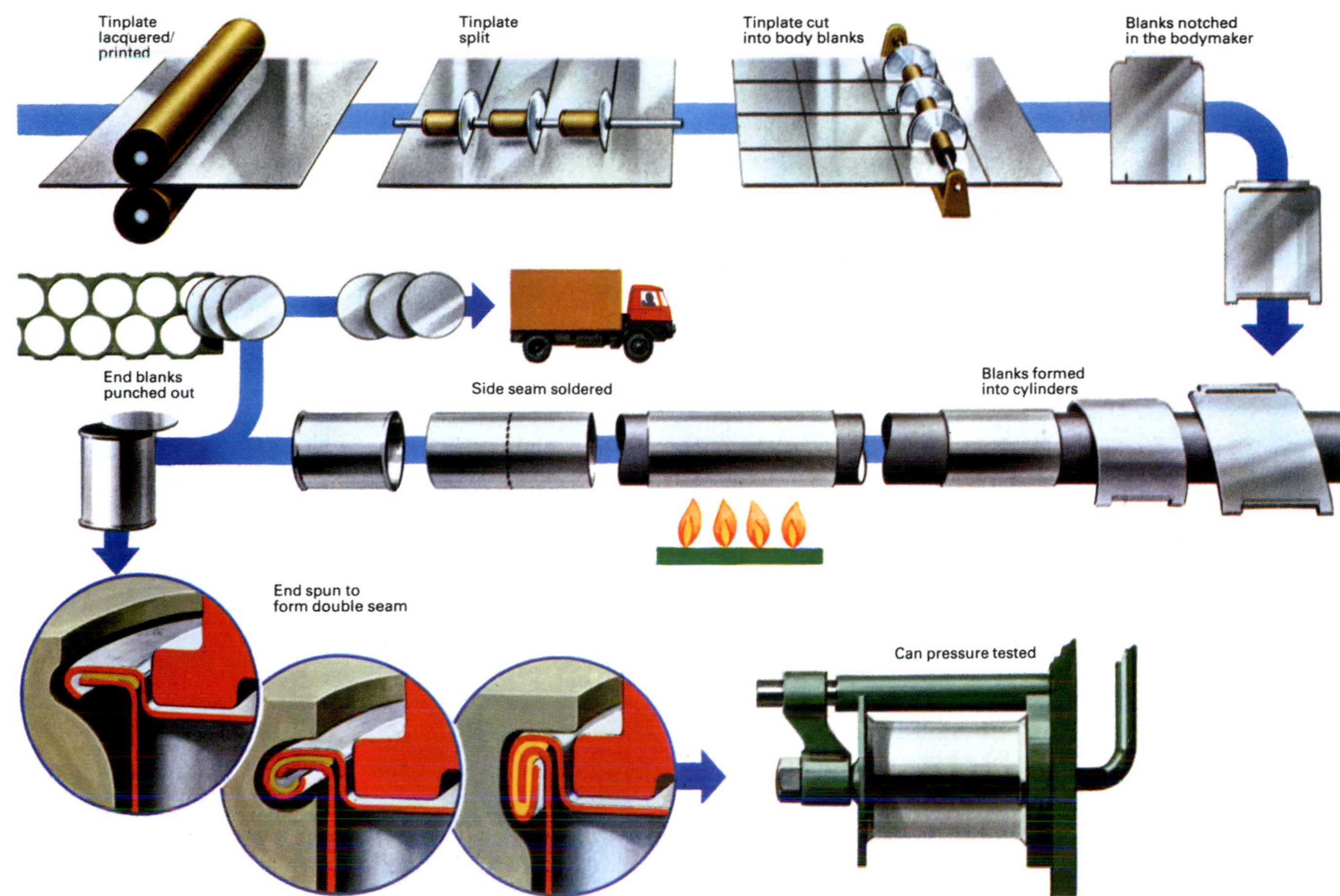

▲ The manufacture of a soldered-seam open-top food can involves 10 separate operations. In many cases, though, the tinplate is decorated by direct printing in stage one, so that the number of distinct stages is reduced to nine.

slits are put in the other side, and the edges appropriately bent. The blank is formed into a cylinder on a mandrel, and the hooked edges are engaged and hammered to give a mainly locked seam with short lap seams at the extremities to facilitate end fixing. The cylinders are then fluxed and preheated to make them easy to solder and carried by magnets or by grippers known as dogs over solder rolls that have been heated to ensure penetration of the solder into the seam. They are wiped to remove surplus solder and finally cooled. The top and bottom edges of the cylinders are flared out to provide flanges. The can ends are stamped out on a press and the perimeter bent under to help the later seaming stage. Finally, the ends may be lined with a synthetic rubber compound. The can is completed by interlocking the flanged cylinder with the end by a spinning process, known as double seaming, precisely enough to give a very tight closure. This process forms a perfect and hermetic seal.

Developments

Since some 60 to 70 percent of the total cost of a can is in the material, it has been important to maintain its place in the market by the introduction of technically proven economies. Thus the thinnest possible tin coating is achieved by differentially coating the plate on each side to the level required. Chemically treated steel plate, usually chrome or chrome oxide protected, known as TFS or tin-free steel, is also used. Container thickness has been reduced in some instances by using stronger double-reduced plate, which is produced using an extra heavy final rolling technique. Modification of can design, for example, by the introduction of beaded bodies ridged for extra strength has also contributed to cost savings.

In the manufacturing process, the use of tinplate and the efficiency and speed of the can-making operation have been highly developed. Perhaps one of the more notable examples is the process by which a long cylinder made on a standard body-maker is divided on a special parting machine into two or three separate cylinders, so doubling or tripling the line speed.

Welded or adhesive-bonded seams are being used increasingly for beverage cans. Such seams are even stronger than the metal itself. The adhesive used is a type of polyamide and is preapplied to the specially lacquered tin-free steel plate before the blanks are heated and formed into cylinders. On the lap side, the seam is bumped together with highly chilled tools to set the hot adhesive. It

WIDGETS AND BEERMAKING

▲ The free-floating widget is a development of early widgets, which were fixed to the can. The widget is able to move around the can and jet nitrogen into more of the beer, knocking carbon dioxide and nitrogen out of suspension thus creating a surge in the bubbles and forming a creamy head on the beer.

▶ The "rocket" widget used in bottles operates differently from widgets used in cans and is designed for people who like to drink out of the bottle. When the top of the bottle is removed, pressure in the bottle drops and causes the gas inside the widget to jet down to the bottom, triggering bubble formation. As the bottle is tipped for each mouthful, the widget floats back to the bottom, causing mixing and a small amount of resurge.

A widget was invented by the Irish brewer Guinness as a way of achieving a good head on canned beer. The British and Irish like beer to have a low dissolved CO_2 (carbon dioxide) content when poured—that is, not gassy, but with good head, which is created by large numbers of gas bubbles during pouring. With draft beer a head is achieved by passing the beer through a venturi nozzle, which introduces lots of air bubbles when pouring. Canned beer needs to have a higher internal CO_2 pressure to ensure that the cans have sufficient strength for stacking and also to provide some form of head when poured. The problem was to develop a way of getting the dissolved gas out of solution rapidly when the can was opened, to produce the creamy head and low gas content that is typical of draft beer.

The Guinness widget consists of a hollow capsule fitted at the bottom of each can. Each capsule has a very small hole in it, through which some liquid enters at the high pressures involved in filling the can. When the can is opened, the liquid in the widget, which is still under pressure, is forced out through the very small hole. This action causes a large number of very small bubbles to be formed from the dissolved CO_2, resulting in a creamy consistency and thick head. The main problem with this design is that the amount of bubbles produced depends on the temperature. Unless the can is cold when opened, excessive amounts of foam are produced with messy consequences.

The Whitbread widget, developed by a British brewery, uses sophisticated materials engineering to overcome this problem. High-pressure nitrogen gas is injected into the widget through a one-way valve before it is placed in the can. The can is then filled, sealed, and pasteurized at 144°F (62°C). When the can is opened, the nitrogen in the widget has to get out the wrong way through the one-way valve. This is possible because the temperatures achieved during pasteurization change the properties of the widget material, making it more flexible and allowing the nitrogen to escape through the one-way valve after the liquid pressure above it has been reduced on opening.

Since the advent of widgets in cans, widgets have been designed to produce the same effect in bottles. Guinness' "rocket" widget moves up and down as the beer is drunk, causing bubbles to form.

The materials used in widgets have to satisfy stringent requirements—they have to be nontoxic and compatible with beer; easily molded to accurate dimensions; cheap; light (to reduce transport costs); and made of a material that does not gradually stretch at storage temperatures, as this would allow gas to escape. To get the exact level of relaxation required at 144°F (62°C), a plastic is needed. Polypropylene satisfies most of the criteria well, though extremely careful control of its properties is needed to ensure the widgets operate consistently well.

is most important that the cut edge of the side seam is protected either by the bonding material or by applying a separate, protective side stripe.

Another commercial development, which became popular in the mid- to late 1970s, is that of the two-piece drawn and wall-ironed (DWI) can used for beer and soft drinks made in aluminum or tinplate. This process basically consists of blanking out a disk from a sheet of metal, drawing a cup, and finally forcing it with a punch through a number of rings. The clearances between the punch and rings become progressively less, thus ironing the walls to a thin section but leaving a thick base. The can is then given a reduced-neck form at the top and flanged to allow an aluminum easy-open end to be seamed on once the can has been filled.

Cans must be lacquered internally to prevent contamination of the contents. On seamed cans, the lacquer coating is applied by roller to the tinplate before the can is made, and on the DWI can, the lacquer is sprayed on after drawing. Decoration and labeling of cans take place after the cans have been filled and closed.

Carbonation

The fizz is introduced to canned drinks by the addition of carbon dioxide gas under pressure. The first use of artificially induced carbonation dating back over 250 years, was for the preservation of drinking water and to improve its quality. The process used to introduce carbon dioxide today is undertaken after the can is filled with a beverage. The gas is injected into the drink in a carbonator machine immediately prior to sealing the can. While under pressure and chilled, the drink may absorb up to four times its own volume of carbon dioxide. The pop heard when a drink can is opened is caused by the rapid escape of carbon dioxide gas caused by the sudden release of pressure on the beverage.

Bottling drinks

A much older technique for packaging liquids is bottling. Glass is the most traditional material used, but it is heavy, particularly if large volumes of liquid have to be accommodated. Plastic bottles are much lighter and thinner, but they are less environmentally friendly than glass, which can easily be recycled.

Bottles arrive at the packaging plant where they are visually and electronically checked to ensure that no foreign bodies are present and that there are no cracks or splits. After inspection, they enter the filler. If fizzy drinks such as beer or soda are being processed, bottling takes place under constant pressure to prevent the loss of carbon dioxide. The bottle then passes to a crowning, or capping, machine to be sealed. Between filling and capping, the fizzy beverage is forced to release some gas, which makes the liquid froth slightly and displace any air that may have entered the bottle after filling.

The bottles undergo another check to make sure they are properly full. Drinks that are prone to spoiling, such as beer, then have to go through a pasteurization process to kill any microorganisms. Labels are automatically pasted onto the front and back of the bottle, which is then given a final check for leakage before being put into crates ready for dispatch.

▼ Bottles have to undergo a number of inspections as they pass along the production line. First they are checked for cracks and flaws before they are filled. After filling, bottles pass in front of light boxes so that inspectors can check that they are filled to the correct level, that there are no foreign bodies present, and that labels are on properly.

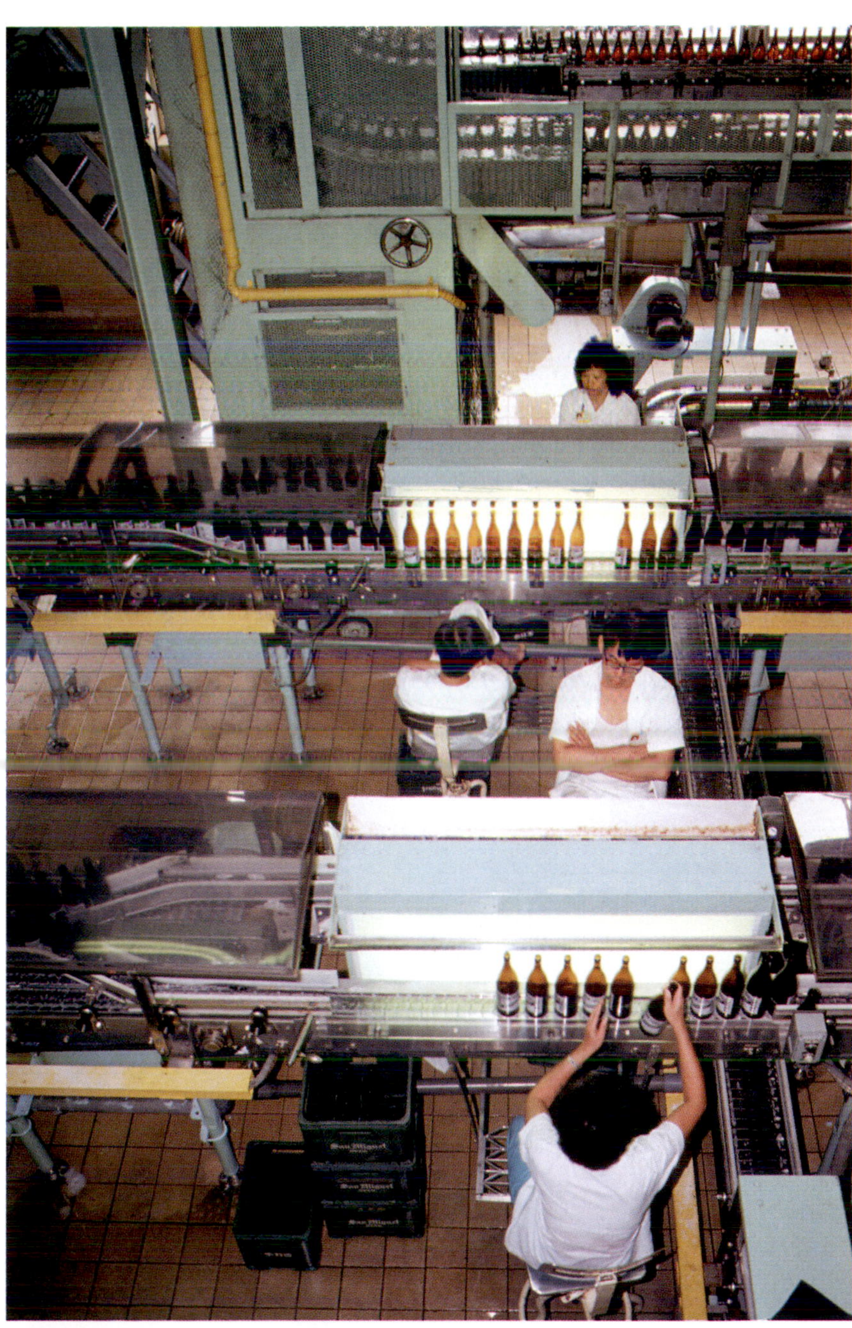

SEE ALSO: Assembly line • Food preservation and packaging • Glass • Metalworking • Plastics

Capacitor

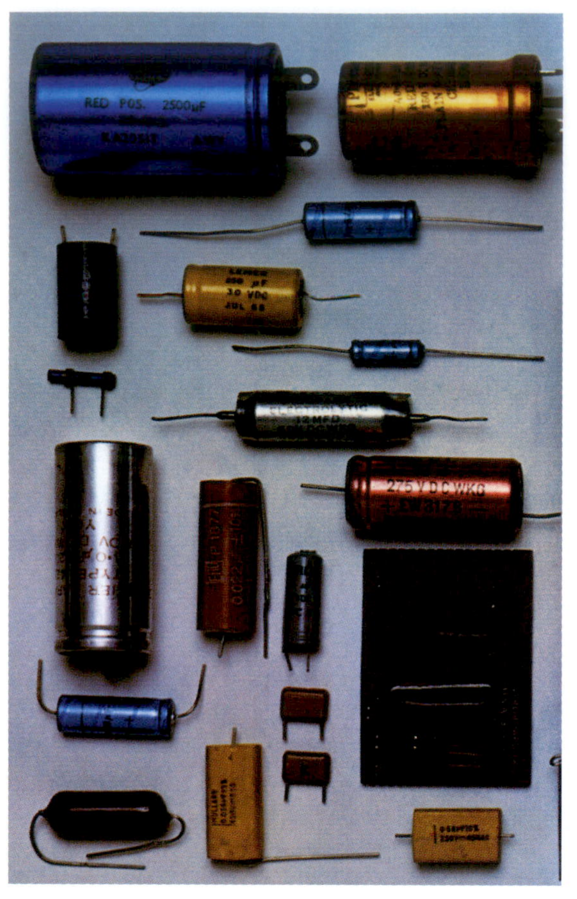

▲ An array of capacitors of various vintages, including several electrolytic (silver), nonelectrolytic (flat amber), and ceramic (gray).

Electrical capacitance is an electrostatic phenomenon and is concerned with the storage of electrical charge. Devices that use this phenomenon are called capacitors (formerly known as condensers) and are widely used in electronic equipment. They consist essentially of two parallel plates, separated by an insulating material, which possess a certain "capacity" to store electric charge.

The capacitance of a device is determined by dividing the charge stored on the plates by the voltage the charge creates across the plates. By increasing the capacitance, more charge can be stored at the same voltage.

Capacitance can be increased in three ways: by increasing the area of the plates, by reducing the separation distance between the plates, and by using a better insulating medium, or dielectric, than air between the plates.

Dielectric materials

If an insulating material, or dielectric, is introduced between the plates and a voltage is applied across the plates, polarization will occur in the material. Polarization is the rearrangement of electric charges in the material to form dipoles, which are opposite charges very close together lined up in the material in an orderly fashion. These dipoles produce an internal field that cancels part of the field created by the applied voltage, enabling more charge to be stored for a given applied voltage.

Introducing a dielectric therefore, increases the capacitance, and the ratio of this new capacitance to that with an air gap is called the relative permittivity, or dielectric constant, of the material (symbol ε—the Greek letter epsilon). This constant varies for different materials.

Some typical materials with their dielectric constants are a vacuum, $\varepsilon = 1$; air, $\varepsilon = 1.00059$ (normally assumed to be one); polytetrafluorethylene (PTFE), $\varepsilon = 2$; polystyrene, $\varepsilon = 2.6$; barium titanate, $\varepsilon = 6000$. Using barium titanate as the dielectric means that, for a given capacitor size and shape, the capacitance can be increased 6,000 times.

Capacitors in electrical circuits

If a battery, switch, resistor, and capacitor are connected in series in a simple electrical circuit, the following voltage–current relationships can be observed depending on the switch position.

When the switch is closed, there is an initial current, or flow of charge, equal to the battery voltage divided by the resistance of the resistor, according to Ohm's Law. Charge soon builds up on the capacitor plates, increasing the voltage between them. Like charges repel, and so the buildup of charge eventually slows. The current in the circuit dwindles to zero, leaving the voltage across the capacitor equal to the battery voltage. This is the charging process.

If the switch is now opened, the capacitor will retain its stored charge. In theory, it will do this indefinitely, but in practice there will always be some leakage or loss, and the charge stored and the capacitor voltage will slowly decrease.

If the battery is removed and replaced by a piece of wire there will be an initial current, in the reverse direction, equal to the voltage across the capacitor divided by the resistance of the resistor. The current dwindles as the capacitor voltage drops to zero. This is the discharge process.

When an alternating (AC) voltage source is used instead of a battery in the above circuit, the capacitor goes through repeated charge–discharge cycles. As the frequency of the alternating voltage is increased, the capacitor has little time to accumulate charge before the second half of the cycle—the discharge cycle—begins, and the maximum voltage across the capacitor gets smaller and smaller. Thus, with increasing frequency, the capacitor has less and less effect in the circuit and the current approaches the source voltage divided by the resistance of the resistor.

The behavior of a capacitor in an alternating current circuit will be different from that in a direct current circuit. When a capacitor is charged by a direct, or DC, voltage, the accumulation of charge on the plates provides a means of storing energy that can be made available on demand. An example is the capacitor used in a camera flashgun.

The frequency dependent properties of a capacitor in an AC circuit lead to several important applications, including pulse shaping and smoothing and radio-interference suppression (as in the ignition system of cars). The capacitor allows high-frequency currents to pass through it but at the same time blocks the low frequency and direct currents.

So far, only ideal capacitance has been discussed, whereas in practice all dielectric materials have a certain electrical resistance. For example, when a DC voltage is applied across a capacitor, a small leakage current will flow continuously through it. In actual circuits, allowances have to be made for the capacitors being less than perfect.

There are two major types of capacitors—fixed and variable—both of which are used in a wide range of electronic devices. Fixed capacitors can be further subdivided into electrolytic and nonelectrolytic types and represent the largest proportion of the market. Capacitors are sometimes still referred to as condensers, their original name.

Electrolytic capacitors

Electrolytic capacitors have a much higher capacitance, per cubic centimeter, than any other type. This is achieved by making the effective plate separation extremely small by using a very thin dielectric (insulator) between 200 and 10,000 angstroms (0.02 and 0.001 mm) thick. The dielectric is an oxide layer that is formed on either a tantalum or an aluminum plate by electrolysis—passing an electric current through a liquid called an electrolyte. The capacitor is liquid-filled, so that the process continues all the time it is working. The tantalum or aluminum plate is always made the positive plate (the anode) in electrolytic capacitors, and the process of oxidation is sometimes referred to as anodic oxidation. The negative plate (cathode) is usually copper. Because the electrolyte is a good conductor of electricity, the effective plate separation is only the oxide layer, which is an extremely good dielectric. Generally, acids such as sulfuric acid or salt solutions like glycol borate are used as electrolytes.

Nonelectrolytic capacitors

Of the nonelectrolytic capacitors, only paper, film, mica, and ceramic types are of any significance. Older types using, for example, glazes, vitreous enamel, glass, and certain ceramics have all but disappeared, having been replaced with film types.

Mica is a naturally occurring dielectric and has a very low dissipation factor—that is, a very high resistance. The capacitors are constructed of either stacked sheets of mica with silver coatings for electrodes or with tinfoil electrodes inserted between layers. These capacitors are particularly useful in high-voltage and high-frequency applications such as radio transmissions. Because of the control that can be exercised over the chemical composition of ceramic dielectrics, there is a wide range of possible capacitor properties. The high permittivities (dielectric constants) that can be achieved give very high capacitance per unit volume, but these are generally low-voltage types.

Paper and film capacitors are constructed using a similar technique of rolling the dielectric and metal electrodes into a cylindrical shape. The metal electrodes can be either aluminum or tinfoil or, alternatively, a layer of metal, either aluminum or zinc, vacuum-deposited onto the paper or film. The most commonly used film is polyethylene terephthalate, which is used in the metallized form. The wide capacitance range available and the temperature range of –67 to 257°F (–55–125°C) make the capacitors suitable for most applications.

Variable capacitors

Variable capacitors generally have air or a vacuum as the dielectric, although ceramics are sometimes used. The two main subgroups are tuning and trimmer capacitors. Tuning capacitors, so called because they are used in radio-tuning circuits, consist of two sets of parallel metal plates, one isolated from the mounting frame by ceramic supports, while the other is fixed to a shaft that allows one set to be rotated into or out of the first set. The rows of plates interlock like the fingers of two hands but do not quite touch.

Trimmer capacitors are made of flat metal leaves separated by a plastic film; these can be screwed toward each other. They have a smaller range of variation than tuning capacitors and are used where only a slight change in value is needed in a particular application.

▼ These solid tantalum capacitors, sometimes called slugs, are formed of fused powder and have been coated with various thicknesses of dielectric material.

SEE ALSO: Atomic structure • Electricity • Electronics • Resistance

Carbohydrate

▲ Carbohydrates are found in a wide variety of foodstuffs, such as bread, potatoes, and pasta. Together with fat, carbohydrates fuel all the body processes that require energy. Glucose, the main product when complex carbohydrates are broken down by the body, is an essential brain food.

Carbohydrates are a group of naturally occurring compounds that include a variety of foodstuffs and fibers. Natural sugars, starch (found in bread, corn, potatoes, and other vegetables), and cellulose (in cotton, wood, and many natural fibers) are the best known carbohydrates. Carbohydrates were originally classified together when analysis showed that they contained only three elements, carbon, hydrogen and oxygen and that the proportion of the hydrogen and oxygen atoms was the same as that in water, H_2O. As compounds that contain water are known as hydrates and the general chemical formula of this group is $C_x(H_2O)_y$, carbohydrates were originally called hydrates of carbon. Later research showed that this formulation is an oversimplification.

Structure

Like most organic compounds, carbohydrates have a structure based on a carbon chain, with other atoms, in this case hydrogen and oxygen, arranged around this chain. In carbohydrates, the hydrogen and oxygen are also found as the hydroxyl group (–OH), which is the characteristic group of the alcohol family.

Monosaccharides

The simplest carbohydrates are the monosaccharides, which contain only a few carbon atoms. These compounds are generally sweet tasting, hence the name, which comes from the Greek word for sugar, *sakkharon*. The more complex carbohydrates are formed by linking monosaccharides together. These monosaccharides are divided into different groups according to how many carbon atoms they contain. The best known groups are the pentoses, with five carbon atoms, and the hexoses, with six carbon atoms in their molecules. Monosaccharides with other numbers of carbon atoms exist, but these are less common.

Glucose

Glucose, ($C_6H_{12}O_6$), which is soluble in water and has a sweet taste, is the most abundant hexose. It plays a vital role as an energy source in both animal and plant metabolism. Sunlight is used by plants to make glucose from atmospheric carbon dioxide (CO_2) and water (H_2O) by a process known as photosynthesis. Rather than storing glucose in solution, it is much more conveniently stored in nature as polymers (long-chain molecules), which are largely insoluble in water. These polymers—glycogen in animals and starch in plants—are made by linking glucose molecules together, and as each link is formed, a molecule of water is eliminated. Although starch and glycogen are formed by the same link between the glucose molecules, there are about twice as many branches in glycogen as there are in the starch chain.

Glucose was first prepared synthetically by the German chemist Emil Fischer in 1887, but it is so readily available from natural sources that no commercial process for its manufacture has been developed. One of the major difficulties in chemical synthesis of monosaccharides is that for any combination of carbon, hydrogen, and oxygen atoms a variety of different structures, each known as an isomer, is possible. Glucose, for example, is one of sixteen possible monosaccharides all with the formula $C_6H_{12}O_6$: only three of these isomers exist naturally. Natural synthesis uses specific enzymes (naturally occurring catalysts) that can produce one isomer to the exclusion of all others.

Laboratory chemical processes, however, tend to be less specific, and mixtures of the different isomers are produced that are difficult to separate. Glucose is prepared commercially by hydrolyzing starch, that is, breaking down the polymer links and restoring the missing elements of water to reform glucose. Mineral acids can be used to hydrolyze starch, but increasingly, a process using commercial preparations of natural plant enzymes is used.

Disaccharides

When two monosaccharides are combined, with the elimination of a molecule of water between them, a disaccharide is formed. So when glucose and another hexose, fructose, which is found in many fruits, are joined in a specific way, a disaccharide is formed called sucrose, commonly known as sugar. Sugar is an essential food ingredient, and its consumption in developed countries of the world exceeds 76 lbs. (34.5 kg) per person per annum. Sugar is obtained by the extraction of sucrose from sugarcane, sugar beet, and sugar maple.

If sucrose is hydrolyzed, a mixture of glucose and fructose is obtained called invert syrup. The name was given to the mixture because a solution of it rotates polarized light in the opposite way to a sucrose solution.

Germinating grain, where the breakdown of the stored starch is incomplete, contains another disaccharide, maltose, which is two glucose molecules linked together. Milk has a small amount of a disaccharide, lactose, made from glucose and another hexose, galactose. Lactose is obtained by evaporation from whey, which is a by-product in cheese-making.

Polysaccharides

Polysaccharides are powdery compounds usually insoluble in water and tasteless. They consist of monosaccharides combined to form compounds of high molecular weight.

Starch and cellulose occur abundantly in plant material. Starch is found stored in seeds and tubers as a future food supply, while cellulose is the chief constituent of plant cell walls. Both are formed by the polymerization of glucose, that is, the linking together of many glucose molecules, but the geometry of the polymerization is different in each and every individual case.

In starch, the link makes the polymer take a helical form, so that starch molecules tend to pack together as granules. In cellulose, the glucose units adopt a straight-chain structure, which gives

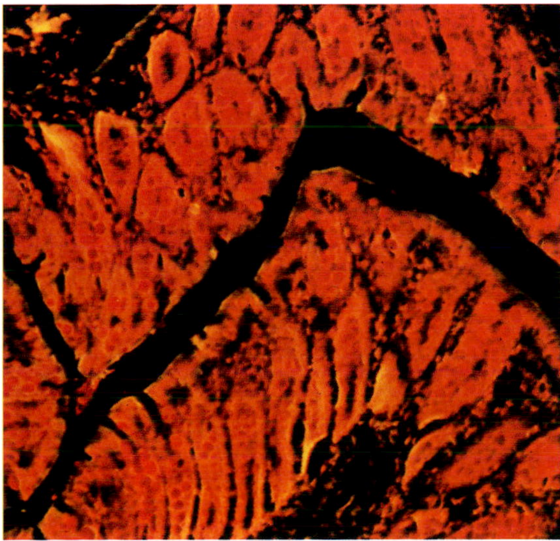

◀ Part of a human colon stained with fluorescent dye to reveal the presence of carbohydrates.

it a fibrous character. Bread contains about three parts of a branched form of starch (amylopectin) and one part of an unbranched form (amylose).

Starch is also used in a number of industries, for example, in the dressing of fabrics and in giving specialized types of finish to paper (known as sizing). Partial breakdown of starch and cellulose provides a range of adhesives, such as dextrin or "British gum." Glycogen, or animal starch, occurs in the liver and muscle tissue and is necessary for muscular action.

Cellulose is the main constituent of natural fibers such as cotton, wood, flax, and hemp. Several other useful products can be obtained if cellulose is modified chemically. Nitrocelluloses (more correctly known as cellulose nitrates) are obtained if cotton is treated with a mixture of nitric and sulfuric acids. One of these highly nitrated celluloses, guncotton, explodes on impact or when strongly heated. Two high explosives, nitroglycerine and guncotton, are blended together with a little petroleum jelly to give another explosive—cordite. Cellulose nitrate, containing less nitrogen (formerly called collodion cotton), is not explosive and is used to make artificial silk, imitation leather bookbinding cloth, and in lacquer production. A solution of collodion cotton in a mixture of ether and alcohol is called collodion and is used for coating metals and, in medicine, for covering wounds. The first artificial silk, Chardonnet silk, was made from collodion in 1884, and the first plastic, celluloid, was made in 1865 by mixing collodion cotton and camphor in alcohol.

Other modified celluloses have been used as ingredients in slimming foods. They provide the bulk that makes the dieter feel full, but as the body is unable to break them down, they pass through the system and therefore have no nutritional value.

The artificial fiber rayon is made from cellulose either by forcing a viscous solution of cellulose acetate in acetone through fine holes into warm air where the solvent evaporates leaving fine threads of cellulose acetate or more usually, by the viscose process. Here cellulose and caustic soda react with carbon disulfide to give a xanthate called viscose. Extrusion through fine holes (in a spinneret) into an acid solution produces rayon threads. By extruding the viscose through rollers in an acid medium, a film, better known as cellophane, is formed.

STARCH

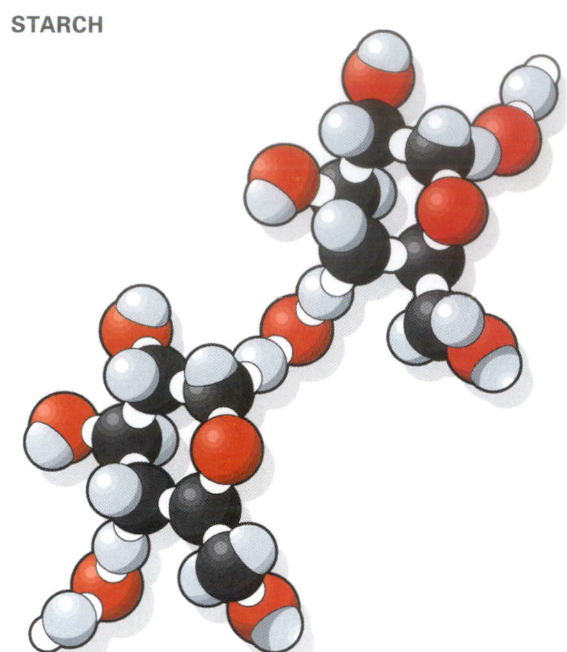

▶ Starch is a complex formation of a large number of sugar molecules, called a polysaccharide. The manner in which the sugar molecules link together gives starch a helical structure, which packs it into granules. The presence of starch in a food can be detected using iodine solution, which turns blue if starch is present.

SUCROSE

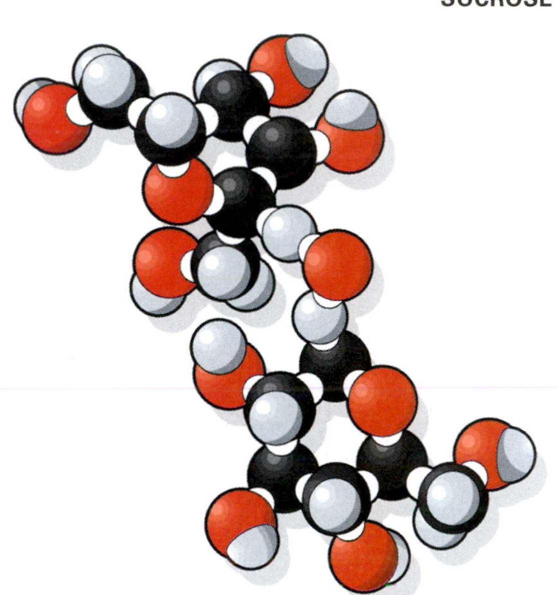

◀ Sucrose, more commonly known as sugar, is a disaccharide, that is, it has been formed from two simpler hexose or pentose sugars, in this case, glucose and fructose.

▶ Potatoes and other root vegetables are a major source of starch and complex carbohydrates. They are often a key part of a human diet because they are filling and take time to break down in the digestive system, whereas simple sugars are absorbed almost immediately. Many athletes eat high-carbohydrate meals before endurance events.

SEE ALSO: Cell biology • Digestive system • Fermentation • Nutrition and food science • Sugar refining

Carbon

◀ Diamond, a form of carbon, is the hardest known substance. Each of these diamonds is a single crystal in which each carbon atom is covalently bonded to its four neighboring carbon atoms. The unusually high refractive index of carbon is responsible for the internal reflection of light that produces the sparkle of a cut diamond, while the angles of the cuts are designed to enhance this reflection. Minute traces of impurities give certain diamonds a hint of color.

▼ A photomicrograph of the surface of a diamond reveals its crystal structure.

Carbon is unique in that no other element forms the huge variety of compounds that carbon can form with other elements. All forms of life on Earth are based on carbon compounds, as are most plastics, drugs, and dyes.

The preeminence of carbon in the ranks of more than 100 elements has long been recognized by chemists, who have divided the subject into two broad classes: organic and inorganic chemistry. Organic chemistry concerns the chemical reactions of compounds that contain carbon and usually hydrogen, while inorganic chemistry concerns compounds of the other elements. Although this might seem an unbalanced division, there are many more compounds of carbon than all the conceivable combinations of all the other elements—and by a huge factor.

Properties and occurrence

The atomic mass of carbon is approximately 12 times the atomic mass of hydrogen, the lightest of all elements. Each carbon atom has six electrons: two in an inner shell and four in an incomplete outer shell. A carbon atom tends to find four more electrons to complete its outer shell of eight electrons; in most cases, this bonding is achieved by sharing electrons in covalent bonds with other atoms. Because of this tendency, chemists say that carbon has a valency of four, meaning that it could bind with four hydrogen atoms, for example, each hydrogen atom donating an electron to its bond with the carbon atom.

Carbon is present as a mere 0.3 percent of Earth's crust. Most of this carbon is bound up in carbonates such as limestone and chalk or in fossil fuels such as coal, gas, and oil. The fossil fuels formed through the action of bacteria, heat, and pressure on the remains of plants and animals over many millions of years. Coal derives from vegetation, while petroleum and natural gas derive from the decomposed remains of marine organisms.

Slightly impure carbon is formed when organic matter is heated in the absence of air. Heating wood in the absence of air drives off gases and volatile liquids to leave charcoal, for example, while treating coal in a similar way produces coke.

When ignited in air, charcoal glows at a high temperature forming little smoke, making charcoal ideal for cooking food in barbecues. Until the industrial revolution, charcoal was the main source of heat and carbon for producing iron from iron-oxide ores. Since then, the use of coke for the same purpose has permitted iron to be made on a much larger scale because coke is hard enough to support the weight of the charge in a blast furnace, whereas charcoal would not be.

Allotropes of carbon

A small proportion of the carbon in Earth's crust is present as the element—an ability shared by few other elements, of which gold is the best-known example. Pure carbon occurs in two physical forms, called allotropes, and each corresponds to a different arrangement of carbon atoms.

Carbon is not alone in being allotropic: phosphorus exists as two allotropes—white and red phosphorus—that also have different atomic arrangements. What distinguishes the allotropes of carbon—diamond and graphite—is the vast difference between their properties. Diamond, for example, is a colorless transparent solid that is the hardest of all known substances, while graphite, on the other hand, is a soft dark-gray material used in the lead for pencils and as an industrial lubricant. Diamond is a poor conductor of heat and electricity, while graphite is a good conductor of both, though not as good as a metal. The contrasting properties of graphite and diamond are due to their different structures.

The fact that diamond and graphite are two forms of the same element can be confirmed by burning them: the product is carbon dioxide in either case. The French chemist Antoine Lavoisier first performed this experiment in 1773.

The difference between the properties of the two allotropes of carbon stems from their different arrangements of carbon atoms. Each carbon atom has four electrons that are available for forming bonds. In diamond, each of these electrons forms a bond with a neighboring carbon atom, and the neighboring carbon atoms lie at the points of a tetrahedron with the first carbon atom at its center. Each of the carbon atoms in the tetrahedron connects with four other carbon atoms—including the first—and so on, so every carbon atom in a diamond is held firmly in place by four bonds. In a way, a diamond is one giant carbon molecule: there are no free-bonding electrons, and since electrons are responsible for conduction, diamond is neither a conductor of heat nor of electricity. The strength of bonding in a diamond makes it the hardest substance known—a great advantage in cutting applications.

The carbon atoms in graphite, however, are arranged in flat planes of hexagonal rings stacked one on another. Each carbon atom bonds to just three others within the plane. The remaining bonding electron wanders relatively loosely between the planes, accounting for graphite's conductivity. The planes are held together by weaker attractions, a fact that is reflected in the larger separation between planes than between adjacent carbon atoms within a plane. The planes can slip over each other easily, making graphite soft and a useful lubricant. The free electrons in graphite are capable of absorbing and reflecting all frequencies of visible light, thus making graphite both dark and shiny. In contrast, bonding electrons of transparent colorless diamonds do not absorb light at visible frequencies.

Graphite can be turned into diamonds when temperatures of at least 4530°F (2500°C) are combined with a pressure of 700 tons per sq. in. (99 tonnes/cm^2). Scientists at the U.S. General Electric Company first achieved this conversion in 1955. Synthetic diamonds made in this way are used to make cutting tools.

CARBON IN IRON MANUFACTURE

A blast furnace, a tall brick-lined structure, uses coke—an impure form of carbon—to convert iron-oxide ore into metallic iron. Coke is obtained by heating coal to around 2000°F (around 1500°C) in the absence of air to drive off gases and volatile liquids. Blasts of hot air from jets around the base of the furnace provide oxygen for coke to burn, producing heat and carbon monoxide. The hot carbon monoxide reacts with iron oxide to form liquid iron, which runs to the bottom of the furnace, and carbon dioxide, which escapes in the blast furnace gases. Limestone (calcium carbonate; $CaCO_3$) reacts with impurities in the ore to form a liquid slag that floats on the liquid iron in the bottom section of the furnace. Iron and slag are tapped, or run off, from the blast furnace from time to time, and more iron ore, coke, and limestone are charged through a double-bell arrangement at the top of the furnace. The double bell prevents poisonous gases from escaping to the atmosphere.

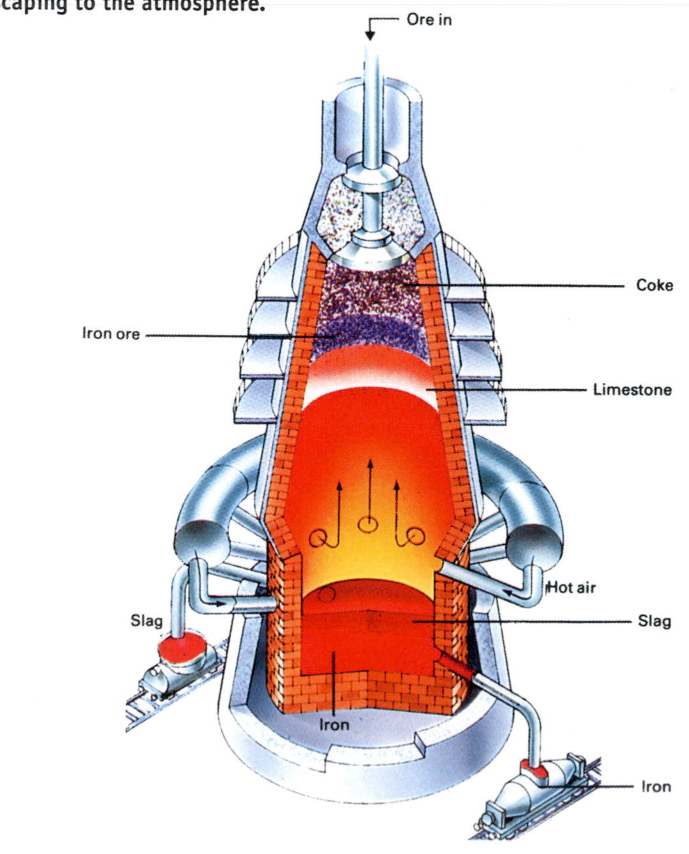

Isotopes of carbon

All carbon nuclei contain six protons, and thus all carbon atoms have six electrons. In nature, carbon nuclei may contain six, seven, or eight neutrons. These different forms of atoms are called isotopes. Carbon-12, with six protons and six neutrons, is by far the most common isotope: it accounts for nearly 99 percent of naturally occurring carbon. Almost 1 percent of carbon is present as carbon-13, while there are only small traces of radioactive carbon-14.

Carbon-14 forms by the action of cosmic rays on nitrogen atoms in the upper atmosphere. It has a half-life of 5,760 years, which is the time taken for the half number of carbon-14 atoms in a sample to decay. A balance between the rate of formation and the rate of decay of carbon-14 leads to an almost constant proportion of carbon-14 in the atmosphere, although atomic weapons testing and the burning of "old" carbon in fossil fuels has shifted this balance in recent centuries.

While an organism is alive, it exchanges carbon with the atmosphere, and its balance of isotopes matches that of the atmosphere. Once dead, the decay of carbon-14 atoms changes the isotope balance. This discovery is the basis of radiocarbon dating, a technique used by archeologists.

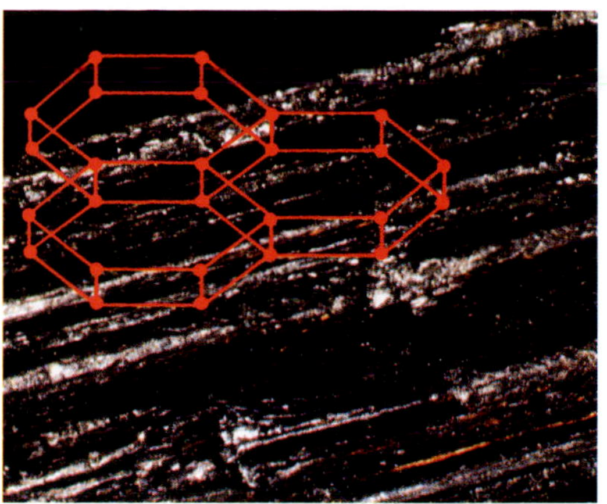

◀ In graphite, carbon atoms link together in sheets of hexagons. These sheets slide over each other with ease, making graphite slippery. Only three of the four bonding electrons of each carbon atom are used in bonds with neighboring atoms. The other bonding electrons form delocalized bonds similar to those in metals, which is why graphite is a good conductor.

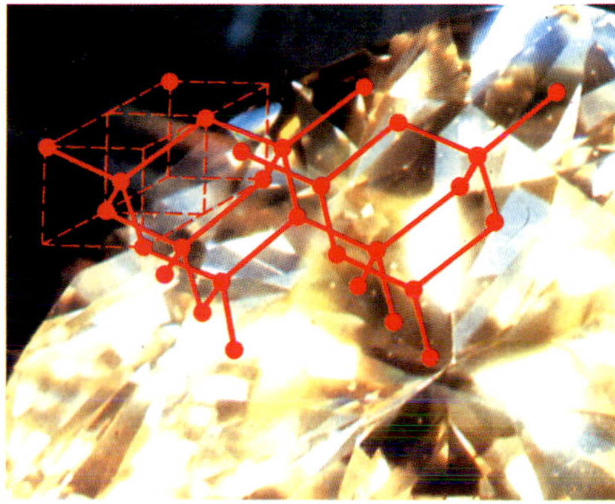

▶ The diamond structure is radically different from that of graphite. In a diamond, each atom uses all four bonding electrons in covalent bonds with its four closest neighbors. These atoms are arranged in a regular tetrahedron around the central carbon atom, and each of them is surrounded by four carbon atoms in a similar pattern.

FACT FILE

- *Experiments suggest that diamond, like silicon, gray tin, and ice, has a melting point that reduces with pressure, and that diamond melts to form a metallic liquid denser than solid diamond under these conditions. If this is the case, carbon present in Earth's deep mantle and core may exist in the form of a metallic liquid.*

- *Wind erosion has revealed carbon-rich meteorites, known as carbonaceous chondrites, frozen into the ice of the polar plateau of the Antarctic. These meteorites were probably formed in the beginning of the Solar System, and analysis of their original matter suggests that the Solar System started to form some 4 to 5 billion years ago.*

- *Iapetus, the outermost-but-one of Saturn's moons, is composed of a combination of elemental carbon and ice. Photographs of the 900-mile (1,450 km) diameter moon, taken by NASA's* Voyager 2 *space probe, reveal a black-and-white striped surface.*

Carbon chains

The multitude of carbon-containing compounds exists by virtue of the ability of carbon atoms to form chains. Carbon is not unique in being able to form more than one bond with atoms of the same element: oxygen atoms form two bonds with other oxygen atoms, and nitrogen atoms form three. The difference is that while other elements form multiple bonds between small groups of atoms—O_2 and N_2, for example—carbon has a stronger tendency to form single bonds with other carbon atoms because a pair of single carbon–carbon bonds is stronger than one double carbon–carbon bond.

Another important consideration is the tendency of carbon atoms to form bonds with atoms of oxygen, since oxygen is reactive and abundant in Earth's atmosphere. The carbon–oxygen bond is stronger than the carbon–carbon bond, and thus charcoal releases heat as it burns and carbon–oxygen form in place of carbon–carbon bonds. The difference in bond strengths is small, and carbon compounds must be heated before they can start to burn.

SEE ALSO: Atomic structure • Carbon fiber • Chemical bonding and valency • Chemistry, organic • Chemistry, organometallic • Element, chemical

Carbon Fiber

◀ Polyacrylonitrile fibers darken during heat treatment as their carbon content increases.

Carbon fibers are filaments that consist of almost completely pure carbon. The tensile strength of such fibers can be up to five times the strength of steel, making them extremely useful where a combination of strength and lightness is needed.

One of the earliest uses of a form of carbon fiber was in the incandescent lamp of the U.S. inventor Thomas Edison in 1879. Edison charred cotton thread to drive off water from the cellulose of the cotton. The result was a carbon-based material that glowed white hot as it conducted an electrical current.

Carbon is an excellent refractory material owing to its high vaporization temperature of 6700°F (3700°C) and its resistance to chemical and physical change even at high temperatures. These properties make carbon-fiber felts, wools, and papers useful for the filtration of hot corrosive fluids, for high-temperature insulation, and for catalytic purposes in industrial processes. Early carbon fibers were brittle and lacked mechanical strength, thus they had limited uses.

During the 1950s, a method was developed for making carbon fibers from viscose rayon filaments. The fibers so produced had sufficient mechanical strength to make them useful for reinforcing phenolic resins such as Bakelite. In the 1960s, advances in carbon-fiber technology led to techniques for producing low-density fibers of great stress resistance and tensile strength.

Starting materials

All methods for producing carbon fibers start with polymer-based fibers called precursors. These precursors are carbonized (converted into high-carbon materials) by controlled pyrolysis (decomposition by heat). The carbonization product retains the fibrous structure of the precursor.

A variety of natural and synthetic materials have been used as precursors for the manufacture of carbon fibers. Natural cellulosic fibers, such as cotton, hemp, and flax, produce a low carbon yield and poor-quality fibers; viscose rayon—a semisynthetic cellulosic precursor—produces carbon fibers that are somewhat superior to those based on natural cellulose.

The most significant advances were made by using polyacrylonitrile fibers as precursors. Polyacrylonitrile, or PAN, is the material used to make commercial acrylic fabrics.

Other potentially important synthetic precursors include polyvinyl alcohol, polyimides, and polyamides. Various fibers based on pitch, wool, and bitumen are also practical starting materials.

Manufacture

The conversion of precursor fibers into carbon fibers of consistently high quality requires heat treatment under strictly controlled conditions of timing, temperature, atmosphere, and tension. In batch processing, a bundle of many thousands of fibers is subjected to a variable heating schedule in a single furnace; in continuous processing, the fibers travel through a sequence of heating zones at different temperatures.

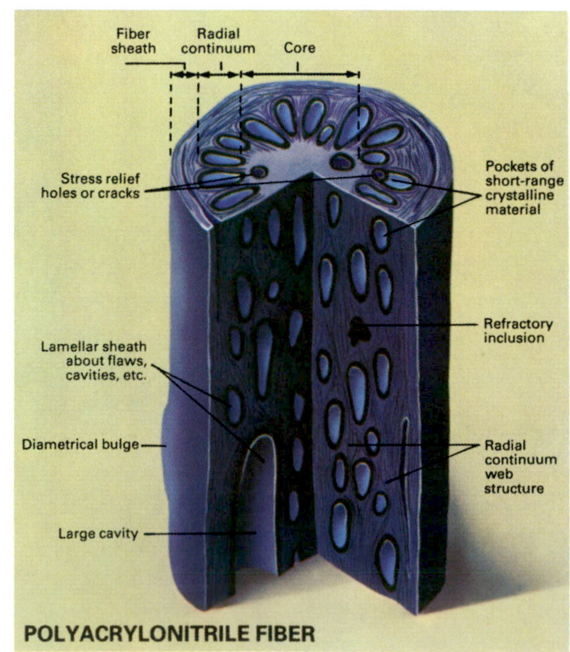

▶ A carbonized polyacrylonitrile fiber consists of a porous core and a smooth skin. The pores in the core result from the formation of gases during the process of carbonization.

A typical sequence for the conversion of a polymeric precursor begins with a pretreatment, such as stretching in steam. After pretreatment, the fibers are heated to between 390 and 570°F (200–300°C); this strengthens the fibers by linking together neighboring polymer chains through chemical bonds called crosslinks. The crosslinked fibers are then carbonized by heating to around 1800°F (1000°C) in an atmosphere of an inert gas such as argon. The decomposition of the precursor polymer causes the fibers to shrink and releases gases that are carried away by the inert atmosphere. During the carbonization of PAN, for example, ammonia, carbon dioxide, water vapor, hydrogen cyanide, and nitrogen are given off. The final stage is the graphitization of the fibers by heat treatment at 3600 to 5400°F (2000–3000°C), which promotes the formation of graphite crystals within the fibers.

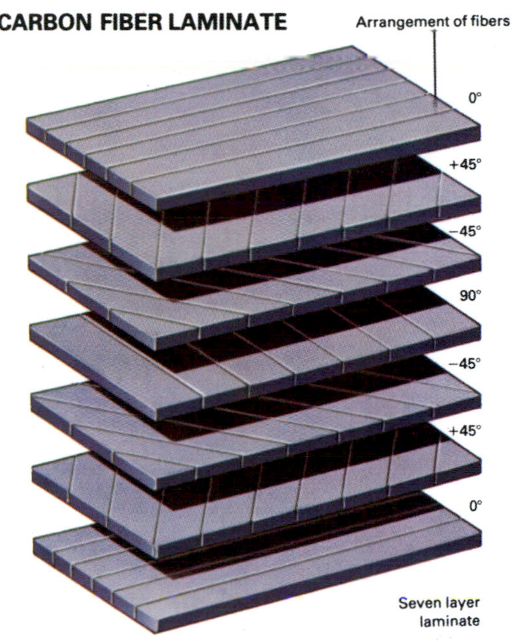

◀ A sheet of carbon fibers has a greater tensile strength along the fibers than across them. Stacking sheets so that the fibers in each sheet are oriented at 45 or 90 degrees to the fibers in adjacent sheets produces a composite that is equally strong in all directions. A polymeric resin bonds the stacked sheets together.

The structure of carbon fibers

As an element, carbon can exist in a variety of forms, each with distinct properties. Diamond is hard and crystalline but only forms at extremely high temperatures and pressures.

Graphite consists of sheets of carbon atoms that are bonded strongly together in a repeating pattern of hexagons; these sheets stack together in a close-packed layer structure. The binding forces within layers are much greater than the forces between layers, so the mechanical properties in the direction of stacking are different from those in the plane of the sheets. (The variation of properties according to direction is called anisotropy.) Amorphous forms of carbon, such as soot, coke, and charcoal, have no definite structure, and their mechanical properties are far inferior to those of diamond and graphite.

The fibers produced by the carbonization of precursor fibers are largely amorphous, which explains the poor mechanical properties of early carbon fibers. During heat treatment at temperatures above 3600°F (2000°C), the carbon atoms arrange themselves into minute crystals of graphite. If the precursor is spun and drawn so that it has an ordered molecular structure, the crystal layers are aligned parallel to the fiber axis. After graphitization, a network structure of tiny graphite fibers (fibrils) is obtained, each typically 50 angstroms (5 nm) deep—equivalent to around 15 crystal layers—150 angstroms (15nm) wide, and extending for 10,000 to 100,000 angstroms (1,000–10,000 nm). A similar degree of order can be achieved from less-ordered precursors, such as pitch, by stretching the fibers during graphitization at 4000 to 5250°F (2200–2900°C). This process is called strain graphitization.

Fiber cross sections can be circular, irregular, or even dog bone-shaped, and fibers usually have a mean diameter of 6 to 15 µm. Surface appearance varies depending on the precursor, tending to be smooth in PAN-based fibers and longitudinally grooved in rayon-based fibers.

The adhesion of resins to carbon fibers can be improved by oxidation processes, which produce surface pits, or by "whiskerizing," in which whiskerlike crystals of silicon nitride are formed on the surface of the carbon fibers.

Properties and uses

Graphitized or partially graphitized carbon fibers are remarkable for their strength and stiffness. The strongest fibers have the greatest proportion of graphite fibrils aligned along the fibers. Resistance to stress increases with heat treatment in the range 2200 to 5400°F (1200–3000°C), reflecting increasing graphitization. Density increases with graphitization from 1.5 to 2.0 g/cm^3. Carbon fibers are moderately good conductors of electricity, with electrical resistances around 500 times that of aluminum.

Carbon fibers are most often used in composites with flexible resins, to which they contribute tensile strength. Such composites have found use in the manufacture of strong lightweight sports equipment, bicycle frames, and aircraft components. They are much stronger but much more expensive than glass-fiber-reinforced equivalents.

SEE ALSO: Aircraft design • Boat building • Carbon • Fiber, natural • Fiber, synthetic • Glass fiber • Polymer and polymerization

Carburetor

The carburetor is an important part of the internal combustion engine: it is the device used to mix the air and gasoline vapor. This mixture is fed into the engine under a variety of operating conditions from cold weather starting to increasing acceleration.

The first carburetors appeared at the end of the 19th century and were known as surface carburetors. They worked very simply by drawing air over the surface of the fuel and mixing its vapor with the air to form a combustible mixture that was then fed into the engine. The wick carburetor, developed next, was similar, but instead of the air being drawn over the fuel, it was drawn over wicks that had one end immersed in the fuel, which soaked into the wick and vaporized into the air. To assist evaporation, hot air from the engine was used. Various versions of these designs were made until the development of the two basic types of carburetor used today: the fixed-jet and variable-jet carburetors.

Carburation

A carburetor works by suction from the engine, which helps to atomize (break up into tiny droplets) and vaporize the fuel. The amount of fuel drawn into the airstream in the carburetor to obtain the required air-to-fuel ratio is controlled by a narrow passage called the choke (barrel), or venturi. As the air flows through this passage, its speed increases and consequently the pressure drops, causing fuel to be sucked into the airstream from a hole or jet at this point.

The fuel atomizes and is mixed with air, usually in the ratio of about 15 parts (by weight) of air to 1 part (by weight) of fuel. In cold-weather starting, however, the mixture may need to be much richer, say 2 parts of air to 1 of fuel.

The amount of fuel–air mixture allowed into the engine is controlled by a butterfly valve, or throttle, that is positioned after the venturi. The valve is a simple device, that when opened (when the accelerator pedal is depressed) allows large amounts of the mixture through, and if it is closed cuts off the supply. The throttle therefore controls the speed at which the engine runs. The gasoline–air mixture is sucked into one cylinder of the engine, where a valve closes to seal it in. The piston rises to compress the mixture before it is fired by the spark plug. The force of the burning mixture pushes the piston down, the valve opens, and the cycle starts all over again.

The fixed-jet carburetor

The fixed-jet carburetor has several jets of a fixed size and an accelerator pump that is used to boost the fuel supply when necessary, as in sudden accel-

▼ A bank of three Mikuni constant-vacuum (CV) carburetors from a multicylinder Suzuki GT750 engine.

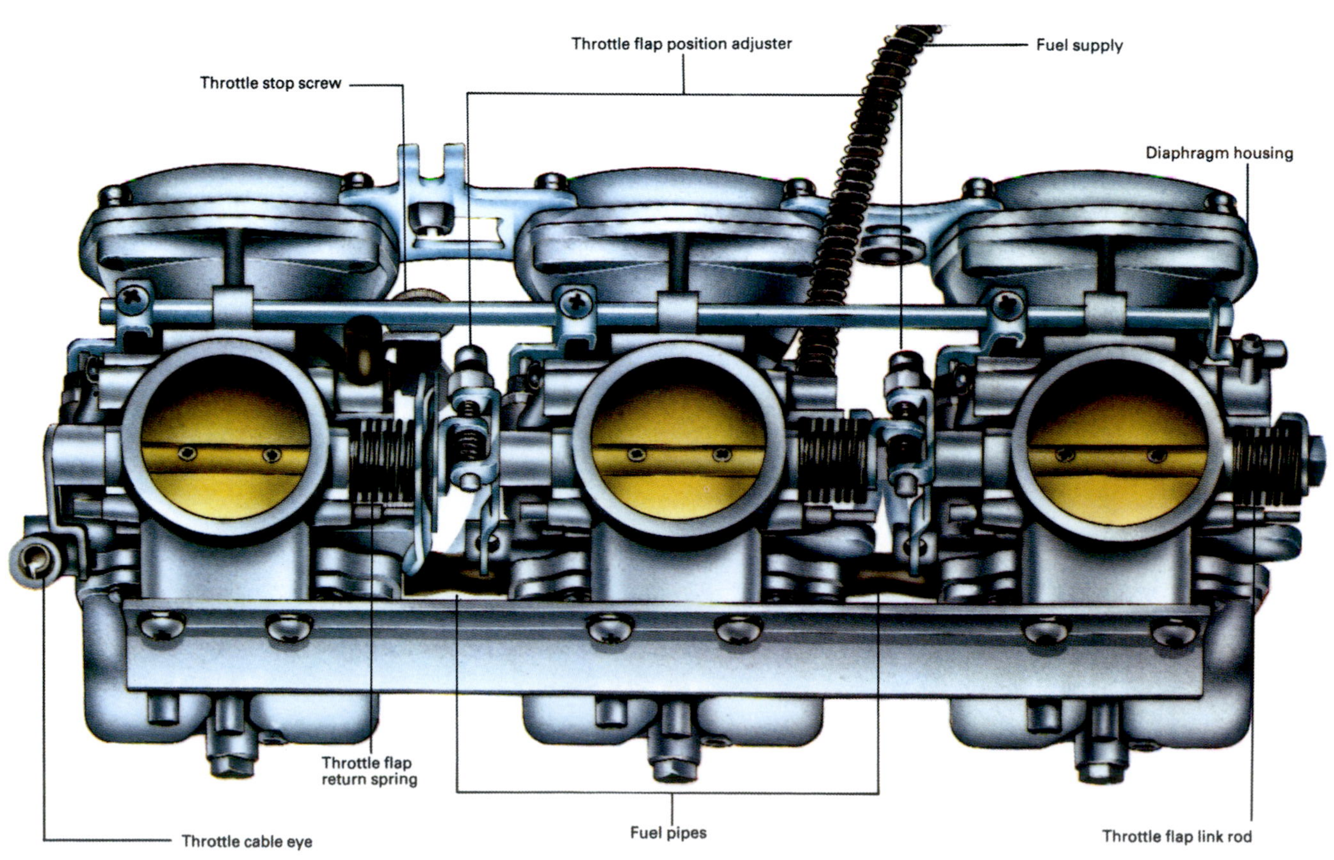

eration. Each jet has a function. The idling jet bypasses all of the other jets and allows a constant small flow of fuel to reach the air flow. It is used to keep the engine turning over at low speeds. The other jets are designed to mix correct quantities of fuel with the incoming air under other conditions, such as acceleration and fast driving. They include the main jet, which operates once the butterfly valve is opened, supplying fuel for constant high-speed running, and the compensating jet. This jet functions when the butterfly valve is opened to supply extra fuel to the engine and enables it to accelerate to a high speed, at which time the main jet takes over. There may be more jets found in this type of carburetor, but basically they just assist the three jets mentioned.

The variable-jet carburetor

The variable-jet carburetor works on the suction of the engine and also depends on the butterfly valve to control engine speed. It consists of a main jet and a tapered needle, mounted on a piston. In this type of carburetor, the air is usually drawn in from the side of the carburetor, while the piston and needle move vertically. They are mounted through the air tube or the venturi. The tapered needle sits in the main jet, and as the butterfly valve is opened, the suction from the engine is increased; this suction acts on the top of the piston, which is sucked upward. As the piston rises, it pulls the tapered needle out of the main jet, and more fuel is allowed to flow through and mix with the air. A damper on top of the piston slows its rise when a richer mixture is demanded for sudden acceleration.

Attached to both types of carburetor is a small reservoir tank of fuel called the float chamber because it has a float that rises with the fuel level until it reaches a certain level. At this stage, it cuts off the fuel supply from the main tank. This action also stops too much fuel from being passed into the carburetor and so acts as a control valve.

If a better performance is wanted from an engine, as in racing cars, one of the first things to be modified is the carburetor. Engines may have two or more carburetors instead of one or a carburetor with two or four chokes side by side. These modifications give a better distribution of the mixture to the engine. Short open pipes may be fitted to the air intakes of the carburetors; called ram pipes, they improve the air flow to the venturi at certain engine speeds to give a better mixture. Sometimes larger main jets are fitted to allow more fuel to flow. Other high-performance engines have fuel-injection systems, where fuel and air are precisely metered and mixed in the engine itself.

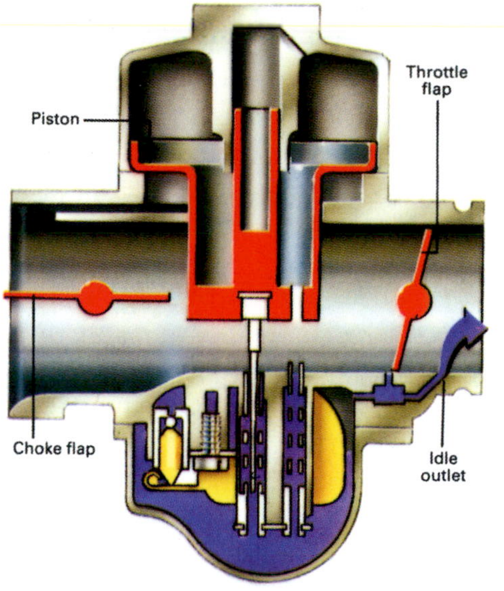

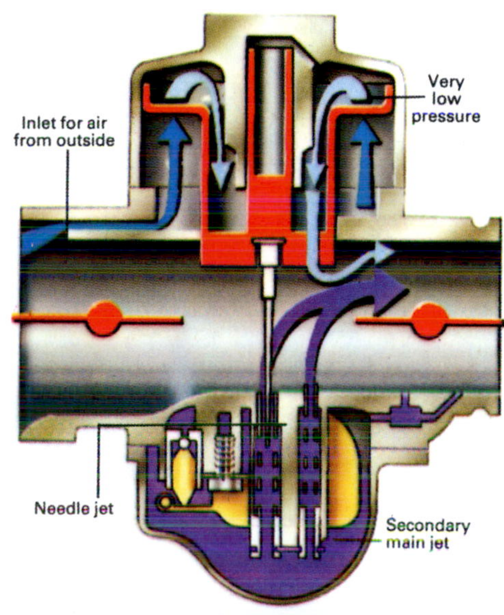

◀ The operating principle of a constant-vacuum carburetor. At closed throttle (top), the pressure drop is not quite enough to lift the piston and slide, and at full throttle (bottom), venturi depression is at a minimum and the pressure drop lifts the slide.

Controlling emissions

As engines have been developed to give better fuel economies, attention has also been paid to controlling emissions from various engine components. Hydrocarbons evaporate continuously from the fuel tank and the carburetor, so engines now incorporate an evaporative control system that recycles them. Essentially, this system consists of a canister of activated carbon that can hold up to 35 percent of its own weight in fuel vapor. When the engine is running, vapors from the carburetor are consumed, but when it stops, they flow through the air cleaner to the canister for storage. The process reverses when the engine is turned on, and they are burned in the combustion chamber.

SEE ALSO: Air • Automobile • Automobile electronics system • Fuel injection • Ignition system, automobile • Internal combustion engine

Car Wash

The first car-washing facilities appeared in the United States in the 1930s and were little more than conveyors along which the car was pulled while gangs of workers cleaned it by hand. One group applied detergent while another, farther along the line, rinsed it off. The space required, coupled with labor costs, made this an expensive operation. The first fully automatic car-washing machine was made in the United States in 1938; such machines did not appear in Europe until a German firm began production separately in 1964. Since then, a number of firms have produced variations or innovations.

A typical machine has three large cylindrical cleaning rollers made of very dense but flexible polyamide or polyethylene strands, the ends of which are splayed out. It is claimed that these bristles tend to flick away the dirt, whereas hand-cleaning methods are more likely to grind the dirt into the paintwork. The brushes rotate at speed, so that the strands stand out about 12 in. (31 cm).

The rollers, which are about 6 ft. (2 m) long, are arranged with one horizontal, to clean the upper surfaces of the car, and two vertical, to clean the sides. As they rotate, water and detergent sprays wash the car. The car is moved by a device such as a small roller, which is located behind one of the car's wheels, or else the car remains stationary and the roller frame moves over it. The latter system is cheaper and requires less space, but the moving-car system allows a continuous line of cars to be dealt with, giving a higher production rate.

Most sets of rollers are equipped with limit switches, usually operated by simple levers that control the action of motors. When the rollers meet with some resistance, such as the front of the car or even a fixed wing mirror, the movement of the roller over the car is stopped, and the motors drive the roller upward or to one side, "feeling" the way round the obstacle. When the obstacle is overcome, the limit switches stop the motors, and the motion of the car through the rollers continues.

In one system, the vertical rollers are pivoted at the top and are free to swing apart easily. The horizontal roller is counterbalanced so that very little effort is needed to push it up, though it will move downward slowly if left to itself. These rollers have no limit switches or motors, but "crawl" their way around the car as it moves by virtue of their rotation.

After the brushes have cleaned the car, either it can be driven away to let the water dry off naturally, or with the more expensive machines, driers are used. Some driers blow warm air onto the car to evaporate the moisture away. Others blow the water off while the car is still in a mobile state, using intense jets of air directed downward and outward. This method is more economical, as the volume of air blown and heating required is rather less than in the other system. The final rinse may have a chemical added to lower the surface tension of the water, thus aiding the drying.

Some machines may have small separate brushes equipped with separate switches that clean the car's wheels. Pillars containing sprayers that treat the lower half of the car with a degreasing fluid before the wash takes place, are also available.

Brushless washers

Commercial vehicle fleets sometimes use brushless machines, which consist of a narrow rectangular frame suspended from a hoist. On the inside of the frame are a large number of jets that produce a strong, finely divided spray. One of the cross members can be adjusted to the varying lengths of different vehicles in a single commercial fleet.

In operation, the frame is lowered around the vehicle and then raised, during which an acidified detergent is sprayed on. After a pause of about a minute to allow the detergent to activate, the process is repeated using an alkaline detergent. Ten seconds later, the vehicle is rinsed thoroughly with water and the frame is removed.

▼ An automatic car wash in which the revolving brushes move over the stationary vehicle.

SEE ALSO: Automobile • Detergent manufacture • Water supply

Cash Register

▲ A modern electronic cash register combines data from a bar code scanner, a keyboard, and a stock database to tally sales, calculate change, and provide information for stock control.

The first cash register was patented in 1879 by James Ritty, a restaurant owner of Dayton, Ohio. He intended his invention to discourage staff from stealing from the till by making the value of every transaction visible. Dayton's device had keys for registering the amount charged. A dial similar to a clock face displayed these amounts: the "hour" hand showed the number of dollars and the "minute" hand showed the number of cents. One complete revolution of the cent hand moved the dollar hand on to the next number. The design was inspired by a ship's propeller revolution counter: inside the case was a tamper-proof wheeled mechanism that accumulated totals.

In 1882, James Ritty and his brother John set up the National Manufacturing Company to build cash registers. Their machines were never commercially successful, however—in fact, they were widely regarded as something of a joke—and in 1884, the brothers sold the controlling interest in their company for $6,500 to John Patterson, who founded the National Cash Register Company. By that time, the Ritty brothers had produced a model that established the broad design principles of cash registers for the next 90 years. It had pop-up flags that appeared at the top of the case, making the price visible to the customer and assistant alike, and a paper roll that was pricked by pins in a coded sequence when the keyboard was operated. The roll provided the storekeeper with a way of checking the contents of the till against a printed record of the registered sales.

In 1906, a U.S. electrical engineer, Charles Kettering, added an electric motor to drive the calculating and printing mechanisms. Through continual additions and modifications, electromechanical cash registers based on Kettering's design survived until the mid-1970s, when cheap electronics sounded the death knell for mechanical cash registers. The first electronic registers heralded the arrival of information-gathering functions that storekeepers of Ritty's time could not even have dreamed of.

Mechanical cash registers

Prices are composed on a mechanical cash register by pressing keys for the cents, tens of cents, dollars, and tens of dollars as needed to make up the value. Pressing another key raises the pop-up flags or turns the numbered drums that signal the price, advances the tallying cogs by a number of positions that correspond to the digits of the price, and prints the price on the till rolls. When a cog completes a rotation of ten positions, it causes the adjacent cog to advance; so, when one cent is added to nine cents, the cents cog advances to zero and causes the tens-of-cents cog to advance by one position. In this way, individual prices are added to a running total that is displayed and printed by pressing a subtotal key. Pressing a total key at the end of the transaction sets the cogs to zero and releases the cash-drawer catch so that a spring can push the drawer open.

A second set of cogs keeps a running total of all sales, which can be displayed by turning a key to a position that is usually marked "X." At the end of trading, the total is displayed and the counter reset to zero by turning the key to a position marked "Z." The key that enables these functions is held by the managers or owners of the store.

More complex electromechanical cash registers have separate sets of cogs to record cash, check, and credit card sales. Further sets of cogs record refunds and "no sale" transactions, and the most sophisticated models can keep separate tallies for each checkout operator, department, or type of item. By the 1970s, even the most basic mechanical cash registers had more than 2,500 precision-engineered parts, which were mainly levers, toothed wheels, cams, and linking rods.

▶ Shown here without its cover, the Sweda Class 5000 was typical of the electric cash registers that were in widespread use until the 1970s. A cog mechanism calculated totals and change, and a separate device printed details of transactions on two strips of paper. One strip issued a printed receipt for each customer, while the other strip wound onto a roll used for auditing purposes.

Electronic cash registers

By the late 1970s, the complexity of functions expected of a cash register combined with the falling costs of electronics to ensure the demise of the electromechanical cash register, although many are still in service in smaller stores. In an electronic cash register, microchips and computer memory replace thousands of the moving parts of an electromechanical cash register; an electric keypad replaces the mechanical keys, and a digital display replaces the numbered drums.

The program of an electronic cash register supplies all of the functions of the most complex electromechanical cash registers and offers many more besides. Each item appears in the appropriate subtotals for the transaction itself, for the operator or shift, and for the method of payment. The cash register calculates the change due and prints a receipt that lists the individual prices and change calculation together with the date and time of the transaction. At the end of trading, the manager or store owner can print a report of total sales and subtotals by operator or method of payment.

Itemized keypads

In theory, each item in a sale could be registered by pressing separate keys for price, item type, department, and so on; in practice, so many keypad operations would overtax the operator and slow the pace of sales. Fast-food restaurants and other retailers who have a limited range of goods overcome this problem by using keypads that have a key for each item. The operator presses a single key that adds the price of the item to the running total of the sale as well as adding it to the sales tally for that item. The information entered on itemized keypads can be used to generate orders in a restaurant's kitchen or to call up goods from stock when an order is taken in a showroom.

This type of system makes price changes simple—the old price is changed in the memory of the cash register rather than on every item—and helps eliminate the keying of incorrect prices.

▶ Since the mid-1970s, electronic cash registers have been the standard transaction-recording devices for stores. This device has a slot at top left, through which credit and charge cards can be passed. Customers' banking details can be read from data stored in the card's magnetic strip.

Other information that can be entered by pressing special keys includes a department number, a credit amount, a discount percentage, the need to add tax, and the amount of cash tendered. In the last three cases, the cash register calculates and displays the discount, the tax, and the change.

At day's end, the shop manager thus gets more than just totals to check against the receipts. The cash register can also print totals and numbers of transactions by sales person, department, cash, check, credit card, and so on, all by specific time of day to the second, if necessary.

Item coding and bar codes

The number of product lines that can be handled by an itemized keypad is limited by the number of keys on the pad. Item coding uses a number to identify products, so a wider range of products can be registered: for example, a four-figure code allows for up to ten thousand different product lines, numbered 0000 through 9999.

The item code represents an entry in a database within the cash register's memory. Each entry includes details such as a price and a product description. When the sales assistant enters an item number, the cash register finds the price and product description in the database. This information is then displayed and printed on a receipt.

In recent years, it has become almost universal practice to represent item codes by bar codes printed on the packaging of products. A bar code is a series of parallel lines of varying thicknesses. The thickness of each line represents a digit of the item code. The bar code is read by a laser scanner: as the laser beam passes across the code, pulses of light are reflected back to a detector by the white spaces between the lines of the code.

The scanner can be a handheld device or it can be mounted in a checkout operator's desk. In the case of desk-mounted scanners, the item must be turned so that its bar code faces the scanner. The bar code is then read as the checkout operator passes the item over the scanner window. If the scanner cannot read a code or if it reads a code that cannot be found in the product database, the operator can attempt to register the item by keying its product number—located below the bar code—into the keypad.

Items that do not lend themselves to labeling include bread, fruit, and vegetables. In these cases, the bar code can be read from a card that has pictures or descriptions of the items next to their bar codes. If such items are sold by weight, they can be weighed on an electronic scale attached to the register. When the bar code is read, the register calculates a price from the weight of the goods and their price per unit weight.

Point-of-sale terminals

In stores that have several checkouts or sales desks, self-contained cash registers are replaced by a single computer that serves a network of electronic point-of-sale (EPOS) terminals. In some cases, the local servers of individual branches of a chain of stores are connected to a main server at a head office by standard telephone lines or by dedicated leased lines.

Such a system provides much more information than cash-flow figures: sales can be broken down by individual EPOS terminals, by individual stores, and by the entire company. These data can be used to identify weaknesses in store layouts and in store locations as well as to highlight operators who might benefit from training. It can be used to discover busy periods, when more sales points or sales staff should be available.

A network of EPOS systems allows price changes to be made on a companywide basis and promotions to be included in the pricing of items. These promotions might include discounts for multiple purchases of single items or for combination purchases of related items, such as meat portions and frozen vegetables.

With precise data available from each store, information about the sales of individual product lines can be used to adjust purchase orders from suppliers. Sales trends can help to gauge the impact of advertising campaigns, of price promotions, or of displaying items in new parts of a store; it can also help identify and discontinue slow-selling items.

EFTPOS

Computer networking has widened the possibilities for instant cash-free transactions using credit and debit cards. The mechanism for transactions of this type is called electronic funds transfer at the point of sale, or EFTPOS. A card-reading device at a point of sale reads information from the magnetic strip of a card to identify the type of card and its issuing company. If the card is a debit card that has no limit, the system simply dials up a central clearing house to confirm that the card is valid and has not been stolen. If the card has a limit, it checks that the value of the transaction does not exceed that limit.

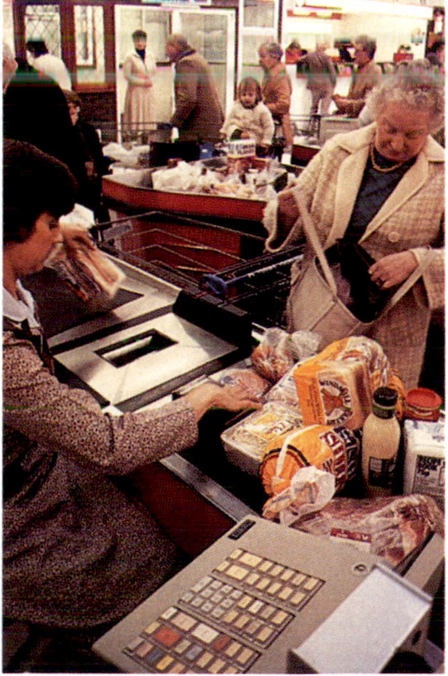

▼ A number of low-power laser beams shine through the glass panel in the desk in front of this checkout operator. When the bar code of an item passes through a beam, the white spaces between the bars reflect pulses of light. A detector below the glass panel identifies the bar code from these pulses. The keyboard is only used to enter sums of money, or if a bar code cannot be read or is not recognized.

SEE ALSO: Automatic teller machine (ATM) • Calculator • Cam • Computer • Computer network • Counterfeiting and forgery • Data storage • Electronics

Casting

◀ Steel wheels for railroad rolling stock are cast in large numbers on a production-line basis.

Casting is a process in which a fluid substance is poured into a mold and allowed to solidify so as to take the shape of the cavity within the mold. Making ice cubes is an everyday example of a simple casting operation. The commercial production, however, of high-quality, often intricately shaped castings required by industry, such as components for hydraulic pumps and engine blocks, demands expertise of a high order. Although certain types of pottery and ceramics are produced by a process called slip casting in which the fluid medium is a thick slip consisting of clay particles suspended in water, this process does not involve true solidification. The term *casting* is generally taken to refer to the solidification of liquid metals and alloys. Casting dates back to antiquity, and sites in Mesopotamia have yielded beautiful ornaments cast in gold, silver, and bronze dating from 2500 B.C.E.

Castings are produced in foundries or casting shops and are shaped according to their intended use. Ingots are the simple often rather rough shapes into which liquid metal fresh from primary extraction is cast. This term is also applied to the equally simple but more precise shapes intended for subsequent mechanical working into wrought components. Ingots are generally cast in metal molds: cast iron is widely used for this purpose, especially in the steel industry, although copper, often water cooled, is also used. An advantage of metal molds is that they can be used many times.

Cast products that will not be greatly altered in shape by any later process are known as castings, and they may also be produced from metal molds, although other mold materials based on, for example, sand, refractory (able to withstand high temperature) cements, or ceramics are probably more important. Castings are usually named after the mold material or casting process—for example, a sand casting is made in a compacted sand mold, and a centrifugal casting is produced in a rotating mold.

Apart from semipermanent ceramic or graphite molds, which can be used several times, molds made from nonmetallic materials are destroyed when the casting is removed. It is therefore necessary to use a pattern to make the mold cavity. This pattern is not usually an exact replica of the desired casting because it must incorporate various devices to facilitate the manufacturing process.

Casting is a versatile metal-shaping process because it enables intricate three-dimensional shapes to be made in one operation. The more complex the shape, however, the more difficult it is to produce the mold. One of the problems is undercuts. An undercut is a reentrant hollow or region that projects in relief, which, if no provision were made, would prevent the pattern from being withdrawn from the mold. There are several ways of dealing with this problem—by using an expendable pattern, for example—but the result is always a more complicated process and greater expense, so the design of castings has to take account of the manufacturing process.

Sand casting

Sand casting is the most versatile of the casting processes: it is used to produce castings in almost all materials in sizes varying from a few grams to several hundred tons, and it represents the major portion of total production. Sand used to make the molds is generally based on silica, although zircon and chromite sands may be used for more demanding applications. A binder such as clay, cereal, or silicate is added to give it strength.

The pattern, made of wood or metal, is placed in a box and the molding sand is compacted around it either by hand or, more commonly, by machine. The pattern is then withdrawn to leave a cavity of the required shape. To facilitate withdrawal, the pattern must be tapered, and its dimensions must allow for contraction when the metal cools. The simplest type of mold has an open top, but usually the cavity is completely enclosed by sand (apart from the small openings through which the molten metal flows): the mold must therefore be made in two or more parts, which are separated to allow the pattern to be withdrawn.

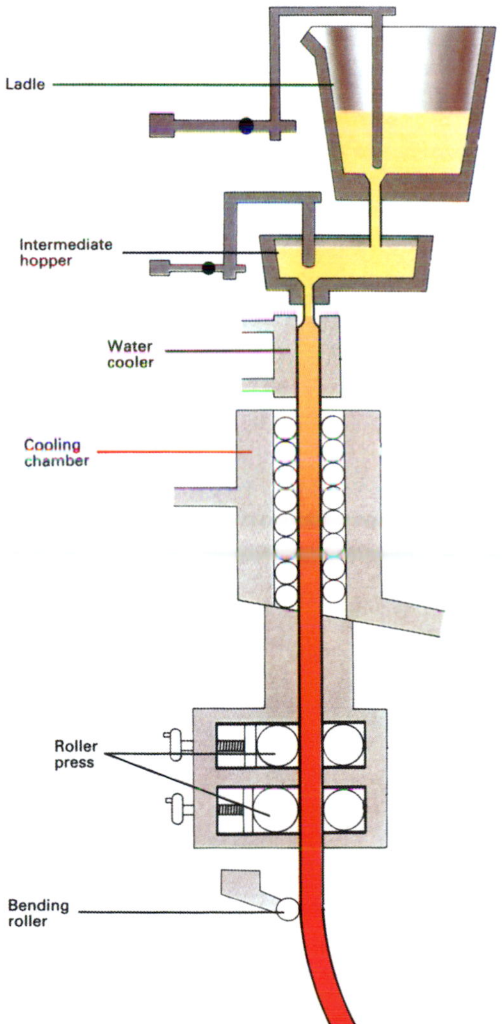

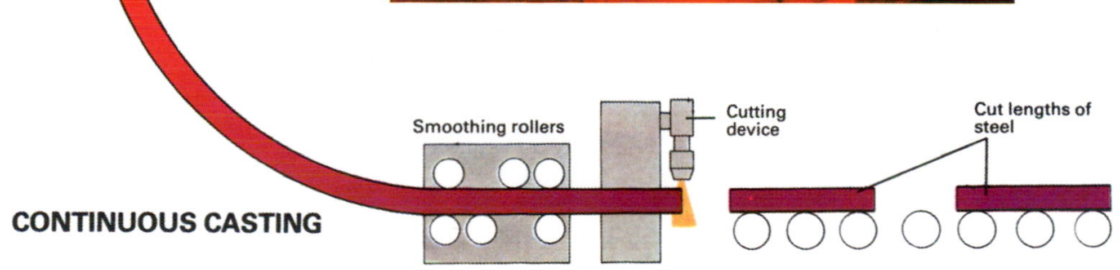

Shell molding

Shell molding, sometimes known as the Croning process, for its inventor, is a modified type of sand molding aimed at simplifying and speeding up the molding process by introducing a kind of mechanization. The patterns, usually of metal, are mounted on plates, incorporated into a shell-molding machine, and heated to about 400°F (200°C). An excess quantity of sand, containing a heat-setting resin as a binder, is then dumped onto the pattern plate. After a few seconds, a small thickness of sand has bonded to form a thin coherent shell. The excess sand is removed by inverting the pattern plate, and the pattern plus shell is cured in an oven at 570 to 850°F (300–450°C). The curing process is complete in about two minutes, and the shell can then be stripped from the pattern by an ejector mechanism. Two or more shells are stuck or clamped together to form the completed mold. This process produces an excellent surface finish to extremely close tolerances. The shell-molding machine and associated equipment are, however, expensive.

Investment casting

Investment casting is an important method of producing very precise shapes, generally in jointless molds, by the use of an expendable pattern. It

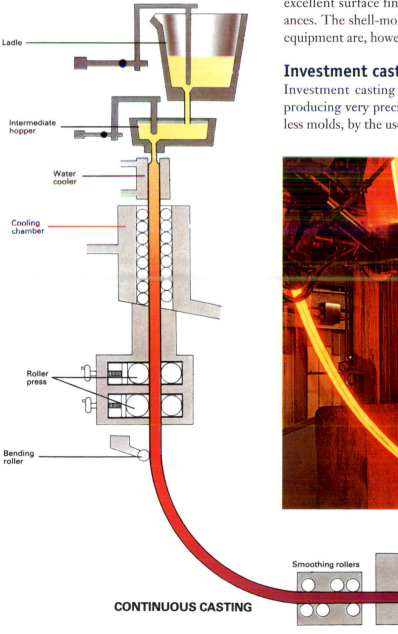

◀ The continuous casting of steel is a particularly useful technique for products such as railroad track. The steel strips emerge continuously from a vertical molding tube and are curved to the horizontal.

Ladle

Intermediate hopper

Water cooler

Cooling chamber

Roller press

Bending roller

Smoothing rollers

Cutting device

Cut lengths of steel

CONTINUOUS CASTING

is also known as the *cire perdue*, or lost wax, process. First used by the early Greeks, it is widely used by artists today for metal sculpture and statuary. The *Silver Lady* mascot adorning the Rolls Royce car is cast by this technique. In industry, it is known as investment casting and is used for the manufacture of precision parts in all branches of engineering, including the gas turbine and aerospace fields, where accuracy is essential.

The expendable patterns are commonly made by injecting wax or plastic into a master die and removing it when solid. Frozen mercury may be used in the same way. Precision castings are often quite small, so several patterns may be attached to a common runner to make an assembly known as a tree. This tree is then dipped into a refractory slurry of very fine silica and ethyl silicate to form a precoat, which may then be thickened by the addition of sand and a binder in a fluidized bed (ceramic-shell process). Alternatively, it may be directly invested into a suitable sand by inserting it into a container and surrounding it with the molding mixture (block-mold process). The pattern is melted out during firing of the mold, which is then ready for casting. For precision, investment casting is rivaled only by pressure die casting. The surface finish is excellent, and final machining is almost unnecessary.

FACT FILE

- *Evaporative casting is a modern technique used with aluminum, bronze, iron, and steel for one-off items such as sculptures and dies. A polystyrene pattern is carved from a block and compacted with sand in a molding flask. The heat from the molten metal decomposes the polystyrene, which exits as a gas from special vents.*

- *Hot isostatic pressing (hipping) is used to heal internal faults in metals such as titanium caused by defects such as shrinkage and porosity. Pressures up to 2000 atm. are exerted at sub-melting temperatures on the casting in a pressure vessel filled with an inert gas. Gas turbine blades can be rejuvenated efficiently and economically in this way.*

- *Intricate computer components can be cast by injecting metal powders mixed with a thermoplastic binder into the mold. The binder is chemically removed before final sintering, and thus one molding operation suffices where over a dozen casting and machining processes were used with previous more conventional methods.*

Die casting

Permanent molds are used for die casting, the molten metal being poured into the mold in a process known as permanent-mold casting in the United States and gravity die casting in Britain. The metal can also be injected into the mold under pressure, a process known as pressure die casting. Many aluminum, zinc, and magnesium alloy components are made by die casting.

▲ Sand castings are not very accurate and must be filed or ground to their final shape.

Gravity die casting is used to produce large numbers of fairly small, simple castings and in principle is similar to sand casting. It is not suitable for very complex castings because, being a manual process, removing large numbers of metal cores would be impossible. In contrast, pressure die casting is used to produce highly intricate, thin-section castings, such as automobile carburetors and mechanical parts for consumer durables.

Melting point

Casting is naturally dependent on the melting point of the metal, and the higher this is, the greater the problems. For example, the melting points of lead and tin, 620°F (330°C) and 450°F (230°C), respectively, are so low that these metals can be melted easily over a simple gas ring. At the other extreme, refractory metals such as niobium and tantalum, with melting points in excess of 3600°F (2000°C), are so difficult to melt that shaped parts are normally produced by powder metallurgy, which does not involve melting at all. Instead, the powdered metal is poured into a die and compressed at a high temperature (but below its melting point), causing the grains of metal to bind together. Sometimes the heating process is carried out separately. In the intermediate range, the temperature required to melt bronze, about 1740°F (950°C), is low enough for casting to have been practiced from very early times, unlike iron, which has a melting point of 2800°F (1540°C), beyond the reach of most primitive peoples.

SEE ALSO: Alloy • Aluminum • Bronze • Furnace • Iron and steel • Metalworking

Catalyst

A catalyst is a substance that speeds up a chemical reaction without being consumed in the reaction. Every year, the chemical industry manufactures millions of tons of products by processes that use catalysts. Important examples are the catalytic cracking and reforming of refinery products to improve the yield of gasoline from petroleum, the catalytic synthesis of ammonia from hydrogen and nitrogen (the Haber process), and the catalytic oxidation of ammonia to form nitric acid.

Concern about environmental pollution has led to extensive research into ways of controlling the level of pollutants; often a catalytic process helps reduce pollution by converting harmful substances into less harmful or harmless substances such as nitrogen or carbon dioxide. The catalytic converters fitted to automobile exhausts are an example of such a use of catalysts.

Many classes of chemical substances can act as catalysts. Examples are metals, such as platinum, nickel, and silver, and metal oxides such as vanadium pentoxide, chromium oxide, and alumina (aluminum oxide).

The substances that are encouraged to react by using a catalyst are called reactants or substrates. The substances that form as a result of a catalytic reaction are called products.

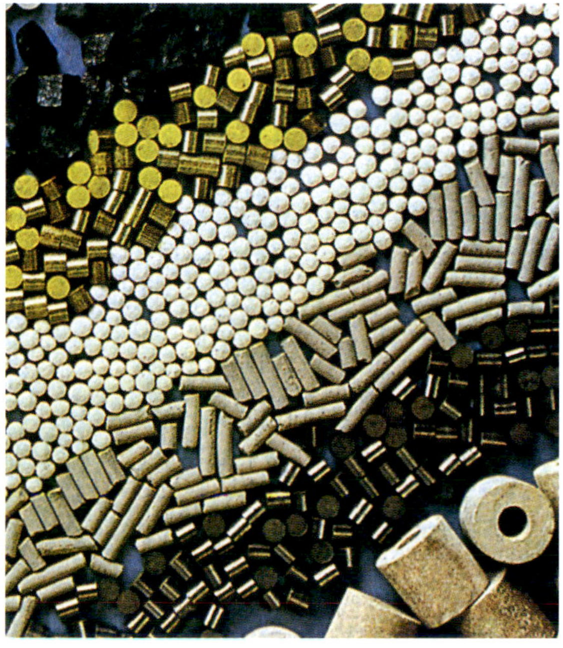

◀ Pellets of catalyst are designed to be packed into columns through which fluid reactants pass as they convert into products. The pellets must be able to withstand the pressure of the reactant flow without compacting together and blocking the reactor. In order to catalyze reactions efficiently, catalysts must present large surface areas, much of which may be within pores in the pellets. Precious metals are often spread on ceramic supports to increase their surface area per unit of mass.

Adsorption

For a catalytic reaction to occur, the reactants must be temporarily attached to the catalyst. In the case of solid catalysts, this attachment is known as adsorption.

The strength of adsorption varies from chemisorption, a powerful interaction in which chemical bonds link atoms in the reactants to atoms in the catalyst surface, to a weaker form of interaction, physical adsorption, where reactant molecules are attracted to the catalyst surface by intermolecular forces of attraction.

The ability of a substance to act as a catalyst depends largely on whether it can form temporary chemical bonds by increasing its valency. This is why many transition metals and their compounds are good catalysts: transition metals change between oxidation states more readily than other elements do, so they can increase their oxidation states to form temporary bonds with adsorbed reactant molecules.

Adsorption weakens bonds within molecules, allowing fragments to break away and drift across the catalyst surface to form new bonds with other fragments. Some combinations form products that then desorb from the catalyst surface.

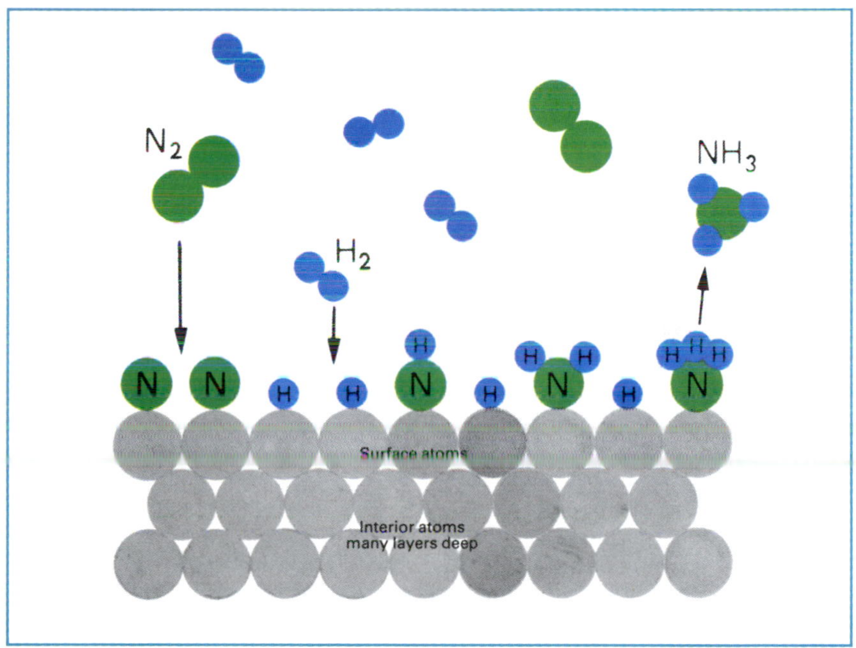

▲ In the Haber process, an iron catalyst accelerates the formation of ammonia by adsorbing hydrogen and nitrogen molecules onto its surface. Once adsorbed, the bonds between the atoms in these molecules break so their atoms can more easily form molecules of ammonia. Once formed, the ammonia molecules are released from the surface of the catalyst.

Although many aspects of catalytic action are imperfectly understood and are the subject of considerable research, it is possible to explain in general terms why iron is preferred for ammonia synthesis, for example. The iron catalyst adsorbs the nitrogen atoms just strongly enough for them to react with the hydrogen atoms. Other metals are less active catalysts for ammonia synthesis because they adsorb the reactant molecules either so strongly that they become unreactive or so weakly that too few atoms are held on the surface for them to have a reasonable chance of reacting together. The choice of catalyst for a reaction depends largely on trial and error.

Activity and selectivity

Catalytic activity is a measure of the amount by which a catalyst increases the speed of a reaction compared to its speed without a catalyst. In general, a mixture of chemicals will be able to react in a variety of ways, depending on conditions. Not all reaction paths will lead to the desired products, however, so an important factor in catalyst choice is how much it promotes the intended reaction relative to side reactions. This property is called catalytic selectivity. Highly active catalysts tend to be unselective, since they promote a number of side reactions as well as the main reaction.

Surface area

Because the surface atoms of a solid catalyst are the only ones to take part in catalysis, methods for preparing catalysts usually attempt to produce as large a surface area as possible.

In the manufacture of margarine, vegetable oils are hardened by hydrogenation—a process whereby a nickel catalyst causes hydrogen to combine with oil molecules. The active catalyst is prepared by first forming an alloy of aluminum and nickel. Treating this alloy with a hot alkali dissolves the aluminum and leaves an open structure with a surface area of around 120 sq. yds. (around 100 m^2) per gram of nickel.

When a precious metal such as platinum is employed as a catalyst, a small amount is spread over special support material so that a large area of platinum is available to act as a catalyst. Highly porous solids such as alumina (aluminum oxide) are frequently used as support materials.

Zeolites

Many oil refining processes rely on the acidity of aluminum oxide to catalyze the making and breaking of carbon–hydrogen bonds. Zeolites are aluminosilicates—minerals that contain aluminum oxide sites in a silicon dioxide network. The structures of zeolites resemble regular sponges formed by channels that widen into chambers where they intersect. Most of the catalyzed reactions take place in these chambers, which promote formation of products with molecular shapes well suited to escaping through the channels. This effect is called shape selectivity, and it can be modified by changing the type of zeolite used to catalyze a reaction.

The zeolite-catalyzed isomerization of xylene (dimethylbenzene) is shape selective. If a blend of 1,2-dimethylbenzene and 1,3-dimethylbenzene is fed through a zeolite at around 750°F (400°C), the product mixture will contain a high proportion of 1,4-dimethylbenzene. The zeolite allows the methyl groups to move around the benzene ring and favors long thin 1,4-dimethylbenzene because it passes through the zeolite channels more readily than its isomers do.

Loss of activity

Although catalysts are not used up in a chemical reaction, they can become less effective with use. For example, the activity of a solid catalyst can be considerably reduced if the catalyst is overheated. Under these conditions, a very porous structure with a large surface area coalesces into larger units with a much smaller surface area.

Catalyst poisons are substances that adsorb so strongly onto the surface of a catalyst that they prevent reactant molecules from approaching the active sites of the catalyst. Sulfur compounds act as poisons for the catalysts used in refinery cracker units, for example, so they have to be removed from the cracker feedstock by a process called hydrodesulfurization, whereby hydrogen converts sulfur compounds into hydrogen sulfide, which is easily removed. Hydrodesulfurization is catalyzed by a mixture of cobalt and molybdenum oxides coated finely on an alumina support.

The active surfaces of catalysts used for hydrocarbon processing can also be deactivated by coking—the formation of carbon deposits.

Regeneration

Poisoned, or coked, catalysts can often be regenerated, or restored to former levels of activity or selectivity, by treating them with hydrogen, steam, and air at high temperatures to remove carbon deposits and poisoning impurities.

▼ Bioreactors like this fermentation tank often use enzymes to catalyze reactions. Brewing is a prime example of a biologically catalyzed reaction—yeast is added because it produces enzymes that break down sugars and starches in grain and turns them into alcohol.

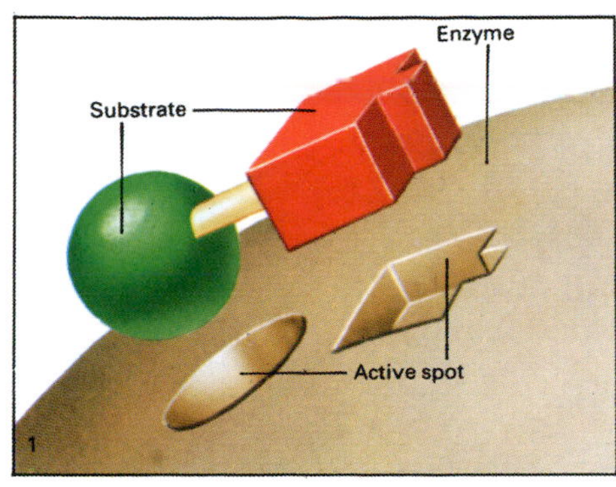

Binding breaking off
Substrate reacts with enzyme
2

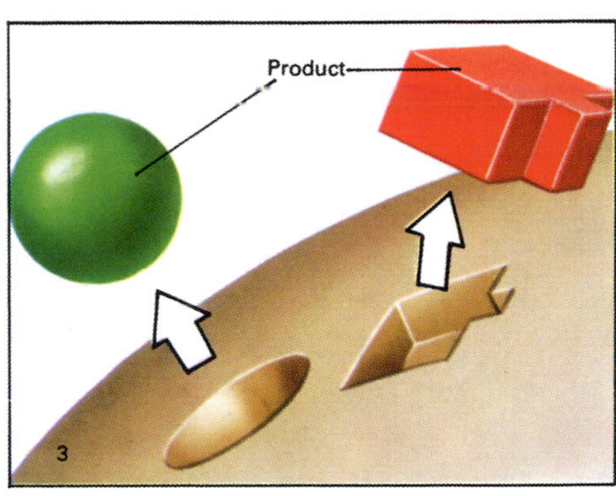

▲ Enzymes are catalysts that function in living systems. Their molecules form active sites whose shapes match their substrates, the substances acted upon. Once the substrate is in place, chemical groups in the enzyme cause the reaction to proceed. The products are then released. The shape-specific active site of an enzyme makes it highly selective for certain substrate molecules.

Promoters

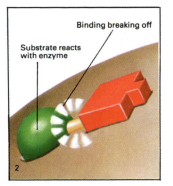

In 1909, after years of practical research, the German chemist Fritz Haber discovered that an iron catalyst prepared from magnetite (Fe_3O_4) mined in Gallivare, Sweden, produces ammonia continuously for longer periods than iron from other sources—thus it keeps its activity longer.

The cause of the sustained catalytic activity of iron from Gallivare is the presence of small amounts of impurities that are absent from iron obtained from other sources. Modern ammonia-synthesis plants use catalyst pellets made from a mixture of finely powdered iron and alumina; the presence of aluminum oxide has a performance-boosting effect similar to that provided by the impurities in Gallivare iron.

Many catalyst systems now include small amounts of substances called promoters that are added deliberately to boost the activity or the selectivity of the main catalyst.

▲ These catalytic converter elements reduce the quantity of palladium and platinum necessary for effective catalysis by spreading the metals in a fine layer on the surface of a porous ceramic honeycomb. The honeycomb structure guides exhaust gases over the catalytic surface without creating an excessive back pressure.

Homogeneous catalysis

The industrial process that uses solid catalysts to promote reactions between liquids or gases is called heterogeneous catalysis; it has the great advantage that the catalyst remains fixed in beds or cartridges, while the gases or liquids flow through, so subsequent separation is unnecessary.

In homogeneous catalysis, the catalyst is in the same physical state—usually gas or liquid—as the reactants. Homogeneous catalysis has the advantage that every catalyst molecule is active, while only the surface atoms or molecules of a heterogeneous catalyst can take part in catalysis.

Catalysis in aqueous solution, where all the constituents of the reaction are dissolved in water, is of growing importance in chemical processing. Ethanal (CH_3CHO), for example, is produced when a mixture of ethene, C_2H_4, and oxygen is passed through an aqueous solution of copper and palladium chlorides. In homogeneous catalysis, the favorable reaction path arises when a loosely bound complex briefly forms between the reacting chemicals and the catalyst. This complex then decomposes to give the reaction products and regenerates the catalyst.

Enzymes

Catalysts that are found in living substances are known as enzymes. They are complex proteins that promote the chemical reactions that occur in cells at temperatures and pressures far lower than those necessary for synthetic catalysts to function.

An enzyme has an active site that catalyzes reactions and is situated in a cavity whose shape is tailored to the molecules that it causes to react. This combination makes enzymes extremely selective catalysts, since they do not accept molecules that cannot fit into their active sites. Enzymes present a great resource for adaptation to industrial processes, for example, the enzymes in yeast are used to make ethanol by fermentation.

Ammonia manufacture • Automobile exhaust system • Chemistry, organometallic • Oil refining

Cathode-Ray Tube

A cathode-ray tube, or CRT, produces a visual display using electronic circuitry. CRTs are used, for example, in television sets, radar displays, and scientific instruments such as oscilloscopes.

A CRT consists of an evacuated (emptied of air) glass tube with a flat screen coated on its inside with a fluorescent material. At the other end of the tube is an electron gun (see below), that projects a beam of electrons down the tube toward the screen. The electrons striking the fluorescent screen excite the atoms of the screen's material and cause it to glow, producing the visual display. The intensity of the glow is proportional to the intensity of the electron beam.

With such a rudimentary tube, in 1897, J.J. Thomson, a British physicist, first identified the rays emitted by a hot cathode: small charged particles we now know as electrons. Using the same tube he was among the first scientists to determine a rough value for the ratio of electron charge to mass.

The above components could not make a useful display. The electron beam leaving the gun is divergent—it spreads out, producing a large dim spot on the screen. It must be focused by a system that makes the electron beam converge to a fine point at the screen's surface. A deflection system is also required so that the electron beam (and thus the spot on the screen) can be moved around.

Electron gun

An electron gun works on the same principle as the electronic valve (vacuum tube). It has three components: a cathode, grid, and anode. The anode is maintained at a high positive voltage with respect to the cathode. When the cathode is heated by a small element, it gives off electrons. Being negatively charged particles, they move toward the anode. In the center of the anode is a small hole through which some of the electrons pass, forming a diverging beam in the direction of the screen. The intensity of the beam is controlled by the grid placed between the cathode and the anode. By varying the voltage on the grid, the flow of electrons to the anode can be precisely controlled as required.

Focusing system

The diverging electron beam can be focused using either an electrostatic or a magnetic field "lens" in the same way that a glass lens is used for focusing light. In both cases, a carefully shaped field pattern is established that bends the electrons mov-

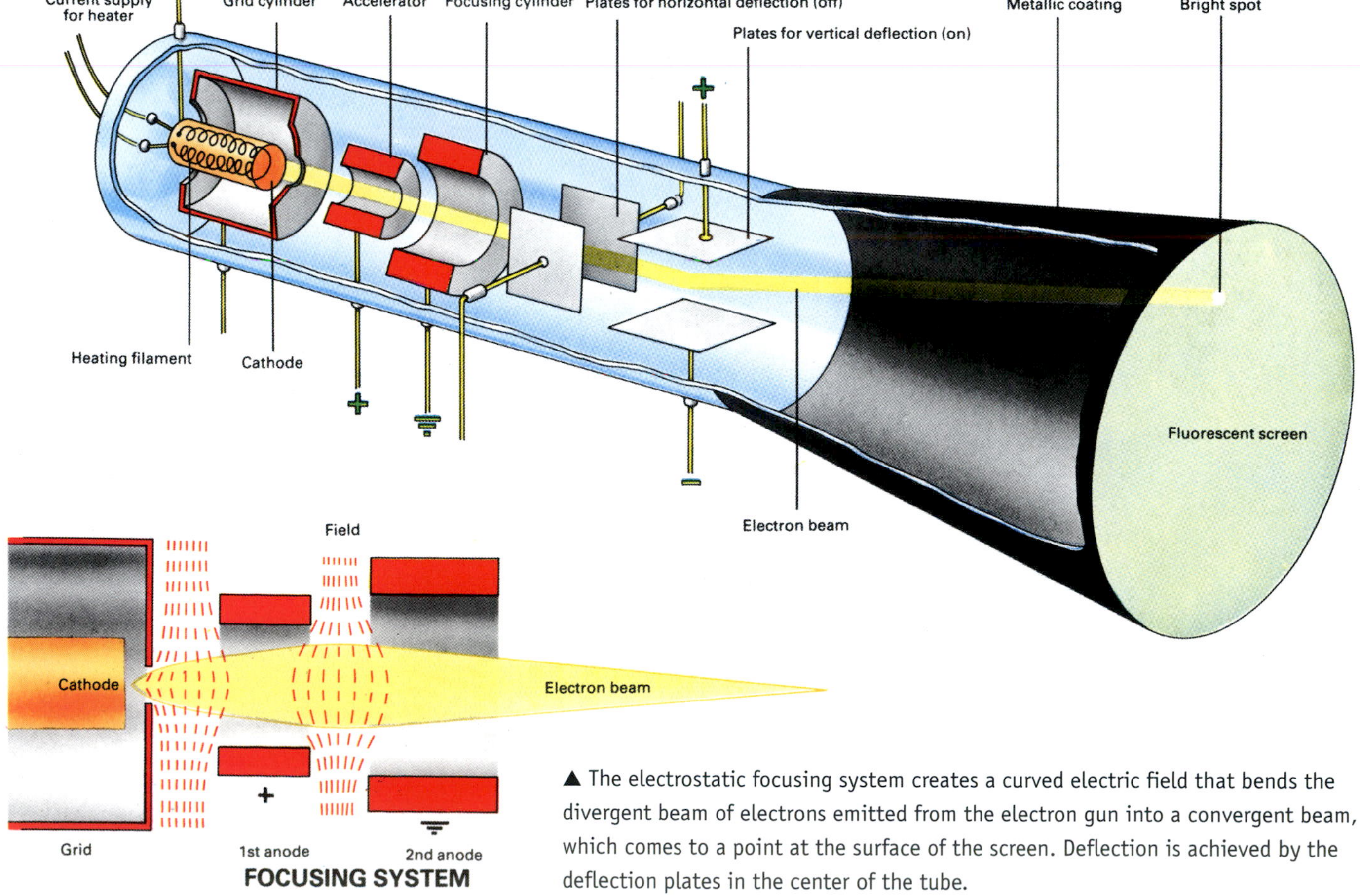

▲ The electrostatic focusing system creates a curved electric field that bends the divergent beam of electrons emitted from the electron gun into a convergent beam, which comes to a point at the surface of the screen. Deflection is achieved by the deflection plates in the center of the tube.

ing through the field into a converging beam. Deflection is also achieved using either an electrostatic or magnetic field. Two such systems are required: one to deflect the electron beam horizontally (left or right) and the other to deflect the beam vertically (up or down). With electrostatic focusing and deflection, the required elements must be positioned within the evacuated tube. With magnetic systems, it is possible to position them externally, making construction simpler and cheaper.

Fluorescent materials

CRTs producing black and white displays commonly use silver-activated zinc sulfide and silver-activated zinc–cadmium sulfide as fluorescent materials. When mixed in the right proportions, they produce a bluish white glow under excitation.

In a television receiver, the appearance of a continuous picture is created by scanning the screen with the electron beam in a series of horizontal lines—varying the intensity of the beam while scanning. Because of the speed at which this is done, the eye sees a complete picture with various shades of brightness—the individual lines being too fine and close to distinguish easily.

With television CRTs, the choice of materials is important because of a phenomenon called afterglow or persistence, in which the material continues to glow for a while after the electron beam has stopped. The persistence of the screen material helps to maintain the picture continuity between scans. Television screens are scanned at a rate of about 25 times a second. If the persistence, or glow time, is greater than 1/25 second, blurring will occur when fast actions are being displayed. On the other hand, a persistence much less than 1/25 second will lead to flickering as the picture fades away before being rescanned. Computer monitors scan down the screen in one go and generally refresh 60 to 85 times per second to improve image quality and prevent flickering. With oscilloscopes and especially radar displays the persistence required can be longer because the rate of change of events to be displayed is lower.

With color television CRTs, the screen is covered with a fine mosaic of three different fluorescent materials that glow with the three primary colors—red, green, and blue. Associated with each color is an electron gun, and these colors are arranged to produce a red, green, and blue image on screen that to the eye merges into one high-definition color picture.

Manufacture

Almost every cathode-ray tube is basically a blown-glass structure with a separate faceplate covering the screen, welded on under either a high-vacuum or an inert gas atmosphere. The small tubes used in oscilloscopes are much easier to make than the big-screen tubes used in radar, PC monitors, and TV receivers. The most complex tubes are those used in color TV sets. The screen, instead of having a uniform coating of material, has to be covered with phosphor dots precisely aligned with small holes in a thin metal shadow mask.

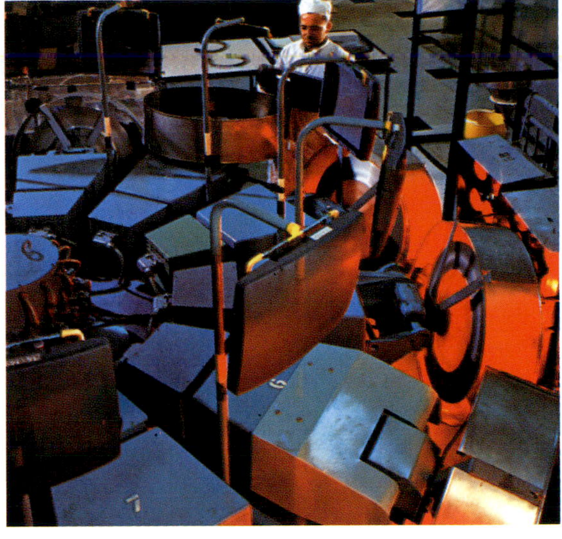

▲ The centrifuges used to deposit the color phosphors on the inside of the faceplate.

This mask is made from a thin sheet of metal—often a nickel alloy—with a light-sensitive coating on each side. Exposure to powerful lights through templates perforated with a fine screen of dots hardens the coating in a corresponding dot pattern, which, after developing and hardening, is etched with an acid spray to leave a precise pattern of some 400,000 0.01 in. (0.3 mm) holes. The sheet is then gently heated in a furnace to remove internal stress and press-formed to a curved shape to match the spheroidal shape of the faceplate.

The shadow mask is then welded into a strong frame that can be fixed to the glass faceplate. The faceplate has to be extremely accurate and free from internal stress. It is coated with a chemical emulsion that glows green when bombarded with cathode rays and exposed to bright ultraviolet light through the shadow mask, and then it is washed. Where the ultraviolet light has hardened the emulsion, a dot is left after washing. This procedure is repeated with phosphors, which will glow red and blue, with the ultraviolet light slightly displaced each time. Each phosphor layer is deposited while the faceplate is whirled in a centrifuge to ensure an even coating. After the exposures and washing, the result is a glass surface coated with dots of the three types of phosphor.

The cone-shaped molded glass part of the tube is made separately. It is tested for accuracy, cleaned, given a coating of graphite at the neck and a thinner graphite coat over the interior, and then edge-coated with a coat of frit (a mixture of chemical solvent and powdered glass) for the bonding of the faceplate at the next stage of manufacture.

Older black-and-white tubes were heat sealed at a high temperature. The delicate pattern of phosphor dots and the metal shadow mask of the color tube make heat sealing impossible. With frit, lower bonding temperatures can be used.

FLAT-SCREEN TV

Microminiaturization techniques have now shrunk the television set to the size of a wristwatch. The limiting factor used to be the size of the picture tube, but developments in tube design and picture display have rapidly reduced screen size. Newer designs of tube put the electron gun axis parallel to the screen. However, the beam clearly cannot scan the screen properly to form a picture without some trickery. A powerful electric field set up between a large pair of metal plates bends the beam sharply around onto the screen. Two pairs of parallel plates nearer the electron source take care of the vertical and horizontal deflection.

Developments in liquid crystal technology allow an image to be created without a conventional tube. When voltages are applied systematically to the liquid crystal filling in the screen's glass sandwich, images form. The molecules in the liquid normally lie randomly; light passes through the display and reflects from the metal foil backing. However, when a voltage is applied across the liquid, all the molecules align themselves with the applied electric field. Light cannot pass through, and the glass appears black.

Liquid crystal technology was initially widely used in digital watches, where the low power consumption of the liquid crystal display (LCD) allows a combination of very long battery life and continuous operation of the display. For the same reason, LCDs are now used in laptop computers.

Japanese technological advances have produced wristwatch-sized displays composed of over 32,000 dots with sophisticated electronics that enable the pattern of dots to show a recognizable and quite finely detailed picture. Although it is not a self-contained television the display module, which can be strapped to the wrist, has a television function in addition to the usual digital watch functions. The television tuner is a separate pocket-sized package connected to the watch by cable, and the antenna is hidden in a pair of headphones.

Another type of solid-state display has enabled full-color flat-screen television. Thousands of tiny transistors can be etched onto the surface of a slice of silicon by the same technique used to manufacture computer chips. Instead of being encapsulated in a protective block of black plastic, the bare surface of the silicon is coated with an electrochromic liquid and sealed inside a transparent envelope. Electrochromic liquid has the very useful property of changing color when a voltage is applied. The particular color produced depends on the size of the voltage being applied. Each of the transistors etched on the silicon slice influences the color of the liquid that is in contact with it.

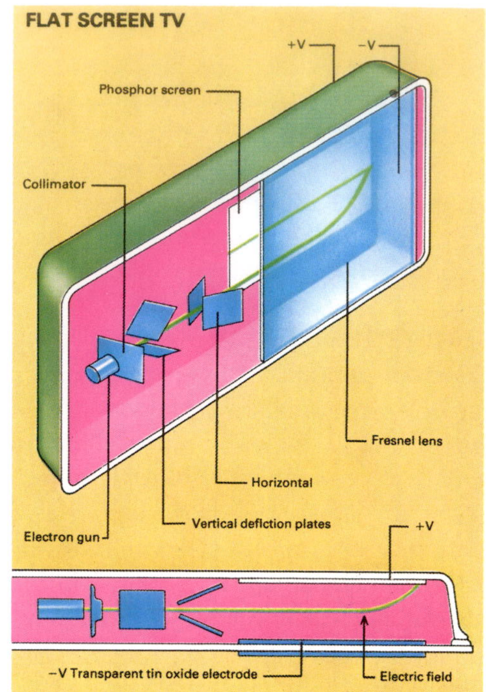

FACT FILE

- *One radar-imaging system developed in Pennsylvania incorporates multiple miniature antennas all over an airfield. Operating together as one huge antenna, they produce a screen image, via a minicomputer, that is so detailed air-traffic controllers can see whether or not incoming aircraft have lowered their landing gear correctly.*
- *Scan conversion tubes are CRTs that can convert radar blips into TV signals to be viewed on a TV screen. The signal comes in at one rate and is emitted for screening at a different rate, which allows an element of "storage." As a result the path of an aircraft is seen as a dotted line rather than as a single blip.*

Finally, the plate and shadow mask are frit-bonded to the conical part of the tube and sealed in an oven, and the joint is tested. The electron gun, with its cathode and its focusing and deflection plates is then fixed inside the neck of the tube. All that remains is to reinforce the tube against implosion (exploding inward).

In the late 1960s, the Trinitron color tube was invented in Japan. In this tube, the shadow mask is replaced by a metal grille with vertical slits from the top of the screen to the bottom. The three electron beams pass through the slits to the colored phosphors, which are formed as vertical stripes aligned with the slits. The grille directs the majority of the electrons through the slits, meaning that a much lower percentage of the electrons is intercepted by the grille, giving a brighter picture.

SEE ALSO: Computer • Electronics • Oscilloscope • Radar • Television receiver • Vacuum tube

Cell Biology

Cells are the basic units of life, the microscopic building blocks from which the human body as well as those of animals, insects, and plants are constructed. All cells share some common features, such as an outer membrane that controls what can enter or leave, but there are also vast differences.

Animal cells

Every adult body contains more than 10 trillion cells, microscopic structures averaging only a hundredth of a millimeter in diameter. No one cell is capable of surviving on its own outside the body unless it is cultured (artificially bred) in special conditions, but when grouped together into tissues, organs, and systems of the body, cells work together in harmony to sustain life.

Body cells vary greatly in shape, size, and detailed structure according to the jobs they have to do. Muscle cells, for example, are long and thin and contain fibers that can contract and relax, thus allowing the body to move. Many nerve cells are also long and thin but are designed to transmit electrical impulses that compose nerve messages. The hexagonal cells of the liver are equipped to carry out a multitude of vital chemical processes. Disk-shaped red blood cells transport oxygen and carbon dioxide around the body, while spherical cells in the pancreas make and replace the hormone insulin.

Structure

Despite these variations, all body cells are constructed according to the same basic pattern. Around the outside of every cell is a boundary wall, or cell membrane, enclosing a jellylike substance, the cytoplasm. Embedded in this is the nucleus, which houses genetic instructions in the form of chromosomes. These chromosomes are essential to the creation and maintenance of human life and personal characteristics.

The cytoplasm, although between 70 and 85 percent water, is far from inactive. Many chemical reactions take place between substances dissolved in this water, and the cytoplasm also contains many tiny structures called organelles, each with an important and specific task.

The cell membrane also has a definite structure, that of a lipid bilayer. Lipid molecules have an ionic head and a hydrocarbon tail. In the bilayer the molecules are tail-to-tail so that the ionic heads are in contact with water on both sides. Protein molecules are embedded at different locations in the bilayer. Some act as channels through which ions and small molecules can flow. Others bind chemical messenger molecules to initiate action within the cell. Some cells have hairlike projections called cilia on their membranes that move in unison to waft substances along in a particular direction.

The cytoplasm of all cells contains microscopic sausage-shaped organs called mitochondria, which convert oxygen and nutrients into the energy needed for all the other actions of the cells. These "powerhouses" work through the action of enzymes—complex proteins that speed up chemical reactions in the cell and are most numerous in the muscle cells, which need an enormous amount of energy to carry out their work.

Lysosomes—another type of microscopic organ in the cytoplasm—are tiny sacs filled with enzymes that make it possible for the cell to use the nutrients with which it is supplied. The liver cells contain the greatest number. Substances made by a cell that are needed in other parts of the body, such as hormones, are first packaged and then stored in further minute organs called the Golgi apparatus.

Many cells possess a whole network of tiny tubes that are thought to act as a kind of internal cell "skeleton," but all cells contain a system of channels called the endoplasmic reticulum. Dotted along the reticulum are tiny spherical structures called ribosomes, responsible for con-

▼ Every day a huge number of cells die and are replaced by mitosis; some cells are more efficient at this than others. Once formed, the cells of the brain and nerves are unable to replace themselves, but liver, skin, and blood cells are completely replaced several times a year. Making cells with half the usual chromosome number in order to determine inherited characteristics involves meiosis, where an exchange of genetic material between chromosomes ensures a unique genetic makeup.

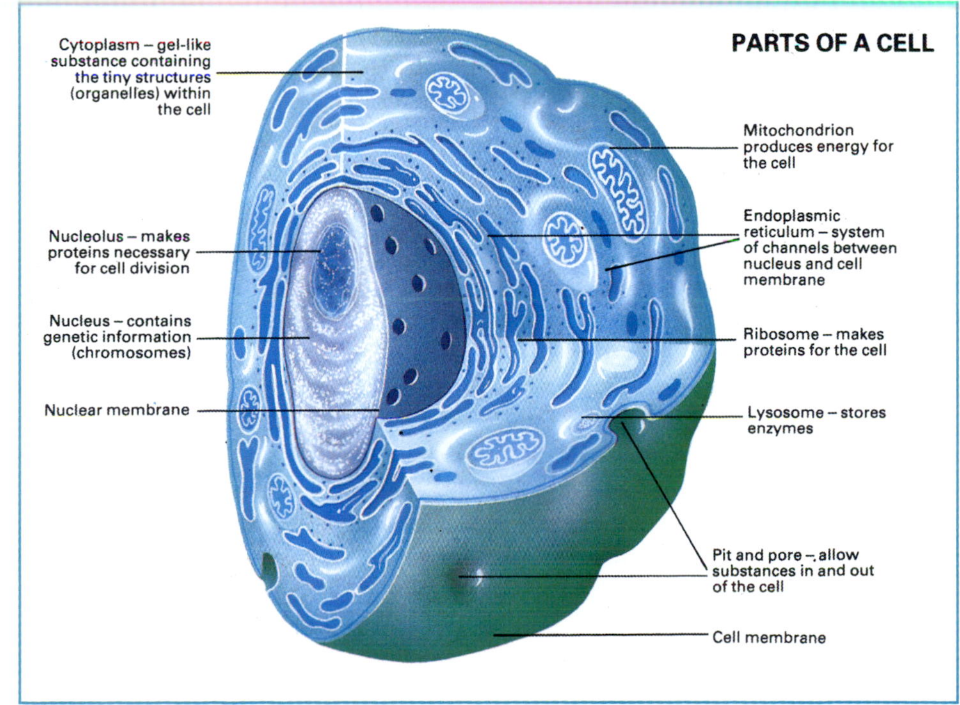

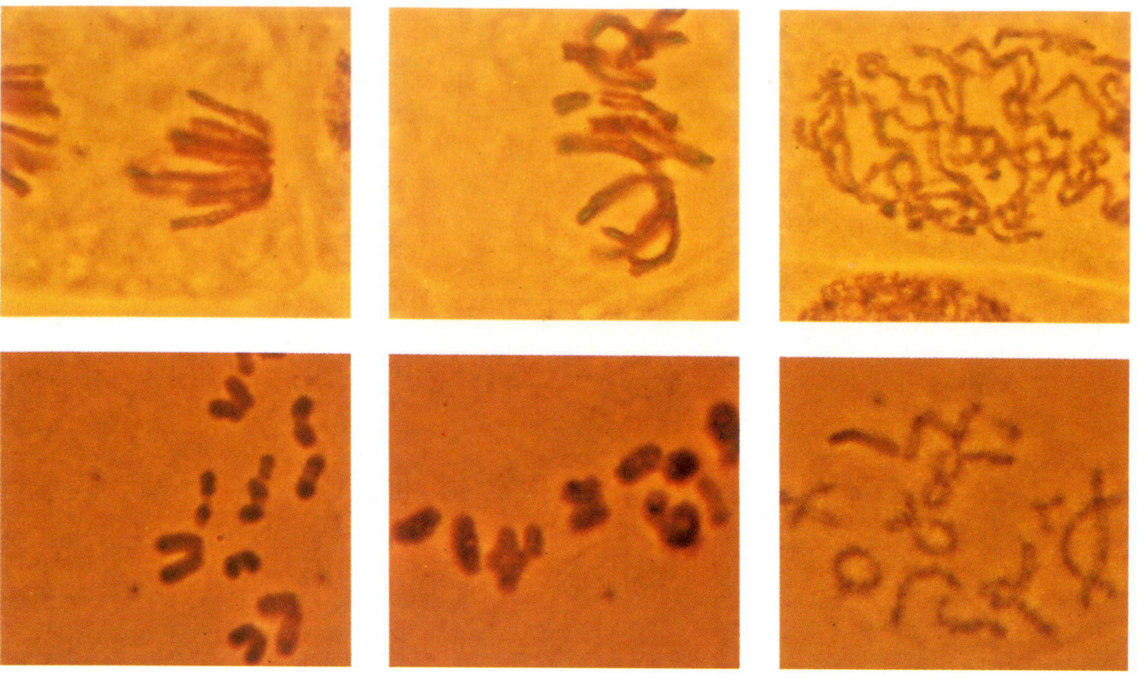

◀ Photomicrographs of the two methods of cell division. In meiosis (top), the chromosomes are duplicated, then pair up and intertwine before pulling apart and dividing to produce sex cells containing half the genetic information needed to produce a human being. In mitosis (below), when each cell divides, the two new cells contain all the genetic information necessary to replace or duplicate existing body cells continuously.

trolling the construction of essential proteins needed by all cells. The proteins are required for structural repairs and, in the form of enzymes, for cell chemistry and the manufacture of molecules such as hormones, to regulate bodily functions.

Plant cells

Plant cells are very similar to animal cells but contain an extra number of specialized components. Unlike animals, plants do not have a hard skeleton to support them, so their cell walls are tougher than animal cells to help give them rigidity. This strengthening is achieved by regular arrangements of cellulose fibers laid in a matrix of polysaccharides.

Inside the cell, much of the space is filled with vacuoles. Vacuoles are very large single-membrane vesicles that can occupy as much as 90 percent of the cell volume. Some are filled with sap and exert pressure on the cell wall to keep it rigid. Others are the location for intracellular digestion, and contain a variety of hydrolytic enzymes to breakdown macromolecules in the sap. Storage of nutrients and waste materials also occurs in vacuoles. Proteins are often stored in the vacuoles of seeds as a food supply during germination. Rubber is another substance stored in vacuoles, as are pigments in petals, scents to attract insects, and noxious chemicals to deter predators.

Chloroplasts are double-membrane organelles found in all higher plants. They are similar to mitochondria but are much bigger and have three separate internal compartments. It is in these organelles that the energy from sunlight is converted for use in driving metabolic reactions within the cell. This process is called photosynthesis and is unique to plant cells. Chloroplasts contain a pigment called chlorophyll, which gives plants their typical green color.

Chromosomes

Each cell nucleus is packed with information coded in the form of molecules of deoxyribonucleic acid (DNA) and organized into groups called genes, which are arranged on threadlike structures, the chromosomes. Every chromosome contains thousands of genes, each with enough information for the production of one protein. This protein may have a small effect within the cell and on the appearance of a plant or animal, but equally it may make all the difference between a person having brown or blue eyes, straight or curly hair, or normal or albino skin. Genes are responsible for every physical characteristic.

In humans, apart from mature red blood cells, which lose their chromosomes in the final stages of their formation, and the eggs and sperm (the sex cells), which contain half the usual number of chromosomes, every body cell contains 46 chromosomes arranged in 23 pairs. One of each pair comes from the mother and one from the father. The eggs and sperm have only half that number so that, when an egg is fertilized by a sperm, the new individual is assured of having the correct number.

At the moment of fertilization, the genes start issuing instructions for the molding of a new human being. The father's chromosomes are responsible for sex determination. The chromosomes are called X or Y, depending on their shape. In women, both the chromosomes in the pair are X, but in men, there is one X and one Y. If an X-containing sperm fertilizes the X egg, the baby will be a girl, but if a Y sperm fertilizes the egg, then the baby will be a boy.

Cell division

As well as being packed with information, the DNA of the chromosomes also has the ability to reproduce itself. Without this ability, the cells could not duplicate themselves, nor could they pass on information from one generation to another.

The process of cell division in which the cell duplicates itself is called mitosis. This type of division takes place when a fertilized egg grows first into a baby and then into an adult and when worn out cells are replaced.

When the cell is not dividing, the chromosomes are not visible in the nucleus. When the cell is about to divide the chromosomes become shorter and thicker and can be seen to split in half along their length. These double chromosomes then pull apart and their members move to opposite ends of the cell. Finally, the cytoplasm is halved and new walls form around the two new cells, each of which has the normal number of 46 chromosomes.

Cell communication

Multicellular organisms are made up of many different kinds of cells working together. In order to achieve this the cells must be able to communicate. In animals, cells communicate by releasing chemical messengers, including hormones that travel through the bloodstream to distant targets and neurotransmitters, which nerve cells use to signal adjacent cells. When these messenger molecules reach a target cell, they usually attach to a receptor, a protein that is part of the cell membrane.

This receptor extends through the membrane. The part exposed on the outside has a structure that exactly fits the shape of one particular messenger molecule; inside the cell, it has a structure that is able to interact with chemicals called effectors. Some receptors cross the membrane only once and are described as single transmembrane domain receptors. Others have as many as seven transmembrane domains. When a messenger molecule binds to the outer part of the receptor, it can change the shape of the entire receptor, including the inner structure. The inner structure then reacts with an effector, often an enzyme, that converts another molecule into a second messenger, which diffuses through the interior of the cell, triggering further reactions. Other receptors transmit their message across the membrane by transporting the messenger molecule itself through the membrane and releasing it inside.

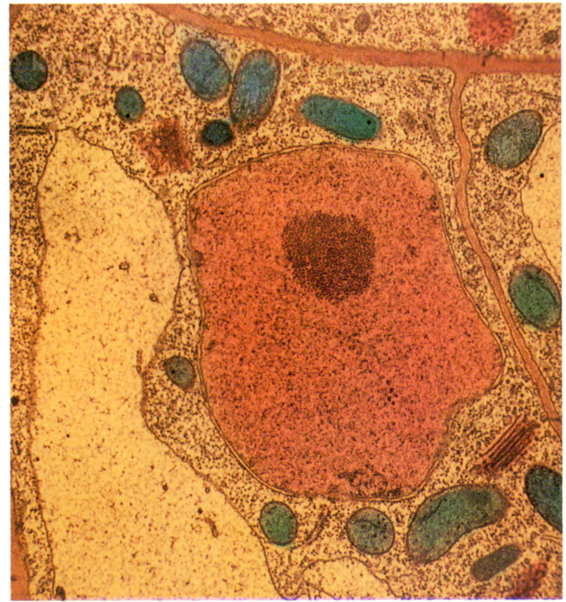

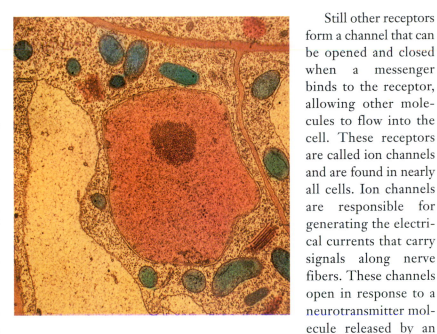

▲ False-color electron micrograph of a plant cell. The nucleus is shown in pink, and the cytoplasm in beige. The circular blue features are mitochondria, while the elongated green parts are chloroplasts. These, the thick cell wall, and the pale holes (vacuoles) distinguish this as a plant cell.

Still other receptors form a channel that can be opened and closed when a messenger binds to the receptor, allowing other molecules to flow into the cell. These receptors are called ion channels and are found in nearly all cells. Ion channels are responsible for generating the electrical currents that carry signals along nerve fibers. These channels open in response to a neurotransmitter molecule released by an adjacent neuron, or nerve cell, allowing sodium and potassium to pass through the channel, generating an electrical signal. In sensory organs, ion channels translate physical or chemical stimuli into electrical signals for the nervous system.

Biological roles of nitric oxide

Most of the body's functions are regulated by large, complex proteins and compounds. However, nitric oxide, a simple gas that is noxious, has been discovered to be an extremely important messenger molecule.

Regulation of blood pressure is a balance between dilation (opening) and constriction (tightening) of blood vessels. Blood vessels are dilated by neurotransmitters such as acetylcholine that cause the muscle layer of the vessels to relax.

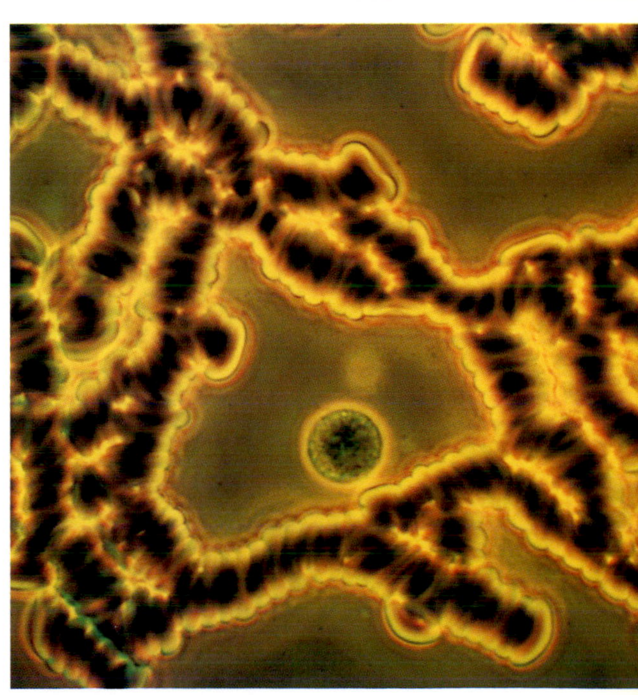

▶ Phase-contrast micrograph of human red blood cells clumped together with a granulocyte—a type of white cell—trapped between them.

Other neurotransmitters, such as norepinephrine, contract the muscle and constrict blood vessels. Because norepinephrine receptors are present on muscle cells, most scientists assumed the cells would also bear receptors for acetylcholine. It was found that acetylcholine acts not on muscle cells but on receptors located on the adjacent endothelial cells that line the blood vessel, releasing a small molecule that diffuses to the muscle layer to relax it. This small molecule was known as endothelium-derived relaxing factor, or EDRF until, in 1987, Salvador Moncada, a scientist at Wellcome Research Labs in England, demonstrated that EDRF is identical to nitric oxide. Nitric oxide is now believed to be the principal regulator of blood pressure.

Nitric oxide appears to play another major role in the brain. Glutamate, a neurotransmitter that is active at more sites in the brain than any other, is now believed to excite cells by a process that uses nitric oxide. The next dramatic observation was that nitric oxide synthase, an enzyme that generates nitric oxide from the amino acid arginine, is found mainly in neurons—specifically in diaphorase neurons, which make up about 2 percent of the cerebral cortex. The reason this distribution is so interesting is that these neurons alone resist the degeneration associated with several diseases. In Huntington's disease, up to 95 percent of neurons in an area called the caudate nucleus degenerate, but virtually no diaphorase neurons are lost. In vascular strokes and in some brain regions involved in Alzheimer's disease, diaphorase neurons are similarly resistant. Knowing how diaphorase neurons resist degeneration might provide treatments for these diseases.

It is believed that the neurons that make nitric oxide release it, and because of its toxicity, it is capable of killing adjacent neurons. However, the cells producing the nitric oxide may have intrinsic defense mechanisms protecting themselves against damage. Bernard Scatton and his colleagues at Synthelabo in Paris found that by injecting small doses of a nitric oxide synthase inhibitor into mice immediately after initiating a stroke, stroke damage was reduced by 73 percent.

Another unrelated activity of nitric oxide is as one of the major weapons of the white blood cells of the immune system, which use its toxic nature to kill bacteria, fungi, and tumor cells. It is also capable of inhibiting blood clotting by preventing the clumping of platelets.

For an apparently noxious compound, nitric oxide is involved in an impressive array of activities. Carbon monoxide, familiar as a toxic gas in car exhaust, is also thought to have some signaling role in a number of brain regions.

▼ Fluorescent dyes are used to stain specific cells in living animals. This is a photomicrograph of neuromuscular synapses—connections—in a mouse. The horizontal bands are the muscle fibers. The mitochondria within the motor nerve terminals appear bright green.

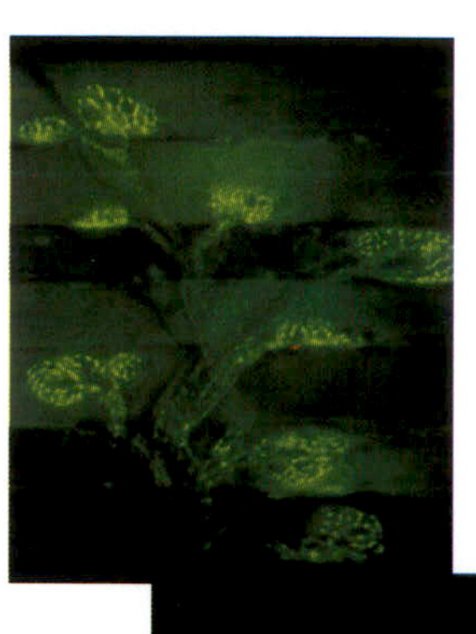

Growing new cells

Perhaps the most excitement in the field of cell research in the late 1990s has been the cultivation of embryonic stem cells in the laboratory. Stem cells are the parent cells of all body tissues, and this discovery may one day lead to replacement materials such as heart muscle, bone marrow, and brain tissue being grown to treat a wide range of human diseases.

The technique has been developed by two teams of researchers at Johns Hopkins University and the University of Wisconsin-Madison. The cells were taken from fetal material and human blastocysts left over from in-vitro fertilization and grown over a "feeder" layer of mouse cells. The cells were able to differentiate into the primary germ lines that make up body-tissue types—endoderm, ectoderm, and mesoderm—which then go on to develop into bone, muscle, neural, cartilage, and gut cells. As yet, this further development into specific types of cell is difficult to achieve in the laboratory.

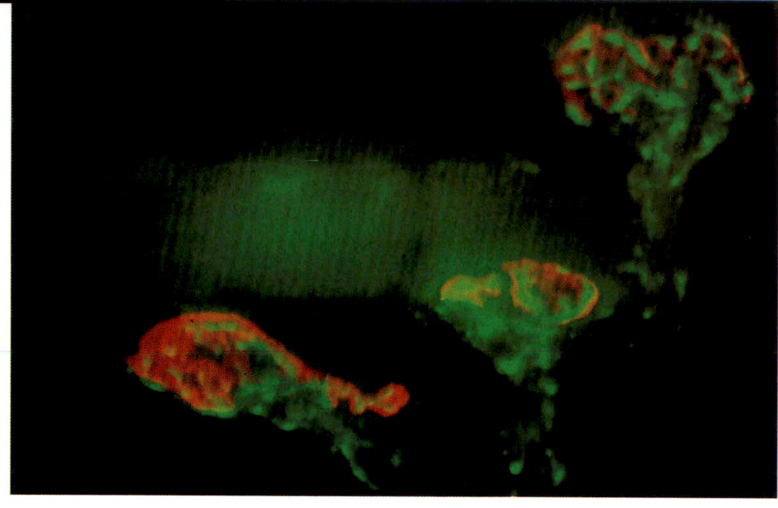

▲ A fluorescence photomicrograph of a young living adult mouse fiber stained to show the motor nerve terminals in green and also stained with rhodamine, which binds to acetylcholine receptors, coloring them red. This photo shows the link between motor nerve terminals and acetylcholine receptors.

Being able to grow different types of cells would open up a number of possibilities for medical treatment. Illnesses such as Parkinson's disease or juvenile diabetes that occur because of defects in a particular type of cell could be treated by replacing faulty cells with healthy ones. Another application could be in developing drugs. Being able to measure the response time of specific cells would improve the testing of new drugs by allowing the rapid screening of thousands of chemicals. Scientists also hope to make discoveries about the early stages of development of human embryos, discoveries that could be significant in preventing infertility, miscarriages, and birth defects.

SEE ALSO: Blood • Botany • Embryology • Genetic engineering • Genetics • Hormone • Life • Molecular biology

Cellular Telephone

A cellular telephone (cell phone) is a communication device enabling direct person-to-person wireless phone contact over the greater part of the developed world. By the year 2000, there were roughly 60 million cell phone users in the United States. It is expected that half the population—150 million people—will be using mobile phones by 2006. The Federal Communication Commission (FCC) is constantly under pressure to provide more bandwidth for this purpose.

The high level of demand for cell phones has also spurred rapid technological development, and cell phones have become simultaneously smaller and smarter. Dedicated digital microchips and improved miniaturized monitor screens have been developed that allow a range of functions, including direct access to the Internet, mobile video communication, and paging and answering service facilities, in a device small and light enough to be carried in a purse or pocket with minimal inconvenience.

One unresolved problem is the number of antenna towers required by the system. In 1996, there were some 25,000 of these towers in the United States, and predictions are that the number may rise by an additional 100,000. Local communities, while enjoying the benefits of a mobile telephone service, have often expressed annoyance at these unsightly towers.

▶ Not only can you talk to friends using a cell phone, it is possible to see them as well. This phone has a viewing screen and a small video camera (the circular object at the top of the phone).

The cellular concept

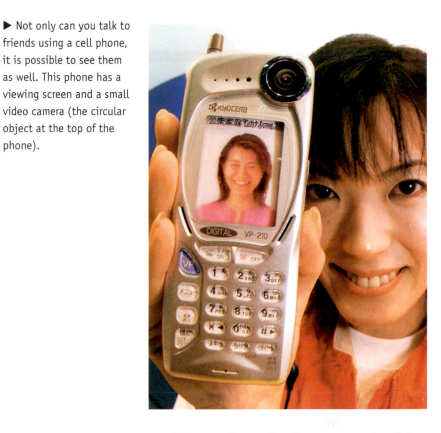

A cellular network is a telephone system that uses a radio link to connect individual users of mobile telephones to the main wired telephone system. Each cell covers a particular geographic area, usually several miles in diameter and has at its center a radio receiver/transmitter station known as a cell site. The site consists of a suitably located mast carrying antennas to receive the signals from mobile phones, to transmit them to other mobiles, and to connect them to the regular phone system. The area covered by each cell depends on a number of factors, especially the presence of obstructions such as high buildings or hills and the number of people using the cell. If, for instance, a particular cell has a higher than usual density of business or other customers using mobile phones, that cell would have to be smaller than average. A cell in a sparsely populated region could be much bigger.

The cellular system must allow for completely free mobility of phone users, but at the same time, it must ensure that there is no interference from other users. To achieve this goal, adjacent cells must use different frequencies. So when a user moves out of one cell area and into another, the move must be detected by the system, and the frequency in use must be automatically changed. This changeover is called handoff. Mobile phones are very low-power devices with a limited range, so a cell—call it cell A—that is separated by several cell areas from another cell—cell B—may safely use the same frequency as cell B. This important fact allows a very large geographic area to be covered by cells without requiring a proportionately large range of frequencies.

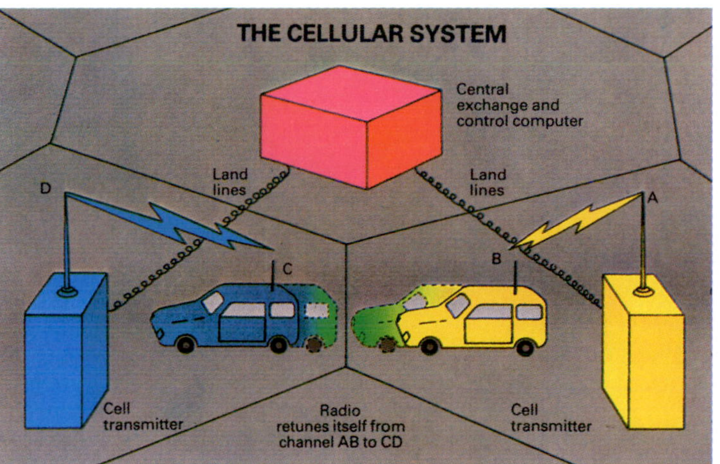

▼ As a mobile user crosses cells in the network, the frequency is switched by the central computer. Each clump of seven cells can reuse exactly the same set of frequencies.

Diagrams of cell systems conventionally show hexagonal cells fitting together, but this is merely a graphics convention. In real life, radio signals vary considerably in their effective range, so the cells are actually very variable in shape.

Technology

Cell phones are radio transmitters operating on a band of frequencies in the region of 900 million cycles per second (900 MHz). This band is capable of accommodating many hundreds of different frequencies. The wavelengths at these frequencies are very short and can be transmitted and received with adequate efficiency by antennas small enough to fit in mobile telephones. The efficiency of an antenna depends, among other things, on its dimensions relative to the wavelength of the signal concerned. Microphones and speakers are conventional miniaturized devices, and every mobile phone contains a central processing unit (CPU) or a smart chip incorporating a CPU and other microelectronics. The phone also includes a frequency synthesizer to provide the transmission signal, with facilities for immediate change of frequency under instructions from the CPU and the cell net; a read-out display; random access memory (RAM) and read-only memory (ROM); and a touch pad for dialling and entering instructions. Internet-access phones incorporate what amounts to a personal computer. A videophone also includes a miniature video camera.

Digital systems

Many cell phones currently in use still work on analog signals of the same kind as old AM radios. An analog signal is one in which electrical levels vary in a continuous manner. An analog electronic signal for a voice message, for instance, varies in step and in amplitude (AM) or frequency (FM) with the changes in the air pressure producing the sound. In a digital system for sound, on the other hand, changes are sampled and measured many thousands of times every second, and the numbers corresponding to each measurement are transmitted one after the other sequentially in binary form as a stream of pulses. Analog phone systems transmit and receive signals that are susceptible to electrical interference—as well as to eavesdropping. The analog system Frequency Division Multiple Access (FDMA) was the original U.S. cell phone system and, as late as 1994, was still in use by almost 100 percent of mobile phone subscribers.

Analog systems are now rapidly being replaced by fully digital systems in which both the control signals and the voice signals are digitally encoded. A digital system is almost entirely secure, produces better voice quality, and provides at least three times as many channels as an analog system. Therefore a service provider need not set up so many expensive cell sites or, alternatively, is able to accommodate many more users per cell. Current digital phone systems include the time division multiple access (TDMA) system and the global system for mobile communications (GSM). The latter system is in widespread use outside the United States, and it has been repeatedly proposed for adoption in America.

With the growing demand for Internet access from cell phones, a third generation of telephones (3G) has arisen using a system known as wideband code division multiple access (W-CDMA) working on the already agreed GSM standards. Very-large-scale integration (VLSI) microelectronics technology allows most of the electronics for such systems to be incorporated into a single microchip. This microchip permits phones with a wider range of facilities but with no increase in size to be manufactured. The third-generation phones include a 32-bit microprocessor with encryption facilities for security purposes, several megabytes of RAM, and transmission rates of up to 348,000 bits per second.

▼ Miniaturization of components and advances in microchip technology have enabled cell phones to be more than just a means of talking to other people. This model incorporates a minicomputer and can connect to the Internet.

Possible dangers

Although the microwave frequencies used for cell phones are significantly lower than those used in domestic microwave ovens and the power levels are very much lower, concern has been raised as to the possible radiational dangers to users of mobile telephones. So far, no positive evidence has been produced to show that the human brain can be damaged by radiation from cell phones. But research has shown that radiation from cell phones does have some effect on the brain. Whether this effect is harmful remains to be seen. A large-scale research project involving the United States, Scandinavia, and Britain designed to investigate whether danger exists, is expected to report in 2003. Until the facts are known, scientists advise that children should only have limited exposure to cell phones.

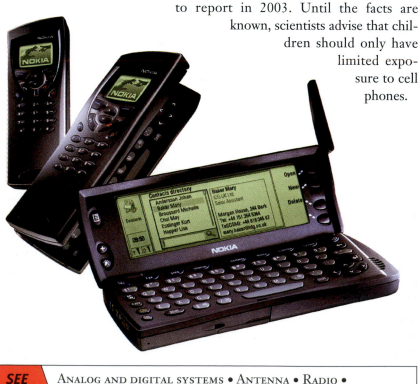

SEE ALSO: Analog and digital systems • Antenna • Radio • Telecommunications • Telephone system • Video camera

Cement Manufacture

◀ A cement works. On the left are the quarries supplying chalk and clay via the conveyor in the center to the plant. On the right are the cement silos, the slurry tanks, and the cylindrical rotary kiln.

The earliest builders tried to find compounds that would hold individual bricks or stones together in a structure so that the loading on them was suitably spread. Such a material is known as a mortar and usually consists of an inert substance such as sand, a binder (i.e., cement), and water, which renders the mass plastic. Cements currently used in construction are hydraulic, that is, they react with water to form a rigid structure, or set, and by continued chemical reaction, this structure hardens and develops strength even when used under water. If a large aggregate of crushed rock or gravel is incorporated, concrete is produced, and this concrete can completely replace stone in large structures. Since concrete is cast as a plastic mass, the opportunities for using it in design and construction are considerable at acceptable cost.

Early cements

The Egyptians used a mortar based on gypsum plaster—obtained by heating gypsum, a calcium sulfate ($CaSO_4{\cdot}2H_2O$)—in building the pyramids, but plaster can be used only in dry conditions. Calcium hydroxide, $Ca(OH)_2$, also known as slaked lime, was used by the Greeks and Romans as a mortar in many of their buildings and made by heating limestone, which is mostly calcium carbonate ($CaCO_3$), to form lime (calcium oxide, CaO). The lime is then slaked, that is, reacted with water. Unfortunately, mortar made with slaked lime tends to crack and crumble when exposed to weather, but both the Greeks and the Romans developed a much more satisfactory hydraulic cement based on lime and a reactive volcanic ash, the latter found in particular near the Italian town of Pozzuoli. Ash, which slowly reacts with lime to set and harden when water is added, is described as pozzolanic. The Romans also used concrete, the Colosseum being an early example of its use. Similar cements, using trass, a material similar to pozzolana found in northern Europe, remained in use until the late 18th century, although quality deteriorated after the collapse of the Roman Empire because the importance of careful formulation and dense compaction were not appreciated. John Smeaton, an English civil engineer who was commissioned to rebuild the Eddystone lighthouse off the coast of Cornwall, Britain, experimented with hydraulic lime made by heating limestone and clay to eliminate water and carbon dioxide and found a product that was superior to pozzolanic cement for underwater use.

In 1824, Joseph Aspdin, an English stonemason took out a patent in Britain on a process for making Portland cement, so-called because of the similarity in color between the set cement and Portland stone. Aspdin's process used a higher temperature than had been used before and produced a cement that had a much improved strength over previous materials.

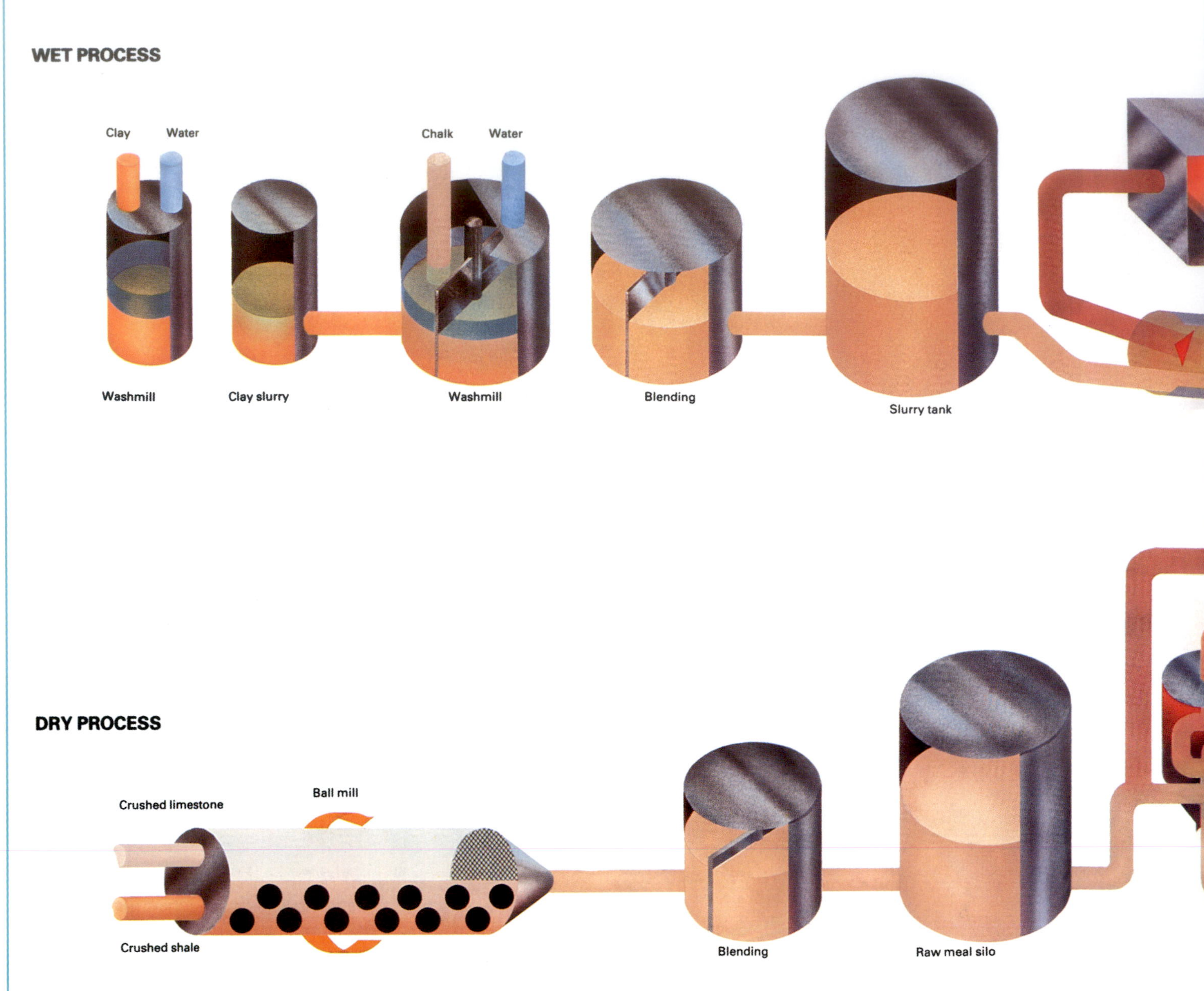

Production

As a manufactured material, cement is relatively inexpensive. The raw materials needed are chalk or limestone, the source of lime, and clay or shale, the source of silica (SiO_2) and of aluminum and iron oxides (Al_2O_3 and Fe_2O_3). Silica is generally present both in the complex clay mineral structure and as quartz. Marl, which is a natural mix of chalk and clay, is often used, but adjustment of the composition by blending is necessary. Small amounts of "imported" raw materials such as sand and iron oxide are sometimes necessary to adjust the composition.

The composition of the input into the kiln is carefully controlled to ensure an end product with suitable properties. The raw materials are reduced in particle size by crushing and grinding and thoroughly mixed. When they have a high moisture content (often in excess of 20 percent in southeast Britain), they are blended as a slurry (30 to 35 percent water), and in the wet process, the slurry is fed directly into an inclined rotary kiln. Heat is usually supplied by burning powdered coal that is blown into the kiln through the firing pipe. Natural gas and oil are less frequently used owing to cost.

In the first section of the kiln, the water is evaporated by heat supplied by the combustion gases. In the middle section, the clay minerals and the calcium carbonate are decomposed as the material temperature rises to 1650°F (900°C). Finally, close to the flame at temperatures of 2550 to 2730°F (1400–1500°C), the lime combines with the other oxides as about a quarter of the materials melts to form the clinker (lumps of cement). A wet process kiln may be up to 600 ft.

▲ Cement can be manufactured either by a wet or dry process. The wet process (top) is used when the materials are chalk and clay. Water is added to the chalk before blending to form a slurry. The mixture is then pumped to a rotary kiln where the water is boiled off and it is converted to

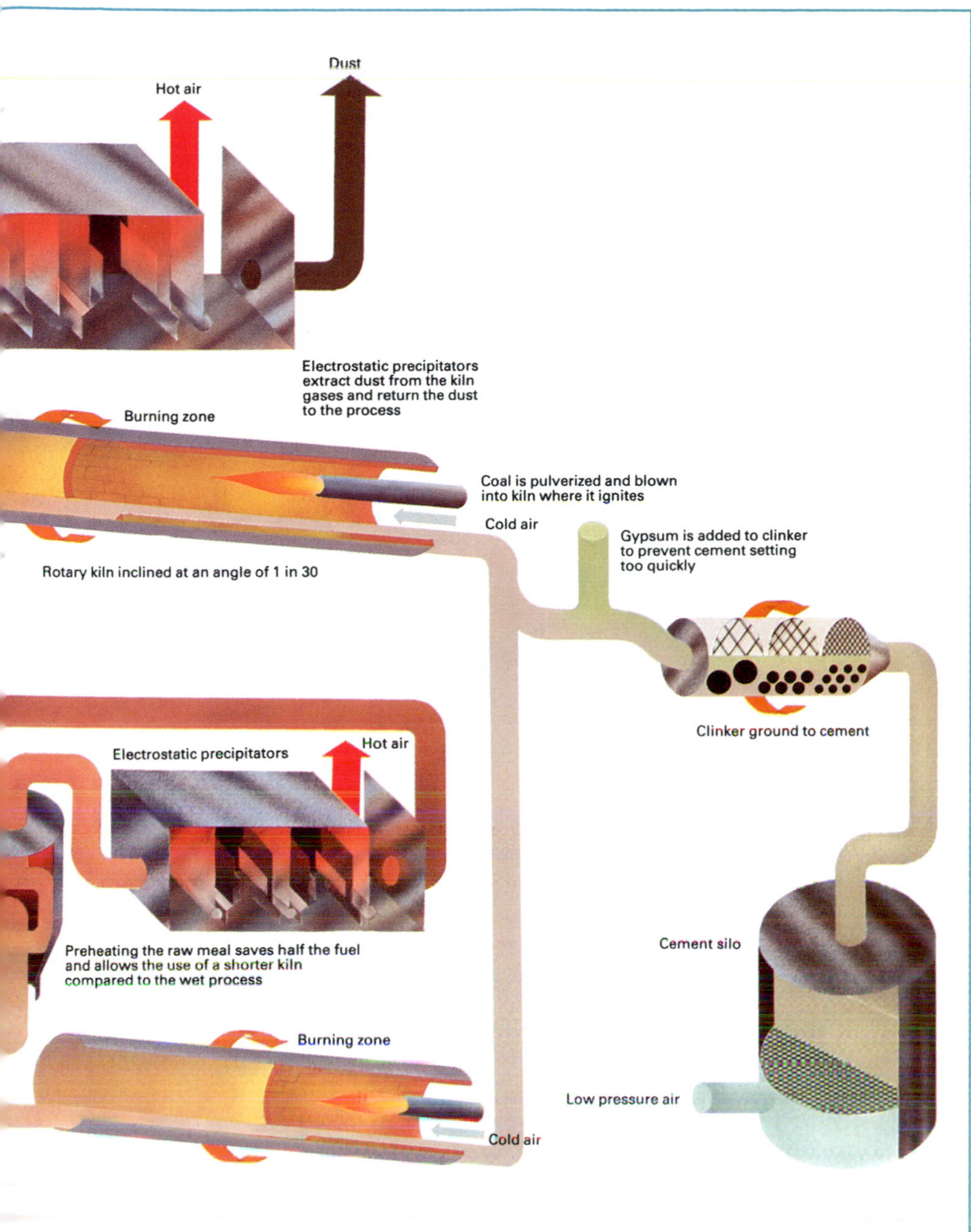
Hot air
Dust
Electrostatic precipitators extract dust from the kiln gases and return the dust to the process
Burning zone
Coal is pulverized and blown into kiln where it ignites
Cold air
Gypsum is added to clinker to prevent cement setting too quickly
Rotary kiln inclined at an angle of 1 in 30
Clinker ground to cement
Electrostatic precipitators
Hot air
Cement silo
Preheating the raw meal saves half the fuel and allows the use of a shorter kiln compared to the wet process
Burning zone
Low pressure air
Cold air

clinker at temperatures of over 1800°F (1000°C). The dry process (bottom) is used for harder raw materials such as limestone and shale. They are ground into raw meal, preheated, and then passed through the kiln. The clinker is then ground to form cement.

(180 m) long by 20 ft. (6 m) in diameter, these dimensions being determined by the throughput required and the amount of heat to be transferred for evaporation of water, calcining, and fusion.

Because the wet process involves the evaporation of a large quantity of water, fuel consumption is high—about 0.2 tons standard coal per ton (0.18 tonnes/tonne) of clinker—and the process is now largely obsolete. In the semiwet process, the slurry is filtered under pressure after removal of the flint if present, and the resulting cake is fed to a shorter kiln to make the clinker.

Where drier hard materials such as limestone and shale are employed, they are crushed, dried, placed into a mill, and ground together. After further blending, the powdered mix is transferred to a short kiln through a system of heat exchangers in which cyclones move the powder against the hot gas stream and capture dust blown back out of the kiln. At its best, fuel consumption approaches 0.1 ton standard coal per ton (0.09 tonnes/tonne) of clinker.

Cement clinker is most often in the form of spherical lumps (nodules) produced as a result of the consolidating action of the melt and rolling in the kiln. It is cooled by passing air through it to provide preheated combustion air. To produce Portland cement, clinker is ground with about 5 percent natural gypsum in a cylindrical ball mill. The energy consumed is considerable. A modern mill will draw more than 4,000 kW and total energy usage is of the order of 30 kWh per ton for ordinary Portland cement fineness.

As the manufacture of Portland cement involves much movement of fine powders, it is necessary to prevent dust emission at all stages. Dust carried out of the kiln system by fast-moving combustion gases (chiefly carbon dioxide and nitrogen) is usually removed from the gas stream by electrostatic precipitators. Particles of dust are charged as they pass through a negative corona discharge produced by an electric potential of 40 to 70 kilovolts (mean), and they are collected when they migrate to the grounded electrodes. Bag filters, which function like giant vacuum cleaners, are favored in the United States for cleaning stack gases, and smaller units are widely used to clean air wherever handling creates airborne dust.

Chemistry

The main chemical constituents of Portland cement are tricalcium silicate (Ca_3SiO_5), dicalcium silicate (Ca_2SiO_4), tricalcium aluminate ($Ca_3Al_2O_6$), and a solid solution with a composition usually approximating to $4CaO{\cdot}Al_2O_3\ Fe_2O_3$, that is tetra calcium aluminoferrite. Very approximate percentages of these compounds in clinker are 60:20:10:10.

During manufacture, the chemical composition is monitored at several stages. A modern plant will employ rapid X-ray fluorescence analysis to check the raw material mix and the clinker produced. Also, before a cement can be sold as ordinary Portland as specified in the national standard, it must meet a number of chemical and physical requirements. In particular, too much unreacted lime can lead to unsound concrete. It must also be tested for minimum strength in a specified concrete mix cured under water in the laboratory for standard defined periods.

Tricalcium silicate is the most hydraulic constituent, and it contributes most to early strength development in the hardening processes occurring when cement reacts with water. This reaction—hydration, or more strictly, hydrolysis—involves the formation of calcium hydroxide and a calcium silicate hydrate with an ill-defined composition approximate to $3CaO_2{\cdot}SiO_2{\cdot}4H_2O$. Particles of the latter are extremely fine but form tightly packed clusters. The gypsum in Portland cement is a regulating agent that prevents the too rapid hydration of tricalcium aluminate, so it prolongs the dormant period during which a mortar or concrete mix remains plastic enough for placing and compaction.

The products of the reaction of cement and water gradually fill the space previously occupied by water to form an interlocking mass of calcium hydroxide embedded in the fine silicate hydrate together with much smaller amounts of hydrated calcium sulfoaluminates, which also contain iron. The forces holding the mass together are not properly understood, but the fine, colloidal nature of the calcium silicate hydrate probably accounts for the wide range of water-to-cement ratios at which useful strength development occurs. However, the lowest ratio compatible with proper compaction should be employed as this not only maximizes strength but also produces concrete with low permeability. While the strength in compression achievable in hardened cement paste is very high (about 150 N/mm^2), that in flexure is low (about 15 N/mm^2), indicating that the bond between the solid particles is relatively weak.

Where concrete is going to be subjected to flexing, steel rods are embedded in it, yielding reinforced concrete. The alkaline nature of hardened cement paste passivates the steel (greatly increases its resistance to rusting), but as carbon dioxide penetrates the concrete, this effect is greatly reduced because calcium hydroxide is converted to calcium carbonate. It is important, therefore, that the concrete covering the steel is of sufficient thickness and high density.

The hydration of Portland cement produces a considerable amount of heat so that when a considerable thickness of concrete is to be poured, as in the construction of a dam, a somewhat more coarsely ground low-heat cement, which has a reduced tricalcium silicate content, is employed, thus avoiding the cracking that can occur on cooling if the core of a structure gets too hot. On the other hand, where smaller precast concrete objects are being manufactured (such as beams or paving), a finer, rapidly hardening Portland cement is usually employed to shorten the time between casting and unmolding.

◀ A rotating ball mill in which limestone and shale are crushed in the dry process to form raw meal. The meal is heated in a kiln to form the clinker—lumps of cement—which is then cooled and made into cement powder by grinding it finely in a mill.

Distribution

Cement is manufactured as close as possible to the quarries supplying the raw materials. The loss in weight accompanying the removal of carbon dioxide from the limestone, structural hydroxyl groups from the clay minerals, and moisture from both is of the order of at least one-third of their total weight, so transport of cement is more economical than transport of raw materials. Nevertheless, cement is not usually manufactured far from its markets because distribution costs are high. Bulk delivery of cement is possible because it can be fluidized by air and then pumped from a tanker at high speed.

Developments in cement

Every age has its own choice materials—from stone, wood, and bronze to steel, concrete, and plastics. Scientists now believe that some of the properties they have discovered about cement could lead to a renaissance in its use.

Stone and other inorganic materials of Earth's crust are easily obtained and provide the most energy-efficient products in the world. If, instead of metals and plastics, cement could be used for similar products, the world's energy bill would plummet. In fact, cement has many attractive features. It is made from the most abundant elements on Earth—elements that occur widely throughout the entire world. Molded easily into different shapes, it is resistant to fire and corrosion, and its extensive use in buildings illustrates its great compressive strength.

Unfortunately, cement is known to have several disadvantages. Chief among these is its outstanding weakness to bending or stretching forces. It is inferior to metals and plastics in both strength and toughness and shatters easily even when dropped on the floor. The first attempts to surmount these difficulties involved reinforcing cement with other materials. Steel rods and nets have been used successfully since the 19th century.

During the 20th century, asbestos, glass, and plastic fibers were used as reinforcement with varying degrees of success. Reinforced cements, however, have a severe limitation—as more fibers are added, the material becomes more difficult to mold. Moreover, the material is highly anisotropic—its properties are different in different directions. Along the length of the fiber, the cement has high-tensile (stretching) and bending strength, but at right angles to this direction, the properties are poor, and they can even be worse than those of the nonreinforced material.

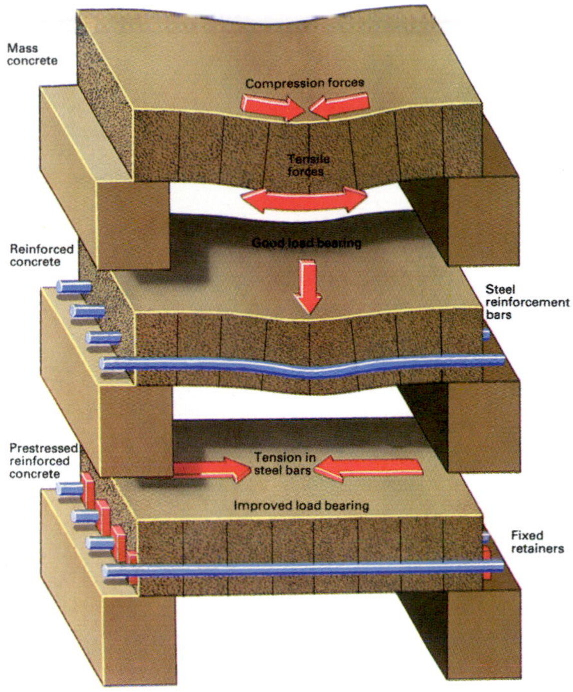

◀ By comparison with MDF cement, structural concrete is weak even when reinforced with steel bars owing to flaws in the molded material that limit the strength of the concrete. MDF overcomes these problems by using different sized particles that pack together more closely, reducing voids in the concrete matrix.

Improving cement's properties

The most recent approach to the problem in the late 1980s was to examine why some of the properties of cement are so inferior. Scientists knew that, in theory, cement could be very strong because it is similar chemically to slate, which has a high flexural strength and can even be machined into intricate shapes. The reason for the weakness in cement, they discovered, lies in flaws or defects in the molded material. These flaws limit its strength, and the larger the flaw, the weaker the material becomes. In fact, it is the largest flaw in the block of cement that governs its properties—reduce the size of the defect and strength should improve.

The first course of action was to establish the origin of the defects. Defects arise from three main processes—poor flow of the cement slurry arising from the flocculation (or sticking together) of cement particles, poor packing of cement grains in the mixer, and air bubbles formed during mixing. To improve the flow, a chemical was added to the mix to bind the cement grains together into a stiff paste and to serve as a lubricant.

The packing problem has been solved by separating out, or fractionating, the cement powder into particles of different sizes. Ordinarily, a normal powder contains a whole range of grain sizes from a few micrometers in diameter to many hundreds of micrometers. By adding different sized fractions in known proportions, the powder can be made to pack closely. To exclude air from the mixture, the dough is pressed between two plastic sheets and cured for seven days. These modifications to the production route remove large air holes from the hardened block, and the product is for this reason known as macro-defect-free (MDF) cement. When the volume porosity of MDF cement is reduced to less than 1 percent, the properties are comparable with those of plastic and aluminum. A sheet of this material only $\frac{1}{10}$ in. (3 mm) thick cannot be broken by hand and remains intact when dropped.

In certain applications, steel sheet can be replaced by an equal weight of MDF cement. Under these weight-for-weight conditions, the cement sheet is almost three times as thick as the metal it has replaced, but it resists bending forces seven times greater and can support a load four times greater before breaking. MDF cement can, unlike its conventional counterpart, also withstand substantial deformations when stressed. Springs have been made from this material that can strain up to 0.5 percent, and it approaches the stiffness of aluminum, one of the stiffest metals.

MDF cement also compares well with plastics. The lubricant added to MDF cement to reduce pore size also allows the material to flow readily into an intricate mold and accurately reproduce fine detail. In fact, on the production line, MDF cement can produce moldings as quickly as can the thermosetting plastics. MDF cement is much stiffer than even the best reinforced plastic. It also has advantages over plastics in another major area—it does not melt or burn even in the hottest fire. MDF cement has natural color and is corrosion resistant and so requires no maintenance.

SEE ALSO: Brick manufacture • Concrete • Plastics

Centrifuge

Centrifugal and centripetal forces occur whenever a body moves in a circular path. If a stone attached to one end of a length of string is rotated about a fixed center at the other end of the string, it constantly tries to fly off at a tangent. This tendency to fly outward can be considered as a force, acting outward and is called a centrifugal force (from the Latin meaning "center fleeing"). The force acting on the stone and preventing it from flying off is inward acting and called a centripetal force (from the Latin meaning "center seeking"). In the above example, the centripetal force is the tension in the string. These two forces, centrifugal and centripetal, are equal in magnitude and opposite in direction and always exist together.

In 1687, the English physicist Sir Isaac Newton published his three famous laws of motion; the first law states that every particle continues in a state of rest or uniform speed in a straight line unless acted upon by a force. Speed is defined as a rate of change of distance with time, but without specifying a direction. Velocity, however, is speed in a specified direction. So in the example, the stone rotating at a constant rate has a uniform speed, because the direction is being changed continually, so is the velocity. Hence, by applying Newton's first law of motion, the stone is subject to a force, the centripetal force, to cause this change in velocity. As acceleration is defined as the rate of change of velocity with time, the stone is being accelerated. This acceleration is not along its circular path but perpendicular (at right angles) to it, toward the center of rotation, and equals the square of the speed around the orbit divided by the radius of the orbit (S^2/R).

Newton's second law of motion states that the force acting on a body is equal to the mass of the body multiplied by the acceleration that the force produces. The acceleration occurs in the direction of the force. So the centripetal force on the stone is found by multiplying its mass by its inward acceleration. This law is true for all moving objects.

Centrifuges are used to speed up certain separation processes. The settling out of a sediment, the physical separation of a solid and a liquid (filtration), and the separation of two liquids that do not mix can be carried out in seconds rather than hours by using a centrifuge. Although a separation usually occurs if the mixture is allowed to stand, the acceleration generated by centrifugal force can be between several hundred and a million times the acceleration (g = 32 ft./s^2, or 9.81 m/s^2) caused by Earth's gravity.

▲ A decanter centrifuge uses a screw conveyor inside a rotating drum to separate semidry solids from liquids. Machines like this are common at wastewater treatment plants, where they are used to dewater sludges.

Spin dryers

The domestic spin dryer is probably the most familiar centrifuge. It is typical of many industrial machines that are used for filtering solids in which a perforated drum is mounted on bearings and driven by an electric motor. It is housed in a casing that guards the rotating parts and collects the separated liquid.

Commercial machines have diameters of up to 8 ft. (2.5 m) and develop accelerations between 300 and 2,000 *g* (300 to 2,000 times Earth's gravity). The rotating axis can be horizontal or vertical. Many machines can be used continuously, which is generally more satisfactory than the batch operation that has to be used in the domestic spin drier. Automatic machines are used in the food, chemical, and mineral industries to remove unwanted water from solids of all types, for example, sugar, starch, and fine coal—an efficient refining process.

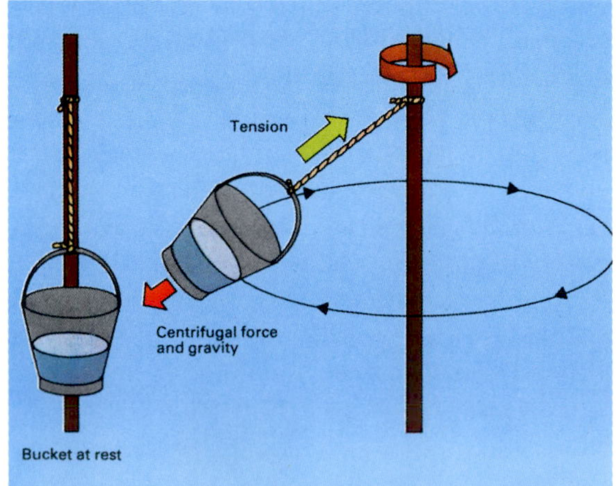

◀ A bucket is prevented from flying off by the tension in the string, which is pulling it inward by centripetal force. The water stays in the bucket through a combination of centrifugal force and gravity, which pulls it toward the bottom of the bucket.

▲ This large centrifuge is used to train astronauts to withstand the high *g*-forces they will encounter during rocket launches into space.

Pushers

In the pusher centrifuge, an oscillating plate pushes out the drained solids, which are then collected. For difficult separations, a three-stage model that has an immediate washing stage is needed. These machines are used in the chemical industry to wash and collect freely draining crystals. Instead of a plate oscillating back and forward as in the pusher centrifuge, the decanter centrifuge uses a screw conveyor. Conical or cylindrical conical machines rotate on a horizontal axis fitted with a screw conveyor inside the rotating drum. This conveyor continuously removes sedimented solids and discharges them in a semidry condition from the cone end of the machine. These machines are often used to dewater sedimentation tanks.

Separators

Gustav de Laval, a Swedish engineer, developed the first continuous separator in Sweden in the 1880s for the separation of cream from milk. These centrifuges tend to operate at higher speeds than the pushers, generating accelerations of 5,000 to 10,000 *g*. A bowl is rotated about a vertical spindle. The feed is pumped in and the separated light and heavy fractions are collected continuously. The separating performance is improved by placing disks inside the bowl, which reduce the distance that the fractions have to travel in the separation. Solid particles that are collected during the continuous operation can be discharged without stopping the centrifuge.

Ultracentrifuges

Very high-speed rotations are needed in certain separations and can be achieved by ultracentrifuges. Small samples placed in glass containers, are accelerated up to 2,000,000 *g*. These machines are used when determining the molecular weights of large molecules such as are found in polymers and proteins, and they are commonly found in laboratories. Ultracentrifuges have also been used to separate isotopes of uranium for the production of reactor-grade uranium 235, as used in nuclear power plants.

▶ An industrial centrifuge used to separate starch from gluten at a maize-processing factory.

SEE ALSO: Gravity • Oscillator • Rocket and space propulsion

Ceramics

◀ Glazing biscuit ware by dipping it into a tank of liquid glaze. After dipping, the ware is put in a firing kiln for the final ghost firing to fix the glaze.

The word *ceramic* is derived from the Greek word *keramikos*, meaning "of pottery," which is itself descended from an even older Sanskrit root referring to a burning or firing process. Today, the term *ceramic* applies to any inorganic nonmetallic solid material that involves heating at high temperature during its fabrication. This definition means that, apart from clay, other naturally occurring materials such as rutile (titanium oxide), and chemically synthesized ones such as silicon carbide may also be classed as ceramic.

There is a tendency to think of ceramics as synonymous with pottery or, alternatively, in the traditional roles of earthenware, porcelain, furnace-lining bricks, and so on. Most of these products start with clay or sand and are then shaped in a wet plastic state followed by firing at high temperature to give the article its final strength. Today, ceramic materials are used in such diverse applications as crockery, insulators, rocket nose cones, machine tools, nuclear fuels, lasers, and magnetic memory cores for computers. These important modern extensions of the uses of ceramics, however, should not overshadow the importance of traditional ceramics to the comfort and convenience of everyday life as we know it.

Properties

Ceramic materials have two important characteristics: they are chemically inert compared with most metals and carbon based (organic) materials, and they have a more complex internal structure. This crystal structure generally involves a number of different elements joined together by strong electrovalent (ionic) bonds. Magnesium oxide (more familiar as the antacid magnesia) is a simple ceramic material that is made up from positive magnesium ions and negative oxygen ions arranged as a cubic lattice.

This structural strength combined with a lack of chemical reactivity gives rise to useful properties. Ceramic materials are harder than metals or plastics and make useful abrasives. Furthermore, although they have the drawback of being brittle in tension, they are very strong in compression, retaining these properties to temperatures close to their melting points (for example, alumina, Al_2O_3, melts at 3630°F, or 2000°C). This property makes them useful where high-temperature strength is required, in furnace linings or rocket nose cones and, if they can be made cheaply enough, as building blocks such as bricks. Ceramic materials have low electrical conductivity, which makes them ideal as insulators, for example, in power-supply substations, and their low chemical reactivity makes them extremely resistant to corrosion in chemically hazardous environments. They are therefore useful for containing molten metals, acids, and alkalis as well as for resisting oxidation at high temperatures.

Heavy clay products

Heavy clay products include building materials such as bricks, roof and floor tiles, and sewer pipes. The raw materials used vary depending on the availability of a clay or hard carbonaceous shale (a type of clay rock). The essential features are cheap raw materials capable of being fired at moderately low temperatures of 1650 to 2010°F, (900–1100°C) to give the required mechanical strength. The trend has been to increase the mechanical stresses on these products, as in the case of bricks used for high-rise buildings, so greater technical expertise is now required to produce optimum strength and erosion resistance.

Pottery whitewares

Pottery includes everything from fine bone china to bathroom fixtures and wall tiles. These products are essentially based on china clay and ball clay (a type of china clay) with other additions such as flint and feldspar (an aluminum silicate rock that is found in granite) for earthenware and bone ash (calcium phosphate) for bone china. The amounts of each raw material used and subsequent firing temperature govern each product's properties.

The evolution from common pottery to bone china occurred because of the continual search for refinement and perfection by potters, who strove to make their pots whiter and more delicate. They first succeeded in doing this by covering the red colors with an opaque glaze, making majolica ware. Then, by selecting clays for white firing material and increasing the firing temperature, they produced earthenware. When sufficient fluxes (a substance used to improve fusion), such as feldspar, and higher firing temperatures were used, fine nonporous translucent materials could be produced, such as porcelain or bone china.

Refractories

Refractories are specifically designed to withstand high temperatures and the corrosive action of their environments. This goal is achieved by using the high melting temperature and chemical resistance of ceramic materials. Early refractories were made from natural clays—the fireclays. Other materials with higher and higher alumina contents were developed to withstand higher temperatures. Refractories are used in most high-temperature industrial processes, including as supports for other ceramics during firing and in the walls of glass tanks and cement kilns, but principally they are used in the iron and steel industry. In the latter especially, changes in the chemistry of the processes used have led to the introduction of basic refractories made from magnesite and dolomite. Other applications call for silica or silicon carbide. Early refractories were made as bricks similar in size and shape to house bricks, but today large or specially shaped blocks are made. Other refractories are installed by spraying or casting concrete, and yet others are available in the form of fibers that can be made into flexible blankets or into rigid boards or shapes.

◀ The two halves of a plaster mold being separated to remove a slip-cast teapot after it has been dried.

Glass ceramics

Glass is another ceramic material from antiquity. Essentially it is made by melting sand, shaping the viscous liquid, and allowing it to cool slowly to produce a material that, while solid, lacks any crystal structure and can be quite transparent to light. In addition to the traditional applications in windows (flat glass) and a wide variety of containers (bottles and jars), modern special glasses are used in chemically resistant wares for laboratory and industrial applications, in vacuum devices from flasks for drinks to electronic equipment, to seal and protect metal and other components, and in a wide variety of other applications.

The intrinsic strength of glass is high, but the strength of commercial glass is limited by internal and surface flaws, which cause cracks. Glass ceramics get over these limitations. They are formed by turning glass into a microcrystalline pore-free ceramic by a controlled heating cycle, which induces crystallization. The product is shaped by traditional glass-making techniques before crystallization, and thus complicated shapes impossible by normal ceramic-forming methods can be made. A conventional clay body could be converted to a glass ceramic by melting it at 3090°F (1700°C) to produce a homogeneous liquid followed by crystallization into mullite and silica. The great advantage of glass ceramics lies

▶ Before the plastic mixture of china clay ingredients can be molded the filter cakes are fed into a pug mill—essentially a giant grinding machine—that mixes the cakes in a vacuum to remove any trapped air bubbles and extrudes solid cylinders of china clay.

in the possibility of varying the properties quite markedly by modifying the composition of the original glass. Very low thermal expansions can be produced, making glass ceramics useful for oven-to-table ware. Their corrosion resistance is useful in heat exchangers, and their uniform dielectric (insulating) properties find applications in radomes (a protective housing for radar) and printed circuit boards.

◀ Before silicon carbide components can be cast into high precision metal machine parts, the volatile constituents must be burned off the ceramic molds.

Modern ceramics

The new materials used are pure compounds, especially oxides, refined from naturally occurring metal ores or chemically made compounds such as barium titanate, silicon nitride, silicon carbide, and the sialons: alloys of silicon nitride with various oxides. Moreover, by careful processing to produce ceramics that are free from the microscopic flaws, which reduce their strength, defect-free cements can be made with much improved tensile strength and thus "springiness."

Alumina (Al_2O_3) is perhaps the best established modern ceramic with the widest range of applications. Other high-temperature (refractory) materials also used to make crucibles and furnace elements include magnesia (MgO), zirconia (ZrO_2), and thoria (ThO_2).

Hard-wearing ceramics, used, for example, in bearings, include alumina, zirconium boride, and silicon nitride. For grinding powders and abrasives, alumina (which occurs naturally as corundum) and silicon carbide (commonly called carborundum) are used. Alumina is also used as the electrical insulator in spark plugs, for "windows" in electronic devices such as klystrons, and as a substrate for printed circuits or a base for power transistors, where its unusually high thermal conductivity, comparable to some metals, helps dissipate the heat. Titania (TiO_2) is widely used in capacitors, and ferrites have a multiplicity of applications, including permanent magnets, transformer cores, antenna rods, and digital store devices for computers. Other ceramics such as beta-alumina and zirconia are used as solid electrolytes in batteries and sensors. Ceramics that exhibit the piezoelectric effect (where external pressure changes the electrical properties), such as lead zirconate titanate (known as PZT) and barium titanate find applications in record player pickups, sonar devices, and piezoelectric spark igniters. Nuclear fuels are usually made from thoria, urania (UO_2), or uranium carbide.

▲ Ceramic is one of the most widely used materials for the manufacture of heavy-duty electrical insulators. Here, an assortment of insulators is being placed in a drying kiln.

Making ceramic articles

Bricks are made by pressing (used in particular for special shapes) or by extrusion, in which process a column of soft clay is forced through a rectangular die and then cut into appropriate lengths by a series of wires in the same way cheese is cut.

There are several ways of making household wares: molding, plastic forming, or casting. In each process, however, the raw materials, say flint, feldspar, and clay in the case of earthenware, are ground to the correct particle size and mixed with water. In making a molded plate, some water would be removed to produce a plastic paste, which is pressed onto a mold. After drying, the formed plate is taken from the mold and fired in a kiln. At this stage, it is known as biscuit ware and needs to be glazed and decorated. The glaze and coloring are applied and the plate returned to the kiln for further firings to develop the colors.

Cups, bowls and similar objects are made by plastic forming or casting. In plastic forming, the plastic clay mixture is shaped by hand, potter's wheel, or machinery. The casting process, also called slip casting, begins with a porous mold. The clay or other material in the form of a suspension in water is poured into the mold, which absorbs the liquid. In this way, a layer of solid is built up on the walls of the mold until sufficiently thick. When dry, the cast wall separates from the mold wall, the mold is taken apart, and the article is removed and fired with subsequent glazing as for a plate.

Tiles are made by pressing dry powdered material into a die of the shape required. The shaped powder is removed from the die, dried, fired, glazed, and decorated in the same way as plates and cups. Tile making has become one of the most automated processes in the ceramic industry, and the dry-pressing process is now being extended to the somewhat more difficult task of making ceramic tableware (plates, saucers, and bowls).

Dry pressing and extrusion are both used to make components from the modern ceramics, but as complex shapes may be required, other processes are also used. In injection molding, a soft ceramic body is forced through a die into a mold.

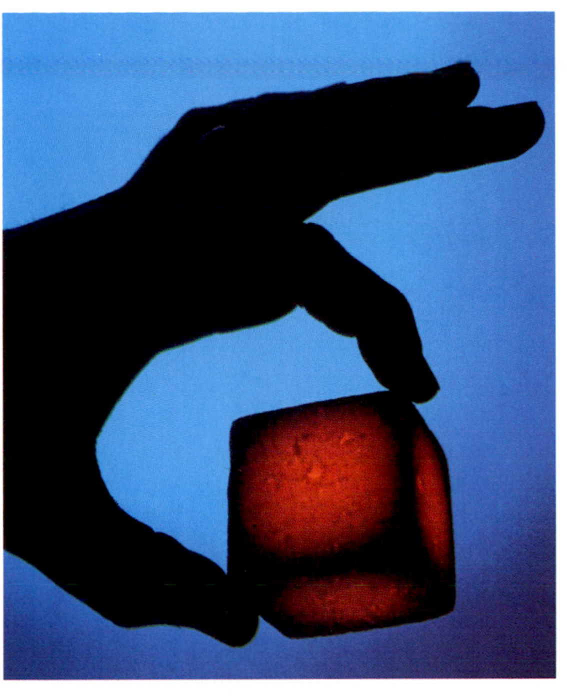

◀ Space age ceramics, such as this silicon compound, were developed to provide a heat-resistant cladding for the exterior of the space shuttle. These materials remain stronger at hotter temperatures than many alloys and have the advantage of being both good insulators and resistant to thermal shock. These materials have great potential in the making of automobile engines of the future, as they can be made lighter and more energy efficient, and so save fuel.

Spark plugs are made from alumina by isostatic pressing. This process overcomes the uneven pressure distribution of conventional dry pressing as used in tile manufacture. By holding the powder to be pressed in a pliable bag made of rubber, plastic, or metal and surrounding it with a liquid that is pressurized, an even pressure is produced around the die. The even pressure gives uniform density and therefore better mechanical and electrical properties in the finished product. The isostatically pressed alumina is removed from the die, trimmed to shape on a lathe, dried, dipped in glaze, and fired. Dimensional stability is important to ensure good fit of the metal parts.

Isostatic pressing is also used for other engineering ceramic components for which further advanced shaping techniques have been introduced. In order to produce dense pore-free ceramics, the application of heat and pressure may be combined using hot pressing or hot isostatic pressing. These techniques are particularly useful for silicon nitride and the sialons, although silicon nitride powder is still expensive. An alternative route to a silicon nitride ceramic, which allows complex shapes to be made to accurate dimensions, is that of reaction sintering in which articles are made by starting with silicon powder.

FACT FILE

- *Hard translucent Chinese porcelain was made from the 13th century onward by mixing kaolin clay with a ground feldspathic rock. The mixture was fired at about 2650°F (1450°C). Despite repeated attempts, European craftsmen failed to discover the correct ingredients and production techniques until some six centuries later.*

- *The scanning laser acoustic microscope (SLAM) is used to test for flaws in ceramic engine parts, which can disintegrate when they fail. Although temperatures up to 2500°F (1400°C) and rotation rates up to 100,000 rpm can be withstood by the ceramics used, failure can occur owing to minute foreign bodies in the material. SLAM makes these inclusions, as well as microcracks and variable porosity, visible on a screen.*

- *In 1983, a team from NASA and General Electric designed and built a prototype for the world's most efficient jet engine. Operating at far higher temperatures and pressures than conventional engines, the E3 (energy-efficient engine) uses a zirconium oxide ceramic in the shroud to deal with the super-heating.*

SEE ALSO: Brick manufacture • China and porcelain • Conduction, electrical • Gas turbine • Glass • Kiln • Laser and maser • Magnetism • Rocket and space propulsion

Chain Drive

▲ An engineer inspects the links of a 4½ in. (11 cm) pitch roller chain, the timing drive of a 28,000-horsepower marine engine in an ocean-going vessel.

A chain drive is a useful transmission system where rotational power has to be transferred from one place to another nearby, the chain linking two or more sprocket wheels. It is often found in machines, from heavy earthmovers to automatic vending machines, though the best-known application is the bicycle chain.

A form of chain was in use 3,000 years ago, made of wooden struts held apart by rope, like a rope ladder. Metal chains with simple interlocking links were used in medieval times, but the first serious uses of chain drives came in the 19th century. The British engineer Isambard Brunel's famous ship, the SS *Great Britain*, used an early form of chain drive to power the propeller shaft.

Roller chain

The familiar roller chain, as used on the bicycle, was invented by Hans Renold in Britain in 1880. This chain has rollers turning on pins separated by side plates. These are arranged to overlap in such a way that there are alternating wide and narrow links, though the pitch—the distance between the roller centers—is always the same. The rollers may be held in place by cotter (split) pins or by splaying the ends of the pins during manufacture.

The use of rollers greatly increases the efficiency of the chain, since when a chain drive makes contact with the sprocket wheel that drives it, there is a considerable impact force. The friction is reduced by the rollers, which totally enclose their bearing surfaces, a good design point. The chain is usually kept well lubricated.

In many applications, the chain is not used singly but in a duplex or triplex form, with two or three sets of links side by side or more if necessary. Where there is a large distance between the shafts of the sprocket wheels being linked—up to 30 ft. (10 m) is possible—a double-pitch roller may be used, with longer side plates and a larger distance between each of the rollers.

The efficiency of roller chains is very high. In a test carried out by Britain's National Physical Laboratory, a roller chain was run under carefully controlled conditions for six hours, with measurements made of the input and output. The efficiency of the drive was found to be between 98.4 and 98.9 percent.

Inverted-tooth chain

The inverted-tooth, or silent, chain was invented by Hans Renold in 1895, though it became more popular in America than in Britain. It consists of a number of thin plates, each cut in an "inverted tooth" rather like a long U-shape, that are assembled side by side in a laminated fashion with pins. The projecting ends overlap slightly. The advantage of this form of construction is that the chain conforms well to the shape of the sprocket as it meets it, giving a more silent run. Guide plates, without the cut-out tooth, are included at the center or edges of the line of chain, and these run in grooves around the sprocket wheel.

This type of chain is used mainly where high power has to be transmitted, such as in cranes and generators. It was widely used in America until the 1930s, when it was largely superseded by the roller chain, which has since become predominant all over the world.

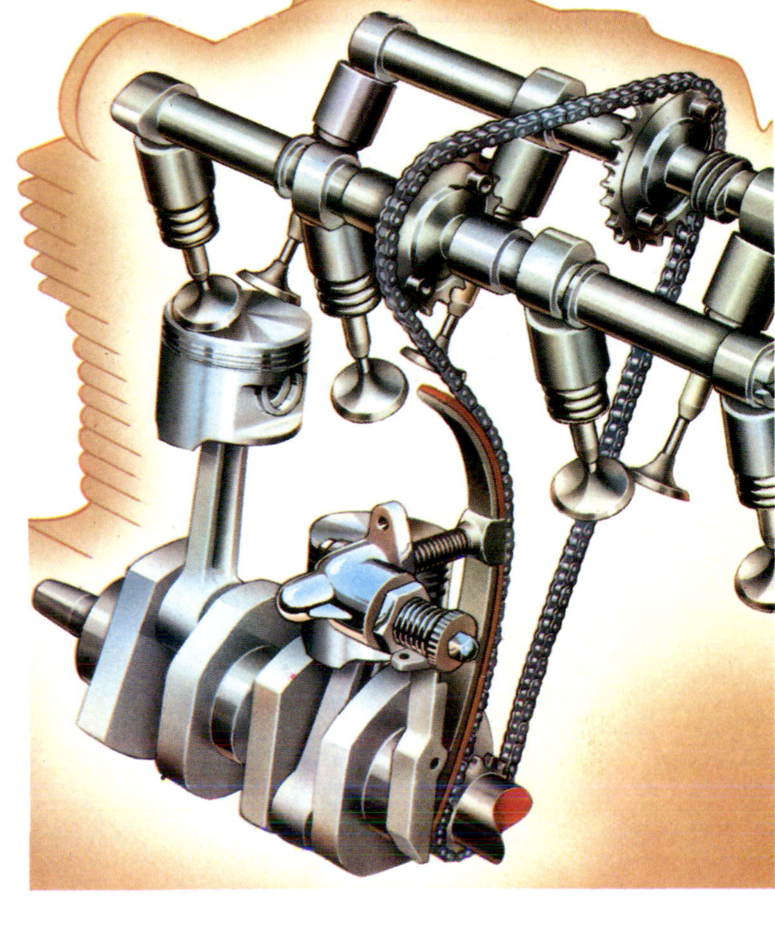

▲ The cam chain arrangement of an overhead cam, four-cylinder Suzuki GS1000.

Other types of chain

Some chain drives have to operate in harsh conditions, such as in earthmoving machinery and chemical plants, where dirt or corrosion would make lubricated chains useless. In such cases, the chains are made more rugged and simple.

The detachable chain is made from identical cast links, each with a hook at one end and a bar at the other. The hook almost completely encloses the bar of the next link. No lubrication is used, as this would tend to trap grit in the bearing surface, resulting in a chain that is less smooth running.

The pintle chain also has identical cast links, each with a narrow barrel at one end through which a pin fits to hold the side plates of the next. The bearing surface is totally enclosed, and no lubrication is necessary. The offset sidebar, or cranked-link, chain is similar, but it has bushings and rollers.

◀ Traditional chain making involved hammering each link closed by hand.

On a smaller scale, bead chains are used—simply plastic beads strung on a cord, fitting in a shaped sprocket wheel. These and other plastic chains are used, for example, in vending machines, tuners in TV and radio sets, and air-conditioning equipment. Aluminum and stainless steel chains of all types are used in other specialized power-transmitting applications.

Chain drives have several advantages over other forms of transmission such as belt drives, which are usually made of fabric or rubber. They cannot slip, an essential feature where synchronization is important, as in car timing chains and printing machines. They are versatile and adaptable: by altering the size of the sprocket wheels, several shafts can be driven at different speeds. The load is also spread over several teeth of the sprocket wheel, giving more even wear. Furthermore, the built-in elasticity of the chain and the film of lubricating oil tend to absorb any shocks.

SEE ALSO: Bicycle • Corrosion prevention • Earthmoving machinery • Lubrication • Metal • Motorcycle • Tracked vehicle

Chaos Theory

The theory of chaos studies ways in which order can be found among seemingly random events, be they natural or mathematical. Although it has become important in several scientific fields over the last few decades, as a branch of mathematics, it was opened up by the distinguished French mathematician Henri Poincaré in 1893.

Poincaré showed that the motion of a satellite attracted to Earth and the Moon could be so complicated that it could not even be drawn. Such motion deserves to be called chaotic, even though it is completely predictable as long as the starting conditions are known exactly.

Progress in chaos theory generally had to wait for the advent of high-speed computers. These revealed chaotic behavior in many areas that had seemed otherwise merely difficult to understand, such as weather prediction. Chaos theory then aims to find order underneath the chaos. For example, Edward Lorenz's equations for modeling the weather can be demonstrated by drawing a curve in space to describe how weather parameters vary one with another—it is like a graph but with more than two variable quantities. The result is a striking butterfly-shaped figure called Lorenz's strange attractor. It shows that only slight alterations at the start of a weather condition can considerably alter subsequent behavior. In effect he is saying that a butterfly flapping its wings in Brazil could set off a tornado in Texas, making accurate long-term predictions impossible.

The pattern does, however, reveal that the evolution of weather is constrained within a limited range of possibilities. The problem is then how to describe them. One way would be to get a measure of how thick the set of possibilities is. Is it a curve (one dimension), a surface (two dimensions), a solid tube (three dimensions), or something in between? Sets with a fractional dimension had been discovered at the start of 20th century and are called fractals. They were brought back to life in the 1970s by the Polish-American mathematician Benoit Mandelbrot at IBM and have subsequently been much studied by many eminent mathematicians.

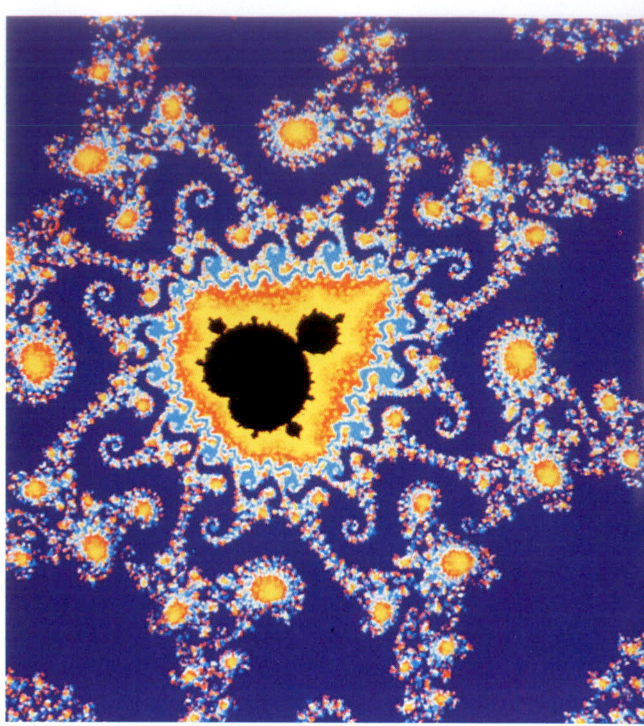

▶ A Mandelbrot set reveals chaotic behavior, with certain points departing from the main structure. The dark shape at the center is characteristic of Mandelbrot sets.

▼ The Lorenz attractor is generated by plotting several variable quantities together. The line, after remaining close to one point, suddenly departs for a different area of the plot, then just as suddenly returns again.

Drawing fractals

A simple fractal is easy to draw as the limit of a series of successive approximations. Start with a triangle whose angles are 30 degrees, 30 degrees, and 120 degrees; the first "curve" is composed of the two shorter sides. Replace this triangle with two smaller ones built from it but having the same angles. The new path is composed of the four equal shorter sides. At each stage, replace the triangles by similar smaller ones in the same way; the curve is formed from all the equal shorter sides. These curves steadily approximate the one we want, that is, a continuous curve that has no tangent—it is truly crinkly. Vary the triangle, and other limiting curves are obtained. Many beautiful computer-generated images have been produced by taking a comparatively simple rule and continuing the process in this way.

Such crinkly sets arise in many areas of mathematics, typically when a number or set of numbers is repeatedly subjected to the same process.

CHAOTIC SYSTEMS

The Lorenzian waterwheel is a simple demonstration of a chaotic system. 1. Water fills a bucket and the wheel starts turning. 2. At a certain flow, the wheel turns steadily. 3. If the water flow increases, the wheel turns faster, the buckets cannot empty in time, and the wheel reverses its motion. This sequence will repeat in random and chaotic fashion.

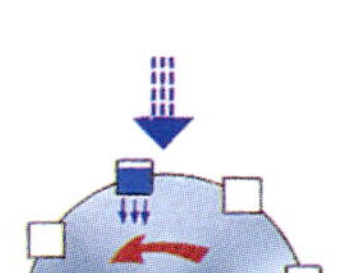
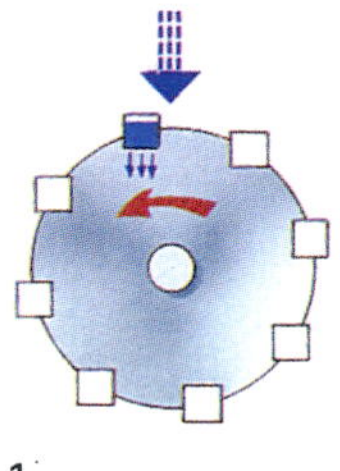

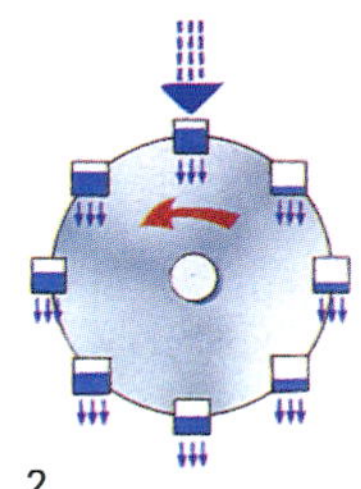
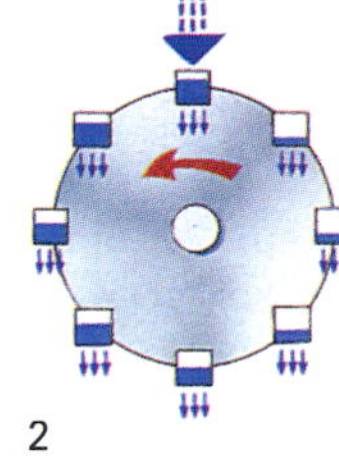

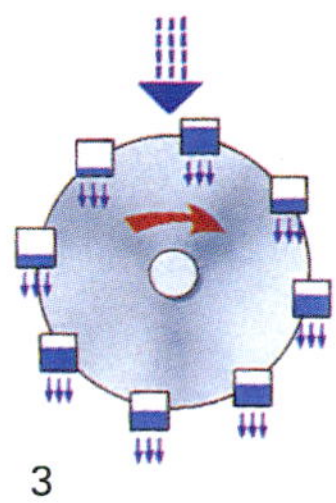
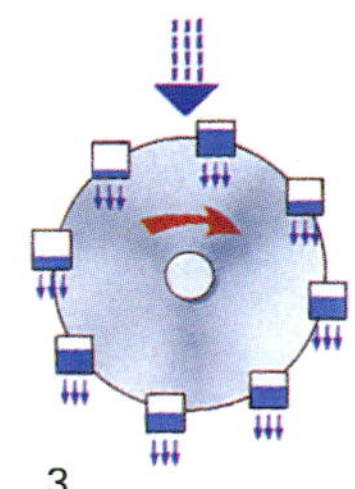

For example, when finding approximate solutions to equations, the output of a formula will be used as the new input until a sufficient degree of accuracy is obtained. Even the simplest examples of iteration (as such a repetitive process is called) are surprisingly delicate. One famous example is an iterative process in which a pair of numbers (thought of as a point in a plane) generates another pair. Points within the main region settle down, points outside move off to infinity, and points on the crinkly boundary move in a variety of ways around the boundary. Such sets are called Julia sets, after Gaston Julia, who was one of the first people to study them.

Some Julia sets come in one piece, others are scattered like dust. The Mandelbrot set describes which are which. Questions about the boundaries of Julia sets and the Mandelbrot set are presently much studied. Are they fractals? Sometimes they are, sometimes not. Julia sets are interestingly similar: if you take a small piece of one and enlarge it, it often looks like the original, which makes the sets very crinkly objects indeed. Remarkably, it was shown in 1991 that the boundary of the Mandelbrot set is not a curve but can be described as two dimensional in a precise geometrical sense.

▼ A Julia set plotted on a computer graphics program by repeatedly carrying out a basic mathematical operation. Small parts of it have a similarity to the longer structures within it.

FACT FILE

- *Mandelbrot posed the simple question "How long is the coastline of Britain?" To everyone's surprise, it was found to be infinite. Using a triangle to approximate the shape of the country, Mandelbrot filled in the outline with smaller and smaller triangles to cover the area more accurately. Because there is no limit to the number of triangles required, the perimeter of the coastline increases but can never reach a maximum, because there is no point at which it can be said the shape defines the coastline exactly.*

- *Manufacturers have not been slow to exploit chaos theory. The first example, a washing machine aimed at producing cleaner and less tangled clothes, used a small pulsator that rose and fell randomly as the main pulsator rotated to create a chaotic effect.*

- *Another washing-machine maker employed fuzzy logic circuits to create chaotic effects. These circuits made choices between one and zero and true and false and were used to control the amount of bubbles, the turbulence of the machine, and even how much it wobbled when rotating.*

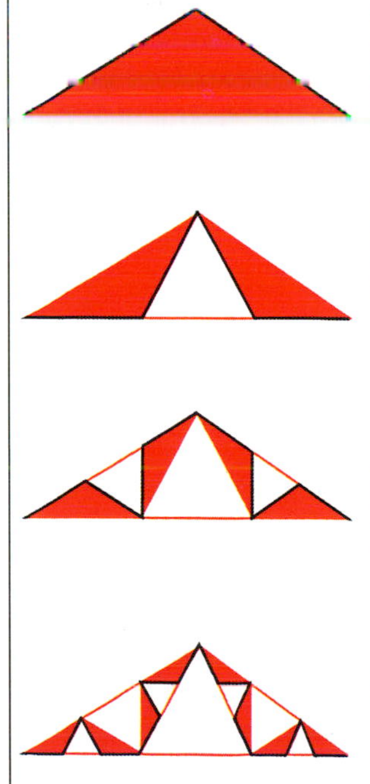

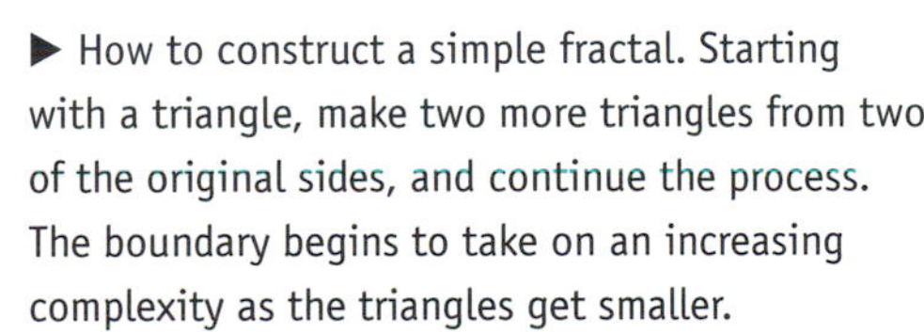

▶ How to construct a simple fractal. Starting with a triangle, make two more triangles from two of the original sides, and continue the process. The boundary begins to take on an increasing complexity as the triangles get smaller.

SEE ALSO: MATHEMATICS • NUMBER THEORY

Charge-Coupled Device

Collecting light for imaging used to be a lengthy business for astronomers trying to capture pictures on photographic film of far away stars and galaxies. All this changed with the electronics revolution and the invention of the charge-coupled device, a light-sensitive silicon chip roughly the size of a postage stamp. Now astronomers can observe objects at the edge of the known Universe with ease, and the charge-coupled device, or CCD, has been found in wide-ranging applications from satellites to supermarket checkouts.

The CCD was first developed at Bell Laboratories in the United States in 1969. Originally it was intended for use in a video telephone that needed a solid-state miniature camera. Video phones did not catch on at that time, but the technology soon found a new home in the video camera. In 1975, Bell demonstrated the first CCD camera with an image sharp enough for broadcast television.

CCDs work by storing charge when light falls onto a transistor gate, or capacitor, called a pixel. Pixels are square pockets of doped silicon arranged in rows. Light falling onto the pixel frees electrons in the doped silicon, and the charge accumulated by each pixel is proportional to the amount of light it receives. The charge stays in the pixel for a fixed amount of time, until the CCD is "clocked." When this happens, the pixel transfers its charge to the next pixel in the row. The process is repeated every time the CCD is clocked until the charge reaches the end of the row. On arrival, the charge is transferred to a low-noise amplifier that converts it to a voltage signal. These signals can be read out or stored on computer.

One advantage of CCDs, their linear response to light, makes it possible to tell how many photons were collected in each pixel, which is useful in astrometry, as astronomers can measure the distances and positions of stars direct from the CCD image. Astronomers usually work with just one CCD at a time, giving a black and white view. However, because the information is stored digitally, it can be manipulated by computers with false colors assigned to specific intensities of light. Home video cameras, on the other hand, have three CCDs, each with a different colored filter. Combining the outputs from the CCDs produces a color picture.

Early CCD arrays were subject to readout noise and were less than 100 by 100 pixels in size. NASA's Jet Propulsion Laboratory, which had picked up on the potential for using CCDs in astronomy, began development of bigger CCDs, culminating in the 800 by 800 pixel units used on the Hubble Space Telescope when it was launched in 1990. Since then, the standard format for second generation CCDs has reached 2,048 by 2,048, with over four million pixels. These state-of-the-art devices can detect photons at as low a rate as one per minute, making them ideal for viewing very faint objects. Multiple arrangements of CCDs known as mosaics have improved the resolution even more.

CCD technology has not been confined to astronomy and video cameras. Today CCDs can be found in other video applications such as the endoscopes used in surgery, security monitoring, videoconferencing, and high-definition television. Other optical technologies have also made use of them—photocopiers, fax machines, barcode readers, and photographic scanners all use the CCD's ability to turn patterns of light into digital images. Digital cameras are the latest application, with photographers able to download their pictures directly from a disk to a computer.

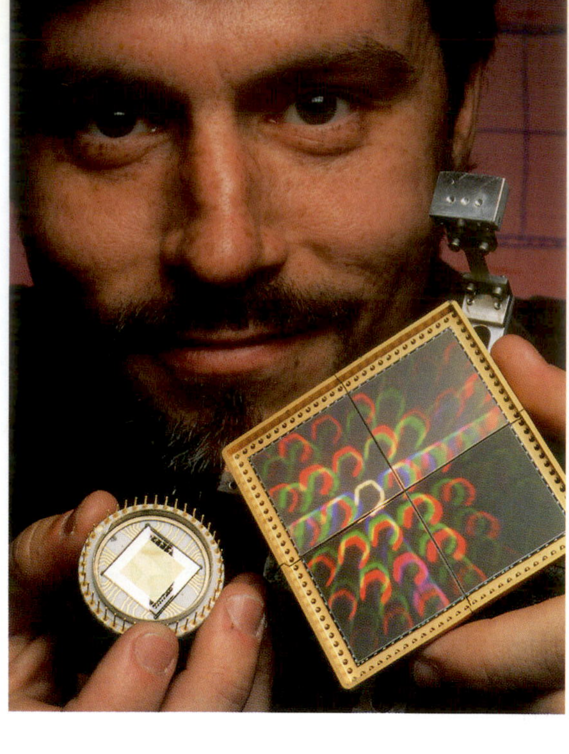

▶ Ordinary CCDs are about the size of a postage stamp, but they can be linked into multiple arrays called mosaics to provide better resolution (the square device at the right). Scientists are already working on more sensitive detectors called superconducting tunnel junctions that can read out each pixel separately instead of shuffling the charge along a row. As a result, scientists will not only be able to register the position of an incoming photon, but record its energy level as well.

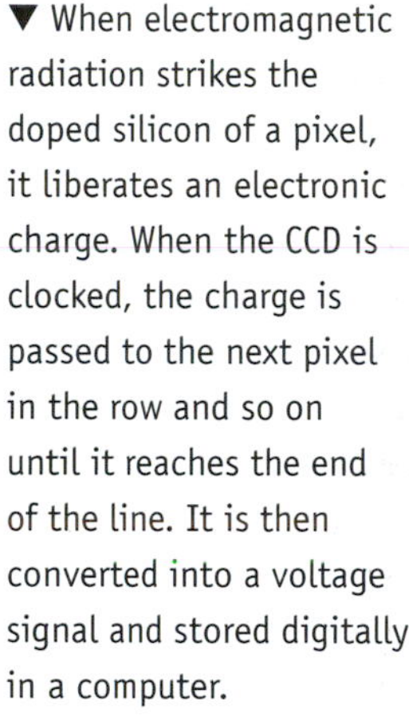

▼ When electromagnetic radiation strikes the doped silicon of a pixel, it liberates an electronic charge. When the CCD is clocked, the charge is passed to the next pixel in the row and so on until it reaches the end of the line. It is then converted into a voltage signal and stored digitally in a computer.

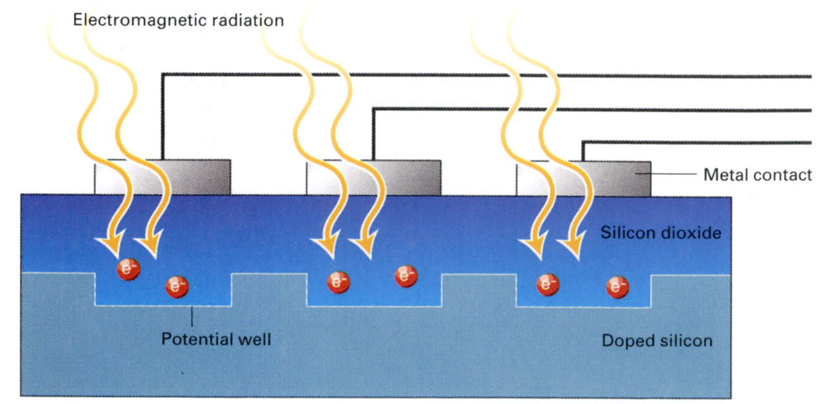

SEE ALSO: Astronomy • Camera, digital • Integrated circuit • Optical scanner • Telescope, optical • Video camera

Index

Page numbers in **bold** refer to main articles; those in *italics* refer to picture captions.

A

Aardvark (flailing machines) *294*
ABS (antilock braking system) 315
abscisic acid 305
acceleration 422
acetylcholine 413, 414
  in plants 305
  receptors *414*
aircraft
  braking systems 314, 315
  wiring used in 346
air-traffic control (ATC), radar 410
alumina *see* aluminium oxide
aluminum
  alloys 332
  uses
    in buildings 336
    cans 385
    in power cables 344
aluminum bronze 332
aluminum oxide (alumina) 407, 424, 426
Alzheimer's disease 414
ammonia, manufacture *405*, 407
analog and digital systems, in cell phones 416
Anderton Vertical Lift 376
animals, cells 411–12
antennas, cell phone 415, 416
antibodies (immunoglobulins), and cancer *380*
antitheft devices 341
aperture size, camera 363
architecture, capsule 338
aspirin, in plants 305
assembly lines *382*, *385*
autoclaves 382
automobiles
  alarms 340
  braking systems 313–15
  catalytic converters 405, *407*

B

babies, skeleton *297*
bacteria, spores 381
bar codes 401
barium titanate 426
batteries, in calculators 360–1
baud rate 354
beer and brewing *406*
  widgets in beer cans 384
beetles, Colorado 303
bicycles, chain drive 428
biobricks 324
biogas, for buses 343
biology
  botany **303–5**
  cell **411–14**
biopsies 378
bioreactors *406*
biotecture 338
biscuit ware 426
blanching 381
blast lamps 339
blood, red cells *413*
blood pressure, regulation 413–14
boat lifts 376
body scanners 312
bombs
  bomb and mine disposal **293–6**
  terrorist 293–5
bone ash (calcium phosphate) 425
bone marrow 298–9
  transplants 380
bones, and fracture treatment **297–300**
bookbinding **301–2**
botany **303–5**
bottling 385
bows and arrows **306–8**
brain **309–12**
  scans *311*, 312
Brain Electric Activity Mapping (BEAM) 312
braking systems **313–15**
  air brakes 315
  aircraft 314, 315
  antilock (ABS) 315
  band 313
  block 314
  cable car 356
  disk 314
  drum 313–14
  dual 315
  electric 315
  hydraulic 314–15
  power brakes *313*, 314–15
  regenerative 315
  train 314, 315
brass **316–17**
brass instruments **318–20**
breathing apparatus **321–2**
bricks 336
  manufacture **323–4**, 426
bridges **325–30**
  erection 330
  materials 329–30
  types
    arch 327–8
    Bailey 328
    bascule *325*
    beam 325
    box girder 325, *329*
    cable-stayed 326, 327, *329*
    cantilever and suspended-span 325
    lifting *327*
    suspension 325–7
bronze **331–2**
bubble and cloud chambers **333–4**
bugles 319
building techniques **335–8**
Bunsen burners **339**
burglar alarms **340–1**
buses (transport) **342–3**
  brakes 315

C

cable cars, aerial 358
cable networks **353–5**
cable and rope manufacture **350–2**
cables
  antitheft 341
  for bridges 326, 327, *329*
  coaxial 354
  power **344–6**
    installation 346
    insulation 345
  submarine (undersea) **347–9**
    manufacture 348, *350*
    power cables 349
  telephone 347
cable transport systems **356–8**
cableways *357*
cadmium sulfide (CdS) cells 368
calcium hydroxide (slaked lime; lime) 417
calcium phosphate 298
calculators **359–61**
calluses 299
cameras **363–9**
  35mm 364–5, 368–9
  autofocus 364
  automatic and semiautomatic 369
  digital **370–2**
  and exposure control 368, 369
  lenses 363, 364, 367–9
  reflex 366–7
    single-lens (SLR) *366*, 367, 368–9
    twin-lens 366–7
  rocket 369
  roll-film 365–6
  shutters 363
    speed 363
cams **362**
canals **373–6**
  locks 373, 375–6
cancer
  causes 377, 378
  diagnosis 378
  formation 377
  immunity 378
  lung *378*
  treatment **377–80**
    antibody-directed drug therapy *380*
    bone marrow transplants 380
    chemotherapy *377*, 379, 380
    gene therapy 380
    hormone therapy 379–80
    photodynamic therapy (PDT) 380
    radiotherapy *378*, 379, 380
    surgery 378–9, 380
  vaccines 380
canning and bottling **381–5**
capacitors (condensers) **386–7**
carbohydrates **388–90**
carbon **391–3**
  activated 322
  allotropes 392
  bonds 393
  isotopes 393
    and carbon dating 393
carbonation 385
carbon fiber **394–5**
carborundum (silicon carbide) 426
carburetors **396–7**
cards
  credit and debit 401
    transaction-recording devices *400*
  identity 341
cargo handling, cableways *357*
car washes **398**
cash registers **399–401**
casting **402–4**
  continuous *403*
  cylindrical casting of brass *317*
  die 404
  evaporative 404
  investment (lost wax process) 403–4
  sand 402–3, *404*
  shell molding (Croning process) 403
  slip 402, *425*, 427
catalysts **402–7**
catalytic converters 405, *407*
cathode-ray tubes (CRTs) **408–10**
  for computer monitors 409
  manufacture 409–10
  in oscilloscopes 409
  in television receivers 409
CCTV (closed-circuit television) 340
cell biology **411–14**
cell membrane 411
cellophane 390
cellular telephones (cell phones) **415–16**
Celluloid 390
cellulose 389–90
  adhesive 390
cement 335
  macro-defect-free (MDF) 421
  manufacture **417–21**
  reinforced 421
central processing units (CPUs)
  in calculators 360
  in mobile phones 416
centrifugal force 422
centrifuges *316*, **422–3**
centripetal force 422
ceramics **424–7**
  piezoelectric 426
  structural 336
  used as insulators *346*
cerebellum 310
cerebrospinal fluid 310
CERN, bubble chamber *333*, 334
chain drives **428–9**
chairlifts *357*
chaos theory **430–1**
charcoal, fuel 391
charge-coupled devices (CCDs) **432**
  in cameras *370*, 371, 432
    video 432
chemicals, carcinogenic 378
chemotherapy *377*, 379, 380
chiasma 309
china, bone 425
china clay (kaolin) 424
Chlamydomonas 305
chlorophyll 412
chloroplasts 412, *413*
choke (venturi) 396
chondrites, carbonaceous 393
chromosomes 411, 412–13
cire perdu (lost wax process) 403–4
clay
  and brick manufacture 323–4
  heavy 424
cliff railways 356–7
clinker, cement 419
cloud chambers 333
coal 391
coasts, length of British coastline 431
cog railways, funiculars 357–8
coins, bronze 332
coking, on catalysts 406
collagen 298
collodion cotton 390
colostomy 379
composites, carbon fibers used in 395
compressed air line apparatus 322
computer printers, printing photographs 372
computers
  and digital cameras 370
  making components for 404
  monitors (VDUs; visual display units) 409
concrete 417
  prestressed 329–30, 335
  reinforced 329–30, 335, 420
  uses
    for bridges 329–30
    for buildings 335, 338
copper phosphide 332
cordite 390
Corinth Canal *374*
corn
  emasculation 303
  genetically-engineered 303
corpus callosum 309
cranequins 308
crops, genetically-engineered 303

crossbows 308
cytokinins 305
cytological specimens, for cancer investigations 378
cytoplasm 411, 413

D

Dacron 350
deaeration 381
dendrites 309
deoxyribonucleic acid (DNA) 412
depth of field 363
dextrin 390
diabetes 414
diamonds
- covalent crystals *393*
- properties *391*, 392
  - melting point 393
- synthetic (industrial) 392

diaphragm, camera *364*
dielectric constants 386
dielectrics 386
digital versatile discs (DVDs) 354
dimethylbenzene (xylene) 406
dimethylether (DME) fuel 343
diodes, light-emitting (LEDs)
- in calculators 361
- in cameras 367
- and fiber optics 355

disaccharides 389
DNA (deoxyribonucleic acid) 412
dogs, sniffer *296*
domes, geodesic *336*
drawing (metalworking) 316
drilling, directional 346
drinks, bottling and carbonation 385
dry-pressing 427
dual-in-line (DIL) package 359–60
ducted installations, of power cables 346
DX coding 369

E

E3 (energy-efficient engine) 427
earthenware 425
Edison, Thomas 353, 394
EEGs (electroencephalograms) 312
EFTPOS (electronic funds transfer at point of sale) 401
electrical circuits, capacitors in 386–7
electrolytic capacitors 387
electron guns 408
electronic point-of-sale (EPOS) terminals 401
electrons, discovery 408
Empire State Building 337
encephalins 311
encephalograms 312
endoplasmic reticulum 411
endorphins 311
endothelium-derived relaxing factor (EDRF) 414
energy resources, fossil fuels 391
enzymes *406*, 407
estrogen, in plants 305
ethanal, production 407
explosive ordnance disposal (EOD) 293
- suits 295

explosives 390
exposure metering 368
extrusion 427

F

fermentation, brewing and *406*
fiber optics
- in cable networks 354–5
- in submarine (undersea) cables 349

fibroblasts *300*
firing, bricks 324
FLAG (fiber optic link around the globe) 355
flailing machines 294
flash tubes, electronic 365
focal ratio (f-ratio; *f* numbers) 363
food
- canning and bottling **381–5**
- carbohydrates *388*, 389, *390*
- genetically-modified 303, 304
- slimming foods 390

fossil fuels 391
fractals 430–1
fractures, bone, treatment 299–300
French-horns *318*
Frequency Division Multiple Access (FDMA) 416
fructose 389
funiculars 357–8
furnaces
- blast 391, *392*
- for brass manufacture 316
- electric arc 316

fuzzy logic, washing machines and 431

G

galactose 389
genes 412
- jumping (transposons) *303*

gene therapy 380
genetic engineering
- gene therapy 380
- of plants and crops (food) 303, 304

geodesic structures, domes *336*
George Washington Bridge 326
g-forces *423*
gibberellic acid 305
gilding metal 317
glass 425–6
glass-reinforced polyester (GRP) 337
global system for mobile communications (GSM) 416
glucose 389
glutamate 414
glycogen 389, 390
GM-CSF, and gene therapy 380
Golden Gate Bridge 329
Golgi apparatus 411
Grand Canal (China) 376
granulocytes *413*
graphite 392, *393*, 395
graphitization, of carbon fibers 395
Greeks, ancient, cement 417
Great Britain, SS 428
guncotton 390
gunmetals 331
gutta percha 347
gypsum 417

H

Haber (Haber-Bosch) process, catalysts *405*, 407
handoff 415
harmonics 318
Haversian canals 298, *299*
hemp 350
hipping (hot isostatic pressing) 404
Hodgkin's disease 379
hormone replacement therapy (HRT) 298
hormones 413
- for cancer treatment 379–80
- plant 305

Hubble Space Telescope (HST), charge-coupled devices 432
Humber Bridge 329
Huntington's chorea 414
hydraulics, braking systems 314–15
hydrodesulfurization 406
hydrogen
- in ammonia manufacture *405*
- in bubble chambers 334

hydrogenation 406
hypothalamus 310

I

Iapetus (moon) 393
identity cards 341
immunoglobulins (antibodies), and cancer *380*
immunology, and cancer 378
indole-acetic acid 305
infrared radiation, in burglar alarms 340–1
insulators, electric *426*
- in power cables 345

integrated circuits (silicon chips; microchips)
- in calculators 359–60
- in cell phones 416
- large scale integration (LSI) 359
- metal oxide silicon (MOS) *361*
- very-large-scale integration (VLSI) 416

integrated transport network 343
interferon 380
interleukin-2 380
internal combustion engines, cams 362
Internet, via cable networks *354*
invert syrup 389
ion channels 413
iron and steel
- iron, manufacture 391, *392*
- steel
  - bridges 329, 330
  - in buildings 335–6, 337
  - cans 382, 383
  - casting *403*
  - for reinforced concrete 329, 420
  - tin-free (TFS) 383
  - tin-plated 382, 383

isostatic pressing 404, 427
isotopes
- carbon 393
- scanning using 378

item coding 401

J

joints (body parts), movement 297–8
Julia sets 431

K

Kevlar, uses, clothing and textiles 295
keypads, itemized 400–1
kilns 323, 324
- for cement manufacture 418–19

L

lactose 389
lasers, used in bar-code scanners 401
LCDs *see* liquid crystal displays
leaded-tin bronzes 332
lead zirconate titanate (PZT) 426
LEDs *see* diodes, light-emitting
leukemia 379
lilies, voodoo *304*, 305
lime (calcium hydroxide; slaked lime) 417
liquid crystal displays (LCDs), in calculators 361
liquid petroleum gas (LPG) 343
locks (in waterways), canal 373, 375–6
longbows 306–8
Lorenz attractor 430
lost-wax process 403–4
LPG (liquid petroleum gas) 343
lungs, cancer *378*
lymph nodes 377, 378
lysine 303
lysosomes 411

M

machine tools, and cam systems 362
magnesium, and flash photography 365
magnesium oxide (magnesia) 424, 426
magnetic resonance imaging (MRI) 312
majolica ware 425
maltose 389
Mandelbrot sets *430*, 431
manganese dioxide 324
margarine, manufacture 406
mats, pressure 340
meiosis *412*
memory (personal) 310
metals
- melting point and casting 404
- metalworking 316–17

metaphyses 298
meteorology, weather modeling 430
meteors and meteorites, carbon-rich 393
microchips *see* integrated circuits
microprisms, in cameras 367
microscopes, scanning laser acoustic (SLAMs) 427
microwaves, uses, movement sensors 340, *341*
Millenium Dome, London *337*, 338
mines, explosive 293
mitochondria 411, *413*, *414*
mitosis *412*, 413
molding, shell (Croning process) 403
moling 346
monoamines 311
monosaccharides 388–9
Morse, Samuel 353
mortar 417
mosaics *432*
movement sensors 340, *341*
muscles, cells 411
musical instruments, brass **318–20**
mustard gas 379
mutes, brass instrument 320

N

nailing, intramedullary 300
natural gas 391
nerve cells *see* neurons
neurochemistry 311
neurology 312
neurons (nerve cells) 411
- in the brain 309, 311
  - diaphorase neurons 414

neurotransmitters 311, 413–14
Newton, Isaac
- first law of motion 422
- second law of motion 422

nickel silver (German silver) 317
niobium 404
- alloys 346

niobium tin 346
nitric oxide, biological roles 413–14
nitric oxide synthase 414
nitrocellulose 390
nitrogen mustard 379
nitroglycerine 390
noradrenaline *see* norepinephrine
norepinephrine (noradrenaline) 414
- in plants 305

notes, fundamental 318
nucleus, cell 411, *413*
nylons, uses, ropes 350–1

O

Ohio Bridge 329
oils, vegetable, hydrogenation 406
optical scanners, bar-code 401
oscilloscopes, cathode-ray tubes 409
osteocytes *300*
osteoporosis 298

P

paperback production 302
Parkinson's disease, treatment 414

particle accelerators 333
pentoses 389
periosteum 298
PET (positron-emission tomography) 312
petroleum (crude oil) 391
pharmaceuticals, development of 414
phosphor bronze 332
phosphorus, allotropes 392
photodiodes
in exposure meters 368
and fiber optics 355
photodynamic therapy (PDT) 380
photoelectric cells (photocells), and security systems 340–1
photographic films
35mm 364–5
DX coding 369
roll film 365–6
photography
aerial, rocket camera 369
flash 365
underwater 369
photomicrography, fluorescence *414*
photosynthesis 389, 412
photovoltaic (PV) cells, in calculators 361
piezoelectric material, ceramics 426
piles, and building techniques 338
pinning, bone fractures 300
pixels 432
plants
cells 412, *413*
communication between 304–5
photosynthesis 389, 412
sense of touch 303–4, *305*
plaster, gypsum 417
plaster casts 300
plastic forming 426–7
plastics
from plants 303
uses
in buildings 337
food and drink containers 382, 385
platinum, as a catalyst 406
plows, underwater cable-laying 349
plywood, uses, for buildings 336
point-of-sale terminals, electronic (EPOS) 401
polarization (electrical) 386
polyacrylonitrile (PAN, Acrilan) 394, 395
polyamides 398
polyesters
glass-reinforced (GRP) 337
for rope making 350–1
polyethylene (polyethene; polythene) 398
polyhydroxybutyrate (PHB) 303
polypropylene (polypropene) 384
polysaccharides 389–90
polytetrafluoroethylene (PTFE; Teflon) *337*
pontoons 328
porcelain 427
positron-emission tomography (PET) 312
potatoes, genetically-engineered 303, 304
pottery 424–5
powder metallurgy 404
pozzolana 417
prefabricated building components 338
printers, computer, printing photographs 372
prisms, in cameras 367
promoters, catalyst 407
propane 334
prostaglandins, in plants 305
pug mills *425*
purifiers 322
pusher centrifuges 423
pylons, electricity 344, *346*

R

rack-and-pinion systems 357
radar
air traffic control 410
for mine detection 293
radiation
cause of cancer 378
dangers from cell phones 416
radio, and cell phones 415–16
radioactivity
and body scanning 378
and radiocarbon dating 393
radioisotopic dating, carbon dating 393
radio tags 341
radiotherapy *378*, 379, 380
railroad systems
casting of components *402*, *403*
tracks *403*
railways
cliff 356–7
funicular 357–8
rangefinders, camera *364*
rayon, manufacture 390
receptors, cell 413
recognition systems 341
"red eye", on photographs 365
refractories 425
regeneration, of catalysts 406
remote handling, bomb- and mine-disposal robots 294, 295, *296*
repeaters, submarine-cable 347–9
respirators 321–2
ribosomes 411–12
rice, lysine in 303
Ritty, James 399
robotics, for bomb and mine disposal 294, 295, *296*
Romans, ancient, cement 417

S

salicylic acid, and plants 305
San Francisco, streetcars 356, *358*
saxhorns 320
saxophones 320
scan conversion tubes 410
scanners, bar-code 401
SCBA (self-contained breathing apparatus) 322
SEACOM network 348
security systems
burglar alarms **340–1**
CCTV cameras 340
movement sensors 340, *341*
selenium cells 368
self-contained breathing apparatus (SCBA) 322
semiconductors, uses, in calculators 359
sensors, in burglar alarms 340
separators (centrifuges) 423
serotonin, in plants 305
shape selectivity 406
shell molding (Croning process) 403
Shinkansen ("bullet" trains) 328
ships, cable-laying *347*, *348*, 349
shutters, camera 363
sialons 427
silicon carbide (carborundum) 426
silicon chips *see* integrated circuits
silicon nitride 426, 427
silk, artificial 390
Silver Lady mascot 404
sintering, reaction 427
sisal 350
skeletons 297
slugs *387*
SmartMedia 370
smell 310
sound
standing waves 318
timbre (tone) 318
sousaphones 320
space shuttles, heat-resistant tiles *427*
space suits, breathing apparatus *322*
spark plugs, manufacture 427
speech and language, and the brain 310
speed 422
spin dryers 422
splints 299
starch 389, 390
steel *see* iron and steel
stem cells, embryonic 414
steroids, in plants 305
Store Baelt Bridge (Great Belt) 329
streetcars, San Francisco 356, *358*
strokes, vascular 414
sucrose 389, *390*
sugar 389
superconducting tunnel junctions *432*
Sydney Harbor Bridge 329
synapses 309, *311*
neuromuscular *414*
synovial fluid 297

T

Tacoma Narrows Bridge 327
tantalum 404
TAT-1 cable 348–9
TAT-2 cable 349
Teflon (polytetrafluoroethylene) *337*
telecommunications
cable networks **353–5**
fiber optics 354–5
submarine cables **347–9**
telegraph
cables 347
history 353–4
telephone systems
cables 347
third generation 416
television broadcasting
cable television (community antenna television; CATV) 354
satellite 354
television cameras, closed-circuit (CCTV) 340
television receivers
black-and-white 409
cable 354
cathode-ray tubes 409
closed-circuit (CCTV) 340
color 409
flat-screen 410
Telford, Thomas 374
tensile structures 338
testosterone(s), in plants 305
tetra calcium aluminoferrite 419
thalamus 309
Thomson, J. J. 408
thoria 426
throttles 396
tiles, manufacture 427
timber, for buildings 336
timbre (tone), musical 318
Time Division Multiple Access (TDMA) 416
tin
tin-plated steel 382, 383
used in canning 382, 383
titania 426
tobacco *304*
tomography, positron-emission (PET) 312
total-containment vessels (TCVs) 296
Tower Bridge *325*
traction 300
trains
brakes 314, 315
Japanese Shinkansen ("bullet" trains) 328
transistors, in calculators 359
transition elements, as catalysts 405
transplants, bone marrow 380
transposons (jumping genes) *303*
trass 417
trenches, cables laid in 346
tricalcium aluminate 419
tricalcium silicate 419, 420
trolleybuses 343
trombones 319
trucks, brakes 315
trumpets 319
tubas 319, 320
tumors 377

U

ultracentrifuges 423
ultrasonics, used in security systems 340
urania 426
uranium carbide 426
uranium isotopes, separation (enrichment) 423

V

vacuoles, cell 412
vacuum, in cans 381
vacuum-servo braking systems *313*, 314–15
valves, mechanical
brass instrument 319
and engine cams 362
for respirators 321
varnishes, uses 385
velocity 422
venturi (choke) 396
Verrazano Narrows Bridge *327*
video cameras, charge-coupled devices 432
video conferencing *353*
video-on-demand 354
videophones *415*
viruses, and cancer 378
viscose 390
Voyager 2 space probe, and Iapetus (moon) 393

W

washing machines 431
waterwheels, Lorenzian *431*
welding, arc 336
wheat, genetically-engineered 303
Wheatstone, Charles 353
Wheelbarrow (robot) 296
wide band code-division multiple access (WCDMA) 416
widgets 384
winches, band brakes for winched loads 313
wind tunnels, to test bridges 327
Woolworth Building 337
World War II
bombs 293
military bridges 328

X

X-ray imaging
bombs 295
bone fractures *300*
xylene (dimethylbenzene) 406

Y

yeast *406*

Z

zeolites 406
zirconia 426
zirconium boride 426